"In her hour of sore distress and peril"

"In her hour of sore distress and peril"

The Civil War Diaries of John P. Reynolds, Eighth Massachusetts Volunteer Infantry

JOHN P. REYNOLDS
Edited by Jeffrey L. Patrick

McFarland & Company, Inc., Publishers
Jefferson, North Carolina, and London

LIBRARY OF CONGRESS CATALOGUING-IN-PUBLICATION DATA

Reynolds, John P., 1840–1919.
 "In her hour of sore distress and peril" : the Civil War diaries of John P. Reynolds, Eighth Massachusetts Volunteer Infantry / John P. Reynolds ; edited by Jeffrey L. Patrick.
 p.   cm.
 Includes bibliographical references and index.

 ISBN 978-0-7864-7599-5
 softcover : acid free paper ∞

 1. Reynolds, John P., 1840–1919—Diaries.   2. United States. Army. Massachusetts Infantry Regiment, 8th (1861)   3. Massachusetts—History—Civil War, 1861–1865—Regimental histories.   4. United States—History—Civil War, 1861–1865—Regimental histories.   5. Soldiers—Massachusetts—Salem—Diaries.   6. Salem (Mass.)—Biography.   I. Patrick, Jeffrey L., 1963– editor.   II. Title.   III. Title: Civil War diaries of John P. Reynolds, Eighth Massachusetts Volunteer Infantry.
 E513.58th .R49 2013
 973.7'444—dc23   2013023006

BRITISH LIBRARY CATALOGUING DATA ARE AVAILABLE

© 2013 Jeffrey L. Patrick. All rights reserved

No part of this book may be reproduced or transmitted in any form or by any means, electronic or mechanical, including photocopying or recording, or by any information storage and retrieval system, without permission in writing from the publisher.

On the cover: Captain John P. Reynolds (courtesy Civil War Library and Museum, Philadelphia)

Manufactured in the United States of America

McFarland & Company, Inc., Publishers
 Box 611, Jefferson, North Carolina 28640
 www.mcfarlandpub.com

Table of Contents

Acknowledgments vi
Preface 1
Introduction 5
John Perkins Reynolds, Jr.: A Biographical Sketch 47
Arthur Forrester Devereaux: A Biographical Sketch 49

1. Off to War 51
2. New York and Philadelphia 57
3. Old Ironsides 62
4. Return to New York 76
5. Washington 87
6. Relay House 100
7. Baltimore 172
8. The Return Home 228

Appendix: Letters of "G.W.B." (George W. Batchelder) ... 243
Notes 261
Bibliography 285
Index 289

Acknowledgments

The editor wishes to acknowledge the invaluable assistance of Brian Leigh Dunnigan, associate director and curator of maps, and Barbara DeWolfe, curator of manuscripts, at the William L. Clements Library, University of Michigan, who cheerfully answered my questions, located and copied important John P. Reynolds material, and provided much-needed support. One journal used for this book is courtesy of the Clements Library.

I owe a great debt to Dr. Herbert W. Jackson of Missouri State University (retired), who read the manuscript and offered suggestions and words of encouragement, and to Lea Ann Kaplan, who shared valuable genealogical information about the Reynolds family.

I would also like to thank Renee Glass and Patti Hobbs, local history librarians at the Springfield-Greene County (Missouri) Public Library, who conducted an extensive hunt for critical Massachusetts newspaper microfilm, and cartographer George Skoch, who produced the excellent maps that appear in this work.

Preface

On April 15, 1861, John Perkins Reynolds, Jr., a resident of Salem, Massachusetts, answered President Abraham Lincoln's call for volunteers to "maintain the honor, the integrity, and the existence of our National Union" and enlisted in Company I, Eighth Massachusetts Volunteer Infantry. The Civil War's first summer was an arduous time for Reynolds and the other members of Company I, also known as the Salem Light Infantry or Salem Zouaves. Fortunately for historians, John Reynolds recorded both his experiences and the daily activities of his company in a personal diary. On August 1, 1861, then-Corporal Reynolds was mustered out of service, having honorably completed his 90-day term of enlistment. Following his return to Salem, Reynolds began copying his diary entries to three small journal books. He intended them as a remembrance for his friend and company commander Captain Arthur Devereux, not as "a historical work, but a simple handbook of reference or journal." In these densely packed volumes, Reynolds preserved the story of the Zouaves, including "various duties, changes of stations, situations, hardships and exposures," along with a "narrative of interesting events, descriptions of places, anecdotes, incidents &c. giving an idea of the duties of the Soldier and a glance at Camp-life generally."

Reynolds left behind a unique record of one company's service during the Civil War. It is readily apparent that despite his denial, he consciously wanted to compile a complete and accurate historical work about the Salem soldiers' activities. Reynolds was quite unlike so many diarists of the era who wrote only brief entries, noting the weather and summarizing, in a few sentences, the events of each day. Reynolds' impressively detailed entries chronicle, in some cases, the regiment's *hourly* activities each day. Not surprisingly, such detailed diaries are rare for Union 90-day units, simply because of the relatively small number of men serving at that time compared to the number of enlistments later in the war. It is important to note that Reynolds wrote with humor

Salem Zouaves, Massachusetts Volunteer Militia, 1861 (courtesy Ron Field and the Company of Military Historians, Military Uniforms in America Series).

and candor as well, never failing to point out the less than respectable actions of his comrades along with their heroic accomplishments.

Undoubtedly, the Reynolds diary may disappoint some readers, as it contains no graphic descriptions of Civil War combat, for the Eighth Massachusetts was not involved in the fighting in Virginia or Missouri in the summer of 1861. The number of gruesome deaths a writer chose to chronicle should not be the yardstick to measure the worth of any Civil War diary, however. Rather, the real value of the Reynolds diary is in the way it provides details about certain events during the first months of the war, details that might otherwise escape the notice of history. The early mobilization and deployment of Union volunteers, Northern and border state support for the Union war effort, the movement of troops to defend Washington, D.C., from an expected rebel attack, the "rescue" of the U.S.S. *Constitution*, raids on secessionist farms in Maryland, and life in the troubled city of Baltimore are just a few of the topics highlighted in the diary.

In addition, Reynolds included many insightful details about Union soldier life and military material culture during the period. Army discipline, religious practices in the ranks, encounters between soldiers and civilians, training, rations, soldier humor and numerous other aspects of the common soldier's existence that is sometimes missing from letters, diaries or memoirs were deemed worthy for inclusion by John Reynolds. In essence, he meticulously chronicled the transition from civilian to soldier experienced by hundreds of thousands of volunteers during the Civil War.

What follows is an exact transcription of the three volumes of the Reynolds diary. Two of the volumes (April through early June and mid–July through August) are in the possession of the editor. The third is part of the James S. Schoff Civil War Collection at the William L. Clements Library, University of Michigan at Ann Arbor. It does not appear that all three volumes are part of the same set, as the page numbers are not consecutive. It is entirely possible that Reynolds completing two sets of the diary, one for his personal library and the other for presentation to Captain Devereux. If such is the case, the location of the other volumes could not be determined.

George W. Batchelder, a fellow resident of Salem, served alongside Reynolds as a sergeant in the Eighth Massachusetts Infantry. His letters, published in two Salem newspapers in May and June 1861, comprise most of the appendix to this work. A post–Civil War letter written by Arthur Devereux, found with the diary, is included in the appendix as well. In this missive, Captain Devereux, Reynolds' company commander, detailed the controversial expedition undertaken by a portion of his command into the Maryland countryside in late May 1861.

"The men, almost at a moment's warning, had left their families unprovided for and their affairs unarranged, trusting to the patriotic humanity of their fellow citizens and of the State, to make all needful provisions for any immediate or final contingency. They had started in the midst of a pelting storm for the first rendezvous, not even properly clad, and thence, not properly equipped, had pushed forward on their perilous errand. It is true they did not have, as they expected, an opportunity of meeting the enemy, although they evinced every disposition to do so, but in the faithful performance of many active and responsible duties required of them, they rendered the cause most effective service, and are worthy of an honorable page in their country's history. To other Massachusetts Regiments is due the honor of having sealed with their blood their devotion to their country ... but while it was not the fortune of the Eighth to be thus honored, to it will ever be ascribed the honor of having opened a route and provided a way for other troops to respond promptly to the call of the President, securing the safety of the National Capitol, and allaying the fears of the Government, besides saving from possible loss, the frigate 'Constitution,' and the 'Old Ironsides' of the War of 1812."
—George W. Nason, *History and Complete Roster of the Massachusetts Regiments, Minute Men of '61*

"We devoutly thank God, my young friends, that having taken up arms so promptly at your country's call, in her hour of sore distress and peril, having so zealously and energetically met every requirement of duty, whether by sea or land, and having gloriously illustrated the name of Massachusetts Volunteer by a discipline and perfection of drill, usually expected only of members of a standing army, He has in His good Providence, returned you to us in safety and high health."
—Stephen P. Webb, Mayor of Salem, Massachusetts, August 1861

Introduction

Boston

Fort Sumter surrendered! The electrifying news spread like wildfire through the streets of Boston. On Sunday, April 14, 1861, after enduring nearly a day-and-a half bombardment, Major Robert Anderson and the small U.S. garrison in Charleston Harbor hauled down the national colors and gave up the post to forces of the Confederate States of America.

The news of Sumter's fall reverberated throughout Massachusetts and the rest of the North. As one historian recalled, Major Anderson's surrender "cleared the air of doubts and uncertainties," and "drew the line sharply between those who upheld the Federal government and its open or covert enemies."[1] Although there was a feeling of despair over the loss of significant U.S. property and a national symbol, a sense of outrage quickly took its place: "Every observing and considering person was sad, but the sadness was overpowered by anger; and while all deplored the event, nearly all denounced those who had insulted the glorious flag of our country, and tarnished it with a temporary defeat," wrote one eyewitness.

Anxious citizens who besieged newspaper offices all day to hear the latest news replaced the usual hustle and bustle along Boston's streets. "In every part of the city," noted the *Boston Herald*, "friends met on the sidewalk, and knots of people collected on the corners, to talk of the news, and without choosing the dainty words of the Saxon language." Some incredulous citizens argued that the reports were exaggerated, unable to bring themselves to believe that Sumter had fallen. Most, however, believed that the central fact of the event was indeed true. At Sunday church services, the city's religious leaders weighed in on the issue. One minister denounced the traitors who had dragged the flag in the dirt; another attributed the entire crisis to the South's attempt to extend the slave "dominion." A third spoke of Southern states emboldened by Northern concessions, with war now necessary to maintain the dignity of the government. One man of the cloth even urged the young men of his congregation to "buckle on their armor and help save their country."²

Because of their unique heritage, the people of Massachusetts found the Confederacy's insult to the Stars and Stripes particularly vexing. The descendants of those patriots who started the American War for Independence at Lexington and Concord and fought for eight years to establish the republic saw the very concept of democratic government at risk. Unlike many Southerners, Bay State residents believed that they owed their allegiance to the national government rather than their state. As Massachusetts militia General Benjamin Butler explained, "There is this difference, I will say, between our southern brothers and ourselves, that while we love our state with the true love of a son, we love the Union and the country with an equal devotion. We place no 'state rights' before, above, or beyond the Union. To us our country is first, because it is our country, and our state is next and second.... Our oath of allegiance to our country, and our oath of allegiance to our state, are intertwined harmoniously, and never come in conflict or clash. He who does his duty to the Union, does his duty to the state; and he who does his duty to the state does his duty to the Union — 'one inseparable, now and forever.'"³

The day after Sumter's fall, President Abraham Lincoln issued a call for 75,000 volunteers to serve for ninety days to "maintain the honor, the integrity, and the existence of our National Union" by giving battle to "combinations too powerful to be suppressed" by ordinary means.⁴ Individual states were assigned specific troop quotas.

Many in Massachusetts urged the prosecution of the war to the fullest and wholeheartedly supported the president's decision. "There is a strong feeling," argued the *Boston Daily Advertiser*, "that the government now must put forth a *strong arm* and crush treason and disloyalty before our liberties are lost forever."⁵ The editor of the *Boston Herald* predicted that a feeling of indignation would arise throughout the country

Engraving of Brigadier General Edward W. Hinks (editor's collection).

"which cannot be easily subdued," and was himself in favor of a "vigorous policy" to end matters as soon as possible, and to show foreign powers that the federal government was capable of maintaining its authority. A strong central government was willing to protect all men and their interests, he believed, and those men would rally to its support. A Southern victory, on the other hand, would only establish despotism. Now, in order to preserve their "glorious heritage," every man should perform "his whole duty." "The people of New England fought for and established American liberty," he continued, "and they will defend it to the last" with a "terrible energy," for "they know how to shoot and are not afraid to smell gun powder." Nevertheless, the same Massachusetts journalist foretold, quite correctly, that the "serious work" ahead would likely result in "immense slaughter."[6] The *Boston Journal* likewise observed that although "These streets were never trodden before by armed men summoned to the dread ordeal of civil war," now citizens would oppose those "who are leagued to overthrow the government under which we have all so marvelously flourished." An "aroused, determined patriotism," the *Journal* believed, was set to crush "audacious treason" forever, for "The old Cromwellian and Bunker-hill spirit, will wear like steel, and shine as it wears."[7]

The "Bunker-hill spirit" was soon on display in the Massachusetts capital as American flags appeared on every street. "The city is as gaily decorated as it usually is on our great national holiday," reported one newspaper, while "New flags are thrown to the breeze every day." One merchant was not content with simply raising a flag, but also engaged a band of music for the occasion.[8] Although public buildings were decorated (the national color was "greeted with three cheers" when unfurled on the dome of the Massachusetts State House), the stars and stripes "are floating from all the flag staffs, are suspended across the streets and from the windows of stores and private dwellings," a Bostonian proudly noted.

Engraving of Brigadier General Benjamin F. Butler, *Harper's Weekly*, June 1, 1861.

Some displays were far more elaborate than simple flags. A representation of George Washington graced the front of one building, for instance, with Justice on the right and Liberty on the left, with the interior of the building decorated as well. In another establishment, a frigate appeared in one window, along with a bust of Daniel Webster, a portrait of Washington, and a conspicuously placed Webster quote: "The Union it must and shall be preserved." Even a horse-drawn omnibus displayed the stars and stripes, and its women riders waved flags. Such outpourings of patriotism offered indisputable evidence that the people of Massachusetts would not "suffer the work of our forefathers to be destroyed without a struggle."[9]

Citizens in smaller nearby towns such as Salem were not to be outdone by those in the state capital. On the evening of April 17, Salem's citizens met in Mechanics' Hall and listened to a powerful address by Mayor S.P. Webb, who called on the people to "forget party differences and uphold the government." Other patriotic speeches were made and resolutions unanimously adopted, including measures to stand by the government, pledge "life and fortune to the preservation of the Union," and to protect the families of those about to go to war. Subscribers pledged several thousand dollars for that cause, and a committee appointed to secure more funds.[10] A few days later, the Salem city council met and appropriated $15,000 for the benefit of the volunteers.[11]

Although such expressions of patriotic fervor were no doubt stirring and welcome, the more practical task of answering Lincoln's call for troops occupied the time of the state government. The Massachusetts adjutant general and

Engraving of Brigadier General Benjamin F. Butler (editor's collection).

governor's offices became beehives of extraordinary activity, as militia officers hurried to offer their services to the commonwealth and Governor John Albion Andrew met with his adjutant general and aides to discuss the state's response.[12] Massachusetts Senator Henry Wilson wasted no time in telegraphing Governor Andrew on April 15, asking him to call up twenty companies of troops (two regiments of ten companies each, or 1,560 men), and a few hours later the War Department reiterated Wilson's request. Andrew ordered four regiments of state militia mobilized in order to fill two to the absolute maximum. Orders went out to the colonels of the Third, Fourth, Sixth and Eighth infantry regiments to form their commands in Boston as quickly as possible.[13] "The call came forth like the fiery cross that was sent through the Scottish Highlands," Massachusetts militia General Benjamin Butler dramatically recalled.[14] Soon after, on April 16, the Massachusetts quota was increased to four full regiments, with the whole force to be led by a brigadier general.[15]

Fortunately for Governor Andrew, the state's well-organized militia was able to respond promptly. Although in existence for many decades, the Massachusetts militia system had been reorganized by the state legislature in March 1840 as the Massachusetts Volunteer Militia (MVM), so that it consisted of active (volunteer) and enrolled (able-bodied, though inactive, except in the event of war, invasion, etc.) militiamen. The members of the active, "Volunteer Corps" were to be paid and called first in times of emergency. Although the MVM experienced various failures and successes through the next few years, by the end of the decade a new, more organized and better-trained militia force was beginning to form. In 1851 Ebenezer W. Stone, the adjutant general, advocated a statewide three-day militia encampment and large "division" camps of instruction. He also argued in favor of obtaining new percussion arms, inspected company armories, sold off condemned weapons, purchased tents, and insisted on correct paperwork in the form of returns and muster rolls. Governor Nathaniel Banks wisely supported Stone's efforts during his term of office (1858–1861). In 1859, the entire state militia took part in one great encampment, with more than 5,000 men in attendance. Stone's successor William Schouler continued his aggressive promotion and management of the militia, and John Andrew, the new governor, likewise sustained the adjutant general.

Although certainly not fully prepared for the coming contest of arms in 1861, the state of Massachusetts was "at least better prepared than the rest of the loyal states," in the words of historian Robert McGraw. Only a few days after he assumed office in January 1861, Governor Andrew issued an order requiring militia company commanders to examine their muster rolls thoroughly to determine who was unable to serve due to age, physical defects, business or family issues, and who could respond immediately in a time of crisis. Those unwilling or unable to respond were to be discharged and new recruits found to fill the ranks. In addition, Andrew ensured that adequate stores of weapons and military equipment were in storage in the state armory. The legislature, (whose term ended just before the attack on Fort Sumter) bolstered his efforts, authorizing $25,000 for military equipment for 2,000 men.[16] Even as late as April 13, as the Confederates bombarded Fort Sumter, Schouler asked U.S. Secretary of War Simon Cameron for 2,000 rifled muskets from the Springfield Armory to arm those soldiers who were still carrying smoothbore flintlock conversion arms.[17]

Many young members of the MVM and potential recruits in Salem were among the thousands enthusiastically ready to answer Lincoln's call. William A. Hill, a clerk in a cotton merchant's office on India wharf in Boston, found a letter waiting on his desk when he returned from dinner. It was an order from the first sergeant of his company to report as soon as possible to the Salem armory. Although his employer was out of his office, the merchant's bookkeeper promised Hill that he would explain his absence, and the clerk left for Salem on the next train.

William Wiley reported to work in South Danvers, only to hear the news of the appeal for volunteers. Wiley's boss entered the room and said, "What is the matter; you look wild?" Wiley said goodbye, telling him that he would be off with the first company to leave Salem. He stepped outside and met a member of the Salem militia company. Together they walked two miles to Salem, where Wiley enlisted. "My home was in Maine and I packed my trunk and sent it there," he recalled many years later.

Joseph M. Parsons was working as a mason when word arrived of the president's call. Parsons immediately dropped his trowel and headed to the town armory.[18]

Two other members of the Salem company were equally anxious to serve — John P. Reynolds, Jr., a 20-year-old clerk at Chandler and Company Dry Goods in Boston, and Arthur Devereux, 24 years old, likewise a clerk in Boston.[19] All these men, as members of the city's celebrated "Light Infantry" militia company, were soon to embark on a three-month military odyssey that took them far from their homes to New York, Philadelphia, and the turbulent border state of Maryland.

The militia company they proudly called their military "home," the Salem Light Infantry (later to be known as the Salem Zouaves), had been organized in 1805. Much of the Light Infantry's history prior to 1861 had been rather mundane, consisting largely of parades for presidential visits, funerals and ceremonies. However, after Arthur Devereux was elected captain on February 7, 1860, the young commander put the company "under strict discipline," with frequent drill sessions to bring the unit to a high state of efficiency.

Upon assuming command, Devereux issued a challenge. "There is a company in Chicago which challenges the world in military drill," he explained, referring to the celebrated United States Zouave Cadets drill team of Captain Elmer Ellsworth. "If you will give me your time and attention for six months, two evenings a week, I will guarantee that you can accept this challenge." Along with the drill sessions, members of the company presented amateur theatrical performances in their armory to raise money for the unit's treasury.

Captain Ellsworth's Zouave Cadets embarked on a tour of Eastern cities that summer, and his company received an invitation to visit Salem. They arrived on July 24, 1860, and the next day, following a parade through the city, Ellsworth's men performed "their novel and interesting drill" on the town common, "all executed with most wonderful quickness and uniformity." Ellsworth's men were so pleased with the reception they received in Salem that they took the company letters from the fatigue caps of the Salem Light Infantry men and fastened them to their own caps as souvenirs.[20]

The new and fascinating drill and uniform of Ellsworth's company inspired the men of Salem. "The visit of the Zouaves marked an important epoch in the annals of the Infantry, the enthusiasm was unbounded, the wonderful and dexterous drill, the easy swinging step of the Zouaves, the dress, and in fact the entire make-up and method of the 'Zous' had fascinated the men of the Infantry," according to a unit history. "Here was something quite new, no heavy cumbersome uniform, none of the stiffness and formality of the old style drill, and in marching the men moved along in an easy swinging style with little or no attention to alignment or uniformity; it was entirely unlike the old drill, and it was no wonder that the Infantry boys found it catching."[21]

The Salem men continued to drill, and passed new rules tightening the unit's discipline, so that on February 5, 1861, Captain Devereux felt confident enough to offer the services of his company to Governor Andrew. On April 9, just a few days before the attack on Fort Sumter, the Salem company planned an exhibition drill demonstration for the governor and other distinguished guests. The militia, appearing in full uniform, gave "variety and brilliancy to the scene," in a drill hall decorated with flags, streamers, and pictures. About 8 P.M., the band struck up "Hail to the Chief" and Governor Andrew entered. The Zouaves, wearing a neat jacket and cap, then gave a two and a half hour demonstration for several hundred ladies and gentlemen, "displaying a proficiency extremely creditable, and which could not have been acquired without close attention and arduous exertion," wrote an eyewitness. "Frequent and hearty applause" filled the hall. "Many, if not most, of the exercises attempted, were, to an unpractised eye, fully equal to the performance of the renowned Chicago Zouaves," according to one spectator. Governor Andrew was impressed as well, and in a formal speech, he not only praised the Salem Zouaves for "the brilliant and beautiful exhibition," but also expressed doubts that any company in the state could equal or surpass the Salem company. Andrew, anticipating that a time of crisis would soon be at hand, alluded to the state of the nation and predicted that Massachusetts men would rally to support the flag under which their fathers had marched to battle. Captain Devereux praised his men for their performance as well, explaining that the citizen soldiers had devoted several hours for two evenings each week during the winter to perfect the drill.[22] The "very successful and interesting spectacle" was the last peacetime event many of the Salem men would know for several years.

Governor Andrew's Special Order No. 14, issued just a few days later on April 15, called out four Massachusetts regiments to meet the government's request for troops.[23] Much like Captain Devereux and John Reynolds, another Massachusetts man was eager to respond to his country's call. As luck would have it, attorney, legislator and militia general Benjamin Butler was trying a court case in Boston when word came for the militia's mobilization. Handed an order for the Sixth Regiment of his brigade to muster in Boston, Butler asked for a postponement of the court case and left immediately for his headquarters. He quickly managed to arrange financing for transporting the troops, and quite naturally asked Governor Andrew for command of the four regiments. Despite the fact that Butler was not the state's senior militia general, he was the most capable, and Special Order No. 21, issued on April 17, placed him in charge of the state's quota.[24]

Although certainly ambitious, Butler was not alone in his attempt to gain the attention of the governor. Edward Hinks, the adjutant of the Eighth Massachusetts Infantry, was also in a fortunate location. On the morning of April 15, he was at the Massachusetts State House, and immediately sent a note offering his services to Governor Andrew. Soon after submitting his offer, Hinks was called into the office of the adjutant general, where he learned that Governor Andrew had been asked to furnish twenty companies. Hinks quickly volunteered his regiment, claiming that five hundred of its members could be ready to march in twenty-four hours, and the entire regiment in two days. Andrew, unsure at that time as to whether he could accept entire regiments, offered to accept six of the Eighth Regiment's companies if they reported to Boston the following day. "After considerable conversation," Hinks recalled, he asked the governor if he would accept all eight companies of the regiment. Andrew finally agreed. That afternoon Hinks sprang into action, sending telegrams to company commanders to prepare their troops, and in several cases notifying the regiment's officers in person.[25]

The troops began arriving in Boston amid a driving rain and sleet storm on the morning of April 16, and the Eighth Massachusetts took up quarters in Faneuil Hall. "The sound of the drum and fife, and the movement of armed men through our streets, have revived a feeling which has not been manifested since the Mexican War," observed one correspondent. "Had any thing been wanting to convince the troops who have hitherto trained for display, that the

Introduction

Map of Area of Operations, Eighth Massachusetts Infantry, 1861.

time for fair-weather soldiering is past, the drizzling storm of rain and hail which has prevailed to-day would be sufficient," he added.[26]

The Salem Light Infantry (actually considered Company A of the Seventh Regiment, but now attached to the Eighth and designated Company I) joined the eight companies of the regiment (one each from Newburyport, Beverly and Gloucester, two from Lynn and three from Marblehead). To make up the required ten companies of the regiment, Company A, First Battalion from Pittsfield was attached as well and designated Company K. That western Massachusetts company was not required to make the lengthy trip to Boston, but would join the troop train en route to the seat of war.[27] The regiment was ultimately destined for Washington, D.C., then vulnerable to a potential Confederate attack.

As the troops assembled in Boston, it was quite easy for both militiamen and civilians to draw parallels between the current state of affairs and the martial glory of the Revolutionary generation. The men who carried the word to the regiments to muster in Boston were the 1860s equivalents of Paul Revere. Faneuil Hall, the old "Cradle of Liberty" where protest meetings were held in the days before the American Revolution, was, quite appropriately, the temporary barracks of the volunteers. Moreover, the presence of so many eager volunteers only stiffened the resolve of the Bostonians, just as the gathering of Massachusetts militiamen outside the city after the fighting at Lexington and Concord in 1775 had served as the basis for the long-serving Continental Army. Although one might hope that bloodshed could be averted, one newspaper editor believed, when the time to strike comes, "let the blow be one from which there can be no possibility of recoil." He thought that the power of the North was undisputable, and the war was groundless, for as a reward for all the North had done for the South, they were given open war. Now, any man who failed to stand by his flag was a coward and a traitor. "The day for tenderness is past," the paper concluded.[28] Despite the raw weather, the men in Faneuil Hall were cheerful, "as was apparent from the blithe songs they sung and the general hilarity which prevailed."[29]

Two days after their arrival, the Eighth Massachusetts men, led by a platoon of the "National Lancers" of Boston and the Salem Zouaves, marched to the State House to receive their colors and listen to farewell remarks by Governor Andrew and General Butler. "The remarkable spectacle of mustering and departing troops for a scene of expected conflict, yesterday threw our city into unaccustomed excitement," according to one newspaper account. Continuous cheers rang out from crowds of spectators, and the absence of military music only enhanced the solemnity of the occasion as citizen-soldiers left to fight "domestic foes." "The scene impressed upon the most careless observer the stirring character of the times," wrote an eyewitness, and "Facts and incidents for history are crowding every minute."[30] One newspaper described the downtown area as a "scene as has seldom been witnessed in Boston." The crowd around Faneuil Hall was so large that it required a large number of police to keep order, while the area in front of the State House was a dense mass of humanity, with every window in the surrounding buildings full of well-wishers. The new soldiers were undoubtedly particularly thrilled by the women at the State House, who wore small American flags on their bosoms, and numerous rosettes of red, white and blue, frequently accompanied by small flower bouquets.[31]

In his formal remarks, interrupted many times by cheers, Governor Andrew told the men, "Yesterday you were citizens; to-day you are heroes.... You have come to be cradled anew one night in Faneuil Hall, there breathing once more the inspiration of historic American liberty, and standing beneath the folds of the American banner." He concluded his remarks with a stirring farewell: "Soldiers, go forth bearing that flag; and as our fathers fought, so, if need be, strike you the blow.... We stay behind to guard the hearthstones you have left.... I speak to you as citizens and soldiers, not of Massachusetts, but of the American Confederate Union. While we live, that Union shall last; and until these countless thousands, and all their posterity, have tasted death, the Union of the American people, the heritage of Washington, shall be eternal. Soldiers, go forth, bearing with you the blessings of your country, bearing the confidence of your fellow-citizens; and ... with stout hearts and stalwart frames go forth to victory. On your shields be returned, or bring them with you. Yours it is to be among the advance guard of Massachusetts soldiers. As such, I bid you God speed, and fare you well."

General Butler summoned God, the Puritans, and Daniel Webster during his remarks. It was the duty of Massachusetts soldiers to maintain the constitutional liberty their ancestors bequeathed, he argued. "To lead the advance guard of freedom, of constitutional liberty, and of perpetuity to the Union, is the honor we claim." "Sons of Puritans, who believe in the providence of Almighty God," he continued, "may he be with us in this strife for the right, for the good of all, for the great missionary country of liberty."[32] "We go forward today to prove that in Massachusetts and in the entire North there is only one sentiment. The Union, it must be perpetuated," he concluded.

Despite the sentries and police, men crowded to get close to Andrew and Butler, and "for a time the most thrilling excitement pervaded the large concourse." A friend of Butler's gave him a parting warning, however, by mentioning that Harpers Ferry, Virginia, and the government arsenal there had already fallen to the rebels, to which Butler merely gave his shoulders a shrug and replied, "'Seventeen Yankees took it once," a reference to the 1859 New England-backed raid of abolitionist John Brown.[33]

All the many years of hard work and dedication by the militia's supporters had paid off. The Fourth and Sixth Massachusetts Infantry left Boston on the 17th, while the Third and Eighth left the city on the 18th. "Truly it was an impressive feat," believed historian Robert McGraw. "In less than forty-eight hours four full regiments of infantry had been alerted, concentrated in Boston, equipped and rationed for active campaigning, and dispatched to the theater of operations."[34]

The Eighth Massachusetts regiment that left Boston that afternoon with General Ben Butler was an eclectic one. Containing companies with such colorful names as the "Cushing Guards," "Sutton Light Infantry" and "Lafayette Guard," "The Essex Regiment" (as the Eighth was sometimes called, due to the fact that nearly all of its companies came from Essex County), had 705 effective men on the rolls, including 59 from Salem. Of that number, 490 were single. The average age of the regiment was 24 years and 10 months, with an average weight of about 145 pounds. The occupations of the troops were varied, and included the typical nineteenth century trades, such as farmer, blacksmith, merchant, laborer and machinist, but also more unusual avocations, including mariner, piano maker, gentleman, fisherman, sail maker, hack driver, ship carpenter, telegraph operator, fish dealer, whalebone cutter and baker, occupations varied enough, in the words of one wag, to colonize Virginia "and establish a live community with its own members."[35]

Like so many early Civil War units, the men of the Eighth Massachusetts agreed to an unwritten social contract with the civilians they left behind. The men, women and children at home agreed to support the troops and assist their families; in return, the militiamen agreed to perform no act that would bring shame upon the people of Essex County. "May God forbid the return of the 8th Massachusetts regiment, if they ever allow this our national emblem to be disgraced in their presence," a newspaper editorial threatened.[36]

The regiment's troop train, drawn by two engines and comprised of seventeen passenger and three baggage cars, moved slowly through the night toward New York. One newspaper reported, "The enthusiasm was very great all along the route from Boston, the cars being frequently delayed throughout the entire night." The same newspaper glowingly described the regiment as composed of all "picked men," in the best of spirits, "sturdy, healthy men, of the sturdy stock that gave such a good account of itself at Concord, Lexington, and Bunker Hill." Perhaps the only truly undeniable statement contained in the report was that "Eastern newspapers can give but a faint idea of the Union enthusiasm" that pervaded the areas from which they came.[37] Enthusiasm was great on board the train as well. Captain Devereux wrote home that it was impossible to sleep on the "long and tedious" trip from Boston to New York because the men were making too much noise.[38]

The train made two brief stops in Massachusetts. First came a halt in Worcester, where General Butler had a chance once again to explain why Massachusetts men had entered the fight: "We are all Americans.... [I]t is only by the sword we can have peace, and only in the Union, liberty."[39] The second stop was in Springfield, where finally the regiment became complete when its tenth company, the "Allen Guards" of Pittsfield, climbed aboard, "as rough-and-ready men as ever walked God's earth," as the Pittsfield newspaper labeled them. Although the "Guards" missed the massive outpouring of emotion in Boston, their departure ceremony from Pittsfield was notable as well, as the *Berkshire County Eagle* explained: "Never, since under the Old Elm the Pittsfield patriots of the revolution bade farewell to their friends, to defend their country and avenge the blood of Lexington, has such a scene been witnessed in Berkshire County as the departure of the Allen Guard.... [O]nly the youthful heroes summoned to the holiest of wars were recognized. The varied partings of husband and wife, maiden and lover, father and child, of friend with friend, never before so well loved — the strong brave man, the bravest in the fight, moved to tears."[40] After waiting for an hour in Springfield for the issue of arms from the federal arsenal, the train chugged on to New York City.[41]

The regiment's early morning arrival in New York on April 19 guaranteed that few would be awake to welcome the men of the "Old Bay State." Although there was cheering from some houses, there were no "very noticeable demonstrations." By the time the regiment had breakfasted and prepared to leave the city later that morning, however, New Yorkers were ready to bid the troops an enthusiastic fond farewell. "The cheering was immense, while thousands of flags were hung from windows and balconies," recalled one member of the Pittsfield company. "Three cheers for the Old Bay State greeted us at every drum tap. Praises for the Old Bay State are in every ones [sic] mouth, as she was the first to respond to the President's call for troops, and the first to shed her blood in the cause of right."[42] Hundreds recognized the popular General Ben Butler, who walked "with steady step and erect head" and was "the subject of a personal ovation of the most complimentary character." The men crossed the Hudson to board a new train in Jersey City, where observers recognized "animation on every face" in the ranks, while "not a regret was visible." Some of the Massachusetts men even boastfully remarked that they were ready, but their only fear was that they did not have enough musket cartridges.[43]

At the Jersey City Depot, A.W. Griswold, a prominent member of the New York bar and a native of Massachusetts presented a "magnificent silk flag, mounted on a massive hickory staff" to General Butler, Colonel Timothy Monroe and Lieutenant Colonel Edward Hinks. In a ritual performed dozens of times by the commanders of regiments in the North and South during the war, Monroe took the banner and swore to "defend it, 'God help me,'" while the men likewise "vowed solemnly to defend that flag with their lives and honor." The cheering that followed was deafening.[44]

The trip south, combined with the support exhibited by the civilian population, thrilled the men of the Eighth and stiffened their resolve. One soldier summarized the feelings of all those in the regiment: "Never in all my life, nor in the life of the oldest inhabitant, was there so much enthusiasm as I have witnessed to-day all through the route, it makes a fellows [sic] blood boil and his hair stand on end to see the old glorious Stars and Stripes so thick from every house top, and cheering the glorious old Bay State boys, and such cheers and shaking of the hand, and blessings fall on us that it makes the spirit of '76 nerve us on to put down rebellion and raise the stars and stripes to its former place and position, out from under the feet of traitors who have trampled it in the dirt." Such an important crusade was certain to require sacrifices, as enlisted man George W. Burbank explained to the folks at home: "We all expect to see fun before we reach Washington. We expect to see some sharp fighting before it is over.... For I will fight till the ground for miles around is covered with my blood."[45]

Philadelphia

Because they arrived in the city in the early evening, the Massachusetts men found the reception in Philadelphia to be far more enthusiastic than the one they enjoyed in New York. "We could not march but a few rods at a time, the crowd was so dense; the cheering for Old Massachusetts, Bunker Hill, &c., is beyond my power to describe," one soldier noted.[46]

The outpouring of emotion so far in the cities of Boston, New York and Philadelphia had made the war seem like a succession of parades to the men of the Eighth Massachusetts. The farther south and the deeper into secessionist territory they moved, however, the more uncertain the situation became. In fact, conditions were about to turn deadly for another regiment of Massachusetts troops attempting to reach Washington.

On April 19 (ironically the anniversary of the 1775 battles of Lexington and Concord), the Sixth Massachusetts Infantry began arriving in Baltimore on their way to the capital. The city had a history of mob violence (most notably in 1812 and 1835), and an unruly pro-secessionist crowd quickly assembled as the thirty-five car train of Massachusetts men arrived at the President Street Station about 11 A.M. There, the cars were disconnected (due to city ordinances barring locomotives from the downtown area) and pulled by four horses down Pratt Street to the Camden Street Station, where they would be reconnected to an engine to continue their journey. Seven of the regiment's companies reached the latter station safely, but not without considerable delay and some injuries, as the mob hurled paving stones and other missiles that smashed train windows and struck soldiers. The regiment's four remaining companies, about 220 men, remained at the President Street Station. There, a mob collected and began yelling taunts, jeers and abuse at the soldiers. The mob also placed obstructions on the tracks, so the Massachusetts officers made the necessary decision to march rather than ride to Camden Street. The troops began marching quickly, with a crowd wielding stones and a few pistols close on their heels. Eventually the soldiers of the Sixth began firing at will, and some hand-to-hand combat took place, until, finally, about 12:45 P.M., the train pulled out of Camden Street and the "Baltimore Riot" was over. Four soldiers were dead and thirty-six wounded, along with twelve civilian fatalities and an undetermined number injured.[47] That evening, an understandably concerned Governor Andrew sent a list of questions to General Butler in Philadelphia, asking about the condition of both Butler's troops and the Sixth Massachusetts. The general responded with a relatively lengthy report, offering what details he had discovered about the attack in Baltimore.[48]

Although Butler was certainly interested in the fate of the Sixth Regiment, he soon had more immediate concerns. A few hours after the incident in Baltimore, the Massachusetts general's chances of successfully reaching Washington decreased dramatically. In light of the "Pratt Street Riot" and the likely possibility that the movement of more Union troops through Baltimore would provoke further violence, some of Maryland's leaders proposed a radical solution—burn or disable the railroad bridges near the city. Baltimore's Chief of Police George P. Kane and Mayor George William Brown visited Maryland Governor Thomas Holliday Hicks late that evening and presented the plan.[49] What the group actually discussed and whether the governor gave his assent has been debated ever since. According to Mayor Brown, Governor Hicks agreed to the destruction. Hicks later claimed that he said he had no authority to authorize the burning, as the bridges were private property, the act was unlawful, and he loved law and order. Hicks supposedly told the mayor that he could act as he pleased, however, as the governor had no power to interfere. On the other hand, Hicks claimed he had no right to interfere with the passage of troops to Washington either, but did join with the mayor in sending a letter to President Lincoln urging that no more troops be sent through Baltimore. In Hicks' defense, the mayor claimed the meeting took place at midnight, but two of the bridges were burned about 1 A.M., so it is likely the plan was already in motion and was going to proceed with or without the governor's consent.[50] Regardless of who authorized the mission, several bridges on the Northern Central and Philadelphia, Wilmington and Baltimore Railroads were partially or totally destroyed.[51]

Butler was now in a quandary. With his orders to reach Washington as quickly as possible still in effect, and the railroad bridges burned and easy access to the capital denied, few choices remained. Marching overland would take days. Moving through Baltimore might spark another riot. His only other option was to move south to Annapolis in some fashion, then seize the depot of the Washington and Annapolis Railroad and hold it open for troops to pass through to the capital.[52] Ironically, a clever plan to transport troops to Washington was already in motion, likely masterminded not by General Ben Butler, but by a civilian railroad executive.

Samuel Morse Felton, president of the Philadelphia, Wilmington and Baltimore Railroad, agreed that no more troops should be sent through Baltimore, but decided that sending troops by rail from Philadelphia to Perryville, Maryland, then by steamer to Annapolis was likely to succeed. He sent word to Captain M. Galloway of the railroad steamer *Maryland*, docked at Perryville, urging him to get the ship ready to sail. That evening, April 19, Felton met with Pennsylvania General Robert Patterson, Pennsylvania Governor Andrew Curtin and Philadelphia Mayor Alexander Henry, among others, to discuss the proposal. All present agreed to the plan. Felton and Navy Commodore Samuel F. Du Pont then went to the Continental Hotel to meet with General Butler. Although Butler initially disagreed with the idea (defiantly and unrealistically stating that he would follow his orders to go through Baltimore, and if fired upon from any house would raze it to the ground), eventually Felton convinced him of the necessity of using the Perryville-Annapolis route.[53]

As Felton arranged to continue the Eighth Massachusetts' journey to Washington, a far more famous regiment arrived on the scene. Colonel Marshall Lefferts and his Seventh New York Infantry (one of the most elite militia units in pre–Civil War America) arrived in Philadelphia about 2 A.M. on April

Engraving of Steamer *Maryland* (editor's collection).

20. Shortly after, Lefferts and his officers met with Felton at his office. Felton shared telegraphs from Governor Hicks and the mayor of Baltimore barring Federal troops from the city, along with messages from railroad agents reporting the destruction of the railroad bridges. Colonel Lefferts considered the idea of going to Perryville as well, as he sent two telegrams to Secretary of War Simon Cameron, one asking for instructions, the other recommending that troops go to Perryville by rail, then by large iron ferryboat to Annapolis, and stating that he was "joined in this opinion" by Patterson, Governor Curtin, and others. Unfortunately, he received no reply, and as the day wore on, Lefferts and his officers delayed making a decision.[54]

With the arrival of the New Yorkers, Butler recognized a unique opportunity to augment his force. He sent a "memorial of plan and reasons for proceeding to Annapolis" to Governor Andrew early on April 20. In the lengthy message, Butler proposed to combine his regiment with the Seventh New York, then march to seize the Maryland capital to "call the state to account for the death of Massachusetts men, my friends and neighbors."[55]

Early on the morning of April 20, Butler left his hotel to meet with Marshall Lefferts and his New Yorkers. The two officers met about 7 A.M. Lefferts explained that he had not made a decision about their route, but was awaiting instructions from Washington. At 10 A.M., Butler returned and learned that the New Yorkers now disagreed with Felton's plan to use the steamer *Maryland*, insisting that the ship could be destroyed or disabled at any time before the regiment arrived in Perryville. In fact, during their meeting, rumors began flying that the *Maryland* had in fact fallen into rebel hands. Their alternative plan was to commission another steamer to take the troops either to Fortress Monroe and then up the Potomac to the capitol, or, if a convoy could not be found to help escort the ship past rebel batteries on the river, it could offload the men at Annapolis and they could travel by rail to Washington.[56]

The general urged them to follow him to Perryville, but Lefferts and his officers were unconvinced; in their minds, their plan was the only realistic way to reach Washington. Not only that, but the New York colonel was less than receptive to the idea of taking orders from a Massachusetts brigadier, and Butler's "appearance, manner, and general conduct," wrote the Seventh's regimental historian, "rendered him extremely unpopular among all with whom he came in contact." The New Yorkers' "unfavorable impression" of Butler came from the general's numerous negative attributes. His personal appearance was "far from attractive," while his manner was "captious and conceited, almost to rudeness"; finally, "his well-known political antecedents, as a Southern sympathizer, and as a supporter of slavery, the cause of the rebellion, were not calculated to secure the confidence of the unconditional and intensely loyal young men of the Seventh Regiment." By 3 P.M., all was ready and the New York troops stuffed on board the small steamer *Boston* to begin their separate journey.[57] The Massachusetts Eighth would travel alone to Perryville, sixty-two miles away, where they would secure the steamer *Maryland* and sail to Annapolis.

At 11 A.M., Butler admitted defeat in a telegraph to Governor Andrew: "I go alone … to execute this imperfectly written plan. If I succeed, success will justify me. If I fail, purity of intention will excuse want of judgment or rashness." About 3 P.M. on April 20, the Massachusetts men boarded a train for Perryville.[58]

On to Perryville

Butler's men anticipated difficult work before them in order to reach the nation's capital. Before the general's announcement that they would take the Perryville-Annapolis route, the men anticipated marching through Baltimore. In light of the "Pratt Street Riot," the news stirred the Bay State men. One Massachusetts clerk sent an enthusiastic letter home: "We have got to push our way through Baltimore in the morning, at the point of the bayonet! But our boys are determined and in for it," he assured his readers. "Our bayonet exercise has got to put the whole regiment through fire and brimstone. To tell you the truth, our boys expect to be split to pieces. But we have all made up our minds to die at our post…. There is an unheard-of hot time before us, and we are furnished with no ammunition as yet, and we are to rely on our bayonets and revolvers solely…. But what is more glorious than to die for one's country?" Despite their bravado, many in the regiment made out wills, and a large number wrote their name and residence on cards and attached them to their underclothing so their bodies could be identified.[59]

Even though disappointed that they would avoid the place where their comrades had bled and died, there was still the possibility that the Eighth Massachusetts would be forced to fight their way to the *Maryland*. On his way to Perryville, Butler heard rumors that 1,800 members of "a Baltimore mob" were ready to prevent him from reaching Annapolis, and that it was quite likely they had already seized the ship. Butler had ten rounds of ammunition issued to each man and muskets carefully inspected and loaded, while about 40 men "who know nothing about the use of arms" (later dubbed the "corps of sappers and miners") stood ready with axes, pickaxes, and entrenching tools.[60] Some of the rumors flying about the train were even more fantastic. Captain Devereux wrote home that General Butler "sticks to it" that an incredible 10,000 secessionists were waiting within half a mile of the steamer *Maryland*![61]

Butler walked through the cars, examined each man's musket, and stood over him while he loaded it. He told them he would lead the attack on the *Maryland* in person and "share the danger" with them, and called for paper and envelopes so the men could write final letters home. Exhaustion finally caught up with the general, though, and Butler fell asleep. He was startled, however, not by the shouts of an approaching enemy force, but by cries of "man overboard." One of Butler's sergeants, unnerved by the thought of facing the foe, ran across the fields, dressed only in his trousers and shoes. Although some men went in pursuit, Butler ordered the recall sounded and offered a reward of $30 to track-men on the railroad if they captured him (which they soon did). Obviously not every member of the Eighth Massachusetts was ready to "see the elephant."[62]

About 6 P.M., Butler and his troops disembarked from the train and approached the *Maryland*. Captain Devereux's Salem Zouaves were deployed as skirmishers on both sides of the road, supported by the Pittsfield company 100 paces in the rear. They were immediately followed, in turn, by the men with axes and hatchets. The remainder of the regiment followed in solid columns 50 paces to the rear, ready to "throw themselves into the boat by the weight of the column." "The Company then marched steadily forward, not a man blanched or faltered," Butler recalled, "indeed the prospect of meeting those in battle who had murdered our brothers in Baltimore seemed to give them pleasure."[63] As they advanced, the men called out such exclamations as "Fight savage, boys!"[64] No secessionist army had control of the *Maryland*, however, and not a shot was fired; the Bay State men marched aboard without incident. Although the troops were disappointed by the peaceful takeover, Butler was not, or so he later claimed, "for it relieved me from a great weight & a fearful responsibility."

The steamer *Maryland* was a large vessel but by no means a luxury ship.

Because there was no bridge across the Susquehanna River at Perryville, trains were forced to stop there, move their cars onto the upper deck of the *Maryland*, which was fitted with tracks, and have the steamer carry them across the river to Havre de Grace, where the cars were unloaded and attached to another engine to continue the journey to Baltimore. In fact, four cars of coal sat on the upper deck and accompanied Butler and his men to Annapolis. It was a means of reaching Washington, though, and as the *Maryland* headed south, the exhausted men threw themselves on their blankets on the deck and were asleep, so that the general found he could literally step on them "without breaking their slumbers."[65] They had secured passage to Annapolis — the next step was to capture that city and open the route to Washington.

Annapolis

Although Butler and his soldiers anticipated taking Annapolis by surprise when the *Maryland* arrived the next morning, the U.S. Naval Academy came to life as soon as the ship came in sight. A rocket sent up from a picket boat and lights dancing on shore made the Massachusetts men uneasy, so the *Maryland* wisely came to anchor two miles below town, and Butler sent his brother Andrew and Captain Peter Haggerty from his staff, dressed in civilian clothes, to reconnoiter a landing spot in town.

Butler soon had visitors. About an hour after the *Maryland's* arrival, the general saw a boat with five men making its way toward him. He called out, "What boat is that?" and received the reply, "What steamer is that?" Butler's answer was unequivocal: "None of your business. Come alongside or I will fire into you." Lieutenant Edmund Orville Matthews, the Naval Academy's mathematics instructor, climbed aboard the *Maryland* and was closely questioned by Butler.

Such a comedy of errors, ("an almost ludicrous game of bluff" as Captain Devereux called it) existed because Butler had every reason to believe that the Naval Academy had already fallen to the secessionists and that he was interrogating a rebel officer. On the other hand, Lieutenant Matthews thought that he had been taken aboard a boat filled with secessionist reinforcements, whose mission was to reinforce those on land who would then move to capture the Academy. An hours' worth of vigorous questioning and pleading convinced Butler that Matthews was in fact a loyal Union officer.[66]

At the break of day, Andrew Butler and Captain Haggerty returned to the *Maryland* with a guest — Naval Academy superintendent Captain George S. Blake.[67] Blake had spent several anxious days since the war started waiting for help to arrive. He had outlined his dire predicament in a letter to Navy Secretary Gideon Welles on the day Lincoln called for troops: "This point is not

Middies Learning the Ropes at the Naval School on Board the *Constitution*, Annapolis, *Harper's Weekly*, May 11, 1861.

defensible against a superior force, and that the only force at my command consists of the students of the Academy, many of whom are little boys, and some of whom are citizens of the seceded States." Blake had an additional worry—the safety of an American icon. The Naval Academy was the home port of U.S.S. *Constitution*, "Old Ironsides," the heroic frigate of the Quasi-War with France, the Barbary Wars and the War of 1812. Although used as a school ship for training the midshipman since August 1860, rather than as a warship, the sacred relic of U.S. naval history could not be allowed to fall into the hands of the secessionists. In his letter to Welles, Blake suggested loading everyone on board the U.S.S. *Constitution* and either mounting a defense from the ship, or putting to sea and abandoning the academy. Welles approved his plan, but urged him not to move prematurely. Five days later, on April 20, Welles urged Captain Blake to "defend the *Constitution* at all hazards. If it can not be done, destroy her," and the same day the Navy Secretary "respectfully" asked Secretary of War Simon Cameron to furnish a military force to protect the "much exposed" ship and school. On April 22, a still worried Blake wrote Welles that "it is the determination of a great many people of this State that the *Constitution* shall be the first ship of war to hoist the flag of the Confederate States" due to her "very defenseless condition."⁶⁸

Now, with Union reinforcements on hand, Captain Blake, tears running down his cheeks "like rain," according to Butler, asked the general to help him save "the *Constitution*." At first Butler believed he meant the document rather than the ship, and answered, "Yes, that is just what I am here for." Butler quickly realized Blake's meaning and that he was "considerably alarmed" for the safety of "Old Ironsides."⁶⁹ Butler too had a "strong desire" to keep the old vessel "out of the hands of those who would be but too happy to raise their Confederate flag upon the *Constitution* as the first ship of their hoped-for navy."⁷⁰ With an inadequate number of sailors to sail the ship to New York and out of harm's way, Blake would need Butler's help. Fortunately for both, Governor Andrew's instructions left Butler "a latitude for the exercise of my discretion," so he was, in effect, on his "own hook."⁷¹

Blake first invited the general ashore for breakfast. Before the officers left the *Maryland*, however, Navy Lieutenant Matthews handed Butler a note from Maryland Governor Hicks. Addressed to the "Commander of the Volunteer Troops on board the steamer," Hicks "most earnestly" urged Butler not to land his troops at Annapolis and to take them elsewhere "as the excitement here is very great."⁷² But Ben Butler would not be deterred by such an impolite message from another state's governor. He would save Old Ironsides, land his troops, and rescue the national capital.

The most pressing issue was the safety of U.S.S. *Constitution*. Butler's plan was to first move the ship out into the bay, away from the academy, then sail her out of danger. At 6:30 A.M. the steamer *Maryland* came alongside "Old Ironsides," and the warship received the Salem Zouaves, the "Allen Guards" (Pittsfield's Company K), and the approximately 40-man "sappers and miners" company that had been assembled in Philadelphia.⁷³

According to both the Massachusetts men and the Navy's midshipmen, the *Constitution*'s condition was dire. She lay in the mud, secured by four heavy anchors, with a narrow footbridge connecting the ship to the shore. The once proud warship now consisted of a berth-deck for eating and sleeping, while the gun-deck forward of the cabin was divided into three study rooms by bulkheads running fore and aft, and the spar deck, over the main hatch, had a small "house" or building with two rooms used for student recitation. There were six 32-pounders on each side of the quarterdeck, while additional guns had been brought from shore. The ship's force consisted of 101 men (25 sailors and 76 midshipmen), but many of the latter were inexperienced and Southern born or of questionable loyalty.⁷⁴ The Academy contained midshipmen of various political sentiments, from secessionist "fire-eaters" to abolitionists and those in between. "Each and every one appeared to feel himself standing at the crater of a volcano which might at any moment commence an eruption," remembered one midshipman.[75] Because of the small number of trained sailors aboard, and the lack of a proper marine force to protect the ship in case of attack, Butler's men would serve both purposes—his two Marblehead companies, composed of veteran sailors, would operate the ship, while the well-trained Salem Zouaves would act as a marine detachment. As Butler explained, "They will sail the *Constitution* as their fathers did before them."[76]

The ship required considerable preparation before it could sail, however. The heavy guns would need to be removed in order for the *Constitution* to clear the shallow harbor. About 9 A.M. on April 21, under the immediate supervision of "Old Ironsides" commander Lieutenant George Washington Rodgers, the men began the process of transferring the upper deck guns and carriages to the *Maryland*, and then hauled up the ship's anchors (stuck several feet in the mud).[77] When *Constitution* broke free, the deck was showered in mud. "I never saw so much mud on deck before," one midshipman noted, and every one who had any thing to do forward was minus a suit of clothes."[78] While their relatives back home made their way to Sunday morning church services, the Massachusetts men were engaged in the work of war, removing ten of the *Constitution*'s 32-pounders in order to float her off.[79] According to Devereux, even as they unloaded the guns from the *Constitution*, a regiment of hostile Marylanders looked down on them from the heights above, but did not attack.[80]

About noon, after three hours "working like a dog for a good cause," as one member of the regiment described it, the guns were transferred and the *Maryland* was ready to tow Old Ironsides out into the harbor.[81] Their voyage was short-lived, for at 3 P.M. the frigate grounded on a bar, and the disappointed Massachusetts men dropped anchor to await the tide. The *Maryland* then tried to return to Annapolis, but found herself grounded as well. Butler would not allow both ships to remain helpless, however. According to eyewitnesses, Butler and his men made every effort to lighten the *Maryland*, even throwing the coal trucks overboard. "We saw them start the truck for the stern with a cheer," wrote an eyewitness. "It crashed down. One end stuck in the mud. The other fell back and rested on the boat. They went at it with axes, and presently it was clear." The soldiers tramped forward, aft, and danced on her decks, and Butler himself smashed a drumhead in his frantic efforts to keep time, but the *Maryland* would not budge. The Massachusetts men were "all grimy with their lodgings in the coal-dust. They could not have been blacker, if they had been breathing battle-smoke and dust all day."[82] Another observer agreed that the men of the Eighth "presented a most forlorn aspect, and looked as little like soldiers as want of uniformity, loss of sleep, and coal-dust could well make them." To make matters worse, drinking water and food on the *Constitution* were scarce. The little water on board was in musty tanks (some men offered fifty cents and a dollar for a drink of water) and some provisions that had

Landing of the Seventh Regiment at the Wharf of the Naval Academy, Annapolis, *Frank Leslie's Illustrated Newspaper*, May 11, 1861.

been aboard for years were worthless, although at least some men took a piece of raw fat pork, spread it on a hardtack biscuit, and "proceeded leisurely to demolish the tempting morsel." "'Rather rough!'" as one Bay State man expressed it.[83]

Despite what one soldier characterized as "the hardest day's work I ever did," the fact remained that both ships were still vulnerable to attack, and the Eighth Massachusetts was a divided command, with troops aboard both vessels. To heighten their anxiety, at 9 P.M. the men on Old Ironsides were called to quarters, and told to expect an attack by 2 steamers and 5,000 men. Cutlasses and revolvers were issued and boarding pikes kept at the ready.[84]

As if to fulfill that prophecy, the men on board Old Ironsides saw a ship approaching at daylight on April 22. Fortunately it was a friendly vessel — the *Boston*, carrying Colonel Lefferts and his Seventh New York militiamen. The colonel had attempted to follow through with his original plan to sail up the Potomac to the capital, but after hearing that rebel artillery batteries awaited him on the river's banks, he held a council of war, and the New Yorkers decided to come to Annapolis instead.

As the effort to rescue the *Constitution* continued, General Butler tackled the problem of getting his men to Washington. In a letter to Governor Hicks on April 22, Butler again asked for permission to land his troops at the Naval Academy and pass quickly through Maryland to Washington, in accordance with Lincoln's wishes. He also pointed out to the governor that his men were not *Northern* troops, but part of the "*militia of the United States, obeying the call of the President.*" He also asked the governor for permission to relieve his men from "the extreme and unhealthy confinement of a transport vessel not fitted to receive them" and "supply their wants." Hicks responded, again calling Butler's decision to land his troops "an unwise step," but urging them not to stop in the city if they did so.[85]

In addition to exchanging formal correspondence, Butler had a personal meeting with Governor Hicks, but the encounter did not go well. The governor again urged Butler not to land his troops, and informed him that even if he did, the Annapolis and Elkridge Railroad (leading from Annapolis to Annapolis Junction, where travelers could then board a train for Washington) had been wrecked. Butler replied that his orders were to reach Washington, but he could not do so without provisions, so he would need to buy some. The Marylander countered that no one in town would sell provisions to the Yankees. The exasperated general threatened to unleash his men to seize provisions, and the meeting ended with no resolution.

With the arrival of Lefferts and his Seventh New York, Butler now had to worry about unloading and provisioning more than just his own regiment.[86] It became painfully obvious that neither Butler nor Colonel Lefferts could keep their men on board crowded ships in Annapolis Harbor indefinitely. At 5 P.M., despite the governor's pleas, the *Boston* disembarked the New York troops at the Academy, and then sailed out to free the *Maryland*, which then unloaded the Eighth Massachusetts.

The recently landed New York and Massachusetts men found Annapolis to be "a picturesque old place, sleepy enough, and astonished to find itself wide-awaked by a war." The Naval Academy buildings stood along the Severn River, with a green plateau toward the water and a lovely green lawn toward the town.[87] "The playing of the bands the cheering of the troops [sic] taken with their grey uniforms and bristling muskets, was a sight long to be remembered," wrote one Massachusetts man.[88] Despite the bucolic surroundings, there was great uncertainty. General Butler claimed later that the Academy was "almost in a state of siege from the 'plug uglies' of Baltimore," while a New York soldier wasn't certain whether a seemingly inoffensive knot of civilians would, at the tap of a drum, "unmask a battery of giant columbiads, and belch blazes at us, raking our line." Even if the Federals were mistaken and Annapolis was indeed secure, conditions in Washington were unknown. "Nobody knew whether Washington was taken. Nobody knew whether Jeff Davis was now spitting in the Presidential spittoon," worried one member of the Eighth, and there was still a long march to reach the capital.[89]

With their men safely ashore, the issue of getting them to Washington remained paramount for Butler and Lefferts. Two options were possible—

either take the most direct route to the capital by marching down the wagon road, or move up the Elkridge Railroad, repairing it as they moved, so that other Union troops could follow. Butler favored the latter option. Anticipating secessionist opposition, however, Butler knew that the Seventh New York would be needed on the thirty-nine mile journey to the capital.

Although rebuffed in Philadelphia, Butler now tried again to convince the New Yorkers to march with him. Despite his "unsoldierly dress, dumpy figure, unprepossessing face, and political antecedents," the unpopular general made a convincing case that the New Yorkers should join his regiment. The scene was "worthy of an historical painting," according to an eyewitness, as Butler used his "brilliant oratory" to persuade them. He then suggested to Colonel Lefferts that in order to begin the advance, he should detach two companies of his regiment to seize the local railroad depot.[90]

The New York men agreed with Butler's basic premise, and enthusiastically agreed that they should move on to Washington. Lefferts and his officers, however, were more than a bit miffed by Butler's second blatant attempt to seize command of their regiment. Making relations even more strained was the fact that Butler had already issued several "brigade" orders, implying that the Seventh New York was now a part of his command.

After Butler's inspiring speech, the Seventh's officers held a meeting. They all agreed that the wagon road would be the fastest route to Washington, not the railroad, and that they should refuse to cooperate with the Massachusetts general in order to send a clear message. Colonel Lefferts sent Butler a formal note on the evening of April 22 stating that they would stay put, using the reasoning that they carried little ammunition and were sure to face opposition on the road by a large enemy force.[91]

The following morning, when Butler discovered both the note and the fact that his orders to capture the depot had not been carried out, he "fumed and blustered" to Lefferts, threatened arrests and court-martials, and "spared no effort to injure the reputation of Colonel Lefferts, and indirectly stigmatize the Seventh Regiment." The New Yorker stood his ground. His orders from his state's governor directed him to report to General-in-Chief Winfield Scott. Although he was willing to cooperate with Butler, he would not take orders from him, and besides, his regiment was the first to land at Annapolis and deserved the honor of leading the march, not serving as a railroad depot guard. Rebuffed, Butler gave the depot assignment to two of the Eighth Massachusetts' companies. When a messenger from the War Department arrived at the Academy, however, urging the Federals to repair the Annapolis and Elkridge Railroad on their way to Washington and thereby open a way for the passage of more troops, the situation changed. Lefferts finally agreed to cooperate with Butler's plan and take the "longer and more tedious railroad route."[92]

Even though his future was far from certain, Ben Butler was quite proud of his accomplishments. In a letter to his wife penned on April 23, he explained, "I have worked like a horse, slept not two hours a night," but "have saved the 'Old Ironsides' Frigate from the secessionists, and have landed in the Capital of Maryland against the protest of her Government.... I think no man has won more in ten days than I have. We will see, however."[93] Now he intended to march to Washington, and if opposed, "shall march steadily forward."[94]

Despite the less than cordial relationship between their commanders, the men of the Seventh New York and Eighth Massachusetts struck up an instant friendship. After the *Maryland* unloaded her human cargo, a group of New York men shared their hardtack and salt pork with a famished group of Bay State men, cementing the bond. The New Yorkers were equally impressed by their new comrades.[95] Thanks to their hard work on the *Maryland*, the Massachusetts men were certainly less impressive in appearance than the elite Seventh New York, but that made little difference. "What a figure they cut," wrote one New Yorker of the bedraggled Massachusetts troops. "Nobody could decipher Caucasian, much less Bunker-Hill Yankee, in their grimy visages. But, hungry, thirsty, grimy, these fellows were GRIT," pronounced New York soldier Theodore Winthrop.[96]

Finally, on Friday, April 26, one of Butler's major headaches disappeared when the steamer *R.R. Cuyler*, chartered by the War Department as a troopship, arrived from New York. The *Constitution* weighed anchor, and by noon, the *Cuyler* had started to tow "Old Ironsides" on her lengthy journey to safety at the Brooklyn Navy Yard, with the Salem Zouaves aboard.[97] With the *Constitution* out of harm's way and on her way to New York, Butler could take pride in the fact that one of his goals had been accomplished. In a lengthy message, he recounted the reasons for all their hard work to save the ship: "The frigate *Constitution* has lain for a long time at this port substantially at the mercy of the armed mob which sometimes paralyses the otherwise loyal State of Maryland. Deeds of daring, successful contests, and glorious victories had rendered 'Old Ironsides' so conspicuous in the naval history of the country that she was fitly chosen as the school-ship in which to train the future officers of the Navy to like heroic acts. It was given to Massachusetts and Essex County first to man her; it was reserved for Massachusetts to have the honor to retain her for the service of the Union and the laws. This is a sufficient triumph of right and a sufficient triumph for us. By this the blood of our friends shed by the Baltimore mob is in so far avenged. The Eighth Regiment may hereafter cheer lustily on all proper occasions, but never without orders. The old *Constitution*, by their efforts, aided untiringly by the U.S. officers having her in charge, is now ... safe from all her foes."[98]

"And we have done it," echoed Captain Devereux triumphantly on board *Constitution* on April 23. The men of the Eighth had brought out "Old Ironsides," "in the face and eyes of a regiment of the enemy." "I am now on board, in command," he proudly noted, "and am to bring 'Old Ironsides' into New York *safe. We shall do it, or blow her up!* She never goes into the hands of an enemy."[99] Salem Zouave John Reynolds gave credit to the *Constitution's* officers, who would have blown up the ship rather than surrender her, and the Allen Guard and sappers and miners.[100] The *New York Herald* was likewise effusive, although it only paid tribute to the "splendid young men" of Salem who had saved the *Constitution*, and ignored the other men aboard.[101] Captain Blake, in turn, complimented the men of Butler's command, who had deterred any secessionist force from seizing the ship.[102]

Rumors were rife aboard "Old Ironsides" as she sailed to New York: "It is very amusing to hear the speculations of the men upon the various matters of interest to us — the mess tables are all alive with all sorts of Rumors, Speculations, Assertions, denials and guesses, and we all rise quite as wise as we sit down and a good deal more mystified; until all have come to the conclusion to wait for something to turn up, Micawber like," wrote Captain Devereux. "We hear so many that we disbelieve them all."[103] Finally, at 12:30 P.M. on April 29, the U.S.S. *Constitution* appeared off New York.[104] A U.S. Navy legend was now secure.

While Captain Devereux's company sailed north on "Old Ironsides," General Butler began the effort to leave Annapolis and move up the Annapolis and Elkridge Railroad for Annapolis Junction, where they would find a Baltimore and Ohio train to Washington. His plan called for two companies of the Eighth to first seize the depot. After midnight, two companies of the Seventh would join those companies, followed by the rest of the regiment, then the remainder of the Eighth. When Lieutenant Colonel Hinks and two companies of the Eighth (along with a party of "skilled workmen") arrived at the depot, they discovered secessionists disassembling a locomotive and hiding the pieces. Leaving some machinists to put the engine in working order (incredibly, one of the Massachusetts soldiers had helped *build* that very locomotive), Hinks took the rest of his men and started out on the railroad. Pushing a handcar laden with tools and materials, the Massachusetts men repaired about three and a half miles of track before they enjoyed a fitful night's sleep, interrupted by at least one alarm. According to plan, at 2 A.M. on April 24 an advance force of two companies of the Seventh New York and part of a third armed with a howitzer met the Massachusetts mechanics at the depot. Gathering all the rolling stock they could find, at dawn a train of two open platform cars (formed by sawing the tops off two old cattle cars) carrying the howitzer and caisson in front of the engine, and two small passenger cars carrying the two companies of the Seventh, moved out of Annapolis toward Annapolis Junction. Just up the railroad, they found Lieutenant Colonel Hinks and his men and shared the contents of their haversacks with the famished Massachusetts troops, again confirming that they were "firm friends."[105]

Introduction 33

While the New Yorkers scouted ahead to foil any possible ambush or drive off parties of rebels trying to destroy the track, the Massachusetts men moved slowly forward, repairing the damaged rail line. One eyewitness described the stirring scene as the Federals made steady progress: "There stood Homans [the soldier who helped repair the engine], with his hand on the lever of the engine; on each side of him a soldier, with fixed bayonet; the birds-singing in the trees beside the gleaming track.... Sledge and crowbar were wielded by resolute men under the warm and sultry sun. Bridges and track were rebuilt with a will."[106] Although the New Yorkers shared their rations with their Massachusetts comrades (word spread quickly so that "the Seventh have almost been worshipped"), the men also "lived off the land," as two butchers from Newburyport went into the nearby pasture and drove an ox back to the railroad where the men were working, slaughtered the animal and butchered it.[107] At about 9 A.M.,

ABOVE: Men of the Eighth Massachusetts Regiment Repairing the Bridges on the Railroad from Annapolis to Washington, *Harper's Weekly*, May 11, 1861.

OPPOSITE: The Eighth Massachusetts Regiment Repairing bridge on their route from Annapolis to Washington (top); Frank Pierce, one of the Eighth Massachusetts Regiment, diving for a missing rail on the road from Annapolis to Washington (bottom); *Frank Leslie's Illustrated Newspaper*, May 11, 1861.

Opening the Road to Washington (William Swinton, *History of the Seventh Regiment, National Guard, State of New York, During the War of the Rebellion*, 1870).

after advancing about six miles, the combined New York-Massachusetts detachment halted to wait for the rest of both regiments to catch up, and the men flopped on the ground in the shade of nearby trees to smoke their pipes, eat their breakfast, and discuss whether they would reach Annapolis Junction alive.

The remainder of the Seventh New York left the Naval Academy at 7 A.M. and, after marching through extreme heat "'like hot lava,'" reached the halted contingent three hours later. Then the column pushed on, and moving at the rate of one mile per hour, they reached the Millersville Bridge about 2 P.M. and found it destroyed. It was rebuilt and finished after sunset, but not before a violent thunderstorm thoroughly drenched the men. The rest of the Eighth Massachusetts caught up with the column at the bridge, and as they rested, the Seventh New York moved on ahead and marched through the night. The exhausted soldiers stumbled over railroad ties and blundered through the nearby woods and fields in search of missing rails. Some of the men collapsed and slept until the repairs were completed, but were then ordered to push or drag the platform cars carrying the howitzer and caisson (the engine had been sent back to keep the road open). The night turned cold, completing their misery, and the tired, hungry and wet soldiers tramped on. Early the next morning the New Yorkers marched unopposed into Annapolis Junction. The entire Seventh New York boarded a train there at 10 A.M. on April 25 and arrived in the capital at noon.[108] The Eighth Massachusetts reached the junction that morning as well, and the following day headed toward Washington, where they arrived about 1 P.M.[109] The Seventh proudly marched in column down Pennsylvania Avenue and reported to Lincoln at the White House. When the Eighth Massachusetts marched into the city, the men looked "sunburnt and weary, but they marched square to the front, and "Colonel Tim. [Timothy Munroe] seemed as spry as a lad of eighteen."[110] The next day, the president paid tribute to the Bay State men: "Allow me now to express to you, and through you to the officers and men under your command, my sincere thanks for the zeal, energy and gallantry, and especially for the great efficiency in opening the communication between the North and this city, displayed by you and them."[111] According to one account, President Lincoln appeared when the Eighth entered Washington and said, "Three cheers for the Eighth regiment of Massachusetts, who can build locomotives, lay railroad tracks and re-take the *Constitution*."[112]

Despite numerous obstacles, the New Yorkers and Bay State men had restored the railroad from Annapolis and, as they believed, helped save the capital from falling into Confederate hands.[113] The secessionists had been bested: "They fancied the Yankees would sit down on the fences and begin to whittle white-oak toothpicks" instead of repairing the track, wrote one New Yorker.

The fact that the Eighth Massachusetts and Seventh New York had worked together to open the road to Washington continued to foster a spirit of great camaraderie between the two units. Major Theodore Winthrop admiringly wrote, "We of the New York Seventh afterwards concluded that whatever was needed in the way of skill or handicraft could be found among those brother Yankees. They were the men to make armies of. They could tailor for themselves, shoe themselves, do their own blacksmithing, gun-smithing, and all other work that calls for sturdy arms and nimble fingers. In fact … I have no doubt, if the order were, 'Poets to the front!' 'Painters present arms!' 'Sculptors charge bayonets!' a baker's dozen out of every company would respond."[114] U.S. Congressman Samuel Curtis, traveling with the Seventh, admired the Eighth Massachusetts for their "endurance, intelligence, and courage they manifested; and General Butler is a man of great zeal, energy, and intelligence."[115]

The Eighth Massachusetts Regiment bivouacked under the Capitol dome, and ironically, the old Senate Chamber, where Massachusetts Senator Daniel Webster argued against nullification and Charles Sumner was brutally assaulted, became a hospital for Massachusetts volunteers.[116] The day after their arrival, the New Yorkers treated their comrades to "a grand collation," with twenty kegs of lager beer, crackers, cheese and sandwiches.[117] In return, the Eighth Massachusetts unanimously passed resolutions celebrating their "close intimacy and companionship" with the Seventh New York. They thanked the New Yorkers for their hearty welcome at Annapolis, for sharing their rations, for the collation on April 27, and "their many favors." Finally, they pledged that the Massachusetts men would go wherever the Seventh went, and "if ever their colors go down before the hosts of the enemy, the Eighth of Massachusetts would be first to avenge their fall with the heart's blood of every man."[118] Northern newspapers were thrilled to print the resolutions of thanks, as they brought out some of the best characteristics of each unit, and illustrated that combination of qualities that would "override all obstacles and break down all opposition."[119]

After a pleasant if uneventful stay in Washington, the regiment received orders to return to Maryland. On May 15, they left for the Relay House.[120]

Relay House

The regiment's new temporary "home," about nine miles from Baltimore, was not simply "one of the most beautiful spots the eye could rest upon" and "beautifully romantic," in one soldier's opinion, but also a strategic railroad junction.[121] The Relay House, the local landmark, "is an old wooden tavern," wrote one unidentified visitor, "small and dingy, with a broad piazza along its front." Opposite the house was the railroad depot, and between them, the tracks of the Baltimore and Ohio leading from Baltimore. A few rods west of the depot the track divided. The Washington Branch crossed the Patapsco River on a massive stone viaduct and ended in the nation's capital; the other bent westward, hugging the northern bank of the river, to rebel controlled Harpers Ferry and disputed western Virginia. Steep, easily defended hills commanded the junction.[122] General Butler considered the Relay House position "impregnable against any force which may be brought against it."[123] The Federals were able to "have the odds against any attacking force, however large," and cut off all railway communication, if necessary.[124] A portion of Cook's Massachusetts Battery took position near the viaduct, in order to sweep both the Washington branch and main line, while the rest of the battery held the other side of the viaduct, commanding the road to Harpers Ferry.

The Massachusetts encampment was located a short distance from the Relay House, on the opposite side of the Patapsco near the village of Elkridge Landing, the viaduct, and the Washington Branch of the railroad. Two prominent hills were located there, about 150 feet above sea level, with a parade ground between. The Eighth was encamped in Camp Essex, southwest of the viaduct, on the hill nearest the route to Washington, "almost upon the lawn of a handsome country seat," in a clean, grassy grove, while the Sixth Massachusetts was located on the other rise.[125] "The camp was not arranged precisely according to 'regulation,'" wrote one Massachusetts man, "yet nearly enough to give an idea of the ideal law," with rows of tents for the quartermaster, commissary and hospital, the colonel and his staff, the major and the surgeon. The regiment's chaplain shared a tent with the paymaster, so that a man of the cloth slept between a box of rifles and one of money, and "arms, gold, and the Gospel" came in close contact. The captains occupied a row of tents as well, with the quarters of the enlisted men, more "densely populated" than the others, erected at right angles to the captain's quarters. Nevertheless, "many who in wealth, culture, and position were fully the equals of their military superiors" filled the enlisted ranks, wrote one soldier, including the son of a former U.S. senator. Each enjoyed his "undivided fifteenth part of the canvas ten-footer with fishermen and shoemakers, carpenters and sailors."[126]

In addition to guarding the railroad and preventing a rebel attack from the direction of Harpers Ferry, on May 10, General-in-Chief Winfield Scott ordered Butler to have his troops at the Relay House examine the baggage of passengers going west from Baltimore, and to seize all "caps and munitions of war," along with provisions. Groceries could pass through if deemed expedient.[127] Although the troops at the Relay House were described as "having an easy time" by one soldier, they had in fact earned a bit of "soft" service after having had "all the 'bounce' of militia training knocked out of them, and having acquired the steady bearing and solid movement of regular troops." They were "for the most part cheerful, contented, and eager for action."[128]

Some soldiers may have considered the Eighth's lengthy stay at the Relay House as merely a period of mundane drudgery, but it did give the men an opportunity to perfect their drill and become more accustomed to the routine of army life. Many of them would put such skills to good use during the bloody campaigns in Virginia during the coming months. "The life of a soldier is one of real and regular work," explained a Massachusetts soldier. "His hours of rest and labor may not indeed be uniform, but they are none the less regulated. It is not the ten-hour system of the factory, but all-hours system of the ship. The details of the programme of a day in camp can not be as fixed as in other forms of labor; yet its general outlines are the same day after day."[129] Wearing their havelocks (a white cloth cap cover, with a cape to guard the back of the neck) the Zouaves frequently marched to a large grass drill field on the high ground on the north side of the Patapsco to keep their skills sharp.[130] The Salem Zouaves received particular notice for their attention to martial exercises. "Neither here nor in Washington have I seen a company that could compete with them," wrote a member of Cook's Battery. "Their drills are one of the chief attractions for military men. The manual, the firings, and the maneuvres, are executed as if the men were parts of a piece of machinery. Early and late, and in all sorts of weather, they are hard at work. Salem should be proud of them."[131]

The training regimen varied somewhat and was not without excitement. "We have been performing the double quick to-day at charge bayonets, cheering as we advanced," reported a member of the regiment on June 8, and "the men seemed quite excited and marched on as if the imaginary foe was a real one." A round of instruction in "street firing" (a maneuver necessary if moving through an urban setting, such as Baltimore) was performed "much to the amusement of all who witnessed it," he added.[132]

When not on the drill field, the Zouaves became familiar with other aspects of a soldier's life, including long periods of separation from home and loved ones. Mail call became one of the most important and popular events in an army camp, as it provided one of the few tangible links between the men in the ranks and their home communities. If the soldier was fortunate enough to receive a missive from home, it provided a great boost to morale. "If our friends at home could but appreciate the great amount of pleasure we derive from the receipt of their letters they would write more often," explained one soldier, who also threatened to stop writing until letters arrived from friends and loved ones. Despite the regiment's proximity to the national capital, however, there was no guarantee that the precious notes would reach their readers. On one occasion, the regiment's mail was stolen in Washington, but was eventually recovered in one of the city's canals. Much to the soldiers' disappointment, however, all the money was missing from the letters, and many that contained nothing of value were ransacked as well.[133]

Adequate food and the timely arrival of army wages proved to be just as important to a fighting man as a letter from home. As was the case with mail delivery, despite easy access to Baltimore, Washington and the rail lines, the soldiers at the Relay House were not always supplied with adequate rations, and were occasionally forced to buy food locally in order to supplement their meager fare. A member of the Eighth wrote home on June 5, for instance that the men enjoyed fresh beef three times a week and soft bread, but "most of us have money and can buy at the pea nut stands what Uncle Sam fails to furnish." Many of the boys have "fatted up," he continued, but no thanks to Uncle Sam, and their purses suffered heavily, for the soldiers would have gone hungry on many occasions if the government rations were all that could be procured. Even when plentiful, the army rations proved to be less than popular. One soldier lamented the issue of hardtack, the army bread ration: "'Only 64 days more,' some of the boys exclaim with a sigh as they vainly attempt to imprint their teeth in a Bomb proof biscuit." As their supply of cash vanished with unplanned purchases of supplemental rations, the Massachusetts men eagerly awaited the arrival of the paymaster. "Our pocket-books present a deplorable picture," reported a member of the regiment in mid–June, "and it would take several like mine to make a good shadow."

Although many men felt inconvenienced by the bland rations and constant drilling, for some life at the Relay House proved to be far more unpleasant. Illness, the bane of Civil War armies, made its appearance there as well.

Extremely hot weather, with the temperature rising on several occasions to more than 100 degrees, caused heat casualties. "All have felt the heat intensely," wrote one soldier. Nevertheless, soldiers also noted the effects of other disorders, including rheumatism, fevers, and "bilious complaints." The fact that the men had no choice of physicians, as they would at home, and were forced to either accept treatment from medical men they perceived as less than competent or go without, no doubt caused distress among both the sufferers and their comrades.[134]

Frequent rumors that the troops were about to leave the Relay House for more "active" service buoyed the spirits of the men, but also caused great disappointment when those rumors proved to be false, engendering a deep suspicion of such reports. On May 25, one of the men wisely noted, "the fact is Bear has been cried out so often since leaving home, that when the animal really makes his appearance, and not until, will they believe that active service is before them."[135] "We are, to be sure, very comfortably situated at the Relay," admitted another, "but this constant state of inaction, only varied by a hard and sharp two hours drill in the hot sun, makes us envious of anybody who can have something to do, no matter how difficult or dangerous." Despite the inactivity, there was no lack of resolve among the men of the Eighth. "Would to God this war could end, and all traces of division be swept away," begged one soldier. "But I wish it not, till some settlement can be had with those *traitors* who have misguided and deceived a once well meaning, loyal and chivalrous people."[136] In one soldier's case, all it took was music to refresh his patriotic spirit. "Heard Gilmore's Band of Boston, and as they performed the Star Spangled Banner and Hail Columbia," a Pittsfield soldier reported, and "felt that revival of patriotism within us, which characterized first starting for war, but which monotonous life here had almost extinguished."[137]

As the new soldiers settled into the routine of army life, they found that the camp began to assume more of a professional military air. Guards who had been lax about a soldier's travels grew stricter, so that the men could not enter or leave camp without passes. Some men tried altering their old passes by changing the date, while others claimed they were merely going to wash themselves nearby, but all failed to fool the sentries. The discipline forced some to take drastic measures. One of the Massachusetts men became "unruly," struck at the colonel of the regiment for some unknown reason, was subdued and placed in the guard tent in irons.

In mid–May, the men were finally formally mustered into service, but not every man was comfortable with taking the Oath of Allegiance to the United States. Two members of the Salem company initially refused, then relented under considerable pressure. Some officers and enlisted men had little use for those who refused to take the oath. "Much indignation was expressed" in one company, and they proceeded to drum the reluctant men out of camp.

Others were far more understanding. "Many enlist in the service under the great excitement which always prevails at such times, who, after gaining a little insight and personal knowledge of soldier's life, repent the step which they have taken," one soldier explained. Any man who wished to retire when the time came to take the oath, he believed, "should have the privilege of doing so honorably." If those at home were quick to criticize, then perhaps when the civilians had a little personal experience with army life they would judge the soldiers with more mercy. "I have too much pride left for my native State to wish to see her ... assume or endorse an enforced enlistment" which would place her on a level with "the most fanatical of the Southern States," he added. The principal, according to this soldier, was the same, whether men were forced to enlist out of fear of condemnation by public opinion, or by physical force.[138]

Baltimore

On June 26, the Salem Zouaves and their comrades in the Eighth Massachusetts were thrown into "great commotion" by orders to leave the Relay House. Their destination was the very city where their comrades in the Sixth Massachusetts had fought the "Pratt Street Riot" only a few weeks before.

Much had changed in Baltimore since the trial by fire of the Sixth Massachusetts soldiers. On May 13, General Benjamin Butler, acting without orders, had brought a force of Union troops into the city and onto Federal Hill. Butler explained that he had learned that there were rebel military stores hidden there, that he had promised the men of the Sixth Massachusetts that he would lead them back to Baltimore, and, after all, he had no direct orders NOT to enter the city. In a proclamation to the citizens, Butler claimed that his troops were there to enforce "respect and obedience to the laws."[139] The *Baltimore Sun* disagreed, arguing that the heavy-handed Butler did not manage his command "in a manner likely to conciliate the people, or serve the true interests of the government." Butler was soon transferred to Fortress Monroe, Virginia.

Citizens expected "Ben's" successor, George Cadwalader, to be a different sort of commander. Unlike Butler, the 55-year-old Pennsylvania officer was regarded as "a gentleman of courtesy and high character" who was "well-known to our people."[140] Although a "gentleman," Cadwalader soon ran afoul of Supreme Court Chief Justice Roger B. Taney. John Merryman, a local secessionist, was arrested by Federal troops on May 25, and unfortunately for the Marylander, President Lincoln had suspended the writ of habeas corpus the month before. Taney ordered Cadwalader to appear with Merryman and show cause for the latter's incarceration. Neither the general nor Merryman appeared, so Taney issued a writ ordering Cadwalader to appear and explain why he should not be held in contempt. The general failed to appear again, but Cadwalader remained in command until June 11, when he received a field command.

Now, as members of the Eighth Massachusetts arrived in the city, they found themselves under the command of Nathaniel Prentiss Banks. The 45-year-old Massachusetts native was a former Congressman and governor, and, despite a lack of military experience, a newly minted major general of volunteers.[141] Although at first Banks adopted a conciliatory attitude toward the secessionists of Baltimore, he gradually hardened his stance. On June 17, Banks moved several Union units to the outskirts of Baltimore in order to "exercise an important moral effect upon the disaffected inhabitants of the city," and, if necessary, allow him to promptly forward troops to Washington.[142]

His next move was far more provocative, and sparked a highly charged exchange between Banks and some of the city leaders. While the former believed that he was suppressing secessionist activities and securing the city for the Union, the latter saw the general's pursuit of a largely non-existent secessionist element as merely an excuse to establish a military despotism.[143]

Fortunately for Banks, he had the backing of his superiors in Washington. By June 24, 1861, General-in-Chief Winfield Scott became convinced that secessionist sympathizers in Baltimore were "by far more active and effective than the supporters of the Federal Government," and believed that a blow needed to be struck at the city's leadership, "to carry consternation into the ranks of our numerous enemies." Accordingly, Scott ordered Banks to arrest Marshal George P. Kane and the four city police commissioners. Three days later Banks carried out a portion of the order when his troops seized Kane and hauled him away to Fort McHenry in Baltimore Harbor. In a proclamation to the citizens, the Massachusetts

Captain John P. Reynolds, 19th Massachusetts Infantry (courtesy Civil War Library and Museum, MOLLUS, Philadelphia, PA).

general explained that he believed the marshal was protecting parties of secessionists who were stockpiling arms and ammunition and carrying on a contraband trade with Confederate forces. When Banks appointed Maryland Colonel John R. Kenly as the city's provost marshal, the police board ordered their force disbanded. In response, Kenly organized his own police force of "good men and true," and early on the morning of July 1, Banks arrested the four members of the police commission as well. He also claimed to have found a "concealed arsenal" in the police headquarters and elsewhere, including several artillery pieces and several hundred small arms.[144] The Lincoln administration condoned Banks' actions, and in a memorandum written later that July, proposed that Baltimore "be held, as now, with a gentle, but firm, and certain hand."[145] Despite some grumbling by civilians on the city's street corners, there was no repeat of the "Pratt Street Riot."

The Eighth Massachusetts infantrymen pitched their camp on the seized country estate of Maryland Militia General George Hume Steuart (also the home of his son, a Confederate brigadier of the same name) on West Baltimore Street, about two miles from the city's center.[146] There they celebrated the Fourth of July in proper style, buoying the hopes of the city's pro-Union citizens and demonstrating to any local secessionists that the city was firmly under Federal control.

Due to his apparent success, Nathaniel Banks was destined for a greater command in a more active department, and on July 23, 1861, a new commander arrived at Fort McHenry—Major General John Adams Dix. In the wake of the Union's disastrous defeat at Bull Run, Dix found Baltimore to be "ripe for revolt; the Confederate colors were worn in the streets, the Confederate flag was displayed," and reports were circulating that a strong Confederate force was on its way to liberate Maryland. The day after he formally assumed command, Dix asked for reinforcements, arguing that there should be 10,000 men "here and at Annapolis," as the Bull Run defeat had "brought out manifestations of a most hostile and vindictive feeling" in Annapolis and Baltimore.[147] Only a few weeks later, Dix recommended that the Federals greatly strengthen their fortifications in Baltimore, as "the hostile feeling" which existed in the city, "which does not even seek to disguise itself," called for such action. To those who thought such efforts to "overawe" the city would increase bad feelings toward the Union Army, Dix was unequivocal: "I do not think the secessionists could be more intemperate than they are now, and the Union men would be encouraged and strengthened by such a demonstration."[148]

The men of the Eighth shared some of the concerns of their commander, expressing their support for the city's Unionist population while casting a suspicious eye on other residents who were less enthusiastic about the presence of the Federal army. Nevertheless, by late July, the Massachusetts soldiers began to realize that, despite several apprehensive days that month, Baltimore was firmly in Union control, and that they were to serve as "a reserve, which will be drawn upon from time to time as government [sic] may see fit to place them in the field."[149]

End of Service

With their 90-day enlistment almost at an end, the men of the Eighth Massachusetts looked forward to returning home, having faithfully fulfilled their terms of service. When it came time to break camp, they not only loaded their tents and camp equipage onto the train, but also many souvenirs, including cats, dogs, captured muskets, and "quite a number of colored servants," some reputed to be "contrabands" (escaped slaves). They also took several flags, including the one presented to them at Jersey City, one given to them by the friends of the Seventh New York Regiment, one from the loyal citizens of Baltimore, and one presented to the members of Company F by the Native Americans of Baltimore.[150]

As Colonel Hinks and his men bounced along on the train back to Boston, they were confident that they had not only done their duty, but were now regarded as heroes by both the citizens at home and the national government. As one member of the regiment explained, "If we have not been called into an engagement, it was not our fault; we went with the expectation of meeting the enemy, and if we did not it is their fault."[151] The rapid mobilization of the Eighth and other three-month units and their creditable service had vindicated the nation's militia system. "A long cultivation of the arts of peace," the false predictions that the country would come to ruin if a certain presidential candidate were elected, and the existence of well-organized police forces had convinced the general public that

John P. Reynolds, postwar (courtesy Massachusetts Commandery, Military Order of the Loyal Legion and the U.S. Army Military History Institute).

the militia system was costing more than it was worth, argued the editor of the *Salem Gazette*. Its extinction, he continued, would have been felt only "in the emotions of very good men wedded to annual musters from long habit," rather than by the body politic. Nevertheless, the present war had proven such sentiments entirely false.[152] The citizens of Massachusetts and pro-war civilians throughout the North would undoubtedly have agreed with members of the U.S. House of Representatives and specifically Congressman Owen Lovejoy, whose resolution of thanks to the Eighth Massachusetts, approved on July 31, 1861, read as follows: "Resolved, That the thanks of this House are hereby presented to the eighth regiment of Massachusetts volunteers for their alacrity in responding to the call of the President, and for the energy and patriotism displayed by them in surmounting obstacles upon sea and land which traitors had interposed to impede their progress to the defence of the national capital."[153]

The people of Massachusetts were understandably eager to welcome their heroes home. "Every body wants to see the boys who opened the road to Washington and held it until the Capital was safe," trumpeted the *Salem Register*. These were, after all, the men "who rescued Old Ironsides; who fellowshipped with the New York Seventh; whose exploits were immortalized by the glowing pen of the lamented [Theodore] Winthrop [of the Seventh New York]; and whose varied practical accomplishments have been the theme of many a stirring essay over the length and breadth of the land."[154]

The regiment was scheduled to be mustered out at a formal reception in Boston. There, the men impressively "marched half across the Common with battalion front, as straight as a chalk-line could have made it," wrote one observer. The Zouaves in particular were "attacked by a large number of young ladies who hurled boquets [sic] and smiles into their ranks with very disorganizing effect." Colonel Hinks, with cracking voice, bade farewell to his men, and

Lieutenant Colonel Arthur F. Devereux, 19th Massachusetts Infantry (courtesy Massachusetts Commandery, Military Order of the Loyal Legion and the U.S. Army Military History Institute).

hoped they would not forget their old commander.[155] He shook the hand of each of his officers, and when he took Captain Devereux's hand, "addressed him personally, with much feeling." When the regiment gave Hinks three rousing cheers, there were few dry eyes in the ranks.[156] Nearly all of the regiment's members had returned safe and sound. In all, of the 711 men who served in the Eighth Regiment, only one man deserted, six were discharged for promotion, and twelve were discharged for disability.[157]

Soon the Salem Zouaves boarded a train one more time for the last leg of the trip home. At 3:45 P.M. on Thursday, August 1, 1861, the company arrived back in Salem, their arrival announced by the ringing of bells and the firing of a salute. "Dense crowds lined the streets," reported the *Salem Register*, "salutations innumerable were exchanged, and bouquets in rich profusion were thrown among the boys from fair hands." The Zouaves "looked finely," and appeared to "have greatly improved in muscular development since they left home."[158] The men of Salem were welcomed home "with the most cordial enthusiasm not only by friends and acquaintances but by the public generally. The demonstrations of good feeling have been quite universal."[159] Many of the Zouaves, such as Devereux and Reynolds, would quickly re-enlist in newly formed regiments, and would put the experience gained with the company to good use on some of the most horrific battlefields of the Civil War.[160]

Even though many of them survived the bloodletting at Antietam and Gettysburg, the soldiers of the Salem Zouaves always regarded their time in Maryland with Captain Devereux with a certain fondness. In October 1897, the surviving Zouaves met in Boston to celebrate the centennial of the launching of U.S.S. *Constitution*. In a more poignant gathering, in April 1911, John Reynolds and eleven veterans of Captain Devereux's "famous company" gathered at the Salem Armory, then marched through the streets of the city in front of thousands of spectators to the Broad Street Cemetery. There they dedicated a bronze tablet to the memory of their commander. In April 1918, as Americans struggled through yet another war, eight of the twelve surviving Zouaves held a reunion and dinner in Salem, and doubtless many stories of "Old Ironsides," the Relay House and Baltimore were told. Only a year later, John Reynolds joined Captain Devereux and the rest of the fallen Salem Zouaves at their bivouac in the afterlife.[161]

John Perkins Reynolds, Jr.:
A Biographical Sketch

John Reynolds was born in Salem, Massachusetts, on June 1, 1840, the son of John Perkins Reynolds, Sr. and Sarah Rebecca (Roberts) Reynolds. Although working as a clerk when the Civil War began, Reynolds was a member of the Salem Light Infantry, and had only to look to his ancestry for inspiration to continue a military career. His paternal great-grandfather served on board a privateer during the American Revolution, while his maternal great-grandfather was a member of Captain John Parker's militia company that confronted the British at Lexington Common on April 19, 1775. Interestingly, Reynolds' militia ancestor had reputedly followed some British officers the night before the opening shots of the American Revolution, and like the more famous nightrider Paul Revere, had been captured and held until the following morning. Both of Reynolds' maternal and paternal grandfathers served in the War of 1812, and "from them he inherited his strong and enthusiastic military spirit." In 1859, he joined the Salem Light Infantry (Company A, Seventh Regiment, Massachusetts Volunteer Militia).

Only two days after he was mustered out of service in August 1861, Reynolds not surprisingly became one of the men selected from the Salem Zouaves by Lieutenant Colonel Arthur Devereux to be drillmasters in the newly formed Nineteenth Massachusetts Infantry. Many of Reynolds' old comrades accompanied him into the Nineteenth, including its colonel, Edward W. Hinks. In fact, one newspaper boasted, "nearly every company [of the Nineteenth] had a private or sergeant from the Salem Zouaves as lieutenant," as the Zouaves were "capable of officering a new regiment."[1] By the end of August 1861, when the Nineteenth was mustered into service, Reynolds received a commission as a second lieutenant in Company D. That November he was promoted to first lieutenant, and was raised to captain in February 1863.

Reynolds had a relatively short but active career with the Nineteenth Massachusetts. He participated in the Battle of Ball's Bluff, Virginia, in October 1861, and all the battles of the Peninsula and Seven Days Campaigns the following spring. At Antietam, Maryland, on September 17, 1862, he was severely wounded in two places (in the left ankle by a bullet and in the right elbow by a shell fragment).[2] He rejoined his unit in March 1863, but was soon sent home again on leave due to his wounds "breaking out." Reynolds tried once again to return to his command, but was finally obliged to resign in November 1863. Not wishing to leave the army entirely, he appeared before a Board of Examination and was commissioned an officer in the Veteran Reserve Corps in March 1864, subsequently serving in Washington, D.C., Detroit, and Kalamazoo, Michigan, and commanded the post at New Albany, Indiana. He was mustered out of service in June 1866.

Following the war, Reynolds continued to be active in both military and veterans' affairs. He commanded the Salem Light Infantry from 1868 to 1873 and was prominent in the Grand Army of the Republic, the Military Order of the Loyal Legion of the United States, the Society of the Army of the Potomac, and the Massachusetts Minute Men Association. He also led the regimental associations of the Eighth and Nineteenth Massachusetts and the Salem Light Infantry. From 1883 to 1911 he worked in the Massachusetts Adjutant General's Office, and, after 1868, as the manufacturer of "Reynolds Escutcheons of Military and Naval Service," which were elaborate formal certificates sold to Union veterans and their families for placement in the home "for expressing at a glance, on the army (or navy) regulation principle, the record of an officer, soldier or sailor."[3]

Despite his active postwar career, Reynolds' wartime wounds caused him great distress. As his physician explained in 1913, "The injuries are permanent and have greatly handicapped him through all these years."

Reynolds died on June 19, 1919, after an illness of several days, and now rests beneath a simple government-issued headstone in Harmony Grove Cemetery in Salem.[4]

Arthur Forrester Devereux: A Biographical Sketch

Arthur Forrester Devereux was born in Salem on April 27, 1836, the son of George Humphrey and Charlotte Story Forrester Devereux. His father, a Harvard graduate, represented Salem in the Massachusetts House of Representatives, commanded the Salem Light Infantry, and was adjutant general of Massachusetts from 1848 to 1851. Young Arthur attended Harvard and the U.S. Military Academy, but was supposedly suspended from West Point for six months for an infringement of the rules. When he returned and was ordered to join the next class, Devereux resigned from the academy. He took a course at the Lawrence Scientific School at Harvard, but in 1854 went to Chicago in employ of the Chicago and Galena Union Railroad. While in business in Chicago as a solicitor and promoter of patents, he also had a large interest in a factory for producing stamp machines. When the "Panic of 1857" wiped him out, Devereux returned east and became a bookkeeper.

After his service with the Eighth Massachusetts, in which he had "made an exceptionally brilliant record," Devereux was commissioned lieutenant colonel of the Nineteenth Massachusetts Infantry.[1] He was conspicuous in the repulse of Pickett's Charge at Gettysburg, where his regiment captured four Confederate flags. Placed in command of a brigade in the Army of the Potomac's Second Corps, Devereux resigned from the army in February 1864 because of "imperative family considerations." He received a brevet promotion to brigadier general, U.S. volunteers in March 1865 for his service. Following the war, Devereux had a business in Boston as a dealer and contractor in railroad and mill supplies. He served as governor of the Marion (IN) Branch of the National Home for Disabled Volunteer Soldiers (1890–91), and then moved to Cincinnati, where he worked for the Cleveland, Columbus, Cincinnati and Indianapolis Railroad, and was elected to the Ohio legislature.

Devereux was described as "quick in thought and decided in action, and once feeling assured that he was right, neither argument nor influence could change him." A man of honor, he was "loyal to his superiors, fair to his equals, and just to his subordinates." As a tactician, his contemporaries believed him to be "clear-headed, original," and one who "commanded by his impressive presence." "Discipline was innate in his own make-up," according to one biography, although he was "most companionable" and fond of music.

Devereux died in Cincinnati, Ohio, on February 13, 1906, and is buried in that city's Spring Grove Cemetery. Devereux's tie to his old comrades "was a source of happiness to him to the end of his life." The Salem Zouaves sent a beautiful floral piece to his funeral, a symbol of "a devotion as keen at the end of 40 years" as it was when he led the Zouaves to war.[2]

1

Off to War

Journal
Giving a full and detailed account of the various duties, changes of stations, situations, hardships and exposures of the Salem Zouaves (S.L.I.)
Capt. Arthur T. Devereux
Attached to the Eighth Regiment Massachusetts Volunteer Militia during the three months campaign at the commencement of the Rebellion. Containing also a narrative of interesting events, descriptions of places, anecdotes, incidents &c. giving an idea of the duties of the Soldier and a glance at Camp-life generally
Carefully prepared from notes kept at the time by the writer, Corpl. John P. Reynolds. Salem, Mass. 1861.

Apology.
Though these pages are not to be placed before the public, the writer has no objection to their perusal, by such as desire it, but claims it as his privilege by way of an introductory to remind the readers that the manuscript before them is not a historical work, but a simple handbook of reference or journal, kept by himself while a Corporal in the Salem Light Infantry (more familiarly known as the Salem Zouaves,) during the three months campaign of the Eighth Regiment Massachusetts Volunteer Militia, at Washington D.C. afterward at the Relay House Md. and finally at Baltimore Md. at the commencement of the Great American Rebellion. It is often pleasant to look back upon one's younger days, review the pleasant scenes and sociabilities of former times, and recall to mind the scores of familiar and happy faces now passed away. But to look back upon days spent in the service of one's country is not only pleasant, but an honor of which to be proud. This motive perhaps more than any other actuated the writer to the perplexing task of keeping a journal, a task indeed when we consider the limited opportunities

and poor facilities of the camp for such a purpose. Since its completion this manuscript has furnished valuable information for the completion of the records of the Salem Light Infantry while in the United States' service. It is possible some errors may be found, but the information and narration generally will be found reliable, being completed from notes kept at the time. The first half dozen pages are naturally of more interest to the writer than any one else, and might be passed over altogether, by the reader, but they refer to a very bright personal experience of the author of these chronicles, severed for a time by the duties of the hour.

Corpl. John P. Reynolds

Boston Wednesday Apr 17, 1861

The country was wild with excitement, the proud banner of freedom, had been for the first time in our history suddenly lowered at the bidding of traitors. A call had been issued by the executive, for seventy-five thousand troops, to enforce the national authority, and bring back to their allegiance, the states that had seceded from the Union. The old Bay State was among the first to respond, and her militia was at once placed on a war footing, and some regiments already had received marching orders. I proceeded to my duties at the store (of Chandler & Co. Dry Goods, Summer St.)[1] in the morning as usual, and on my return from dinner, received a notice from Capt. Devereux, through fourth Lieut. Putnam, to proceed without delay to Salem, and report to the armory of the Salem Light Infantry, to which company I then belonged, for military duty.[2] Accordingly I (made a hasty settlement of my affairs with Mr. Capen, who promised to retain my situation for me until my return, and) took the three o'clock train for Salem, arriving at a quarter to four, and reported as I had been ordered.[3] The scene here was very exciting. The armory was filled with people, and many of the boys already appeared, "armed and equipped as the law directs," and were highly complimented for their promptness. It was reported that the company was to leave Salem that night, and proceed at once to Washington, but I soon ascertained that we had received no definite orders, excepting to hold ourselves in readiness for any order which might be issued. (After spending an hour at the armory, talking over the events of the day and future prospects, I called at Mrs. C---s on Washington St. where I spent the next half hour very agreeably in the company of Mr. & Mrs. C. Annie A---, N---, and Mrs. G---.[4] The latter two had started on a visit to Mrs. B---s in Lynn, but having missed the two and a half p.m. train, were spending the afternoon at Mrs. C---s, until the arrival of the next one at half past five. I made known to them my intentions of entering the service, and they were much surprised at the announcement, particularly N--- who was of course rather more interested than the rest in my movements, and I held a lengthy interview with her on the subject, until a few moments before the time for the train to arrive, when I accompanied her with Mrs. G--- to the depot, where I accepted their invitation to join them at Mrs. B---s by the next train, saw them safely aboard the cars, and returned home to tea. Here I made known to the folks my intentions, and they were also much surprised, but though they expressed much regret at my leaving, they did not object, or attempt to dissuade me from my motives, when they considered the nature of my departure, and the necessity for prompt action on the part of the people. I therefore received their consent, with a fathers blessing and a mothers prayers. After tea I made some few trifling arrangements, then put on my uniform and proceeded again to the armory, a company drill having been ordered. Soon after my arrival, however, I sought permission of the Captain to be absent for the evening, (it being one of the bye-laws, that "any member desirous of being absent from any drill, must previously obtain permission, or be fined in consequence"), which permission was granted,) and I took the quarter past seven train from Salem, arriving at Lynn at half past. I at once proceeded to Mrs. B---s to make good my promise, and spent the evening very pleasantly in company with Mrs. B--- and family, N--- and Mrs. G---. During the evening we were highly entertained with a mammoth music box, which discoursed in all about twenty-five pieces, "The Anvil Chorus" and various waltzes and schottisches being among the number. Music on the piano also added to the pleasures of the evening. I was also introduced to Mr. B---, who entertained us in jokes in conversation. At about half past eleven I took my leave, promising to call on them again before leaving with the company (as they were to remain all night,) and walked briskly to the depot to await the arrival of the eleven-fifteen train from Boston. It came in on time, and I stepped aboard, arriving home at about twelve o'clock.

Thursday April 18th

(It was a beautiful morning, the sun arose in all its splendor, and hardly a cloud was visible in the heavens. A cool breeze from the South East re[n]dered the air bracing and comfortable, and the citizens were about at an early hour. I arose at half past six, and after breakfast called on Harry H--- across the street to learn the movements of the company.[5] Sergt. Gray was also there, and informed me that the company were under orders to appear at the armory at eight o'clock, and would leave for Boston at nine. I remained here about half an hour, then returned to the house to make arrangements for my departure. At half past seven I took a hasty farewell of the folks, and called at the residence of the Sergeant in Mall St. with whom I proceeded to the armory. On the way I stopped into the stores of J.B. & S.D. Shepard, (Dry Goods), and Wm. B. Ashton's, (Clothiers,) and made some purchases of under clothing, &c. to complete my outfit, arriving at the armory a few moments before eight. I immediately obtained permission from the Captain to take the eight o'clock train for Lynn, and join the company there on its arrival, at nine o'clock or soon after. Arrived at Lynn at fifteen minutes past eight and proceeded to Mrs. B---s, where I found my friends in good spirits, and I spent nearly an hour with them in the pleasantest possible manner. They expressed a wish to see the troops pass through on their way to Boston from Salem, and at nine o'clock we adjourned to the depot. Here the excitement was intense, and the people were full of enthusiasm. We found it next to impossible to proceed a step, the crowd filling almost every inch of room. The train was somewhat late, and while awaiting its arrival, we enjoyed ourselves in conversation and merry jokes, and I was quite pleased with the good spirits and cheerful manner of my friends, so entirely foreign to the majority of people on such an occasion. As a slight memento they each presented me with a pocket handkerchief, charging me to keep it to remember them by. This I assented to and stuffed the handkerchiefs under my jacket. At a quarter before ten, the train came slowly into the depot, and the excited crowd pressed in dangerous proximity to the cars, and were with difficulty kept from being injured. I bade a hasty adieu

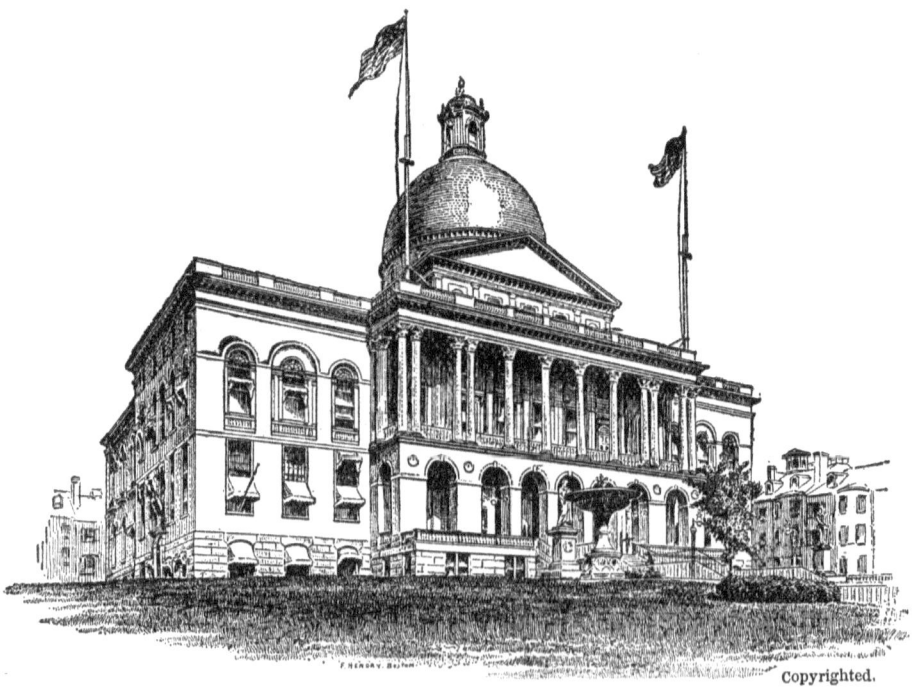

Massachusetts State House (*Butler's Book*).

to my friends, and elbowing my way through the crowd, stepped upon the train, already crammed to its utmost capacity, and many hanging from the railings on the platforms. I was somewhat surprised to learn that the company numbered sixty four members, but on inquiry learned that thirty new members had been voted in at the meeting last evening, and were then with the company, but without uniforms. Most of them were clad in such portions of the old infantry uniform as they could obtain. Some had on the old thick-breasted swallow-tail coat, others the pants, with the wide old fashioned stripe. No two of them were dressed alike, but the people were too much absorbed with other thoughts to notice their comical appearance. I was also informed that the departure of the company from Salem, was a most affecting scene. At the armory, prayers were offered by the Rev. Mr. Wildes of Graces church, and remarks were made by several prominent gentlemen, among whom were Mr. Webb, mayor of the city, and ex-Gen'l. Devereux (father of the captain, who also had two other sons in the company, Charles the orderly sergeant and John).[6] At the depot and on the streets hundreds were gathered to take a farewell of their sons, brothers and friends, and many were the tears shed on that memorable occasion. At ten o'clock we left the depot in Lynn, amid a most deafening shouting from the crowd on all sides, and arrived in Boston at a quarter before eleven. Disembarking from the train we formed on Causeway St., in front of the depot, and proceeded under the escort of a detachment of the Salem Cadets, to the State House, where we were furnished with knapsacks, overcoats and some underclothing, and a blanket each.[7] We remained in the rotunda of State House a couple of hours, during which time we were drilled by the Captain in load & fire, before a crowd of spectators. We then proceeded to Fanuel Hall with the balance of the regiment, packed our knapsacks and were furnished with dinner. This was the grand <u>rendezvous</u> for the troops, passing through on their way to the seat of War. At about four o'clock, the regiment entire were marched back to the State House, where we were addressed by His Excellency Gov. Andrew, in an appropriate and feeling manner.[8] At the close of his remarks, we returned again to Fanuel Hall, and took supper, and at five o'clock took up our line of march round the common, through Tremont, Court and Washington streets to the Worcester Depot, where we embarked in the half past five train for New York. All the streets through which we passed, were lined with people, and we were greeted with cheers and shouts at every corner. On our arrival at the depot we were received with the same enthusiasm and thousands blockaded the track and passage ways, eager to witness our departure. As the train slowly started, parting words were exchanged and hands shaken rapidly, and we left Boston amid the waving of handkerchiefs, and boisterous cheers. All along the road at the several stopping places, the same excitement prevailed, and bonfires, booming of cannon, ringing of bells &c. announced our arrival. At Worcester the people were crazy with excitement, and made loud and rapid calls for Gen'l Butler, who I should have before mentioned was with us in command. The General stepped upon the platform, and responded in a patriotic manner for several minutes, and we again moved on. At Springfield, several illuminations were visible to us, in the immediate vicinity of the depot, and we remained here some time.[9] Refreshments consisting of hot coffee and sandwiches were freely distributed through the train, which were very acceptable. All night long the boys were in the highest spirits, and sleep was not thought of by many. Some of the boys sang songs, others danced and all kept up considerable noise. (At four o'clock in the morning I was detailed for guard and remained on duty until our arrival at New York).

2

New York and Philadelphia

Friday April 19th
(The morning air was quite cool, and a thick fog enshrouded us. Heavy clouds bearing a threatening appearance were also visible, but disappeared with the fog soon after sunrise. Continuing our journey we arrived at the depot of the New York and New Haven rail-road, on Fourth Avenue at seven o'clock, and marched through Fourth Avenue, Twenty-Sixth street, Waverly Place, and University, down Broadway to the Astor House, where we partook of an excellent breakfast, after which the company were dismissed for an hour, which was spent in repacking our effects, bathing, writing, &c.[1] At half past eleven we were ordered to fall in again, and took up a short march under the escort of a posse of the New York city police, through the City Hall park and Courtland street to the ferry, crossed the Hudson (or North) river and took the cars on the New Jersey Central road for Washington. We started without delay, and I found much to take up my attention as we whirled along. The country was very level, and the early vegetation contrasted greatly with the dead surface of the locality we had started from. We had gone but a few miles when it was rumored through the train, that "hot work" was no doubt before us, and accordingly our arms were inspected, and every precaution taken against surprise. This was the first glimpse of the reality of our position which crossed our mind, for the excitement attending our departure, was sufficient to destroy all sober reflection. Notwithstanding, however, this somewhat gloomy report, our boys continued in the same lively mood. The Conductor, a very patriotic individual, now entered the car in which I was seated, and entertained us in a very pleasant manner. He was a native of the Bay State, and said he was proud of that honor. Also informed us that he was in the service in 1812, and give us a number of interesting anecdotes concerning his experience in soldiering. He was a good singer withal, and gave us a number of patriotic airs in the

style of a professional singer. (My attention was now again drawn to the scenery around us. The rail-road ran parallel with the Delaware river canal for several miles, and I watched with considerable interest the numerous boats passing in either direction thereon, drawn by mules. It was the first thing of the kind I had ever seen, (for we have no canals east) and I found it an interesting novelty.[2] At half past two o'clock we arrived at New Brunswick, which with its numerous factories and canal bridges presented a lively and interesting sight. A short distance before reaching the depot, the road passes over a bridge, I should think a hundred feet in height, directly underneath which large factories were built. As we crossed it we had a beautiful view of the surroundings for some distance. As the train stopped we were greeted with considerable enthusiasm, and hundreds of factory girls waved their aprons from the windows, while the male and juvenile portion of the operatives streamed towards us in swarms. We remained at the station about fifteen minutes, and took our departure again amid a deafening roar of shouts and yells, resuming our journey to Campden arriving at about six o'clock. Here we at once crossed the Delaware in the ferry-boat, to Philadelphia. We were here met with an overwhelming reception, surpassing anything since our departure from home. Cheer upon cheer rent the air, and the people pushed and crowded around us in the highest state of excitement, and were with the greatest difficulty made to "stand back" by a posse of police, who escorted us to the Girard House, then unoccupied and which was assigned to the regiment as quarters. From the ferry to our quarters it was a continual uninterrupted ovation. Chestnut street was so densely packed that we proceeded with difficulty. Windows were crammed to their utmost capacity, and the buildings were profusely decorated with bunting, streamers and mottoes. At almost every visible point on the route flags were thrown to the breeze, and a vast sea of waving handkerchiefs accompanied us the whole distance.[3] Upon our arrival at the Girard house we were dismissed, and marched in turn by companies to the famous "Continental" directly opposite, and were furnished with an excellent supper which was duly appreciated. The negro waiters were also most lavish in their attentions, and our every wish was gratified. The evening was passed in different ways. Some strolled about the city, others threw themselves flat on the floor and spent the time in writing. Among other features about twenty of us gathered on the balcony in front, and gave a rousing "seven" for the ladies at the windows opposite. This "seven " was a novel sort of cheer or response, which we had adopted with our appellation of Zouaves, and was more familiarly known as the "Zouave cheer." It consisted of counting in concert as far as seven, then repeating the words, tiger and Zouave at the same intervals of time, concluding with the person or object cheered. Thus on this occasion it was "one"—"two"—"three"—"four"—"five"—"six"—"seven"—

"tiger"—"zouave"—"ladies." When a member proposed a cheer he would say "seven for this" or "seven for that," and the cheer that followed would be given as just described, in boisterous tones and perfect time. Before retiring for the night, we were informed by the Captain of the attack on the Sixth regiment by the mob, in Baltimore, and that General Butler intended to push through that place in the morning at the point of the bayonet if necessary. We were therefore placed in readiness to fall in at an early hour, and turned in with the determination to do our whole duty if called upon.

Saturday April 20th

At one o'clock in the morning, we were aroused from a quiet slumber by the Orderly, and ordered to pack our knapsacks with all possible speed, and without so much as a whisper. In fifteen minutes were ready to execute any orders required and marched, or rather crept from our quarters to the lower hall, where we marked time awaiting the Allen Guards, who were the only company of the regiment besides ourselves who had been disturbed. (All the while I suffered with a violent headache, and every movement I made jarred my brain like a thunder bolt. I would at any other time have gone back to bed, but on this occasion was determined to see the fun, if any there was to be.) Various thoughts coursed through my brain as we stood here before the outside door of our quarters. We were unable to ascertain the nature of the duties before us, but it made little difference, for most of the men were in good spirits and prepared for the worst. As soon as the Allen Guards were ready, the door was thrown open and the order double quick given, and we started with muskets at right shoulder shift, at a tearing pace which we did not slacken until we arrived at the depot of the Philadelphia Wilmington and Baltimore Railroad on Broad street.[4] It was a pretty tough stretch for us, and our position was rather ludicrous, for our knapsacks thumped heavily against our backs at every step threatening our equilibrium. Private Charles H. Mansfield suddenly brought his toe in contact with something which sprawled him in the road, while his knapsack and musket kept him company and rattled about on the pavements. The situation of the next dozen that followed, one on top of the other, was laughable in the extreme. Mansfield regained his feet in a moment however, happily for him none the worst for his fall. Upon our arrival at the depot we found the famous Seventh Regiment of New York, Col. Lefferts, on board the cars ready to start for Baltimore. They numbered one thousand men, all finely equipped, and had with them also a couple of brass howitzers. It was supposed that they were to accompany us but for some reason they left the cars, and we afterwards learned that Col. Lefferts had decided to go by water from Philadelphia to Annapolis. From two o'clock in the morning until eleven in the forenoon, we remained in the depot waiting the decision of the gallant (?)

Colonel, during which time we were furnished with something called a ration, which consisted of a couple of slices of salt-junk, the same of dry bread, and mustard enough to keep it for eternity. Although we were pretty hungry this was most too much of a good thing and we left it untouched. An hour after some unknown friend sent some warm loaves to us which were very welcome. Having waited in vain for the Seventh, Gen'l Butler was determined to go through without them, and accordingly at ten o'clock we were joined by the balance of the regiment from the Girard.[5] A band of Sappers and Miners, made up from detachments of each company excepting the right and left, was organized and furnished with the necessary implements.[6] At eleven o'clock we left Philadelphia in the cars evacuated by the Seventh, amidst the shouting of a countless multitude of people assembled along the road for considerable distance. Of course we responded in a hearty manner and gave them many a <u>rousing</u> "seven," the balance of the regiment joining in the old fashioned three cheers. As we streamed slowly along some of the boys struck up "America," "Star Spangled Banner," "Red White and Blue" &c., much to the amusement of our friends outside. We were soon far away from the crowds, and whirling over the country at a rapid rate, and I occupied my attention with the scenery about us. For miles we followed the course of the Delaware, and the more forward condition of the vegetable kingdom indicated our rapid approach to somewhat warmer regions. We were soon in slave territory, and our attention was often attracted to the groups of negroes assembled along the fences, who greeted us with their broad grins, and manifested considerable pride in saluting us. As we neared the junction at Wilmington, it was reported and afterward confirmed, that the bridge south of Havre de Grace had been burned, and the track torn up for several miles. Also that the ferry boat at Perryville was in the hands of rebels to the number of a thousand, who were however poorly armed, having only one hundred guns among them. Arrangements were accordingly made for seizing the boat by force, in which we were afterward to proceed down the river to Annapolis. We were furnished with ammunition — thirty rounds to a man — and ordered to load.[7] The captain then addressed us in a few words, assuring us that there was every indication of trouble before us, and that blood would no doubt be spilt before our purpose was accomplished. Notwithstanding this flattering prospect of things, the utmost coolness and determination prevailed, for which we were afterward complimented. We were the right flank company of the regiment, and of course as skirmishers would be the first to come upon the enemy. We were therefore divided into squads, each man numbered and assigned to his position, ready to jump into it the moment the train should stop. One would suppose that a set of inexperienced soldiers like ourselves, would be overcome with fear on being so suddenly called upon to take the position of the fighting soldier, but it is but in justice to the entire regiment to say, that there was little or no exhibition of any such thing, for in less than half an hour, the majority were sleeping as calmly as if nothing had happened to test their courage. About half a mile from Perryville the train "broke up," and leaving our baggage and knapsacks in the train we leaped out, and formed platoon front directly across the track. As soon as the men were in their places the order "forward" "double-quick" was given and away we started to meet our fate. To make a clean sweep the Captain yelled in loud tones "two files on the right and left over the fence," and being on the extreme left I scrambled up the bank with the rest, and we jumped the fences in a moment, landing in a puddle of clay and water some inches deep on the other side, which in our hurry and excitement we could not avoid. Not a soul met our eye, and we had a good opportunity to laugh at our besmeared condition, and indulged in an outburst. We kept on at a lively pace to the ferry, which we expected to be the scene of considerable sport, but on our arrival we were not only happily disappointed, but somewhat surprised to meet but a few unresisting civilians. Some of the boys claimed to have seen people retreat with arms behind the buildings, but there was no evidence of any thing of the kind. Our safe and unmolested arrival we could hardly account for, and while enjoying the "sell" it occurred to the minds of some of the boys that there might be a lurking force below on the boat, waiting to draw us into a trap. This we soon ascertained to be incorrect for we were marched below without delay to find none but the hands belonging to the boat, and we felt quite secure again. It was reported that the captain of the boat was waiting for his secession friends, and therefore refused to get under way for us, but Butler brought the man to his senses, by giving him choice between a dose of cold lead, and compliance with his order. This had the desired effect and we soon launched out upon the waters of the Susquehanna. The river was calm and clear, not a breath of air could be felt, and our sail was delightful.[8] We had much to take up our attention in the changing scenery on either side, and at about seven o'clock emerged from the broad mouth of the river into the Chesapeake bay, stretching away to the horizon before us. The moon now lent her silvery charm to the scenery about us, and we remained on the upper deck until a late hour. The excitement and fatiguing labors of the day finally took a strong hold upon us, and we spread our blankets and turned in.

3

Old Ironsides

Sunday April 21st.
The men were summoned at an early hour, and the non commissioned officers of the company were detailed by the captain to drill the recruits on the upper deck. At the expiration of an hour we formed company again, broke ranks and rations were served out to us for breakfast. It was a most delightful morning, enlivened by a brisk southerly breeze, and not a cloud was visible in the Heavens. We were at anchor in the tranquil waters of Annapolis harbor. The huge hull of the old Constitution lay within a gun shot of us at her moorings, her black sides towering above the waters edge, and her port holes thrown open from which her "long toms" protruded as if to threaten our safety. A short distance in rear of her was the Naval Academy to which she was attached as a practice ship for the midshipmen, and from which she was reached by a narrow foot bridge. We soon discovered her to lower a boat, which put directly for us to discover who we were, and we learned from the inmates that the captain of the frigate (Rogers) had taken us for a posse of Baltimore roughs, who he had expected in the same boat which contained us—the Maryland.[1] At nine o'clock we hauled alongside of her, and preparations were immediately commenced for removing the ship from the dangers of being seized, as was hourly expected, by the secessionists of Annapolis, to the navy yard at Brooklyn, N.Y. The Allen Guards, Sappers and Miners and our own company were detailed as her convoy, and also to furnish the necessary hands to work her. The harbor of Annapolis was very shallow, and there was great danger of running her aground at any moment, and thus not only delaying her rescue, but rendering it much more doubtful. Accordingly some of her heaviest guns were hoisted out, and placed temporarily aboard the Maryland, in order to lighten her and render her capable of passing over the bar.[2] Some three hours were occupied in this difficult job, and at twelve o'clock noon we

General View of Annapolis, with the *Constitution* in the foreground, *Harper's Weekly*, May 11, 1861.

weighed anchor, and the Maryland took us in tow down the harbor. We made but little progress as the tide was rapidly running out, and a strong head wind was blowing all the time. At three o'clock we grounded on the bar as we had feared, and several attempts of the Maryland to haul us off proved unavailing, and we dropped anchor to await the next tide.[3] The Maryland then drew in her hawser and directed her course back to Annapolis, but had proceeded a short distance only before she grounded also. She made several attempts to extricate herself, and finding it impossible to do so, Gen'l Butler ordered her coal cars to be thrown overboard, but she was obliged to let go her anchor and remain till next tide.[4] We were now in an exposed condition. Our Reg't was divided, a portion on the Constitution, and the rest aboard the Maryland half a mile or more distant. It was reported and some believed, that the pilot of the latter was a rapid secessionist, and ran the boat aground intentionally.[5] As night drew near, precautions were taken to secure against surprise, and a guard was detailed and divided into three reliefs, each relief being placed under the supervision of a corporal. The sentinels were posted at every quarter, and were relieved every two hours. I was detailed as corporal of the third relief, and while on duty an unknown light was reported by the sentinel on the forecastle, which I in turn reported to Capt. Rogers, who ordered the "call to quarters" to be beaten and every man summoned on deck. The order was obeyed with the utmost confusion, and Captain Rogers threatened to shoot every man who spoke a word. Quiet and coolness was soon restored, and we were ordered to place a cap on our muskets already loaded.[6] The big guns were then set, ready to be run out as soon as the ports were opened. It was an exciting suspense and every mouth was hushed, awaiting the result of the discovery. As soon as the light arrived within speaking distance, Capt. Rogers spoke the craft and we ascertained it to be the steamer Boston from Philadelphia with the New York Seventh on board. She was ordered to heave to by the Captain, and lay near us at anchor all the next day. We were then dismissed and ordered to turn in, which was a most welcome order, as the sky was thickly overcast and rain was expected any minute.

Monday April 22d.

The clouds rapidly disappeared at an early hour, and we were favored with another beautiful day. The morning air was rather keen but comfortably cool and bracing. At five o'clock reveille was beaten and we were soon up and ready for duty. This was the first time we had heard the loud stirring reveille, and our curiosity was not a little excited by it. After roll call I had occasion to enter the state-room of Capt Devereux, who informed me that we had effected a narrow escape in removing the Constitution, and that we were as yet not entirely free from danger. That six hundred Rebel troops were stationed in the vicinity of Annapolis, and that it was their intention to seize the Constitution, and turn her over to the Rebel authorities. That if our troops had been three hours later, her doom would have been sealed. Had such been the fate of "Old Ironsides" who so nobly supported and defended the Republic in its infancy, and covered herself with laurels,[7] and whose very name caused the fires of patriotism to kindle, it would have indeed been "a sad termination of a glorious career," which would have been deeply felt by all true and loyal Americans.[8]

We lay at anchor in the Chesapeake bay, a mile or two from Annapolis, with the Maryland and Boston near us at a short distance. Our boys spent the time in an easy manner about the decks some writing, others smoking, while others who had become somewhat fatigued by the various duties which we had encountered since our departure, and the privations which befell us, gave them selves up to "tired nature's sweet restorer"— Sleep.

For my own part I found considerable pleasure in watching the numerous sailing craft, passing and repassing in the distance around us, upon the broad expanse of water, and enjoying the cool delightful breeze from the water. All seemed to enjoy our situation much, the only thing to mar it, being the food, a misfortune which came very near being serious. Salt junk and pork which hogs might have found fault with, hard tack (as the sailors call it) which <u>might</u> have been baked in 1812, being about the consistency of brick-bats, and a thin black decoction called coffee, but more like common senna, constituted the sum total of our rations.[9] Two meals a day of this stuff was all we could obtain. There is no doubt we subsisted upon the best the ships larder afforded, for she had for a long time been so situated as not to require a store of provisions aboard, and the sudden arrival of our troops, so unexpected, prevented her officers from making the necessary preparations for so many. Yet with all this consideration the change from the ordinary habits of our lives was so great and so sudden, that we couldn't stand it, and accordingly set up an indignation meeting. Capt. Devereux heard of our proceedings and summoned us before him, demanding an explanation, which we were not slow in giving. After hearing our complaint, he said he could not blame us, and in order to provide us with as many necessaries as possible, he told the non-commissioned officers to go into a state-room, choose a commissary from our number, and make out a list of such articles as we needed for the trip, promising us a full supply as soon as a boat should leave for the shore. This we considered a great kindness and appreciated it accordingly. Towards night the Boston put ashore at Annapolis, and landed the Seventh, and the Maryland soon after floated off and landed her troops at the same place.

At half past seven retreat was beaten by the drummer and fifer of the Constitution, after which dress parade took place on the quarter deck, Capt. Devereux commanding and Lieut. Putnam acting as Adjutant. The moon shone beautifully and her soft light lent a charm to the scenery about us. It was too pleasant to turn in after ranks were broken, and most of us collected on the fore castle deck, and spent the time in a joyful manner, indulging in "sweet notes of song" until two bells, (nine o'clock,) when we dispersed to our quarters.

Tuesday April 23d

We were aroused from our snug quarters in the house-on-deck, by reveille which was beaten at five o'clock, and were allowed an hour or so to ourselves. The weather of the morning was fine, and appearances indicated a beautiful day until about ten o'clock, when the air grew thick and hazy. This lasted but an hour or so however and it cleared away again warm and pleasant. At the customary hour of seven o'clock we marched down to breakfast, but our table was no more inviting than usual, no change in the diet having as yet manifested itself. Dissatisfaction perched upon every countenance and we could not refrain from grumbling, while some actually complained of being sick. We were obliged however to make the best of it, and of course "pitched in," starvation being the only alternative. After breakfast I spent an hour in the ward-room and wrote a couple of letters. While here a report was circulated that Washington had been captured and was in the hands of the Secessionists, and that we were at that moment surrounded by the traitors who numbered thousands, and were stationed in and about Annapolis. This report occasioned much excitement but proved to be a mere rumor without the slightest foundation whatever. At about nine o'clock the Maryland came alongside and we proceeded to retake the guns aboard, which gave us a chance to try our hands at the capstans. The manner in which the

66   "In her hour of sore distress and peril"

Grounds of the Naval Academy, Annapolis, *Frank Leslie's Illustrated Newspaper*, **May 25, 1861.**

capstans were worked was a new thing to us. When all was ready, we were ordered to leave, and the fifer commenced a lively air, and bracing ourselves to the bars, away we went, forward march, around the circle again and again, keeping time to the soul stirring music of his fife. It was indeed an interesting novelty, but soon became tedious in the extreme.[10]

It was necessary to have a guard about the ship as usual, to warn us of approaching danger, and I was detailed Corporal of the guard for the day. This duty prevented me from pulling many ropes, but I was not sorry, for it was tough work and I was glad to escape it. At four o'clock we had succeeded in getting all the guns aboard and mounted on their respective carriages, and we now felt doubly secure against any attack. At half past four the company was formed and we drilled for a short time in the bayonet exercise, load & fire and manual, which caused the big drops of sweat to roll from our foreheads and the inner man to cry for re-inforcements, but we dared not think of the latter for the ship afforded no such substantials as our sharpened appetites craved. On the contrary our evening meal was more scanty than ever, and to add to our discomfort, the company were served last of all. We called on Capt. Devereux and presented to him this new grievance, and he immediately interceded for us, the result of which was good hot coffee and plenty of it. This I will confess wrought a great change in our humor, and we took possession of the forecastle deck where we spent the evening in a pleasant manner, singing, smoking &c. under the sweet silver rays of the moon, until tattoo which beat at two bells (nine o'clock) and we turned in. We were not sorry for being interrupted, for the boys had undergone a hard days work at the capstans, and a good nights rest was very desirable.

    At eleven o'clock I was routed for guard duty and summoned my relief. The boys were quite vexed at being disturbed and I pitied them. The moon still shone in all her silvery luster, as we took our posts about the deck, and a warm southerly breeze swept over us. Not a sound disturbed the profound silence, save the occasional slap of a tiny wave against the sides of the ship. To gaze upon the broad expanse of water, reflecting like a sea of silver, the brilliant orb over our heads, was a scene I had seldom witnessed, and I enjoyed my situation much. At one o'clock a.m. a boat drew alongside, and the few on deck were rejoiced to find that it contained a good stock of provisions and for us. The Captain's promise was fulfilled indeed, and our mouths watered at the prospect of good things again, for a time at least. The stock consisted of potatoes, mackerel, hams, tongues, eggs, butter, cheese and sugar. How we longed to make a hole in them. We were not slow in getting them aboard and placing a guard over them, to protect them from the ravages of our hungry fellows. At the proper time our relief was called in, and we retired to snuff the savory mouthfuls in store for us, in dreams.

Wednesday April 24th.

Reveille again rattled in our ears at the usual hour, and we reluctantly left our hard but comfortable beds, and commenced our daily tasks, by first making our rough toilets which occupied the time until seven o'clock, when we fell in for breakfast. The morning air was beautiful, rendered doubly charming by a brisk balmy breeze from the southward. The golden rays of "old Sol" as he arose above the horizon, were but the forerunners of the beautiful day that followed. At an early hour, a number of steamers were visible making towards us from the south-east, and their movements were closely watched by all on board. They soon arrived near enough for us to distinguish them, and we counted eleven, all having the stars and stripes floating from their mast heads. As they approached nearer we discovered them to be loaded with troops, and among them we distinguished the Ariel, Baltic and Harriet Lane.[11] We expected that the Mechanic Light Infantry, and

City Guards of Salem were on board one of them, and we watched eagerly for our friends. They sailed in all directions around us, and came to anchor as if seeking protection under our guns, and cheer upon cheer rent the air and were rapidly responded to, as one by one they steamed by us. Two other steamers from Baltimore soon passed us on their way to Annapolis, which we also cheered. It was estimated that since we first saw the fleet approaching, eight thousand troops had passed the old frigate Constitution on their way to Annapolis and Washington. As soon as the excitement occasioned by the arrival of the steamers had ceased, our company fell in and roll was called. We were then drilled in the manual, bayonet exercise and load and fire in all its branches, by the Captain. Much wonder and delight were expressed by the officers and midshipmen, particularly the latter, who stood staring at us with mouths wide open, as we went through the several motions, and who applauded in a rough boisterous manner. After the drill our muskets which had been loaded since the recent night alarm, were discharged one by one in a kneeling position from a port hole on the starboard quarter. Ranks were then broken and we were called together, and inspection of knapsacks of all the men on board took place, as a number of men had complained of having their property stolen, a very common affair among soldiers. A list of their missing articles was given to the Captain, and every knapsack was opened and its contents displayed upon the deck, while the men stood in line behind them. After considerable investigation a majority of the missing articles were found, and restored to their proper owners, who had been in a majority of cases neglectful of their property, and allowed it to get misplaced. During the inspection a boat came alongside the ship, loaded with small articles of lunch, which were eagerly purchased at exorbitant prices by the men, who dove at them like starved beasts. Their hungry condition was taken advantage of by the sellers, and twenty-five cents was charged for a small package containing a few small crackers and bit of cheese, while everything else rated in proportion. The men did not stand for prices, and patronized liberally, a change to anything from our daily rations being far preferable to money, which like Crusoe's pieces of eight might be as dross, but for this.[12]

    We now packed our knapsacks again, and fell in for dinner at half past twelve. Soon after dinner black clouds appeared in the south eastern horizon, which rapidly spread over the entire firmament, accompanied by violent gusts of wind. In a few moments after, rain commenced falling in large scattering drops, which were followed by a heavy shower which continued for half an hour, and we were not slow in retreating under cover, where we remained. I resorted to the ward room and spent considerable time writing. At about four o'clock the clouds began to disappear and the sun soon shone as bright as ever. Retreat was beaten at five o'clock and shortly after the line

was formed on the quarter-deck for evening parade. During this ceremony a
boat came alongside from the steamer Ariel, bringing two members of the
company, Private George O. Stevens and Private Samuel H. Smith, who as
they came aboard inform[ed] us, that though they could not leave Salem with
the company, they were determined to join us, and left with the Mechanic
Light Infantry, who they said started with ninety-six muskets, and the City
Guards with over sixty.[13] They brought with them several letters and papers
for the boys, and after welcoming them with due ceremony, they fell into
ranks and drilled with us. Inspection of arms then took place and we were
dismissed. The evening was spent in pleasant conversation with the two
arrivals, and we learned from them some news. Among other things they
informed us that a company called the Home Guard numbering fifty-four
men, mostly ex-members of the company, was organized in Salem, under
the command of ex-General Devereux, who used the armory for drilling
purposes. At tattoo we answered to roll-call and turned in.

Thursday April 25th.

The morning was somewhat cool, but clear and bracing. A high wind from
W.N.W. was blowing when we turned out at reveille, and our overcoats were
quite comfortable. A barque from Baltimore, loaded with flour, which had
been seized by Capt Rogers during the night, lay a short distance from us
on the port side, and it was reported that a part of her cargo was to be taken
aboard the ship, and the balance sent to Annapolis for the benefit of the
troops. After roll call the company was divided for convenience into messes,
and a captain chosen to each mess, who was held responsible alike for the
proper care of the dishes and victuals, and the conduct of the men at the
tables. The non-commissioned officers constituted one mess, and at seven
o'clock we took breakfast under this new arrangement, for the first time. At
eight o'clock the colors were hoisted with due ceremony, and saluted in the
customary manner by the drummer and fifer. At half past ten the company
was ordered to fall in, and after inspection of arms we drilled for an hour.
As we broke ranks a boat came alongside loaded with eatables and the boys
patronized as eagerly as usual. We purchased a couple of shad for the N.C.O.
mess which we had cooked in excellent style. Arrangements were now made
for the embarkation to New York, and at noon Capt. Rogers and Lieut.
Upshier went ashore to procure the necessary articles for the ship's outfit.[14]
At one o'clock we marched to dinner which was quite an improvement on
our meals generally, and soon after a steam tug came alongside with sails,
rigging, anchors &c. and we immediately were detailed to assist in getting
them aboard, which gave us another chance to tug at the capstans. In a
short time the deck was strewn in every direction with the truck, and it
was almost impossible to move about. The ship's cooking apparatus came

among other things, but it was of no use as parts of it were lost, and it was impossible to put it together. This was a great disappointment to us, for we had been promised better facilities for cooking as soon as this could arrive. Hammocks were distributed during the afternoon, and we commenced at once to string them for use. At seven o'clock the officers returned to the ship, and at half past seven we marched to supper. At eight o'clock one hundred and forty midshipmen arrived on board from the naval academy, varying in age from twelve to twenty years, and their manner caused some ill feeling among our boys. They manifested a haughty air towards us, and after selecting the best quarters the ship afforded, in some cases even removing us, they commenced giving their orders to us with the air of a General officer. This was a sad mistake for them, for our boys showed them that they were entitled to no better treatment than ourselves, and after knocking over one or two of them, they returned to their senses, and we had no more trouble from the midshipmen. At an early hour I retired. The moon shone beautifully, and the evening was spent in a joyful manner by all hands.[15]

Friday April 26th

(At the usual hour we were summoned for duty by the loud stirring music of the reveille. The atmosphere was again cool and bracing. The utmost stillness prevailed, and all nature was wrapped in the most profound silence). We soon learned that the Allen Guards were to leave us, having been ordered to join the regiment by Gen. Butler. This we regretted very much for the Guards had been detailed with the company, and we had kept together during the whole journey and had become greatly attached to each other as companies. At an early hour they commenced making their preparations for departure, and at half past seven went on board the steamer Josephine, which stopped on her way from Baltimore to take them to Annapolis. As they left the ship we gave them a rousing "seven," and cheer upon cheer in response rent the air, from the Pittsfield boys.[16] The Middies (as we called them) also took it up and gave several loud parting cheers for our friends. We watched them until they were nearly out of sight, waving our hats after them, until our attention was called in another direction by a steamer making directly towards us which proved to be the R.R. Cuyler from New York, and which had been sent for to take us in tow, for which preparations were immediately made. Two large howsers were run out over the bow of our ship and made fast to the stern of the Cuyler. At about twelve o'clock the huge anchors were drawn up, and the Constitution left her moorings in the Chesapeake for New York. A strong head wind prevented us from making very rapid speed, and we coursed along at about eight knots per hour. New attractions one by one presented themselves as we passed the various points on the coast, and we soon left Annapolis completely out of sight behind. At two o'clock dinner was served up, and we fared rather better than usual, mackerel and potatoes, luxuries to us then, being provided and in ample quantity. During the afternoon we amused ourselves in various ways about the decks, watching the various changes in the scenery of the coast as we coursed along. At about four o'clock assistance was called for aloft, and some of our boys who had had previous experience in sea faring life, volunteered their services at once, and Simey Dalrymple and Private Luscomb, were in a jiffey, at home among the rigging.[17] A contest soon ensued between our boys who were at work on the foremast, and the sailors and middies on the mizzen mast and the boys proved themselves decidedly the smartest, finishing their job and gaining the deck a full half hour before the middies, for which they were complimented by Capt. Rogers. At half past six the company fell in, and we drilled for an hour then took supper. In the evening I enjoyed myself in a pleasant manner in the quarters of the midshipmen. A number of them were musicians, and formed a fine orchestra consisting of two flutes (first and second,) a violin and a guitar, and during the evening they discoursed some excellent music. At nine o'clock I turned in but at half past two a.m. turned out again for guard duty with my relief. Our tour was a pleasant one, as the moon shone beautifully and the air was warm and comfortable. Towards four o'clock the steamer Harriet Lane which had thus far accompanied us, hailed an unknown schooner from Baltimore and ordered her to heave to, but for some reason she did not obey, and the Harriet Lane immediately gave chase, came up with her in a few minutes, fired a gun across her bow with brought her to in double quick time. At half past three we spoke the steamer Monticello from New York, bound for Annapolis.[18]

Saturday April 27th.

The eastern sky soon began to light up, and the grey streaks bespoke the dawn of day. One by one the stars vanished from sight to their snug little hiding places, and the sweet lustre of the moon faded gradually away, as if shrinking in terror from the more brilliant "King of Day" who now gradually appeared above the horizon, as if emerging from the depths of the water beyond us. I witnessed this spectacle with interest and pleasure, for I had often heard of the grandeur of sunrise at sea, and though not exactly at sea, the effect was equally as grand. At first his face was of a magnificent crimson hue and much larger than the ordinary size, but as he traversed his daily path towards the zenith, he seemed to contract his dimensions, assuming a more golden hue, until I was obliged to turn away from his dazzling brightness.

The ship moved on under her powerful escort, steady and firm. The surface of the water was comparatively smooth, disturbed only by gentle ripples caused by a light westerly breeze, and our sail was pleasant in the extreme. At nine o'clock some little excitement was occasioned by the breaking of one of the hawsers and the slipping of the other, which caused some little delay, but these injuries if they may be so called, were soon repaired and we moved on again. We coursed along at the moderate rate of about ten knots per hour, and at about ten o'clock launched out from the bay into the broad Atlantic, leaving Cape Charles on the left and Fortress Monroe in the distance on the right. The scene now grew more interesting and exciting, the waves ran higher and the ship rolled with the long dizzy swells of the ocean. The boys enjoyed it much and perched themselves upon the rails of the ship, and in the portholes on the gun-deck, from which the sea looked beautifully. Some however were sadly afflicted with the nausea of sea-sickness, and the unfortunate victims lay strewn about the decks, exposed to the ridicule and laughter of their comrades. During the afternoon an amusing scene took place on the spar deck. A pair of boxing gloves were procured, and several of the men on board amused themselves and the crowd, in sparring. Two little fellows among the midshipmen* proved to be quite expert at it.[19] They appeared to be from ten to twelve years of age, and the manner in which they handled the gloves was surprising. The skillful licks which each at times dealt his opponent, elicited frequent applause from the bye-standers. This sport lasted about an hour when the "sponge was thrown up." At about seven o'clock we took supper, after which the company was divided into two watches for the night, the front rank constituting one and the rear rank the other watch. (Being in the second watch I retired at the usual hour, but had been asleep but a short time when the ship gave a sudden lurch upsetting the bench upon which I was lying in the house on deck, and landing me sprawling on the floor. I jumped up and finding myself unhurt, replaced the bench and laid down to rest again. At twelve o'clock we were routed for duty, and went on deck to relieve the first watch, where we remained until four o'clock. The ship rolled and pitched tremendously with the impetuous waves, and fears were entertained that the connecting hawsers might snap, and we were obliged to watch them closely. It was impossible to walk or even stand up on deck without support, and we managed the best we could until four o'clock a.m., when we were relieved and retired again to quarters.)

Sunday April 28th.

(The company did not turn out until seven o'clock, and when we did we had no duty to perform, and after attending to a few personal matters awaited breakfast. The sky was dark and overcast and a dense fog was visible at the eastward, which soon closed so thick around us, that it was impossible to see for any distance. The air was cold and chilly from a southerly wind, and we were obliged to put our overcoats to keep comfortable. At about half past five rain commenced falling, and there was every prospect for a stormy day. At one time the sun was partially visible through a veil of clouds, and seemed as if striving to shed his golden rays around us, but his attempts were unsuccessful, and he was soon obscured by the clouds again. At half past seven we were ordered to fall in, and marched down to breakfast, after which I returned to the spar-deck and discovered that a pilot-boat had arrived from New York, with a Pilot for the Cuyler. I remained on deck but a short time, and went below again to the ward room to write, but was soon interrupted by some most beautiful music from a melodeon in the quarters of the midshipmen, and laying aside my writing materials went to join them. A crowd soon collected from all quarters of the ship, and we indulged in a variety of songs, until we were routed by the officers of the ship, who coolly informed us that we were making too much noise, and that it was impossible to hear a word on deck, so we were of course obliged to give it up. We scattered in various directions and I took possession of Lieut. Brewster's state-room and indulged in a nap, but had been lost in the arms of Morpheus but a few moments, before some mis-

Colonel Elmer E. Ellsworth (courtesy Wilson's Creek National Battlefield, National Park Service, WICR32622).

chievous rascal disturbed my dreams by nearly jerking my leg off, and yelling to the top of his voice, "fall in for dinner" I first thought to retalliate, but came to the wise conclusion that dinner was far preferable to a knock down, and fell in with the rest.) Soon after dinner the wind increased to a perfect gale, and it being considered inadvisable to proceed farther in the fog, we dropped anchor, and the Cuyler cast off of our hawsers and anchored at a short distance also. We now lay off the heights on Jersey shore, the ship riding heavily on the waves, at times rolling furiously, and the rain falling thick and fast, while the wind continued to blow and whistle through the rigging, and the fog seemed to grow thicker and thicker. We remained in this position for a couple of hours, but at three o'clock the fog began to disperse, and we weighed anchor, and were again taken in tow by the Cuyler. This time we put on but one hawser, but the wind blowing dead a-head it was feared this would be insufficient to hold us, and sails were put on to lesson the strain. At six o'clock we passed Sandy Hook and the steam frigate Niagara at anchor, also an English steamer laden with troops which we cheered heartily.[20] We now changed our course a little, and sped along at a rapid rate up the outer bay of New York harbor, and soon entered and passed through the "Narrows" into the inner harbor. We were now within a few miles of the great Metropolis, and the scenery on all sides grew more attractive and interesting. On one side of the bay lay the rapidly grown city of Brooklyn, with its many attractions, among which could be seen the beautiful hills and glades of Greenwood cemetery, situated on Gowanus heights and covering an area of some three hundred and thirty acres. Immediately south lay Fort Hamilton numbering eighty guns. On the opposite shore lay Staten Island, a favorite resort for summer residence, with the Forts Richmond and Tompkins, numbering respectively one hundred and forty, and forty guns, and the batteries Hudson and Morton numbering sixty guns. Governors Island on which is situated Fort Columbus, Castle William and South Battery, with an aggregate strength of one hundred and eighty two pieces, and Bedloes Island with Fort Wood numbering sixty-seven guns, were objects of interest as we passed them. We now rapidly neared the venerable crescent shaped battery so familiar to New Yorkers, and at half past eight dropped anchor where we lay all night. It was now quite dark, and the myriads of lights from New York directly before us, Brooklyn on the right and Jersey-City on the left, all blended together in one continuous line, formed a novel and interesting sight, not unlike a monstrous torchlight procession. We found much to interest us during the evening, though some of the boys spent considerable time preparing letters to forward the first opportunity. For my own part it was pleasing to watch the various colored lights, and listen to the numerous bells of the steamers and ferries, passing and repassing in every direction. At about nine o'clock

Capt. Devereux and Lieut. Austin embarked in a small boat for the shore, and many of the boys desired to go ashore also but no man was allowed to leave the ship. After listening for half an hour to some music from the Midshipmen, Corporal Williams and myself occupied Lieut. Austin's state-room and turned in.

4

Return to New York

Monday April 29th.
(At an early hour we were up and ready for duty, and after finishing our duties of the morning, I ascended to the spar-deck to view the sights around us. The Battery before alluded to and formerly celebrated for its picturesque delights, was but a stone's throw before us. Small craft of every description sailed or steamed on their way in all directions around the old Frigate Constitution. Brooklyn and Jersey City, the Hudson and East rivers and the harbor, furnished numerous attractions for the eye, and I enjoyed the surrounding prospect in the highest. At seven o'clock I was interrupted in this enjoyment by the order "fall in for breakfast" and of course obeyed it, and after breakfast I spent considerable time writing.) At ten o'clock two tug-boats the Oliver M. Petit and James A. Stevens came alongside and prepared to take us in tow to the Brooklyn Navy Yard.[1] A high wind was blowing, and the ship hove round stern fore most in a contrary manner, and nearly an hour was spent in properly heading her. With a powerful tug at each side however this was soon accomplished, and we weighed anchor and were soon rapidly nearing our destination. (While watching these maneuvers, I had the misfortune to lose my cap overboard, and the satisfaction (?) of seeing it float rapidly down the harbor, in spite of all efforts to secure it. As we entered the mouth of East river, a wonderful panorama met our eyes. Far as the sight could follow all was life and action. Great ships bearing the flags of almost every country on the globe, crowded the wharves, their forests of masts and spars concealing from view the walls and roofs of the city beyond. Numerous ferry boats passed and repassed in seeming confusion. Skiffs, pleasure boats and tugs, moved back and forth, the whole forming a scene of crowded and tumultuous movement.) At twelve o'clock noon we arrived at the Navy Yard, and soon after the Captain returned with orders for us to pack up immediately, preparatory to going ashore. We

executed this order in double quick time, and when we were in line Capt. Rogers addressed us in a few words, complimenting us for the manner in which we had conducted ourselves during the trip, and expressing his regret at the poor and scanty fare the ship afforded, and the limited accommodation we had received, assuring us that under the circumstances the best had been done for us. At the conclusion of his remarks we gave him a hearty "seven," and stepped aboard the ferry-boat which already lay alongside to receive us, (taking with us our utensils, and a quantity of coffee and sugar that remained of our stock of provisions.) In less than half an hour we landed at the foot of Beekman Street and proceeded, route-step, to the Astor House, where divesting ourselves of our equipments and baggage, we marched into an excellent dinner.[2] The tables presented something of a contrast to those we sat at on the Constitution, and the dinner was duly relished. After dinner we were dismissed for a short time and the boys strolled in every direction about the city to "see the elephant." At about four o'clock Col. Ellsworth's celebrated regiment of Fire Zouaves, composed exclusively of New York firemen, came around the city-hall park on their way to Washington and we formed line in front of the Astor to greet them. They were a bold looking sett of men, armed with short rifles with sabre bayonets, and dressed in a neat light grey uniformed trimmed with red. They numbered about eleven hundred men, and were escorted by several thousand active firemen of the city.[3] Cheer upon cheer rent the air as they passed up Broadway, and we gave them several hearty "sevens." (While here I came across a friend from Salem with whom I enjoyed a pleasant conversation. He informed me that he was about to return and kindly offered to take home parcels, letters or any word from any of the boys, and a number accepted his offer. At five o'clock Lieut. Brewster, Private Douglas and myself, took a short walk to the United States Hotel, and spent a short time very pleasantly, returning to the Astor at about six o'clock. On the way we stopped into a military store, and Lieut. Brewster purchased a curious looking article called a fez-cap, consisting of a mere bag of thick red cloth, square at the top with a very bright blue tassel hanging over the side from the centre. At half past six we had a roll call, then went in to tea, after which Corporal Williams and myself took a walk up Broadway as far as Eighth street, and on our return visited Laura Keene's to see the famous "Seven Sisters," which was a highly entertaining performance.[4] One remarkable feature of the play was a drill of twenty five female Zouaves, under the command of Laura Keene, which was loudly applauded. At about eleven o'clock we returned to the Astor, formed company and proceeded to the temporary barracks in the city-hall park, where we were quartered for the night. Whittredge furloughed for 20 days.

Tuesday April 30th.

At six o'clock we turned out and after roll-call and morning duties generally, resorted to the Astor for breakfast. The morning air was cool and bracing and the sun brilliant and charming, and there was every prospect for a most beautiful day. Breakfast over we occupied ourselves in various ways about the house, some smoking and chatting, others reading, some writing and all of us awaiting the arrival of the mail, which soon occurred and the wished-for letters were shortly at hand. I was at last fortunate enough to be in luck and received my first letters from home. After perusing them the company was ordered to fall in, and after roll-call we proceeded to the city-hall park nearly opposite, and gave an exhibition of the bayonet exercise to a tremendous crowd of spectators, which judging from the applause we received, must have been very satisfactory to them. At half past nine we were dismissed, and a squad of us took a short walk about the city. I visited several hat stores and military establishments, and endeavored to purchase a new uniform cap, to replace mine which I lost overboard, but could find nothing anything like what I wanted. We next patronized the barber under the Astor and called at Meade Brothers to sit for a photograph, after which we returned to the Astor and dined.[5] At about two o'clock I strolled up Broadway with Private Harry Hall, and called on some friends of N---s at 753, where we spent an hour very pleasantly. On our return we passed down Clinton and Waverly places, which with the above were places of peculiar interest to myself only. Thick black clouds now suddenly made their appearance, from which rain soon commenced falling, and we made the best of our time back to Broadway, hopped into a Bus just in season to save a ducking and returned to the Astor at about half past four. We had a most refreshing shower, and after it was over we started out again, called at the Metropolitan, St. Nicholas and La Farge returning just in season for tea. At half past six the company were ordered to fall in, and after roll was called we marched down to the salon in the basement, where we drilled for half an hour and were dismissed. (Some half a dozen of us now started out to attend some place of amusement, but were unable to determine which offered the greatest attractions. Pending the decision, we visited the celebrated "Taylors" and after enjoying one of those world renowned ice creams, decided in favor of Winter Garden where we afterward resorted.[6] The programme for the evening was "Jenny Lind," and "Governor's Wife" in which Mrs. John Wood and Jefferson appeared in all their glory.[7] At the close of the performance we returned to the Astor. During the day we had made arrangements to occupy some of the rooms in the upper story for quarters, which was a great improvement of course on the close bunks at the barracks where we had before slept. On the way to my room I met a brother of Corporal Williams on the stairs who had just come on from

Salem, and who brought me another letter from home. I spent half an hour in pleasant conversation with him, then wrote in my journal and retired.)

Wednesday May 1st

A cool but clear and beautiful morning. Arose at half past six, and on the arrival of the mail at eight o'clock, was much pleased to receive another letter from N---, which I at once read and answered. At nine we took breakfast, and soon after were ordered to fall in, and after roll call were drilled for an hour in the bar-room. At ten we broke ranks, and I called at Meade Brothers for the photographs I had ordered, and sent three of them home. After some difficulty I purchased a red zouave cap, somewhat different in trimming from the company pattern, which Mrs. Austin, mother of the Lieutenant, then visiting at the Astor, kindly trimmed with some gilt braid, to correspond with the rest. At about twelve o'clock clouds appeared, obscuring the sun, and rain fell quite fast. At half past one I partook of an excellent dinner, after which a party of us visited "Barnum's" where we spent the afternoon very pleasantly. On entering the museum I was much pleased to meet three midshipmen from the Constitution, also a member of the New York Seventh who was with us at Philadelphia with his regiment, but had returned on account of ill health. The latter kindly furnished us with tickets for reserved seats at the dramatic performance, which consisted of the celebrated play the "Hidden Hand," which had been running there for some time. At the close of the performance we examined the variety of curiosities including the "Bears," "Seals," "Sea Lion," "What-is-it," "Tom Thumb," "Albino family" and in fact all the interesting features of the museum.[8] At half past five we returned to find the weather again delightful, the rain having ceased, and the sun shining beautifully. During our absence, a quantity of Camp and Garrison Equipage arrived for us consisting of haversacks, canteens, and rubber blankets. At six the company fell in for roll call and a short drill, after which we took tea. During the evening a squad of us strolled up Broadway, called at the St. Nicholas and round to the "Fifth Avenue" returning to the Astor at half past nine when we turned in, but not to sleep, for no sooner had we extinguished the lights then a half dozen of the boys burst into our room, and commenced upbraiding us for retiring so early. Although it was pitch dark it was easy to distinguish that they had been out "calling," but as six of us occupied the rooms in three beds, we felt equal to them at least. They were bent on a good time generally, and commenced very unceremoniously to remove the bed clothes from us, whereupon we "pitched in," and for an hour all was hub-bub and confusion. "Every dog will have his day," and the boys having got their fill, left us and retired at a late hour.

Thursday May 2d.
(This affair rather trespassed upon our hours of sleep, and the sun was high up before we awoke at all in the morning, and even then we did not turn out until we were attracted by an unusually loud noise in the entry, announcing the arrival of Charlie Dearborn of Salem — a member of the Salem Cadets, who had come on to join the company. Dearborn brought with him a number of letters for the boys among which were three for myself. Of course I did not lay abed long after that. The sun shone beautifully, and the morning was made doubly charming by a cool northerly breeze. After enjoying a hearty breakfast, I returned to my room and spent the greater portion of the forenoon reading, and answering my letters from home. At about twelve o'clock Private Archer Stimpson and myself, called at the celebrated bakery of Erastus Titus & Co. on Washington street, near Chambers, and spent an hour very pleasantly. Mr. Titus was an elderly gentleman and an old acquaintance of father's, and paid us marked attention.[9] He very kindly escorted us over his immense establishment, the largest of the kind in the city at least, occupying the whole of the building five or six stories in height. In the basement were the great ovens where the bread was baked, also novel and ingenious machinery for kneading, rolling, cutting, stamping and preparing the dough for the ovens, all of which were the inventions of Mr. Titus himself, saving an immense amount of labor, delay and expense. The steam engine furnishing the motive power for this machinery was also here. The upper stories were occupied for assorting, packing, branding, storing and shipping the various kinds of hard and soft crackers, comprising twenty different varieties, not the least among which might be mentioned the best quality of "hard-tack," for which Mr. Titus has taken several premiums at different fairs and exhibitions. At one o'clock or soon after we took leave of Mr. T. and called at the immense Dry Goods and Clothing establishment of H.B. Cloflins & Co., said to be the largest in the world, where I purchased a pair of laced marching boots with which a majority of the boys were already furnished. At two o'clock we returned to the Astor and dined, after which Archer and myself took another stroll up Broadway, returning at about four o'clock. Soon after four we were ordered to fall in, and after the roll was called descended to the barroom where we drilled for a short time, awaiting the arrival of some field music which had been sent for. They arrived in a few minutes and we proceeded to the city-hall park and drilled for an hour nearly, in the different branches of load and fire, before a throng of spectators who frequently applauded the movements. During the day an invitation had been extended to the company, through the Captain, by Mr. Wm. R.L. Ward, father of Private Ward, to visit his residence No. 22 West Sixteenth street, and partake of a collation. This invitation was accepted by the Captain, and at about five o'clock we marched

up Broadway, arriving at Mr. Wards at about half past five. We at once stacked arms and went inside. The tables were set in excellent style with many tempting articles, and the occasion was enlivened by the smiling countenances of a number of beautiful ladies. After satisfying the "inner man" we formed line on the pavement and entertained Mr. Ward and his friends with a short exhibition of the bayonet drill which drew from them loud bursts of applause. We wound up by giving him a hearty "seven," and retraced our steps by a circuitous route to the Fifth Avenue Hotel, where we were again assailed by Mr. Savory of Salem, an ex-member of the company, who insisted upon our accepting refres[h]ments (?) again.[10] We stacked arms and spent a few moments with him inside, after which we drilled a short time on the pavements in front. At about seven o'clock we retraced our steps down Broadway to the Astor, marching <u>for convenience</u> at rout-step. The excitement of the day, and the march and drill, used us up a little, and most of us turned in at an early hour. "<u>Honi soit qui mal y pense</u>."[11]

Friday May 3d

(At seven o'clock I arose having enjoyed a good nights rest, and in half an hour after went in to breakfast. The weather continued pleasant until about nine o'clock when the wind shifted to the South, and appearances indicated rain. After breakfast I purchased a blank book for the purpose of keeping the records to compose this journal, and spent most of the forenoon writing and copying.) During the afternoon, arrangements were made for having photographs taken of the company in line, as it was expected that we could not remain much longer in the city, and many desired such a picture while there was an opportunity. Accordingly after dinner which we took at the usual hour, we were ordered to fall in with overcoats, and proceeded at once to the city-hall park for this purpose. One half of the company were recruits, and unversed in the different tactics, and were therefore placed in the rear rank, leaving the front rank composed entirely of the more experienced members. We were then drawn up in open order, and the picture was taken with the front rank kneeling at the position of "ready," in load and fire kneeling, the rear rank standing at the position of order arms. The weather was anything but favorable, rain falling quite fast all the time we stood there. After one or two attempts however, our artists (Meade Brothers) succeeded in getting a very good negative. At half past three we returned to the Astor and were dismissed. It still continued to rain quite fast and I went up to my room to improve the opportunity to write, but had just seated myself when loud huzzas, music and drums, drew me to my window, which opened out to Broadway and afforded an excellent opportunity of witnessing whatever might be going on below. The excitement at this time proved to be the Ulster County Regiment passing down Broadway on their way to Washington.[12] They numbered about five hundred men. During the afternoon the Twenty-Second New York also passed with twelve hundred strong, and as fine a looking regiment as we had thus far seen anywhere. It was a wet and uncomfortable evening, and at seven o'clock I took supper and at an early hour retired.

Saturday May 4th.

At half past seven I arose and soon after sat down to a heavy breakfast. Pleasures cannot always last in this world, and to day is one that will be remembered, by every member of the Salem Zouaves. For a week we had enjoyed the hospitality of one of the best hotels in the city, receiving more than the usual attention from the gentlemanly proprietor Mr. Stetson, an ex-member of the company. We had visited the principal "lions" of the city, and had come in contact with many friends from home, some of whom stopped at the hotel with us. We formed many acquaintances, and gave the citizens of New York frequent exhibitions of our manual and bayonet exercise, never failing to draw from them loud bursts of applause, and well deserved compliments to our gallant commander, Arthur F. Devereux. All this was soon to end, and we were to leave these "gay and festive scenes," to rejoin the regiment at Washington.[13] The reluctance with which this intelligence was received, was followed by a feeling almost of sadness, the weather contributing to give us the blues, for it was cool and disagreeable, rain fell quite fast, and at intervals during the forenoon we were visited by frequent spits of snow. Soon after breakfast the expected order came, to "pack up," and we heard that we were to embark on board the steam frigate Niagara at eleven o'clock. This however proved to be a mistake. The scene at the house was unusually lively for a short time, and we were soon ready to move. We were no sooner in line, than the order was countermanded, and "unsling knapsacks" was obeyed with uncommon promptness. We broke ranks again and I improved the last opportunity to write a few lines in my journal, until dinner when we partook of a sumptuous feast, and our last meal at the Astor. Soon after dinner we were ordered to fall in a second time, and slinging knapsacks we proceeded to the bar room, where we waited orders in line. At three o'clock they came, and after giving a deafening "seven" for our friends and the Astor, we bid farewell to both and proceeded by the shortest route, to the steamer Roanoke, at her dock on the Hudson.[14] We went aboard at once and while waiting for her to steam up, were much pleased to see our friend Mr. Ward on the pier, who afforded considerable amusement, by tossing the contents of a huckster's basket among us, consisting of apples, oranges, &c., which caused a scrabbling among the boys, and a good deal of sport among the lookers on. In their eager desire to secure the fruit, many lost their equilibrium, and rolled about the deck convulsed with laugher. After the excitement had subsided, we disembarked from the boat at the request of some of the spectators, and give a short exhibition of the bayonet drill on the wharf. Again we went aboard, and at six o'clock precisely we steamed away from the pier, amid the cheers of the crowd which we did not fail to return, till we were nearly out of sight. We enjoyed a most beautiful sail down the harbor, watching the receding city of New York, until one by one the spires, and the shipping faded from our vision, and all was lost in a misty cloud. Staten Island and Sandy Hook were soon far behind us, and we were once more on the broad Atlantic.[15] The smooth surface of the harbor and bay, was now followed by the sudden surge of the ocean, and our little steamer rolled and pitched far more violently than the Constitution, for the waves were unusually turbulent, and produced the never failing effect, to persons unused to the sea, on nearly all on board. I did not escape the calamity, and retired to my berth in all the miseries of sea-sickness. I could hear the clattering of doors and the splashing of waves distinctly, which did not add much to my comfort.[16] Suddenly a loud crashing as of crockery, broke upon my ears, and I learned that the dishes had all been swept from the tables, and broken in a thousand pieces. After a while I fell asleep, and enjoyed a comfortable night's rest.

Sunday May 5th.

I did not wake until aroused by the entrance of Capt. Devereux in my stateroom, when I arose and joined the company, in line. After breakfast I went up on deck to enjoy the surrounding scenery, and was much pleased with the view before us. With the exception of a few tiny white clouds, the sky was clear and spotless. The bright sun shone in all its brilliancy, and the scene was enlivened by a balmy breeze from the south-west. We were a second time upon the broad surface of the Atlantic — wholly out of sight of land, with no object to attract our attention save the white sails, and occasional columns of smoke, from the various craft in the distance. The blue canopy of Heaven above, and the darker blue surface of the water beneath, joining in a complete unbroken circle around us at the horizon, was to me an object of interest, of which I had often heard, but never till then witnessed. We sat in groups about the deck until ten o'clock, when we were ordered to fall in to attend divine services, which took place in the saloon below, and were the first we had attended since our departure from Salem. They were conducted by Private Harry S. Hall, and consisted of the following order of exercises:

1. Prayer from "Episcopal Service."
2. Selection from 15th Psalm.
3. Missionary Hymn.
4. Reading of 5th chap. of Matthew, by Hall and company alternately.

5. Reading of 5th, 6th & 7th chap of Proverbs, by Conductor of Services.
6. Prayer.
7. Doxology.[17]

At the close of the services I remained in the saloon, and spent an hour writing until half past one, when we fell in for dinner. During the afternoon an amusing scene took place on board, causing fine sport among the boys for an hour. One of the recruits, a tall stalwart individual something over six feet, named Sweatland, but more familiarly known as "Du-dah," was discovered to have on an old coat, with brass buttons bearing the coat of arms of the state of Virginia, said to belong to the Captain of the boat. The boys, always in for a good time, immediately set up cries of "secessionist," "traitor," &c. and chased "Du-dah" about the deck. After some difficulty he was captured, indicted of treason, and an impromptu court-martial convened in the saloon, for his trial. After some deliberation the prisoner was found guilty, and sentenced to be hung by the neck until dead, but no rope being near by sufficient to answer the purpose, the sentence was commuted, and he was condemned to be shot. Accordingly his hands and feet were tied and he was stood up near the stern. Lieut. Putnam then took a revolver, aimed and fired and "Du-dah" rolled over on the deck, with all the grace of reality. As he was taken up many a laugh was indulged in, at the manner in which the joke was carried out. It was now nearly night, and as we were approaching dangerous latitude, a guard was detailed and distributed about the deck, with instructions to keep a vigilant watch for approaching lights. At nine o'clock we came to anchor, near the U.S. frigate Cumberland off Fortress Monroe, blocking James river.[18] At ten o'clock I went on guard but was relieved again at twelve and turned in.

Monday May 6th.

At four o'clock I was routed again by the corporal of the Relief then on duty, and entered upon my duties with my relief on deck. The weather was exceedingly uncomfortable, a cold north-east wind blowing, and rain falling quite fast. As the gray dawn of morning appeared, a boat was lowered from the Cumberland which pulled alongside to speak us. The inmates having satisfied themselves who we were, returned to make report, and we were permitted to approach nearer, which we did, coming to anchor again between the Cumberland and Fortress Monroe, within speaking distance of both. At about half past six Capt. Devereux and Lieut. Putnam embarked in a small boat for the Cambridge, laying at the wharf near the fortress, with the Salem Coast Guard on board, an organization recruited in Salem since our departure, for coast service.[19] At seven o'clock we fell in for breakfast, and soon after we noticed a boat push off from the Cambridge and make directly for us, and as she approached nearer, we recognized the familiar faces of

Charles Pond, Nathan Cutler and Benj. Nichols all of Salem. We assisted them to get board, and spent an hour very pleasantly with them. They mentioned several well known boys as members of the Coast Guard, among whom was Priv. Huntington of our own company, familiarly called "Hunter," who started with us from home, but left the company in Boston, at the solicitation of his father. They informed us that the Cambridge was taking guns aboard to complete her armament, and would accompany the Roanoke to Washington as a convoy.

During the forenoon a merchantman attempted to run by, contrary to orders respecting the blockade, unless she be loaded with U.S. troops or provisions, and without displaying her colors. She was immediately discovered by the frigate, from which a couple of guns were discharged as a signal for her to heave to. The merchantman did not notice the signal, nor alter her course, but kept on apparently unconcerned. The Cumberland evidently did not like this defiance of her authority, and immediately fired a shell, which went hissing into the air with tremendous force, exploding directly over the merchantman, and falling in fragments into the water just ahead of her. This had the desired effect, and she dropped anchor in an instant, and lay under the guns of the frigate.[20] At twelve o'clock we got under way and steamed up the Chesapeake, with the Cambridge a-stern of us. The sky was now rapidly overcast with bleak clouds, bearing a threatening appearance, and at three o'clock a dense fog came up, so thick that it was several times considered impracticable to proceed, we however kept on at a moderate speed, until six o'clock when it gradually dispersed. Our pilot now ascertained that he had mistaken his course, and had been steering in almost an opposite direction, but we were soon righted, and once more steamed at a rapid rate up the bay. We now discovered the Cambridge several miles a-stern, with all sails set endeavoring to come up with us, but the Roanoke was too much for her and she was soon entirely out of sight behind. Soon after seven o'clock we dropped anchor at the mouth of the Potomac to wait for her. I was at this time on guard having been on duty with my relief since four o'clock. The clouds now began to thicken, and the wind increased to almost a hurricane. The captain of the boat came up on deck, took a hasty glance about him and returned below again, saying that he expected we should have an unusually rough night. At eight o'clock I was relieved by the corporal of the next relief, and very fortunately escaped the uncomfortable position of being on duty in the storm, for I had no sooner gone below with my men, than the lightning began to dart in vivid flashes followed by rattling and almost deafening peals of thunder, while the gigantic rain drops which fell few and far between, were but fore-runners of the torrents of rain that followed. The waves were tossed in a frightful manner, and the boat rolled and pitched with such force, that it was impossible to keep a footing without some assistance. The scene was terrifically grand. In the darkness we could discern the snow white caps of mountainous waves, as they came thrashing against the sides of the steamer with dreadful violence, throwing the spray high over our heads, and emitting volumes of that wonder of nature — phosphorescent light.[21] At half past eight I turned in but was routed by the corporal again at eleven, and went on duty with my relief. The weather now began to be quite pleasant again. The clouds gradually disappeared, and one by one the stars peeped from their hiding places, glittering like so many diamonds. During our tour of duty, frequent alarms were caused by the approach of different lights reported at times by the sentries. A[t] two o'clock a.m. we were relieved and turned in.

5

Washington

Tuesday May 7th.
In the morning I arose at the usual hour, notwithstanding the fatiguing duty of the night, and at half past seven went below with the company to breakfast, after which I went on deck to find the scene truly charming. The bright sun's rays fell upon the deck with the genial warmth of midsummer, and the blue canopy of Heaven, was unspotted by even the smallest cloud. Not a breath of air could be felt, and the various objects about us, were reflected with mirror-like distinctness in the smooth surface of the water beneath us. We were steaming rapidly up the Potomac, with the Cambridge a short distance a-stern of us, and the scenery on both sides of the river was beautiful beyond description. The green verdured hills and glens, the thickly wooded forests and groves, the high rocky bluffs, and banks of sand and clay, each in turn lined the crooked stream, while ever and anon the white dwellings peeped from among the trees, to lend an additional charm to the already fascinating picture.

As we were passing hostile shores, it was considered expedient to have sentries posted, to give notice of any movements on shore, which might be construed as sufficient cause for alarm. Accordingly a guard was detailed (and I was on duty as corporal from eleven o'clock till two).

At about three o'clock we passed Mount Vernon, the house and burial place of Washington. The manner in which Nature has crowned this beautiful spot with her many charms, should be seen to be fully appreciated. In accordance with the usual custom, when passing this sacred spot, we stood on deck with uncovered heads, while our bells tolled solemnly in respect for him, whose name will live forever in the hearts of the American people.[1]

At half past three we passed Fort Washington, a short distance above Mount Vernon, on the Maryland side of the river.[2] Here was indeed another attractive spot. The grounds were delightful situated, and cultivated with the taste of a public park, while the massive walls of masonry handsomely built, rose abruptly to the height of several feet, commanding a complete and uninterrupted range of the Potomac, for miles in either direction.

At about four we passed Alexandria, a noted hot bed of secession, and as there was some danger of being fired upon, we were ordered below, and there remained until we had reached safer ground.

At six o'clock we passed the Arsenal at Washington, and on the wharf I recognized a number of acquaintances, members of the Mechanic Light Infantry of Salem, who were on detached service, guarding the Arsenal. Their regiment, the Fifth Mass. Col. Lawrence were quartered at the Treasury Building, a miles distant from the Capitol on Pennsylvania Avenue. We gave them a hearty "seven" as we passed, which was responded to with a will by the Mechanics.[3]

A steam tug now came alongside and took us in tow to the Navy-Yard and Capt. Devereux with Lieut. Austin went ashore for orders, returning at about nine o'clock, and bringing with them several letters which though somewhat old, were none the less welcome. At sun-set we witnessed a battalion drill of the Seventy-first New York Volunteers, who were quartered in the Navy Yard. During the evening I wrote a few letters and retired.

Wednesday May 8th.

At five o'clock we turned out and were ordered to pack up immediately. At seven we went ashore, and proceeded by a different route to the Capitol, where we joined the regiment and were assigned quarters in one of the rooms, on the eastern front of the south wing. This march though but a single mile was extremely fatiguing, for it was mud the entire distance, two or three inches deep of a sort of sticky clay, and of that brick red here, common to the soil in that section of the country, (and which with the heavily laden knapsacks on our backs, retarded our progress considerably.) Arriving at the Capitol, we were cordially met by the regiment and asked a thousand and one questions concerning our trip to New York, all of which we answered in a most satisfactory manner, and they in turn interested us with an account of their exploits during our absence, and informed us that they marched from Annapolis to the junction with the Seventh New York, building bridges, relaying the track &c which had been destroyed by the rebels. They also said that on the march they suffered intensely from the heat, several becoming sick, and one was sun struck. That they were without rations, and also were in constant danger of being attacked by the Rebels, and otherwise suffered from exposure and fatigue. Having taken possession of our quarters we stacked arms and were dismissed, with orders not to leave the building, and while admiring the attractions of our new quarters, our attention was arrested by a loud yell outside, announcing the arrival of several huckster

The Eighth Massachusetts Regiment in the Rotunda of the Capitol, *Harper's Weekly*, May 25, 1861.

women, with baskets loaded with fruit, pastry, &c. We soon closed around them and the baskets were emptied of their contents, which were eagerly devoured, for we had thus far had no breakfast. At the late hour of eleven o'clock, this meal was served up in the enclosure, formed by the basement, and a semi-circular row of arches supporting the paved entrance to the rear of the building, and consisted of fresh bread, coffee and salt-fish. After partaking of this, we were dismissed for an hour and a half, and scattered over the Capitol and its adjoining ground. On the eastern park, a number of companies were drilling in various branches of the tac-tics, and I soon learned that a number of regiments were quartered in the building with us, among which, were Ellsworth's Fire Zouaves of New York.

I was somewhat surprised at the utter confusion and disorder which surrounded the building, and marred the attractions of the grounds. For a distance of several hundred feet, the entire length of the front, lay scattered in all directions, unfinished stone-work, half sculptured pillars and blocks of marble, tons of the different castings which were to form the massive dome yet in embryo, casks of lime and cement, piles of chains and ropes,

Troops in Washington, D.C., drilling in the grounds on the north side of the Capitol, *Frank Leslie's Illustrated Newspaper*, May 25, 1861.

and innumerable other et-cetera appertaining to the structure, which as yet was far from completed. High above the roof were powerful engines, by which with wire cables, the huge parts were hoisted into their places, as fast as they were ready.[4]

(After wandering some time among the machinery and materials, I entered the House of Representatives, and seating myself at one of the desks, spent most of the afternoon in writing, and took in a rough survey of the elaborate finish of this room. The walls were heavily laden with carving, and stucco work in gilt and crimson, with here and there historical paintings sunk in deep panels. The ceiling was arranged in squares separated from each other by heavy pendant ornaments in gilt and colors, the centre being of richly colored glass, divided into forty-five squares, thirty four of which bore the coats-of-arms of the different states, the balance being blank, for the states hereafter to be admitted to the Union. Through this the hall was lighted and in the evening a most brilliant light pierced through, from extensive gas-fixtures concealed from view above. The desks of the Representatives were of black walnut, and completely covered with ornamental work, and arranged in a semi-circle around the Speakers stand. The chairs were of the same material, upholstered with red morocco cushions in the seats and backs. The Speakers' stand was of solid white marble, neatly and elegantly sculptured. A minute description of the place would require a volume by itself, and I must pass over it with this hurriedly justifiable attempt.

At five o'clock we fell in for our second meal, after which we were drilled for an hour on the eastern park, before a large crowd of citizens and soldiers, who gave us several rounds of applause, particularly during the bayonet exercise. At half past six we were dismissed and returned to quarters, after which the following order was read to us by the Captain:

Head Qrs 8th Regiment M.V.M.
Washington D.C. May 8, 1861
Special Order
No.----
Capt. Devereux, Lieut. Putnam, Serg'ts Emmerton, Batchelder and Gray, Corp'ls Evans and Reynolds and Private Hill, are hereby detailed as drill-masters, to drill the officers and men of the other companies of this regiment in Hardee's Infantry Tactics.
By order of Col. Hinks
Comdg. the Regiment.[5]

This was indeed an honor, but I for one tried to escape it, without avail. At eight o'clock we fell in once more and were drilled until tattoo at nine o'clock, when we broke ranks and turned in.

Thursday May 9th.

At five o'clock reveille aroused us from a quiet slumber and we immediately turned out for duty. The morning was rather chilly, but we were cheered with a glorious sun, which soon made it very comfortable. Soon after reveille the bells of the city rang peal after peal, and we soon learned a fire was raging in the vicinity of Willard's Hotel, threatening a good deal of damage. The boys were all in the qui-vive, but no man was allowed to leave the grounds. Ellsworth's Fire Zouaves however could not resist the familiar call, and bolted out en-masse, and were soon far beyond the line of sentries, tearing up Pennsylvania Avenue, and manning the different "machines" as they came along. They were evidently in their element, and it was reported that they did good execution at the fire, in saving the buildings adjoining, though the flames were not extinguished until the burning building was entirely consumed.[6]

At seven o'clock we fell in for breakfast, consisting of beef steak, soft bread, crackers and coffee. At half past nine company was formed, and we joined the regiment on the park, where we went through morning parade, after which the men detailed as drill masters, took charge of the several companies, the Lynn City Guards, Capt. Hudson, falling to me. Our own company also drilled near us under Lieutenants Brewster and Austin. I found my men quite unused to the new maneuvers, having been confined to Scott's Tactics, but they took hold well and did themselves credit.[7] At one o'clock, regimental line was formed, and the companies were dismissed and returned to quarters. At half past one we fell in for dinner, which consisted of roast lamb and beef, with potatoes, which was indeed something unusual. Of course we did not fail to appreciate such a meal.

After dinner a squad of us ascended into the large dome, and climbed to the top of the staging a distance of about two hundred and sixty feet, where we had an excellent view of the city, and of the country for miles around. We remained here about half an hour, during which time, I exhibited a noted characteristic of the Yankee nature, in leaving my initials on one of the beams of the framework. After descending, we strolled through the numerous corridors and halls, and I was amazed at the great skill displayed in the artistic finish of the different apartments. One feature which I could not help stopping to admire, was the staircase leading to the gallery of the new Senate-Chamber, built entirely of polished Tennessee marble, and one of three which together cost the enormous sum of one million of dollars. Covering the entire wall, from the landing half way up the stair-case, to the ceiling, is a gorgeous painting by [blank] symbolical of the rapid growth of the country, and entitled "Westward the star of empire takes its way." The figures are all life-size and most natural, and correct in their proportions. This painting has been admired by hundreds of foreigners, many of whom have pronounced it the finest in the world. We also entered the marble reception room in the north-east corner of the north wing, known as the "Marble Room," an apartment substantial, and beautiful in the extreme. The floor, sides and ceiling of this room are of solid marble from almost every quarry in the world, the only varying material, being the glass in the windows, and mirrors which adorn the walls. Curious as it may seem, there is in one of the blocks which compose the ceiling, a natural portrait of Washington, the features, wig and lapel of the coat being easily discerned, in the blue veins of the marble. After admiring the different features of this room, we went out for a walk in the park on the west side of the Capitol. Here we found many attractions. At the foot of the steps as we left the building, was a large oval pond of pure water, the sides of which are walled with dressed stone, supplied by a continual stream from the aqueduct, and abundant with gold and silver fish. The water is constantly changing, being allowed to rise only at a certain height, and passing out through a pipe into the canal. In the lower grounds are two larger basins, in the centre of which are fountains, which throw the water several feet into the air. Shade trees are abundant, and large and comfortable iron settees, are scattered here and there among them.

OPPOSITE: **Washington Scenes in 1861 (*Butler's Book*).**

WASHINGTON SCENES IN 1861.
1. Pennsylvania Avenue looking towards Capitol.
2. War Department Building before War.   3. Navy Department Building before War.

We were soon interrupted in our ramble by the assembly, and as soon as possible fell in with the company and joined the regiment in the eastern park, where we went through afternoon parade, after which drill masters took charge of their respective companies until five o'clock, when they were recalled, and joined their own company for skirmish drill. We drilled for an hour drawing forth frequent plaudits from the bystanders. At half past six we marched to quarters and fell in for supper, after which I spent considerable time writing.

During the evening I came across an old friend and schoolmate, Mr. Joseph Safford, clerk in the Commissary Department. He kindly escorted me through the vaults in the basement of the Capitol, which were stored full of commissary stores, among which were fifty-six thousand barrels of flour. At nine o'clock I left Safford, and fell in with the company for roll-call. At half past nine tattoo was beaten and the boys turned in. Private Batchelder and myself took a notion that our quarters were rather close, and stole into an adjoining apartment, occupied as Quarter master's department, where we enjoyed a good night's rest.

Friday May 10th.
Reveille beat at half past five and was immediately followed by the customary roll-call. It was another beautiful cool morning, and many companies were engaged at drill on the park, at an unusually early hour. We roamed at pleasure until seven o'clock, when we fell in and marched to breakfast. At nine regimental line was formed, and after morning parade the usual routine of duty was performed viz.— drilling of the several companies under the charge of drill-masters.[8] Having several new recruits in my command, or rather men who were not present with their company at the previous drill, I found it impracticable to make any advancement, and confined myself to movements of the previous day. We had been engaged but about half an hour, when black clouds suddenly appeared, and rain soon fell rapidly enough to interrupt the movements, and we broke ranks and marched double quick to quarters. The mail now arrived, and for an hour we passed the time very agreeably in perusing various letters and newspapers from home. At twelve o'clock noon orders came to fall in, and the company was divided into three reliefs of twenty men each, for guard duty, each relief being placed under the charge of a corporal. I was placed in charge of the second relief. At one o'clock we fell in for dinner, which we took in one of the arches under the pavement, as before mentioned, and used as cookhouses, on account of the stormy weather outside, and immediately after, I posted my relief, relieving the first relief, and remained on duty until half past four.

This tour of duty was exceedingly uncomfortable, for it rained incessantly all the time, and we got drenched through. We remained in the guard room all day and night, and at half past ten my relief went on duty again for the last time.

During the evening we were informed that Colonel Hinks and Captain Devereux, had been ordered to proceed to Annapolis by Gen'l. Butler, on some business the nature of which we did not ascertain.

Saturday May 11th.

As usual at early morning the air was uncomfortably cool, but as the sun came up it gradually grew to be quite warm and sultry. The excessive rain of yesterday made the grounds exceedingly muddy, but by noon most of it dried up and the park was in good condition for drilling purposes. At nine o'clock the company was relieved from guard duty, and we removed again to our quarters. At half past nine roll was called, and soon after regimental line was formed for morning parade, after which the companies were dismissed to the charge of drill masters respectively, our own company occupying a portion of the park by themselves. At twelve o'clock we broke ranks and marched to quarters and at one fell in for dinner. We were then dismissed until three o'clock, and I improved the opportunity to clean my musket and equipments. At three o'clock precisely the assembly beat, and regimental line was formed again for battalion drill. Though the company took their place on the line with the regiment, we were for some unaccountable reason dismissed, and scattered over the park engaged in wrestling, leap-frog and such other athletic sports. At four o'clock the regiment was dismissed and returned to quarters, and my attention was arrested by the solemn requiem of a funeral cortege, passing by up Pennsylvania Avenue. It consisted of a fine body of Regulars, the first I had ever seen, with a fine band of music, also of the Regular service, escorting a handsomely draped hearse, behind which followed a long line of carriages. The name of the deceased I did not learn, but it was evidently some commissioned officer of the Regular Army.[9]

After tea I enjoyed a refreshing ablution in the marble baths. At eight o'clock, orders were issued by the Captain who had just returned from Annapolis, to fall in and be ready to move at a moments' notice. This order was promptly obeyed, and we proceeded with haversacks to the mess room where we were furnished with a day's rations, after which we returned and were drawn up in one of the long corridors, to await further orders. Here we remained a couple of hours, in the most uncomfortable position imaginable. The air was very close, and we had on our overcoats with the usual harness of equipments, knapsacks, haversacks and canteens, preparatory as we expected to [be] starting on some night expedition. But in this we were happily disappointed, for at about ten o'clock our orders were countermanded, and we returned to quarters and turned in.[10]

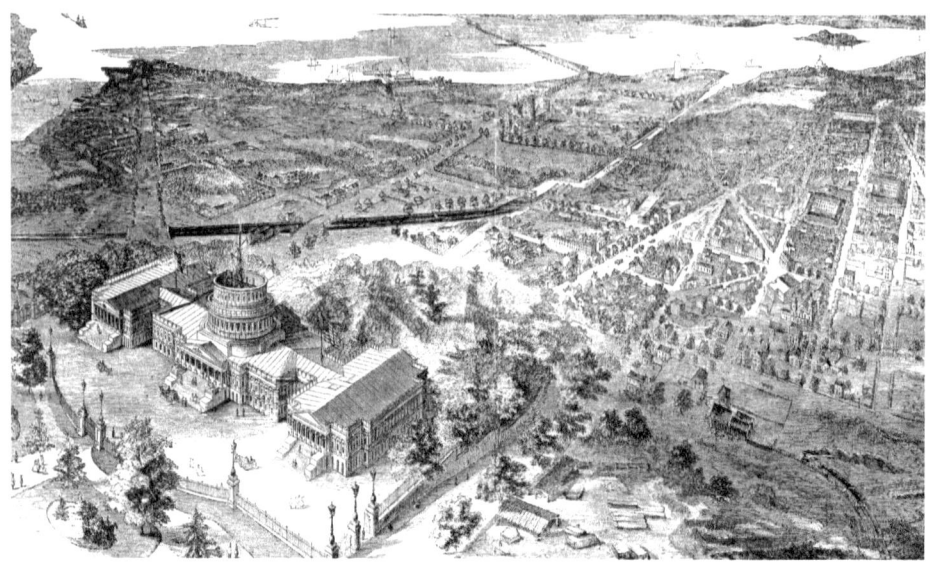

Washington, D.C., *Harper's Weekly*, July 27, 1861.

Sunday May 12th.
A beautiful Sabbath morning, with an unusually clear and bright sun, and hardly a cloud visible in the Heavens. The atmosphere like the previous morning, was somewhat cool and chilly, but as the day advanced, grew to be warm and delightful. At the usual hour of seven o'clock, the company fell in for breakfast, and arriving at the tables were not only surprised, but highly pleased to find them loaded with baked beans. This was a change from the every day ration of hard-tack and fried-up-steak, and of course duly appreciated by us all. Not that there is anything particularly delicious about a dish of baked beans, but to us, having heretofore generally received but a scanty allowance of the poorest kind of food, on account of the limited facilities of the commissary department, to provide for the rapidly increasing army, they were actually a treat.

  At nine o'clock the line was formed, and the entire regiment were drilled, or rather reviewed by Capt. Devereux, in the various movements practiced during the week, drill masters superintending the movements of their respective companies. At ten o'clock we were dismissed, and returned to quarters, divested ourselves of our equipments, and proceeded to the House of Representatives, where we listened to an excellent discourse of about an hour's duration, by the Rev. Dr. Butler of Washington.[11]

  (At eleven o'clock I obtained a pass from the Captain to be absent until roll call, and Private Hill and myself took a walk to the White House, situated at the opposite extremity of Pennsylvania Avenue from the Capitol. It is a handsome building, of marble or white-stone, two stories high with a lofty basement, one hundred and eighty feet long, by eighty-five wide, but not being open to visitors on Sunday, we occupied an hour very pleasantly in the grounds adjoining. The mansion is approached by a semi-circular carriage way and paved walk, the former running under a gable end, supported on tall pillars of white stone, and continuing on to the Avenue again. All of the surroundings were in keeping with the Presidential mansion, but a description of the various attractions which met our eye, would be too great an undertaking here, and I will pass over them, with the mention of one remarkable and attractive feature.

Across the Avenue in the center of Jackson Square, opposite and belonging to the White House, is a fine equestrian statue of "Old Hickory"—General Jackson. This statue is of bronze, mounted on a pedestal of marble, the whole standing about twenty-five feet high, and representing the hero of New Orleans, mounted on his beautiful charger, poised in the graceful position of a canter.

At half past twelve we returned to the Capitol, arriving in season for roll-call and dinner. Immediately after dinner I made use of the stream of water from the fish pond in the western park, to wash out some articles of clothing, and while waiting for them to dry, dropped off into a quiet snooze on the grass. Dan Bruce sent to the hospital.

At half past four the entire regiment were inspected on the park, with knapsacks, haversacks and canteens, after which the company were drilled for an hour by the Captain, in skirmishing, and unfixing bayonets on the double quick. At seven o'clock we fell in for supper.

During the evening a party of us paid a visit to various apartments in the Capitol, among others the Senate Chamber, Senator's Reception and Marble Rooms. At nine o'clock we retraced our steps, attended roll-call and turned in.[12]

Monday May 13th.

This was one of those disagreeable mornings so common in southern localities, the sky was thick and overcast with heavy black clouds, and the atmosphere was very uncomfortable, being close and dead, with not a breath of air stirring. There were many indications of rain, but at ten o'clock the clouds began to disperse, and we were favored with a pleasant but uncomfortably warm day.

At seven o'clock we breakfasted, and a nine formed line for morning parade. Capt. Devereux then drilled the entire regiment again, in company maneuvers for an hour. At ten o'clock we were dismissed and marched to quarters, and at one fell in for dinner. At three o'clock the company received orders to fall in with knapsacks, haversacks and canteens, but the order was

Capitol Dome Construction with Federal troops in foreground, 1861 (courtesy Architect of the Capitol).

countermanded and again issued a second time a few moments after, and we finally fell into line with all our luggage, and joined the regiment already in line on the park. We were however dismissed, and unslung knapsacks again. At 3 o'clk the Regiment under Col. Hinks proceeded to the Arsenal two miles distant, and were furnished with arms and equipments throughout, many of the men being as yet unarmed, the Company were dismissed.

It will be remembered that previous to the secession of South Carolina, the Southern states had availed themselves of an old law of Congress, to draw their quota of arms from the United States, their requisitions being promptly filled by the traitor Floyd, then Secretary of War, thus stripping the arsenals of the North completely, transferring thousands of arms into the hands of the Rebels, leaving the country in an almost utterly defenseless condition, and rendering it necessary to purchase arms of foreign countries, until the facilities of the national armories could be increased. This state of affairs was exceedingly gloomy for the North, nevertheless the people put

Winans Steam Gun, *Harper's Weekly*, May 25, 1861.

the best foot forward, and thousands of Volunteers sprang forward in defense of the national capital, and arrived in Washington as fast as the limited means of conveyance would permit, trusting to the resources of the country to furnish them with arms afterward.

During the absence of the regiment, the company was drilled for a couple of hours by the Captain. At seven o'clock black clouds began to appear, and we were visited shortly after by a delightful thunder shower. At eight the regiment returned handsomely equipped, and armed with Springfield smoothbores.[13] At half past eight we fell in for supper.

During the evening an alarm of fire was occasioned in the city, on account of a bright glowing light in the north-west, which was afterward reported to be the burning of the United States Armory at Harper's Ferry, by the commander Lieut. Jones.[14]

At nine o'clock it being uncomfortably warm in our quarters, Privates Elbridge Brown, Bachelder and myself, took our blankets and sought more comfortable quarters in an adjoining room, where we enjoyed a good night's rest.

6

Relay House

Tuesday May 14th.
We arose somewhat earlier than usual and rejoined the company for fear of being absent at roll call, and being fully impressed with the guilt of our willful violation of orders in sleeping out of quarters. We found the men lively at work collecting and packing their effects, orders having been issued to the regiment to pack up and be ready to move, and we at once followed their example. At seven o'clock we fell in for breakfast, and at nine formed regimental line on the park. At half past nine we took up our line of march by the shortest route to the Baltimore and Ohio Depot, and I now learned that we were to go into camp at the Relay House, nine miles from Baltimore, with the Sixth Mass. Col. Jones, Eighth New York, and the Boston Light Artillery, Captain Cook, who had been encamped there since May 5th.[1]

Before leaving our quarters at "the Capitol," our tall friend "Du dah" took the precaution to guard against short rations, by foraging a pair of plump little pigs, which he nailed up in a box with slats across the top, and smuggled in with the regimental baggage.

The march to the depot though very short, was uncomfortable in the extreme, the sun being very hot and the traveling difficult, on account of the mud which was several inches deep, and caused by the heavy fall of rain during the night.[2] Arriving at the depot we went without delay aboard the train which was already waiting and at half past ten we started for the Relay House. At intervals along the road our attention was attracted to the rough shanties, or huts, built of poles and brush, and occupied by the pickets distributed along the road. Nothing of interest occurred during the passage and in an hour we arrived at the Relay House, disembarked from the train and retraced our steps a short distance over the railroad, crossing the viaduct, a magnificent structure of solid masonry consisting of [blank] arches, nearly a hundred feet in height and spanning the valley of the Patapsco river, and ascended the slope leading to the residence of one Dr. Hall on the hill.³ We passed the encampment of the Sixth pleasantly situated in a delightful grove of shade trees, in the vicinity of which we halted for a half an hour, during which time we received many kind favors at the hands of Mr. Short who accompanied us from Washington, and who generously went himself for several buckets of water, and also succeeded in hunting up some hucksters with refreshments, which were at this time very welcome.⁴

Mr. Short was the inventor of Short's Patent Knapsack, so justly celebrated for its many improvements over all others, and was about introducing it into the Army. This knapsack by its ingenious construction and peculiar arrangement, can be divested of straps entirely, and by means of small handles attached to the top, can be easily and conveniently carried as a hand valise. The straps are also admirably adapted for slinging the blankets in light marching order.⁵

While here we had an opportunity of examining the famous Ross Winans Steam Gun, captured on the 10th inst. at Illchester, six miles from the Relay House on the Frederick road, by a scouting party of the Sixth Regiment, by order of General Butler. This gun though called the Winans Steam

Baltimore (Winans) Steam Gun, *Scientific American*, May 25, 1861.

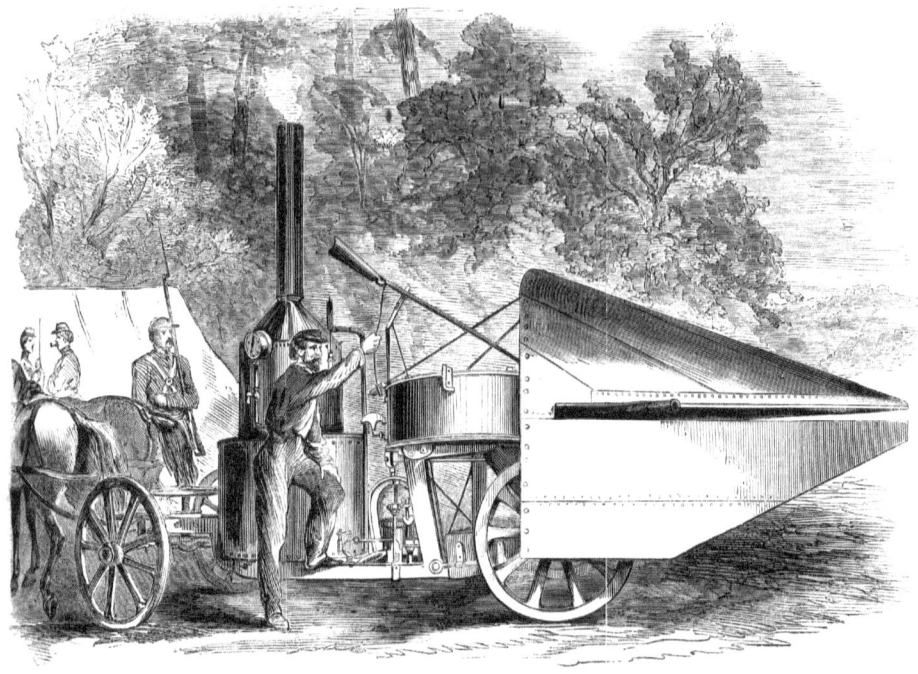

Winans Steam Gun, *Frank Leslie's Illustrated Newspaper*, May 18, 1861.

Gun, was in reality the Dickenson Steam Gun, being the invention of Mr. Charles S. Dickenson of Cleveland, Ohio, and patented August 9th 1859. The only ground for connecting Winans' name with it at all, was the fact that it had previously been sent to their extensive works for repair. The cut opposite is from the "Scientific American," but as the claim to its "superior advantages" as set forth by the inventor in its description is not fully established in my mind, I give an original description from personal observation. To commence with, the diameter of the bore is about three inches, and it is worked on the principle of centrifugal force, thereby requiring no gunpowder. It is loaded at the breach, the shot being introduced by a hopper and passing down through a tube, entering the breach one by one at regular intervals and in quick succession, and being discharged by the horizontal movement of the barrel, which revolves with the rapidity of lightning. A gate in the tube near the breech, prevents the shot from entering until the gun is in the proper position. "It was estimated that the shot from this gun, would cut off a nine inch scantling at the distance of half a mile." The whole is mounted on four wheels and drawn by horse power, and is protected by an iron cone, the sides of which slope at an angle of nearly forty-five degrees, and somewhat resembles the head of a fish, the aperture through which the shot are allowed to escape, representing the mouth. As steam is the power by which the barrel is made to revolve, it would be necessary to have fuel and water accompany the gun at all times, which would be often times inconvenient if not impossible. Then there is no way of altering the range by elevation or depression, and the fire must always be in the same direct line. Again a single glance at the cut, will convince anyone that an enfilading shot could easily render the whole thing unserviceable. If the gun could always be protected from this, and receive a fire directly from the front only, it would possess "superior advantages," on account of the rapidity with which the shot are discharged, it being "capable of discharging five hundred balls per minute." No one can deny that this gun is an ingenious invention, but until the foregoing objections can be overruled, I am of the opinion that it would be of no practical use in the service.[6]

While I was endeavoring to satisfy my curiosity by an examination of this gun, a report reached us that a baggage train, supposed to contain munitions of War and other contraband articles, going through from Baltimore to the Rebels at Harpers Ferry, was momentarily expected at the junction, and the company was at once detailed to repair thither to overhaul it. Orders were given to fall in immediately and we proceeded double quick down the hill, across the viaduct, to await its arrival. We remained here for half an hour, but the train did not make its appearance and we returned again. The sun was melting hot and the perspiration oozed from every pore.

At half past one we moved a short distance to a clear level spot adjoining the railroad, where it was proposed we should pitch our encampment as soon as tents arrived from Washington. Here we stacked arms and were allowed to rest. It was now about two o'clock and as we had thus far had no dinner, most of us began to think a morsel would be acceptable. I was extremely fortunate to receive an invitation from one of the boys to accompany him to the camp of Cook's Battery, but a stone's throw distant, to see a friend of his. Of course I accepted his invitation, and "the friend" invited us (as we expected) to partake of something to eat, and we sat down to a hearty meal which he had cooked for us and which we duly relished. After dinner we took a look about the premises, to examine the position of the Battery. On the north west side of the hill, earthworks were thrown up, with embrasures for two pieces, commanding the railroad across the viaduct. Over the viaduct and near the junction two more pieces were placed, defended by earthworks, and commanding the road from Harper's Ferry. At three o'clock we returned to the Regiment and the afternoon was spent in a leisure manner. At night the company was detailed for guard, and divided into three reliefs, the third relief falling to me.

"Du-dah" now went for his little pigs, which he soon slaughtered and hung up on a tree for the night. The operations were closely watched by the boys, for "Du dah" never failed to make sport in anything he undertook.

At an early hour we spread our blankets and turned in, but at about midnight we were aroused by musketry, and the familiar cry of "Baltimore" which will be distinctly remembered by every member of the regiment, passed loudly and rapidly from one sentinel to another. The alarm soon spread from one to another and the entire regiment were soon under arms.

Without losing any time we moved double-quick up the railroad to the viaduct, where it was reported to the Colonel that Ross Winans had been arrested by the pickets of the Sixth, and confined in the Relay House. A few muskets unnecessarily discharged during the affair, was the cause of the alarm. On learning this we returned again and turned in, and at two o'clock a.m. I was summoned to go on guard with my relief.

Wednesday May 15th.
At four o'clock I was relieved, and soon after the regiment turned out. It was an unusually cool morning, and my overcoat which I had on during my tour of duty, was hardly sufficient to keep me comfortable. But as the sun came up it gradually grew to be quite hot, and I was glad to take it off again.[7] At seven o'clock we fell in for breakfast, and at about eight the company was relieved from guard duty by one of the Lynn companies. No further duty was required during the forenoon, and a number of us engaged in a swimming bath, in the creek near by, which was quite refreshing.

Towards noon "Du dah" took down his pigs, which for a wonder still hung there, and turned them over to the company cooks, one of whom, Private Charles Luscomb, being quite a "tar," converted with some other ingredients, into a dish, known at Sea among the sailors as "lob-skouse." On this the company dined with much satisfaction. M. Douglass furloughed for twenty days.

In the afternoon a squad, myself among the number, got together and it was proposed to put up a shanty to sleep in, as we had no tents, and the nights were very cold with heavy dew. We selected a place on the side of the hill, and after scooping out a place as near level as possible, gathered a quantity of rails from a neighboring fence, two of which we drove firmly into the ground, connecting them at the top with a cross-piece. We then formed a roof of rails laid close together, one end resting on the cross-piece, and the other on the side of the hill. So much for the outside, the next thing was to manufacture a bed. This was easily accomplished with oak leaves, which we brought from the woods close by in our blankets, and spread on the ground to the depth of a foot and a half, and kept from rolling down hill or blowing away by a fender of rails. On this bed we spread first our rubber then our woollen blankets, and like Robinson Crusoe, now had as comfortable quarters as we could wish. Many others noticing our comfort, immediately followed our example, and before dark a row of a dozen shanties were reared.[8]

Some of the boys spent the afternoon, scouring the vicinity for victuals, and towards night some of them returned with frogs, others with fish, but one chap who had been more fortunate than the rest (or, perhaps I should say, more wilful) drove in a large hog which he had foraged.

Just before retreat, a squad brought in a four horse team, with the owner, a live "Reb" who had been a little bitter in his denunciations of the soldiers, also a darkey with him. He was pretty well "sprung," but he was taken before the Colonel, who administered the "Oath of Allegiance" to him and sent him about his business.

At six o'clock a train arrived with Camp and Garrison Equipage for the regiment, and a squad was detailed from each company to unload it. Orders were at once issued to remove the shanties we had built, though the spot selected for the encampment, was not within, five hundred yards. We were greatly disappointed at this, for we had hoped to have the benefit of at least one nights sleep in them, but there was no alternative, and we levelled them all to the ground, and at once set to work to pitch our encampment, which took us till nearly midnight. The spot selected was on the top of the hill, and considerably elevated, commanding an uninterrupted view of the country to the north and east, for miles. A pleasanter spot could not have been found.[9] There was a heavy growth of clover all over it, which worked in admirably for bedding. We were furnished with wall tents of the long pattern, capable of accommodating ten men. Eight were allotted to the Company, one of which was occupied by the four commissioned officers, another by the seven non-commissioned officers, and the remaining six by the rest of the company.

Having pitched the encampment we fell in for supper at a late hour, which consisted mainly of mush and milk, and afterward turned in. During the night we were called out twice, by a few shots among the pickets, discharged at a rail-road switch, and which in the moonlight one of them "<u>was sure</u>" he saw move.

Thursday May 16th.

Reveille was beaten at five o'clock, and the several companies promptly turned out and fell into line for roll-call. At seven o'clock we fell in for breakfast, after which the company fell in again and the camp regulations were published to us by the Orderly. The detail for guard was then made, and we were dismissed. At nine o'clock guard mounting took place, and no further duty was required during the forenoon, and the time was occupied generally in the easiest possible manner.

We had been absent from home exactly a month, and were for the first time fairly established in camp. At about ten o'clock I took a stroll over the premises, to examine our situation which was about as follows. In front of the space occupied by the tents, the ground was very level for a hundred feet or more, constituting an admirable parade, then suddenly sloped downwards to a narrow level strip adjoining the rail road bank. On the right a sudden pitch of twenty or thirty feet, straddled with tall trees, descended to a comparatively level tract on the side of the hill, occupied by a neat white cottage, and outbuildings. In a portion of a good sized barn we located our company kitchen, which also made an excellent Commissary. On either side of the cottage, the balance of the company kitchens were located. In rear of the right flank, the ground was very steep, descending through dense woods to a ravine, through which flowed a fine stream of water, one of the tributaries of the Patapsco. In rear of the centre and left the ground rose very gradually, and under a small clump of great trees was pitched the Colonel's Head Quarters, the tents of the field and staff officers of the regiment extending in a line to the right and left. Back of Head Quarters was an excellent grove of large shade trees, known as Dr. Hall's green, and still further on, the fine residence of the Doctor, owner of the premises. On the left and a little in advance, the Sixth Regiment, Eighth New York, and Cook's Battery were encamped in a thickly wooded grove. A number of springs within the boundaries of the camp, furnished an abundant supply of excellent water. The Sixth and Eighth Mass. and Cook's Battery, constituted a military Post, under the command of Col. Jones of the Sixth, ex-officio. The position was an important one, since it commanded the only approach to Washington by rail-road, and also the road to Harper's Ferry which was in the hands of the Rebels.[10]

At about one o'clock I returned to the company, and soon after we fell in for dinner. At three o'clock the assembly was beaten and we formed regimental line on the parade in front, where we were drilled for a couple of hours in battalion movements by Col. Hinks. After the drill an order from the Secretary of War was published by the Adjutant, announcing the promotion of Brig. Gen'l. B.F. Butler, to the position of Major General in the Volunteer Army. At five o'clock we returned to quarters, and the company was divided into squads, pursuant to Army Regulations, each squad being placed under the charge of a non-commissioned officer.

During the day Private A.C. Douglas received a furlough and took leave of us. He had been unwell for some time, and a change of climate was recommended by the Surgeon.[11]

At about half past five the Sixth Mass. and Eighth New York returned from Federal Hill, Baltimore, having been on duty there since the 13th, when General Butler took military possession of the city. They reported everything quiet there, and said the citizens showed them great attention, and that refreshments were actually forced upon them. This was indeed a great contrast to the reception of the Sixth on the 19th of April, when they were assailed with stones and clubs, by an infuriated mob.[12]

During the evening a meeting was held at Head Quarters, to fill vacancies occasioned by the resignation of Col. Munroe, who had been absent most of the time.[13] Lieut. Col. Hinks was elected Colonel, Major Ellwell, Lieutenant Colonel, and Maj. Ben Perley Poore, of Poore's Rifle Battalion (Savages)—Major.[14] Under other circumstances the Majority would have fallen to Capt. Devereux, who was the right flank captain, and by far the best qualified for it. Later in the evening a squad of singers from the company proceeded to Head Quarters, and serenaded the Colonel, Surgeon Breed and some others, until tattoo, when we returned to quarters, fell in for roll-call, and turned in.

Friday May 17th.

Reveille aroused us at the usual hour and we turned out for roll call. The morning air was cool and chilly, and we scarcely kept from shivering with overcoats on. There was a great contrast between the climate of this locality, and that of New England. No sooner did the sun go down at night, than the heaviest dews began to fall, often times wetting the tents through completely, and it was with the greatest difficulty that we could keep comfortable with both overcoats and blankets till morning, while during the day, we suffered intensely under the scorching rays of the sun, even in our shirt sleeves.

At seven o'clock we breakfasted and at nine the assembly was beaten to form line, after which we were drilled in battalion movements, on the level strip near the rail road, which we termed the lower parade ground. While here the Sixth came upon the ground, and we frequently came in contact with each other while maneuvering, causing some little confusion. At twelve o'clock both regiments left the field, and the Eighth took a short march up the rail-road, turning of on the pike, which we followed a mile or two, across the covered bridge over the Patapsco. The dust was almost insufferable, and the frequent order to double quick, added to the oppressive heat, served to make the march fatiguing and irksome. At half past one we returned to camp were dismissed and fell in for dinner.

During the afternoon a rumor was circulated through the camp, to the effect that six or eight of the notorious "Baltimore Roughs," were stopping at the Relay House, and were loud in their expressions of a desire "to whip any two Massachusetts men." Some of the recruits of the company got considerably excited over it, and wanted to go down there immediately, but the Captain soon quieted them by ordering them into their quarters.

At three o'clock the line was again formed, and we drilled for an hour in battalion movements. At six we formed hollow square, and prayer was offered by the Chaplain, after which we were dismissed and fell in for supper.[15]

At seven o'clock the company was detailed for picket duty, and the

Captain gave orders for us to fill the canteens with water, roll the blankets, and be ready for duty in an hour. Accordingly at eight o'clock we fell in, and proceeded to Head Quarters, where we were ordered to halt and load at will. The Colonel then joined us, and procuring a couple of lanterns from the Quarter Master, we left camp and crossed the viaduct to the Harper's Ferry road. It was a beautiful night and the moon shone in all its splendor, while the evening air was cool and delightful. We hardly knew of what use lanterns could be in the moonlight, but of course we asked no questions. We had an excellent view from the rail road, which ran along a ridge on the side of a hill, for several miles. The bluffs on the right were unusually steep and rocky, ascending to the height of some hundred feet, while on the left about the same distance below, flowed the beautiful waters of the Patapsco, sparking in the moonlight.

A mile up the road a detachment of a dozen, myself among the number, were stationed on duty at the top of the bluff, with orders to stop rail road trains and foot passengers. Other posts were established along the road, to the distance of some seven or eight miles. Our squad was divided into three reliefs, but we might as well all have been in one, from the fact that it was impossible to sleep, the night was so cold. We often had to get up and stir about, to keep comfortable, while our blankets were wet through with dew. There was no disturbance during the night, and we had a quiet but very uncomfortable tour of duty. Soon after daylight the pickets were recalled, and we formed company and returned to camp.[16]

Saturday May 18th.
Immediately on our arrival we descended the hill on the right of the camp, and crossed the stream following along the same until we came to a clear level spot. Here we halted, and fixing a piece of white paper to a tree, made good use of the loads in our muskets, at target practice. This was fine sport made more laughable by the awkward manner in which some of the recruits handled their muskets. It was a new thing to most of us, but we had some good shots in the company, one or two among the recruits, who seemed to be better acquainted with the practical use of the musket, than they did with the manual of arms or any other portion of the drill. Having discharged our pieces we returned to quarters and fell in for breakfast, after which we had no duty to perform until dress parade in the evening. It was the custom for the company which had been on picket, to be excused from all duty during the following forenoon at least.

Although we had now been in service a month, during which time we had been engaged in different duties, yet we never had been actually mustered into service, which was absolutely necessary before we could be officially recognized by the War Department, or receive pay for our services, and during the forenoon a Mustering Officer arrived in camp for this purpose. At half past two the line was formed on the upper parade ground, and the Oath of Allegiance was duly administered by the Mustering Officer, and an opportunity given to those who did not wish to take it, to step two paces to the front. To our surprise two men stepped forward from our own ranks (but I am glad to add that they were both recruits. This action on their part was of course denounced by every member of the company, and after some consideration, they concluded to remain, and serve their country with the rest of the regiment). The muster was to date from April 30th. 1861, and the term of service was three months from that date. We were then dismissed.[17]

At half past five the assembly beat, and the line was formed for dress parade, after which we formed hollow square, and prayer was offered by the Chaplain. The regiment were then dismissed, with the exception of our own company, who remained on the ground and drilled for half an hour under Lieut. Putnam, in the bayonet exercise, and skirmishing with the rallies, at the request of some lady friends of the Lieutenant, who had come into camp to call on him. At about seven o'clock we took supper. Nothing of interest transpired during the evening, and most of us turned in at an early hour, being somewhat fatigued by the labors of the previous night.

Sunday May 19th

At reveille we turned out and attended roll-call. As usual at this hour in the morning, the air was cool and chilly, and we could not help shivering as we stood on the line. At seven o'clock we fell in for breakfast, and no duty was required during the forenoon excepting the usual guard which was mounted at nine o'clock. A squad of us took advantage of this opportunity, to attend divine service at the Episcopal church in the village, at the close of which I returned immediately to camp, and spent an hour or so writing. Unusual quiet prevailed until dinner, which is always a lively occasion among soldiers.

At two o'clock we formed company and drilled an hour in skirmishing, the Regiment at the same time maneuvering near us in battalion movements. At five o'clock we formed Regimental line without arms, and proceeded to the shady grove in front of the Dr's residence (which we termed the lawn) to attend divine service, which was conducted by the Chaplain. A choir made up exclusively from singers selected from the different companies, furnished some very good singing.[18] The chaplain stood on the piazza, his bible resting on the uppermost of three drums arranged in the form of a pyramid on each side of which the colors were planted in the ground, the whole forming a convenient and very appropriate altar. The services were made more interesting, by the presence of a number of ladies, seated on the piazza around the Chaplain. Immediately after the services we formed for dress parade, then broke ranks and fell in for supper.

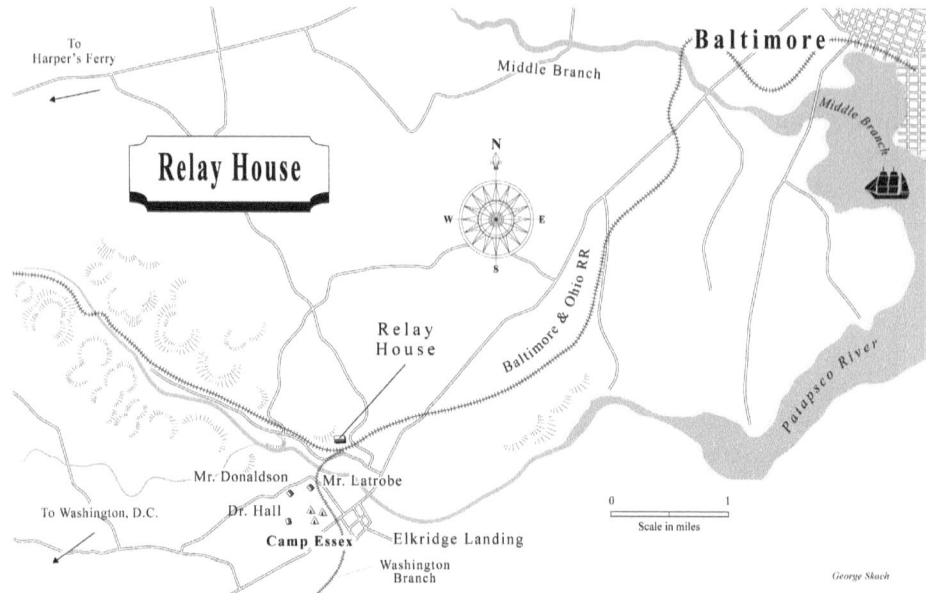

Map of Relay House, 1861.

During the afternoon the sun was several times obscured by heavy clouds, which now grew thicker with strong indications of rain. We therefore set to work digging trenches around the tents to drain the water, but as we had feared, we did not finish before the rain commenced falling, which continued with slight interruptions through the night.

At tattoo we attended roll-call and turned in, but at eleven o'clock were called out by rapid firing among the pickets, who seemed to delight in making all the noise they could, for the sake of turning out the troops. A grave military offense if they did but know it, and punishable by an 'Article of War,' with death. The alarm was as heretofore a false one, and after remaining in line half an hour in the wet, we were ordered to turn in again.

Monday May 20th.

Reveille was omitted in the morning as it rained pouring, and we did not turn out until seven o'clock. The camp was muddy every where to the depth of some inches, and the roll was called in the tents. It continued a cold uncomfortable drizzly day, which was favorable to us in one respect as we had no duty to perform, and spent most of the day in the tents, even taking our meals there. We had an excellent opportunity to write, which most of the boys improved, and by night quite a large mail was made up. This inside confinement was most too much for some of the boys, and in the afternoon

6. Relay House

the "renowned and comical" Ross, sprang out of his tent with a yell that fairly startled us. He was soon followed by the "immitable" Wiley, and some others, who went up and down the company street, yelling to the top of their voices "bouse out here," "bouse out here." Of course the entire company were soon outside splashing in the mud, thinking that something unusual was up. The "sell" was soon discovered and as we had now got out, Ross and Wiley procured the axes from the cook-house, and set about felling some trees, while some of the others, chopped them into logs. In a few moments a rousing camp-fire was built, around which we gathered to enjoy its comforts. The Captain also joined us, and we had a comfortable time. One after another interested the crowd with some thrilling tale, until our attention was attracted towards Private Whittredge, tracking through the mud towards us. He had just returned from a furlough, which he received while we were in New York. He brought several letters and packages with him for the boys, among which was handsome gilt-edged, travelling Episcopal prayer-book for me. A gift from Private Bates of the "pony squad," who was prevented from entering the service with us, by important business requiring his attention at home. The balance of the afternoon was devoted to perusing letters and papers, by those who were fortunate enough to receive them. The rain continued without cessation and at six o'clock we took supper in the tents.

It was our misfortune to be detailed for picket, and at eight o'clock we fell in, and left camp to take our posts of duty. It was a terrible disagreeable night, dark as a pocket, and the mud was several inches deep the whole distance. The grass was also as wet as water itself, and before we reached the rail-road, we were drenched through. The first post was established on the bluff a mile up the road as usual, and the second a half mile further on near the nail-factory. This post was assigned to me, and consisted of six men, which I divided into three reliefs of two each. It was impossible to sleep on account of the mud and wet, and we collected a quantity of wood as near dry as possible, with which after some difficulty we succeeded in making a good sized fire, which we kept up until morning, concealing it as much as possible from observation by huddling closely around it.

The only disturbance during the night was a drum which from the sound appeared to be coming towards us, and which it was reported were a party of the "Baltimore Roughs" (though now good union men). They were halted by the pickets on the bluff, and being without the countersign, were forbidden to pass. They made no resistance, for they were unarmed, and it would have been useless for them to attempt to force their passage. A couple of them were sent back for the countersign, who soon returned with it, and the posse were allowed to proceed. They bivouacked near the nail-factory, but the nature of their midnight tramp, I did not learn. At half past four we packed up and returned to camp, arriving just as reveille was sounding, after a most disagreeable tour of duty.

Tuesday May 21st.

Owing to the dampness of the night, our muskets suffered considerably and by morning were in a rusty condition. Of course the first thing to be done on being dismissed, was to put them in order and we spent the time in this way until the drums sounded breakfast, at seven o'clock. It was a dull morning, and heavy black clouds, were visible until about ten o'clock, when the sun made its appearance, and the rest of the day it was hot and uncomfortable. At nine o'clock guard mounting took place and soon after the regimental line was formed, and the Company were drilled for an hour by the Captain; no further duty was required until late in the afternoon. At the usual hour we fell in for dinner, after which I went down to the stream and enjoyed a good bath, and also washed some articles of clothing, and while they were drying, I sat down on a rock in the shade, and wrote several pages in my journal.

I was here interrupted by the order "Fall in, form Company" and gathering up my materials and clothing, returned to quarters to join the Com-

Relay House, Washington Junction, *Harper's New Monthly Magazine*, April 1857.

pany. The roll was called and we then marched to the lawn, in front of the Dr's residence, where a number of ladies had collected to witness our maneuvers. We had been drilling but a few moments when rain began to fall, much to our satisfaction, for we had as yet not got over our duties of the previous night, and we were in hopes the rain would drive the ladies in doors, and allow us to return to quarters. In this we were disappointed, for after a light shower, the sun made its appearance, and we resumed operations. At six o'clock we returned to our quarters, were dismissed and fell in for supper. Dress parade was dispensed with.

During the evening the moon shone beautifully, and a squad of the Company collected under the trees near our quarters, and enjoyed some good singing, until nine o'clock, when tattoo beat, and after roll call I turned in.

Wednesday May 22d.

At reveille we turned out and answered to roll-call, and an hour after fell in for breakfast. At nine o clock the line was formed on the upper parade ground, and the practice of company drills, under the superintendence of the men detailed for this purpose, which had heretofore been discontinued since our change of station from Washington, was again resumed, and drill masters were ordered to take charge of their companies. In my squad I took up the manual and load & fire, and I was really surprised at the alacrity and zeal, with which the men took hold of this new branch of drill, so entirely different from Scotts Tactics, which they had been accustomed to. Of course, under such circumstances, we could not do otherwise than make good progress, and an hour passed in a pleasant manner.

Soon after ten we were dismissed, and on returning to quarters I ascertained that the whole company had been detailed for guard (an entirely new feature,) and we repaired to the guard quarters for duty. We were divided into three reliefs, the third falling to me. At one o'clock I posted my relief remaining until three. Our tour of duty through the day was a quiet one, and when not on post, I had a fine opportunity to write in my journal, which I improved. The usual routine of duty was gone through with by the rest of the regiment.

The evening was unusually pleasant, the moon was at its full, and her soft silver light fell upon the camp, with almost the brightness of day. Quite a large group of singers, gathered under the trees near our company street, and their "sweet notes of song" floated melodiously upon the still night air, and were distinctly heard by us at the guard quarters, and we listened attentively for half an hour or more.

Suddenly the music stopped short, and was followed by loud bursts of laughter, and shout after shout fell upon our ears, coming from the direction of our company street. Being off duty, I proceeded thither to see what was up, and found considerable sport going on, in the shape of a burlesque on the celebrated Barnum's Museum. There was the "genuine Hippopotamus," crouched under a blanket, and waddling about at the direction of his keeper, who created a good deal of fun by his witty account of the history and capture of the amphibious animal.

Scene 2d. Here was produced six gigantic soldiers, upwards of eight feet in height, who walked with all the ease and grace imaginable, and carried their muskets at support arms. They had on their blankets, which hung from their shoulders in a single fold, and barely reached then to their feet. On turning aside their blankets, we discovered the mechanism of these uncommonly tall individuals, to be nothing more or less than one chap, sitting quietly astride the shoulders of another, the one above carrying the musket, while the other furnished the locomotive power. Some soldiers those!

Scene 3d. A platform borne on the shoulders of a half a dozen men, supported a caricature of Jeff Davis, with a rope around his neck, already to be swung off. This "took" decidedly, and he was carried off with as much indignation apparently as would have been exhibited, had the original Jeff, been before us.

The noise and tumult was now suddenly cut short, by the loud clattering tattoo, and I returned to the quarters of the guard. Roll was called in the various companies, and in a short time the camp was quiet, and "silence reigned supreme." During the night the air was cold and chilly, but we made ourselves quite comfortable, by a rousing fire, which we kept burning until morning.

Thursday May 23d.

A slight fog was visible at dawn but it rapidly disappeared before the warm rays of the sun. The morning air was cool and delightful, and the day was more comfortable and pleasant than common.

At reveille the camp resumed its wonted lively appearance, and the companies were soon out on the line in their company streets for roll-call. At seven o'clock breakfast sounded, and soon after I posted my relief for duty. At nine o'clock guard mounting took place and we were relieved, and as was the custom were relieved from all further duty during the day. It was an unusually quiet day with the Company, though the rest of the regiment went through the customary routine, and the several calls were beaten at the appointed time.

Nothing of interest transpired, with the exception that during the afternoon Capt. Devereux, Lieut. Brewster and Private Palmer procured horses, and rode into Baltimore, but whether on business, or a pleasure excursion I did not learn. At any rate on their return at six o'clock, the Capt. gave orders for the Company to be ready to fall in with haversacks and canteens at eight o'clock. It was evident that some sort of an expedition was on foot, but the nature of it was not made known to us.

It was another beautiful moonlight evening, and the boys were all on the qui vive. At eight we were all disappointed to hear that the order had been countermanded, and at tattoo roll was called and a majority of us turned in.

Friday May 24th.

The reveille sounded at the usual hour, and was immediately followed by roll call of the several companies. The morning was pleasant and comfortable, with a brisk southwest breeze, and at six the Company were ordered to fall in and we drilled for an hour before breakfast. This was something unusual for us, but not uncomfortable, for the air was quite cool and we enjoyed the drill very much. Besides this it sharpened our appetites a good deal, and we partook of breakfast, with greater relish than ever. This was all the duty that was required of the Company until the afternoon, but I was detailed as corporal of the guard at regimental Head Quarters, and after guard mounting, entered in duty with my relief.

By the morning papers we learned that the Union troops, conspicuous among whom was Ellsworth's Fire Zouaves, had occupied Alexandria, and during the forenoon the news of the sudden and unexpected death of Col. Ellsworth, reached Head Quarters. The account was as follows:

"The Marshall House, a hotel kept by James Jackson, was the Head Quarters for Rebel officers, and from a flagstaff on its summit, floated the Confederate flag, so conspicuously, that it had long been discernible by the Federal Executive, from the White House at Washington. Colonel Ellsworth had been the personal friend of the President, and had promised him before leaving Washington, to remove that flaunting insult. He therefore on landing, took two or three men and proceeded to the Hotel, which now with the early dawn, began to show signs of life. On reaching the building Colonel Ellsworth sprang up stairs, followed by the Chaplain of his regiment and Private Brownell, mounted to the roof, hauled down the flag, and began to descend with it, Private Brownell being in advance of him. The landlord was waiting for him; he had armed himself with a double-barrelled gun, and as the soldiers came down to the first landing, fired full at the Colonel's breast, killing him instantly. He fell forward down several steps to the landing, dead."

This news spread through the camp with the rapidity of lightning, causing great excitement, particularly among our own company, for Ellsworth was a warm friend of the Captain. In fact the whole company felt strongly attached to him, for we had received the celebrated "Chicago Zouaves" in Salem, while under his command, and become acquainted with himself and his men. On receipt of the news, all further duty was suspended, the flags were displayed at half mast, and the officers of the regiment, were summoned before the Colonel at Head Quarters. After some deliberation orders were issued to pack up and be ready to move at a moments notice, for the Colonel felt that the affair might cause trouble in Washington and Alexandria, and that all the troops in the vicinity, would be needed in that direction.

At tattoo the regiment were ordered to fall in for inspection, and thirty rounds of ammunition were distributed to each man. Three days rations were also ordered to be cooked, and the cooks were busy at this duty most of the night. At eleven o'clock we turned in, with orders to be ready to fall in at a moments notice.

Saturday May 25th.
There was no disturbance during the night and we slept on until six o'clock, reveille being an hour later, on account of the unfavorable weather of the morning. It rained pouring, and from the appearance of the company streets, which were a complete sea of mud, it must have rained most of the night. We ventured out to breakfast at seven o'clock, but returned immediately after, having no duty to perform until the afternoon. During the forenoon the clouds several times broke away, and closed together again, but at eleven o'clock the sun made its appearance and the remainder of the day was pleasant and comfortable, and the mud began to dry up gradually. At nine o'clock guard mounting took place which was all the duty performed till after dinner.

I spent most of the forenoon in my tent, manufacturing a pair of great coat straps, none having been issued to us with the knapsacks, although they were indispensable. Why there were omitted I know not, but it was evidently a neglect on the part of someone, for with out these straps, it was impossible to pack our knapsacks as required, and each man was obliged to supply the deficiency as best he might.

At noon, news reached us that the body of the lamented Ellsworth, had left Washington for Baltimore, and at three o'clock the entire garrison, Sixth and Eighth Regiments and the Battery were drawn up in line in full uniform, on the lower parade ground near the railroad, to pay our respects to the departed, as the train must necessarily pass the encampment. We were somewhat late however and the train shot by, before we were fairly in position. Nevertheless the colors which had been previously dressed in mourning, were drooped forward, and many stood with uncovered heads. It was a solemn occasion, and though nothing was visible about the train, by which to tell whether anything more than the usual daily freight was on board, yet its appearance had the effect instantly to inspire us with a feeling of sadness.

Immediately after the train had passed we were dismissed, and on entering the company street I noticed familiar faces from Salem. The gentlemen alluded to were Mr. Augustus Hardy of Salem, and Mr. Eben S. Poor of South Danvers. These gentlemen had been on a trip to Washington, and had favored us with a call, being anxious to see how Salem boys stood camp-life and what we were about. Of course we were delighted to see them, and at their request, the Captain ordered us to fall in, and we gave them a specimen of our drill in load & fire kneeling and the same lying, which seemed to please them very much.

At eight o'clock the Company was again detailed for picket, also Company "C," Capt. Martin and both companies proceeded to the old camp of the Eighth New York, where a squad of thirty were selected by Captain Devereux, and distributed at the various picket posts. The balance of us constituted a reserve and turned in here for the night. It was a beautiful moonlight night and we rested admirably, and without being disturbed. At half past four a.m. the outposts were called in, and we joined them as they came along, arriving at camp at five o'clock.

Sunday May 26th.

It was another beautiful day and the warm sun of Saturday had dried up the mud completely. We turned out at reveille and attended roll call, but during the forenoon had no duty to perform, and after breakfast which we took at seven o'clock, a squad of us visited a fine strawberry patch a mile distant in the village, and spent an hour, luxuriating upon this excellent fruit, by permission of the owner. The berries though were few and far between, and visitors had undoubtedly been there before us, at least so we judged from the scarcity of the fruit and the trampled condition of the vines. However we managed to get sufficient to gratify our desires, and returned to camp at about one o'clock, and just as the drums were sounding for dinner, for which we at once fell in.

After dinner we had nothing to attend to, so far as duty was concerned, until three o'clock when the assembly was beaten, and the regimental line was formed for afternoon service, and we proceeded to the lawn, where we listened to an interesting discourse by the Rev. Dr. Babbidge of Cambridge Mass., who was making a tour through the camps, and administering to the spiritual wants of the soldiers.[19]

After the services the line was reformed, and we were drilled in battalion movements by the Colonel, for about an hour, at the expiration of which we were dismissed, and fell in for supper. During the evening we collected various groups from the company in front of our quarters, and spent the time singing until tattoo, when we fell in for roll call and soon after turned in.

Monday May 27th.

Reveille sounded at five o'clock and we turned out promptly for roll call. The morning was clear and delightful, but at about half past eight, thick black clouds came up in the north west and soon encircled the entire heavens. Rain also began to fall and in a few moments increased to torrents accompanied with thunder and lightning, and the shower continued very heavy for an hour or more. At about ten o'clock the clouds gradually began to disperse, the sun soon made its appearance, and the remainder of the day was hot and sultry.

To day the police guard was for the first time made up from details of the different companies, the detail from ours being twenty-six men. Heretofore guard duty had been performed by the various companies in turn, an entire company with its officers furnishing the guard each day, but for some reason the Adjutant had suddenly taken it into his head, to follow the Regulations in this matter, and detail the guard from each of the companies, in proportion to the strength present for duty. Although this took a number of men from the companies every day, thus diminishing the number for drill and other purposes, yet it was by far the better way, partly because the ten organizations were preserved for battalion drill, but chiefly because it was in strict accordance with the Army Regulations.

During the forenoon we thoroughly renovated the tents, throwing out the straw which had been in use every since the encampment was pitched, and which had become very musty, substituting for it cedar twigs which we obtained in abundance from the woods close by, and brought into camp in our blankets. This was a decided improvement, as the cedar was much cleaner than straw, and also filled the tents with its pleasant fragrance.

During the day Willard Phillips, collector for the port of Salem, arrived in camp, and we had a pleasant conversation with him on home affairs &c. In the evening camp fires were built along the front of the encampment, of the rubbish which had been collected during the day, which attracted the notice of a New Hampshire Regiment which passed on the train for Washington at half past eight, and who cheered vociferously, and were answered by the boys with a will. At nine o'clock tattoo was beaten, roll was called and we turned in.

Tuesday May 28th.

At five o'clock we were aroused by the loud stirring beat of the reveille, and were soon on the line for roll call. The morning air was close and sultry and Sergeants Emmerton and Batchelder and myself, proceeded to the stream for a swimming bath. The water was very cold, but by skillful rubbing with a coarse towel when we came out, we got up a vigorous circulation, and felt nicely. Before returning to camp we gathered a number of wild flowers, arranged them into a boquet and sent them to the Colonel at Headquarters. My bath gave me a sharp appetite and I enjoyed breakfast with additional relish. At nine o'clock guard mounting took place, after which the day passed very quietly, we having no duty to perform until four o'clock. At noon Mr. Phillips took leave of us for Salem, taking with him a number of letters, for different members of the Company, and at one o'clock we fell in for dinner.

At about two o'clock Corporal Williams, Lewis (caterer for the Captain's mess) and myself, took a stroll down to the Relay House, to see what was going on, and while here the Ninth New York Regiment passed in a train of eighteen cars for Washington. Like a great many other regiments they had come on without arms, and were to be furnished with them on their arrival at Washington. Half an hour after, the regular train from Washington arrived containing a few of the Seventh New York, who informed us that their Regiment were to start for home on Friday, to be mustered out, their term of service (thirty days only) having expired.[20] I could not help wishing it was our Regiment, although we had been in service a few weeks only. Soon after, the Battery rattled by us, on its way to drill in a neighboring field, and we began to think it was about time for us to be getting back for the same purpose.

At half past four we retraced our steps and on the way met the Regiment en route to a large field, across the Patapsco, and a frequent resort of the Colonel for drill, on account of the room and extremely level ground. I hastened to camp alone, procured my musket and followed double quick, expecting a severe reprimand from the Captain for my absence at roll call, which always preceded drill. About half way to the field I changed my mind and sat down by the roadside to cool off, and while here the Battery came along on its way back to camp, and I jumped upon one of the ammunition boxes, and returned with them.

At six o'clock the Regiment returned, broke ranks and I fell in with the Company for supper. My absence was either not detected, or not reported by the Orderly, at any rate I escaped a reprimand, and considered myself extremely fortunate. Nothing of interest transpired during the evening, and at tattoo we fell in for roll call and turned in.

Wednesday May 29th.

At reveille we turned out and fell in to line for roll-call. It was a charming morning, with a brilliant sun and a delightful atmosphere. At seven o'clock we fell in for breakfast and at nine guard mounting took place. As it had been the custom for a number of days, the regimental drill was dispensed with until the cooler part of the day, and we spent most of the time in the tents, writing and sleeping. In the tent of the N.C.O. we spent most of the forenoon in the latter way, undisturbed except by the frequent call of "Orderly" "Orderly" from various members of the company, who stuck their heads into our tents for this purpose, apparently just to annoy us. If any thing went wrong, officially or otherwise the Orderly was always the first to be called upon, and I must say I did not envy him his position. At twelve o'clock, Private Hill and myself were detailed to drill the recruits in load & fire, and occupied the time in this way until dinner, which we took at one o'clock.

Nothing of importance occurred until half past three, when the Captain gave orders for all men of the Company who could be spared from other duties, to fall in with overcoats, blankets, haversacks and canteens. Accordingly about forty of us were soon in line, and we proceeded to the cookhouse where we filled the canteens, and were furnished with a day's rations, consisting of hard and soft tack and cheese. About forty of the Marblehead Company now came down to their cook-house adjoining for the same purpose, and were to join us. As yet we were unable to ascertain anything definite concerning our destination, or the nature of the expedition before us, but it was rumored that we were to proceed to a certain point on the Baltimore turnpike, for the purpose of intercepting wagon trains, said to be transporting munitions of war to the Rebels at Harpers Ferry. However we did not trouble ourselves much about it, for expeditions of this sort were of frequent occurrence during the campaign, and we had but little interest.[21] The Captain having been unwell for sometime, procured a horse and accompanied us mounted. We now returned for our muskets, and with the Marblehead company, at once left camp by a round about road to escape detection from Head Quarters. Why such precaution was necessary I did not exactly understand, but it was reported that Capt. Devereux had reported to Col. Jones, commanding that Post, that contraband articles were being smuggled over the road from Baltimore to Harper's Ferry, and had volunteered his services to stop it, but Col. Jones disapproving of the Captain's desires, the latter determined to attend to the matter on his own responsibility.

We started in the direction of Baltimore, over an exceedingly rough and hilly road, marching at route step at a rapid rate, in order to place as much distance as possible between us and the camp, before our departure should be discovered, and if possible escape the danger of being over taken and ordered back. In this we were successful, and at five o'clock passed the "monumental city" three miles distant on our right, and also obtained from the high ground, a fine view of the Chesapeake bay beyond. At half past five we halted at a lager beer saloon on the road, kept by a German who was very kind to us. We refreshed ourselves with several glasses of lager, and our German friend furnished us was something to eat also, distributing the supper from his own table which had just been prepared, and which I am obliged to add we accepted and eagerly devoured. But hunger will prompt many bold deeds, and some of the recruits took advantage of our friend's hospitality, and appropriated a dish of apple sauce, which sat under the table, which fairly aroused our indignation, but the German took it all as a joke, and would receive no pay for damages.

A picket guard of half a dozen men, belonging to a Pennsylvania regiment, which was quartered a mile distant at the asylum, were stationed on the road at this point, who informed us that half an hour before our arrival, they had captured some twenty kegs of powder, on its way to Harper's Ferry, and had also obtained information concerning the whereabouts, of several hundred kegs more, concealed for future shipment to the Rebels. On hearing this I concluded that our "game was up," but we were immediately ordered to fall in, and continued on.

A half a mile from here, at the junction of the road with the turnpike, we came upon another picket post of twenty men, who were somewhat startled at our sudden appearance, and who fell in with their muskets and halted us. I for one did not object to this, for I was pretty tired, and enjoyed a good rest during the half hour that we remained here. Upon starting again, we "pressed" a horseman who happened to come along, and took him with us as a guide. At dusk we passed several deserted log huts, and were informed that but a short time previous, they were occupied by Rebel sympathizers who had left for parts unknown, at the approach of Union troops in the vicinity. In half an hour we halted at a small cluster of houses, where we filled the canteens with fresh water, and gathered some information in regard to the road. The thick woods on either side, now shut out what little daylight remained, and darkness finally overtook us.

At half past eight we arrived at a small village, and halted in an open space at the junction of a couple of roads, one of which led to Harpers Ferry, and preparations were made to pass the night. Here our guide took leave of us, and the Company was divided into three reliefs for guard duty, the first relief being posted at once, with orders to stop and search all teams or foot passengers. We were very tired, having marched about fifteen miles, stopping only to enquire the direction of the road, or for some other necessary reason, and at once turned in, with the exception of the first relief before mentioned. But it was impossible to sleep, the night was so cold, and after shivering for half an hour a squad of us turned out, and proceeding to a neighboring wheat field, secured a good quantity of straw, an abundance of which was stacked there, and returned with it. Of this we made a comfortable bed. It was a beautiful moonlight night, but the mournful, and almost deafening song of a hundred whip-poor-whills disturbed us a good deal. We finally fell asleep however and enjoyed a good rest.

Thursday May 30th.

The only arrests during the night, were two or three citizens who happened by. These were searched according to orders, and permitted to pass. One or two vehicles were also searched, the drivers of which though detailed a few moments only, were pretty well frightened. We turned out soon after sunrise, and the morning air being cold and chilly, we set fire to our bedding to keep warm. Two cartloads of bark stood by the roadside, and we helped ourselves to several pieces, with which we replenished our fire. Breakfast consisted of the scanty rations we had left in our haversacks, and after "punishing" this, we fell in and started for the rail road station at Hollingworth, where we intended to take the cars, and return to the Relay House.

The road was a rough and rocky one, and in many places the dust was almost suffocating, which together retarded us a good deal, but of course we had no desire to hurry, for the march of yesterday had used us up a little. In an hour we halted at a farm house at the top of a hill on the road, and filled our canteens with fresh water from a beautiful spring close by. A short distance from the spring was a large dairy, belonging to the farm house, in which were several large pans of new milk, and a quantity of newly churned butter. No sooner was the dairy discovered, than the boys "rallied" on it in double quick time, and commenced devoting its contents to themselves. The work of spoil had hardly commenced, when the good lady of the house came out, and very properly transferred her stock to the house, "out of harm's way" as she said. But we were not to be fooled out of the milk in any such way, so we shelled out what little of the "filthy lucre" remained on hand, and purchased both milk and butter of her. It would no doubt have been more to our credit, had we done this in the first place, but then foraging was so <u>fashionable</u> in the Army, that we could not resist the temptation.

After filling the canteens with fresh milk, we discovered that we were on the wrong road, and retraced our steps down the hill, to a creek running into the Patapsco, by the side of which wound the narrow road, leading to the village of Hollingworth. This we followed for a half a mile or more, which brought us to the Hollingworth station on the Harpers Ferry rail road (and the residence of our guide the night before,) at about eight o'clock. Here we halted for half an hour, quietly waiting for the regular train, during which time we were treated by our friend the guide, to several glasses of new milk.

At half past eight the train came thundering along, and without noticing the signal to stop, shot by us like lightning. We hardly understood this, but a coal train following immediately after, was stopped by Capt. Devereux, and we jumped aboard, and started in a few moments for camp, with a rousing "Seven" for the hospitality of our friend. These cars were built of iron, about half an inch in thickness, and our situation in them was anything but comfortable, there being nothing whatever which we could appropriate for a seat, and we were obliged to perch ourselves on the sharp edges of the sides, or seat ourselves in the plentiful coal dust on the bottom.

The rail road wound along the bank of the Patapsco the entire distance, and the trip to the Relay House was pleasant in the extreme. The scenery was really charming. On either side of the river, the bluffs ascended to the height of several hundred feet, perfectly mountainous, and covered to the top with the thickest growth of trees. These with the numerous dams and mills on the river, were objects of especial interest to myself. We frequently saluted and cheered the operatives of the factories, who waved their aprons and hats to us as we passed. At Ellicott's Mills, about eight miles from the Relay House, we stopped a few moments, and gave a hearty "Seven" for a magnificent silk flag which was stretched across the street near the depot.[22]

At ten o'clock we arrived at the Relay House, and returned immediately to camp. Upon our arrival we learned that the Company had been detailed the night before for picket (as luck would have it,) and that our absence had been reported to the Post Commander, who was greatly enraged at the boldness of Captains Devereux and Martin. Lieutenant Putnam, with what men of the Company who were in camp, and a sufficient number from the other companies to make up the detail, executed the order, and stationed his men as usual along the Harpers Ferry rail road, and here commences another unfortunate circumstance. The regular train from Harpers Ferry, due in Baltimore late in the afternoon, was several hours behind time, and came along while the Pickets were on duty. For some reason Colonel Jones had neglected to instruct Lieut. Putnam, that the train might be expected at any hour of the night. Upon its approach therefore, the Lieutenant after repeated efforts in vain, to stop the train by signaling, gave orders to his men to fire <u>over</u> it. The engineer did not notice this fire and the train continued on. One or two shots entered a car, injuring no one, but damaging the windows and blinds a little, and causing some excitement in Baltimore, upon the arrival of the train at that place. The affair was communicated to Col. Jones, who immediately placed Lieut. Putnam in arrest. He was subsequently released however, a careful investigation of the circumstances, having shown that the Lieutenant had done his duty, and that the blame if there was any, should rest with the Commander of the Post, who was himself guilty of neglect of duty, in failing to communicate to Lieut. Putnam, the knowledge he possessed, of the failure of the train to arrive at the appointed hour.

After ranks were broken, the two companies proceeded to breakfast, and soon after it was reported that Capts. Devereux and Martin were placed under arrest, by order of the Commander of the Post, for leaving camp with their Companies, without orders. This report flew like lightning through the camp, and we soon ascertained it to be true. In obedience to orders the Captains were confined in their tents, and their swords taken to Head Quarters of the Regiment by the Adjutant, but as an expression of the opinion of this conduct on the part of Col. Jones, there entertained, the swords were decorated with flowers, and hung most conspicuously in the Colonel's (Hinks) tent. The utmost indignation was manifested by both officers and men throughout the Regiment, and it was generally acknowledged that the two Captains had done nothing, to justify their arrest. The Company were particularly indignant, and grew bold, defiant and beyond control, and as an expression of their feelings, they formed without orders, marched with arms reversed to Head Quarters of the Regiment, and deposited their muskets loaded and capped, in a huge pile on the ground in front of the Colonels tent. Captain Martins Company soon followed our example, and added theirs to the pile. This was a mutinous act, punishable with death, but it was all the same to the boys, for if it was proper that the Captain should be placed in arrest, or if we were aware of the nature of our proceedings, we were not disposed to confess it. The non commissioned officers, who from a natural sense of responsibility and duty, refused at first to join in this bold manifestation of spirit, now suffered their resolution to give way, and imitating the rest, deposited their muskets upon the pile. The tents were then searched, and every musket and bayonet to be found in them, was collected and thrown on to the pile, nothing belonging to a musket, being suffered to remain about the Company's quarters, as long as the Captain was in arrest. We did no duty during the day, and the greatest excitement was kept up, as the late affairs were discussed.

Our ideas now took a turn in another direction. Somebody had manufactured an effigy, consisting of a suit of old clothes stuffed with straw, with which we amused ourselves, by kicking it about the camp. When the excitement had in a measure subsided, Lieut. Putnam called the Company together, and read to us some portions of the Army Regulations. The boys however "couldn't see it" and had no notion of "backing down." The Colonel then sent us a request, that we should proceed to Head Quarters, and retake our muskets. A request from our gallant Colonel, who was held in such high estimation, by every officer and man in the Regiment, we could not refuse, and we immediately brought our muskets back again, as also did Capt. Martin's Company.

Nothing further was done until evening, when sitting in my tent, conversing with a friend from the Sixth, a huge fire was kindled in front of our quarters, without however attracting unusual notice, it being a common thing with us, to build a camp fire at night. But repeated yells and shouts of laughter, soon drew us outside, when lo! upon a tree close by, hung the headless effigy of Col. Jones. White gloves were attached to the sleeves, and a belt was fastened around the waist, in which was stuck a barrel stave, with the word "coward" upon it in large and distinct black letters. Missiles of all kinds were thrown at the figure, and several jokes were perpetrated at its expense. A half an hour at least was spent in this way, when the boys prepared to burn the effigy by setting fire to the feet, but the straw being packed rather hard, would not ignite, and he was cut down and thrown into the flames. A circle was then formed around the fire, and the boys danced around it with joined hands, all the while keeping up a deafening yell, punching the burning figure with sticks, like so many savages. Two thirds of the Garrison were attracted towards the spot by the clamor of the boys and the gigantic fire. As the flames subsided, the excitement wore away, and Lieut. Brewster (who had doubtless been an eye witness to the whole proceedings, and had enjoyed it as much as any of us) now came out of his tent, and dispersed the crowd, ordering every man into his quarters, and threatening to arrest us all for such "<u>rascally</u> proceedings." This order was promptly obeyed, for we had had our sport, and the game was played out. As it was now ten o'clock tattoo was beaten and the camp was soon quiet. Thus passed an eventful day in the history of our three months campaign, and one which will live till the last hour, in the minds of every member of the Eighth Regiment, and particularly those of the Salem Zouaves.[23]

Friday May 31st.

Reveille was beaten at five o'clock and we immediately turned out for roll-call. At seven oclock we fell in for breakfast, after which no duty was performed by the Regiment until afternoon. The excitement of the previous day was everywhere discussed, and in a great measure renewed, but the release of Capts. Devereux and Martin from arrest adjusted matters, and the duties of camp were discharged as usual. Strange to say the mutinous conduct of the two companies was overlooked by the Post Commander, and we could not account for such leniency.

At ten o'clock I was detailed to drill the recruits of the Company, and while engaged in this duty a letter from home in a mourning envelope, was handed me by the Orderly. Alas! I knew its contents too well, it contained news of the death of my sister Mary. Although I had daily expected it, yet this news fell heavily upon me, for death is always sudden. In the excitement which accompanied the hasty departure of the troops for the seat of War, I left home scarcely bidding her good bye, little thinking that I had seen her for the last time. She had been sick for several months, and I knew her

Washington Junction (Thomas) Viaduct, *Harper's New Monthly Magazine,* April 1857.

earthly career was drawing to a close, but had frequently indulged in the hope that I should be permitted to return home, before Death should throw his icy mantle around her, but Providence willed otherwise, and I could but say "God's will be done."[24]

During the forenoon Private Upton left for home, having received a furlough, on account of the illness of his father. At half past eleven the Company were ordered to fall in, and we proceeded to the brookside under command of Lieut. Putnam to discharge our muskets. A mark was set up, and each man in turn discharged his piece at it. The firing was a great improvement over our last target practice, and some fine shots were made. At half past two the Paymaster arrived in camp, and as this was the first time we had been favored with the presence of such a distinguished individual, his arrival was hailed with considerable satisfaction. The order "Fall in to be paid off" which was immediately issued, was obeyed with wonderful alacrity, and not a man was missing at roll call, the first time I think since our entry into service, that every man was present. One by one the companies were marched to the pay table, and we received about half a month's pay, being state pay to the date of muster-in which was very acceptable.[25]

At four o'clock the Assembly was beaten and the line was formed on the upper parade ground. Private Hill and myself were permanently detailed as Markers, and took our position as such, in rear of the right flank Company. This was rather desirable to me than otherwise, as we escaped the unpleasant duty of guard, and numerous other details. As soon as we had taken our position, the Regiment wheeled into column by companies, and proceeded to the large field (already alluded to) on the other side of the Patapsco, where a couple of hours was spent in battalion movements. At half past six we started on our return to camp via the Relay House where we halted for half an hour to meet the Seventh New York, which was expected in the Washington train for Baltimore, on its way home to be mustered out. The train however did not arrive as was expected, and we continued on to camp.

Upon our arrival we were formed into hollow square, and the Colonel addressed us in very strong terms. It appeared that some of the men had strayed beyond the line of sentries, and even proceeded to Baltimore, where they engaged in riotous proceedings, and otherwise conducted themselves in an unbecoming manner. But their cases had been reported to the Colonel, who now very coolly informed us, that instead of the mild treatment by which he had heretofore governed, he should use violence if necessary, to enforce obedience to orders, and a strict code of camp regulations, was read to us by the Adjutant. A reprimand in orders, of Capts. Devereux and Martin, was also published by the Adjutant, at the end of which the entire Regiment gave three rousing cheers for the two Captains, which Col. Jones might have heard at his Head Quarters had he been listening, and no doubt he did. The Chaplain then stepped forward to the centre and offered prayer, after which we were dismissed, returned to quarters, and fell in for supper.

The evening passed pleasantly, for during the afternoon a number of boxes arrived for many of the boys, and among the load was a barrel of eatables of all sorts for Private Ward, which he generously distributed, to nearly every member of the Company. At ten o'clock tattoo was beaten, and we fell in for roll call and turned in.

Saturday June 1st.

Reveille was beaten at five o'clock, and was followed at once by roll-call, which we attended with the usual promptness. At an early hour Williams T. Fowler of Salem arrived in camp as a recruit for the Company, being one of ten who started for the same purpose, but the balance being for some reason unable to procure transportation, remained behind.[26] This was indeed unfortunate for they would have been quite an accession to the Company. At seven o'clock we fell in for breakfast Fowler joining us.

During the forenoon a Regimental Court Martial was convened by order of the Colonel, for the trial of the unruly scamps, who had brought such a stigma upon the heretofore good name of the Regiment, by their disgraceful actions in Baltimore. No one had any sympathy for them, and it was the unanimous opinion, that the devils might get their due.[27] At ten o'clock, the following list of camp regulations was published, the first since our muster in.

    1 Reveille 5 o'clk A.M.
    2 Roll-Call 5¼ " "
    3 General Police 5½ " "

4 "Peas on a trencher" *(breakfast) 7 " "
5 Guard Mounting 9 " "
6 To the Color ** 9½ " "
7 Company Drills 10 " "
8 "Roast Beef" *** (dinner) 12 " m.
9 Fatigue Call 2 " p.m.
10 Battalion Drill 4 " "
11 Supper 6 " "
12 Retreat Sundown
13 Tattoo and Roll Call 10 o'clk p.m.
14 Taps 10½ " "

*Title of the beat on the drum announcing breakfast from its resemblance to peas dropping on a trencher.
** Formation of Regimental line, the direction of which is indicated by two colors, or markers
***The title of the beat on the drum announcing dinner, but which we at first understood in a literal sense, thereby being sadly disappointed.

At four o'clock the assembly was beaten, and after the line was formed, the Regiment proceeded in column by Company, to the field a mile distant, where they were drilled for a couple of hours in battalion movements. Being slightly indisposed I obtained an excuse from the Captain and remained in camp, and while reading in my tent I heard a terrible yelling, which came from the direction of the Regiment. Upon their return at six o'clock, I was informed that the Colonel had introduced a new feature in the drill, in the shape of a sham fight, which was pretty exciting. The Battery which was drilling close by, was posted in a certain position, with five companies to support it. The other five companies were then ordered forward, double quick, to charge it. At the word of command they rushed upon the Battery with a yell, (which accounted for the noise I heard) and wrenched it from the hands of the supposed enemy, without much show of resistance. The only casualties in the affair, was a scratch received by one of the recruits of the Company, from the point of a bayonet. Private Swasey's bayonet was cut off short at the shank, by bringing it in contact with an Artillery sabre.[28]

Soon after six o'clock we fell in for supper and while thus engaged, it suddenly clouded up and rain fell quite fast for an hour, when it cleared up again, leaving the air close and uncomfortable. At seven o'clock four large cases arrived in camp for the Company, containing a new uniform for every man, also a quantity of underclothing, soldier's companions &c. which were at once distributed. The uniform was precisely the same pattern as the one we were then wearing, which consisted of a loose fitting jacket buttoned up close, and trimmed across the breast with parallel bars of scarlet serpentine braid, terminating at either side in a knot, each bar graduating in length toward the waist; and pants of the same material, with a heavy scarlet cord down the outside seam. The material of the new uniform was a grey mixed merino cassimere, or Kentucky jean as it is more commonly called, and was a decided improvement over the blue flannel, which composed our present one, as it did not show the dust or dirt. Sundry packages, letters &c. helped to fill the boxes, the contents of which were generously distributed by the owners. The evening passed pleasantly, and most of the boys were in an unusually good humor. At ten o'clock tattoo was beaten, roll was called, and a majority of us turned in.

Sunday June 2d.
Reveille sounded at five o'clock and we were soon out on the line for roll call, after which preparations were made for the usual Sunday morning inspection, and we were engaged in policing the grounds, packing our knapsacks, and cleaning our muskets until seven o'clock, when "peas on a trencher" sounded, and we fell in for breakfast. The morning air was very damp, and the camp was rather muddy, rain having fallen during the night, but at nine o'clock the sun made its appearance, and the rest of the day was unusually warm and sultry.[29]

Soon after nine o'clock the assembly was beaten, and the line was formed for inspection, the Company appearing in the new uniform, which attracted some attention.[30] After the inspection was over we were dismissed, and no further duty was required until the afternoon. At twelve o'clock "roast beef" sounded, and we fell in for dinner, after which the time passed quietly until four o'clock, when the line was reformed, and we proceeded to the lawn to attend divine service, which was conducted by the Chaplain. At the close of the service the Regiment were dismissed, with the exception of the Company who were drilled for a half an hour by the Captain in company movements. We were then dismissed and fell in for supper.

At sunset retreat was beaten, and soon after, the Company was detailed for picket and left camp for this duty at eight o'clock. They had been gone but a few moments, when rain commenced falling, and they had a wet time of it. Being somewhat indisposed I remained in camp, and spent the evening in my tent writing. At ten o'clock tattoo was beaten and I turned in, but not to sleep, for the mosquitoes reigned supreme, until having exhausted all my efforts, to conquer these pests, "Morpheus" came to my relief, and I slept sound until morning.

Monday June 3d.
Upon the arrival of the Company in camp, which was soon after reveille, I turned out, and at the early hour of six o'clock we fell in for breakfast. The camp was wet and muddy from the rain during the night, and the atmos-

phere close and muggy. Altogether it was an exceedingly dull and disagreeable morning. The boys who had been on picket, suffered in the usual manner, and returned to camp with their muskets considerably rusted, but as no duty was required of them, most of the forenoon was spent in putting them in condition for use again.

After breakfast I obtained a pass from the Captain, and visited a seamstress in the neighboring village, for the purpose of having chevrons put on the sleeves of my grey jacket, which the tailor had omitted to do, when it was made.[31] At about ten o'clock, rain commenced to fall, and continued for half an hour, when it stopped as suddenly as it commenced. At twelve o'clock "roast beef" sounded and we fell in for dinner, after which I exercised what little ingenuity I possessed in the manufacture of a gun-rack, which took me until nearly three o'clock, and which when finished, I fastened to the rear tent pole. Though rather a rough affair it was better than none at all, and enabled us to keep the muskets up out of the way, instead of allowing them to be kicking about, as is almost invariably the custom.

At four o'clock the assembly was beaten, and Private Hill and myself repaired to Head Quarters for duty as markers, and were posted on the parade by the Adjutant. As soon as the line was formed, the companies were dismissed to the commands of their Captains, and Hill and myself rejoined the Company for drill. We proceeded to the lower parade ground, and were drilled by the Captain in the manual, skirmishing and company movements, until six o'clock, when we returned to quarters, were dismissed and fell in for supper, retreat was beaten at sunset, and soon after the Captain handed me a couple of neat American flags, about twenty-four by forty inches, which were sent him by Major Poor with his respects, for the markers. They were intended to be fastened to the bayonet, in order to point out to the Regiment more distinctly, the position of the markers during the maneuvres.

At about eight o'clock, the assembly again sounded for dress parade, and while the companies were forming, rain commenced to fall which continued in torrents for nearly an hour. We therefore broke ranks, and dress parade, was dispensed with.

During the evening, we were favored in the tent of the non commissioned officers, with a call from Capt. Devereux, Lieut. Coe of the Quarter Master's Dept't. and a number of others, and spent a couple of hours in singing, always a favorite way of passing the evening, with the Captain.[32] At tattoo they took leave of us, and the Company fell into line for roll-call. At taps all lights were extinguished, and we turned in.

Tuesday June 4th.

At five o'clock reveille sounded, and we at once turned out for roll call. It was another dull and disagreeable morning with a slight fog, and a warm, oppressive atmosphere. The camp was still muddy, and so slimy and slippery, as to render it difficult to get about. "Peas on a trencher" sounded at seven o'clock, and we fell in for breakfast, and half an hour after, rain commenced falling, which continued with occasional cessation, throughout the day. At nine o'clock guard mounting took place, and soon after the assembly was beaten, and the line formed on the upper parade ground. It was however considered inadvisable to proceed with the drill and we were dismissed again. We were glad to retreat into the tents, and spent most of the day in reading, writing, at cards &c.[33]

On looking over the "Baltimore Clipper," I noticed the death of Hon. Stephen A. Douglas, which created considerable feeling, not only in camp, but throughout the country, particularly among the democratic party, of which he was a prominent leader. He was an eminent statesman, a true and honest democrat, and a faithful representative of democracy, in its early days. His loss was deeply felt by all parties.[34]

During the afternoon a squad of the Sixth came over, among them Private Charles Fry, an old schoolmate of mine, and we had a pleasant chat with them in the N.C.O. tent. The affair of May 30th when we burnt Col. Jones in effigy was warmly discussed, and the Sixth boys were surprised at our boldness (or "cheek" as they expressed it). I must also confess that we were surprised at our own unruly action, for the affair was actually criminal, and there is no doubt that Col. Jones overlooked it in us, solely on account of our ignorance of the extent of the offense. Strange to say they did not hesitate to express their disapproval of the action of Col. Jones in arresting Capts. Devereux and Martin, and it seemed from their conversation, that the Colonel was very unpopular with his own men.

At six o'clock we fell in for supper and in an hour after, retreat was beaten. At half past seven, the rain having ceased, the assembly was beaten and the line was formed for dress parade, on the upper parade ground, at the end of which we were dismissed.

During the evening Mrs. Hinks, wife of the Colonel, arrived in camp with the Colonel's little boy, from Massachusetts, and a number of the boys proceeded to Head Quarters to serenade them. Their efforts were appreciated by Mrs. Hinks, who presented them with a handsome boquet, which she had brought with her. At nine o'clock we returned to quarters, and at ten tattoo beat and we fell in for roll call, after which we turned in.

Wednesday June 5th.

The weather still continued wet and disagreeable, and the morning was made more unpleasant, by a cold north east wind, which was indeed a great change in the atmosphere. The camp was a perfect bed of mud some inches deep, and we were loth to leave the tents. Orders however must be obeyed

Camp of the United States Volunteers at the Relay House, *Harper's Weekly*, May 25, 1861.

and at reveille we turned out and answered to roll call, retreating under cover immediately after. It rained hard all day, and the duties were of course light. At seven o'clock we took breakfast, and at nine guard mounting took place.

At half past nine the Regimental line was formed on the upper parade ground, and we immediately formed square in four ranks, and the sentences of the prisoners, tried by Court Martial a few days since, were published by the Adjutant. It rained pouring all the time we stood here, and as soon as the Adjutant had finished, we were dismissed and returned double quick to quarters.[35]

During the afternoon a squad of us collected in the Captain's tent, and enjoyed a good time singing. The Colonel soon favored us with his company, having (as he said) been attracted by the music, and as he was a great admirer of a song, we did our best to please him. We had been engaged in this way about half an hour, when loud voices, and the discharge of fire-arms interrupted us, and we instinctively sprang to the door of the tent, and the Colonel returned to Head Quarters. The disturbance came from the village, about half a mile distant, and as near as we could judge, was located in the camp of a Baltimore Regiment encamped there. The tumult increased, and an orderly soon came down from Head Quarters, with an order detailing Captains Martin and Devereux, to proceed with their Companies to the scene of the disturbance, and render such assistance as might be necessary, to restore order and quiet. Notwithstanding the rain which still continued to fall quite fast, we were in line in about three minutes, and proceeded double quick to the camp of the Baltimore boys Major Poore Comdg. the Detachment. Upon our arrival, we learned the cause of the disturbance as follows: A citizen attempting to pass the line of sentinels, was halted by a Guard, and his pass demanded of him in a respectful manner. Not being supplied with this necessary protection, the Guard refused like a good soldier to pass him. The citizen then very foolishly attempted to force his passage, whereupon a scuffle ensued and the soldier was unluckily knocked down. In this position he discharged his musket into the air, and the balance of the Guard came promptly to his assistance, and had it not been for the interference of the Officer of the Guard, the affair might have cost Mr. citizen his life. As it was he received a good pommelling from some of the men, and was allowed to go about his business, having no doubt learned a profitable lesson from his rough experience, which ought to have taught him never again to tamper with a sentinel. The affair rather infuriated the Baltimore boys, and it was some time before they were quieted. On learning the cause of the disturbance, Capt. Martin returned to camp with his Company, while we stepped into a vacant building, formerly occupied as a grocery, and perched ourselves upon the counters, where we remained, about half an hour, awaiting orders. No further disturbance occurred, and as soon as the rain held up a little, we threw our muskets over our backs by the gun slings, and returned to camp.

Upon our arrival, some of the boys procured axes, and felled a couple of trees, which were soon cut into logs, with which we built a large camp fire, to dry ourselves, (for we were wet to the skin) and which we kept burning all night. At six o'clock we fell in for supper, and soon after retreat was beaten but was hardly audible, as the drum heads were badly stretched in consequence of the rain. The evening was spent in a social manner around the fire, jokes were cracked and stories were told, until ten o'clock when tattoo interrupted us and we fell into line for roll call. At half past ten a drummer came round with his "taps" and most of us turned in.

Thursday June 6th

It sill continued wet and stormy and the excessive rain had found its way through the tents, and everything was damp and wet.[36] The camp was a perfect bed of mud, and it was difficult to get about. We turned out at reveille and answered to roll call, but took breakfast in the tents, at seven o'clock. At nine o clock guard mounting took place, and soon after, (notwithstanding the rain and mud,) the assembly sounded, and the line was formed on the upper parade ground for company drills, but the Colonel suddenly returned to his senses, and dismissed us without the usual drill. Towards noon the clouds began to disperse, and appearances indicated pleasant weather, but it soon grew thick and lowery again, and rain fell the greater part of the afternoon and night. At half past twelve roast beef sounded, and we fell in for dinner. At four o'clock the line was again formed and dress parade was gone through with by the Regiment, after which all the companies except our own were dismissed, but we remained "masters of the ground," and were drilled for an hour in company movements and skirmishing.

We were (the Company) an ill fated set of boys, at least so we thought, for while other companies lounged about their quarters, we were invariably drilled at all hours and in all weathers, whenever there was an opportunity. But then "success is the reward of labor," and we enjoyed the reputation of being not only the best and most thoroughly drilled organization in the Regiment, but in the volunteer service, and though we were often led to think we were ill used, we were also forced to admit that our excellent commander, Capt. Devereux, was good in his intentions, that he was without a rival, and that we were lucky in being placed under one so willing to work with us, and devote his whole time to the best interests of his men, in spite of the occasional "hard knock," as the recruits expressed it.

During the drill a new feature was introduced, both novel and interesting, though in my opinion not altogether serviceable, consisting of formation of pyramids in the following manner. Half a dozen of the tallest men on the right were selected, and formed into line, locking arms and bracing themselves firmly together. Half a dozen more shorter in size were then placed behind these, with their heads bowed and firmly braced against the backs of the first row, and their backs curved in such a manner as to present a good foothold. A third row of half a dozen were then placed behind these, in a kneeling position, with their heads braced against the hams of the second row. Still another row crouched on the hands and feet, and braced against the men of the third row, and the pyramid was completed, and thus formed was intended to be used as a bridge or inclined plane, over which the smallest men, selected as being lighter, and fleeter on foot were intended to climb, and thus scale the parapet of earthworks and fortifications generally. This formation would doubtless be of little use, as too much time would be required to render it of any advantage, and as it must necessarily be exposed to a raking fire, a single shot would destroy its utility, and completely frustrate a second attempt to form it.

During the afternoon we were visited by an old friend from Salem. Daniel H. Johnson Jr. who brought with him a large trunk for Private Hill, which among other things contained several packages and letters for the boys, and I was fortunate enough to receive four letters from friends at home. Two large boxes also arrived, one for Serg't Batchelder and the other for Corp'l Williams, and we were treated by them to pastry, fruit and so forth, particularly in the N.C.O. tent. At dress parade Daniel went on line with us and answered to his name — perfectly at home for he was a member of the Salem Cadets.[37]

In the evening a large camp fire was built, by which we dried our clothing and blankets, and after enjoying its comforts for half an hour or so, we adjourned to the tent of the Non Commissioned Officers, and spent an hour singing, where Dan added his voice to the choir. At tattoo we fell into line, answered to roll call, then called on the Captain and passed another hour in a pleasant chat, songs &c. At eleven o'clock we returned to our quarters and turned in.

Friday June 7th.

In the morning it was wet and rainy again, and the air was dreadful close and uncomfortable. At reveille we turned out and answered to roll call, after which we spent the time in a leisure manner until seven o'clock when we fell in for breakfast. The mud was still plentiful, and soon after guard mounting, which took place at the usual hour the line was formed on the upper parade ground. The rain of the past few days had interrupted the daily drills of the Regiment, and most of the time was spent by the companies in their quarters, but to day we proceeded to the lower parade ground, in order to avoid the mud, where a couple of hours was occupied in battalion maneuvers. The wet grass however was about as bad as the mud would have been, and was particularly uncomfortable to Hill and myself, who were obliged frequently to double-quick through it, in the rapid changing of positions. During the forenoon the clouds began to break away, and several times at short intervals the sun made its appearance. At half past twelve we returned to our quarters, broke ranks and fell in for dinner.

The afternoon passed very quietly and I spent most of the time writing. Retreat was beaten at the usual hour, but dress parade was dispensed with. At about seven o'clock the Company was detailed for picket, with Company "C" Capt Martin, and half an hour after we left camp together proceeding in a westerly direction, to a handsome cottage, uninhabited, and about two miles and a half from camp, establishing picket posts of three men about three hundred yards apart the whole distance. The cottage was constituted the <u>rendezvous</u> or headquarters of the reserve, and here those not on post spread their blankets on the piazza and turned in. At about twelve o'clock a wagon came along the road which on being halted, proved to contain a load of peas only, on the way to the Baltimore market. Some of the boys filled their haversacks with the peas, after which the driver was allowed to pass, having paid his toll, and got a good deal frightened, at being stopped by the pickets. This was the only disturbance during the night, and we slept quietly the rest of the time until morning.

Saturday June 8th

At four o'clock we turned out formed companies and returned to camp, taking in the pickets as we came along, and arriving at five o'clock. At early dawn clouds were visible in the east, but soon disappeared and the sun arose clear and bright. Breakfast was for some reason unusually late in the Company, and was not served up until eight [o']clock, which with the return tramp sharpened our appetites a good deal, and we eat with good relish. At nine guard mounting took place, after which the two companies were excused from duty until afternoon.

During the forenoon a quantity of boards from the Quarter Masters department were distributed to the different companies, and preparations were at once made for flooring the tents. This was an improvement and of course hailed with pleasure by us all, for we had heretofore slept upon the ground covered only with straw or cedar twigs to protect us from the dampness.[38] On examining the lumber distributed to the Company, we found it to consist in part of half inch stuff, entirely too thin for flooring purposes, and which part fell to the tent of the Non Commissioned officers. We were about to use it to the best advantage, when the Chaplain happened along and very kindly informed us where we could obtain some better stock by foraging, and tendered us his services as an escort, on condition that he should receive a portion of the spoil, sufficient to floor his own tent. This was a new idea. The Chaplain to conduct a foraging expedition. But as the boards were better than the ones issued to us, and we were bent on having our tent floored, we did not stand upon ceremony, particularly as the Chaplain was in the scrape, so we readily accepted the condition and followed him. We proceeded about a mile from Dr. Hall's residence into the woods, and found a large pile of well seasoned inch hemlock. This was exactly what we wanted, and while getting out a sufficient quantity to answer our purpose, "Du-dah" whom we had brought along with us started off to a neighboring farm house for a team. By the time we had collected them together again, he returned with a conveyance, and we hauled the boards to camp and set to work. We altered the position of the tent a little to bring it on a line with the rest, then floored it nicely, but had no sooner finished than we had an opportunity to test its great improvement over the unlevel ground, for at about two o'clock thick black clouds made their appearance, and rain soon fell quite fast accompanied with thunder and lightning and a high wind. Not a drop of water entered the tent, but a continual stream run under the floor and down the hill. The shower continued for about half an hour, when the sun again came out, as bright as ever.

At seven o'clock the assembly sounded and the line was formed for dress parade, after which the companies were dismissed to their several commanders for company drill and we were drilled for an hour by the Captain in company maneuvers quick and double quick, manual and skirmishing. At eight o'clock we were dismissed and fell in for supper. The evening passed in a quiet manner; at tattoo we fell in for roll call after which I turned in. I had no sooner fell asleep than I was awakened by sweet notes of song from a squad of serenaders outside, and listened attentively for some time but was soon charmed to sleep again. At midnight we were visited by another thunder shower, much heavier than the one at noon though with less wind.

Sunday June 9th

It was a beautiful Sabbath. The day was ushered in with a beautiful sun, and the morning air was cool and delightful. Not a cloud was visible, nor a breath of air stirring. Reveille sounded at five o'clock and we fell into line for roll call, after which preparations were commenced for the usual Sunday morning inspection, which occupied us in a lively manner until breakfast.

An unusual mania seemed to prevail among us on this occasion to have the tents look as elaborate as possible, and the different squads exerted themselves each and all to outdo the rest. To commence with the inmates of each tent selected a name among the various hotels and places with which we had been connected since our entry into service, and painted it on a piece of board, then nailed it up conspicuously on the tent pole in front, with the exception of the non commissioned officers, who confined themselves to the plain N.C.O. Each tent was then profusely decorated with white laurel, which grew in abundance in the woods within a stone's throw of the encampment.

The decorations were about as follows: Commencing with N.C.O. on the right, the pole in front was wound round with laurel, completely covering it from top to bottom. The front was then drawn away and festooned to the corner guy-line on either side, with a band of oak leaves, and the inner edges trimmed with the same somewhat resembling drapery. Under the peak and over the entrance was fastened a handsome wreath of full blown monthly roses. On the summit of the pole in front were perched a couple of non commissioned officer's swords, with a bayonet upright between them, from the blade of which waved the marker flag of the writer, and in the shank of which was affixed a handsome boquet of roses.

Tent No. 2 was decorated in a similar way omitting the ornaments on top, and with the exception of two rows of oak leaves instead of one along the edges of the front, and the addition of a turf embankment with a fan of <u>fleur de leuce</u> leaves at each extremity, in place of the heretofore wooden step. This tent was styled the "Continental," after the famous Continental Hotel in Philadelphia, were we took supper when passing through that city on our way to Washington.

The other tents which we styled "Fifth Avenue," "Astor House," "Zouave Home," "Essex House" and "Hinks Hotel" respectively, were decorated after the manner of the "Continental," with some little variation, with the exception of the "Astor House," which far exceeded in beauty and taste anything on the Company street. The summit of the front pole was crowned with a fan of <u>fleur de luce</u> leaves, under which was a beautiful wreath of the handsomest flowers. Directly over the entrance appeared the well remembered "Astor House" bordered with oak leaves and having a neat little American flag flying at either end. The front was festooned at each side similar to the rest, but completely covered with laurel and roses, and presenting a magnificent appearance. It was fitting that the Astor should eclipse any and every tent on the street, for we had spent a delightful week at this popular establishment, while awaiting orders in New York after having conducted the Constitution to the Navy Yard at Brooklyn, and there was not a member of the Company but that was partial to the name.

Every effort having been made to adorn the outside, the inside of each tent was arranged with the greatest care and precision, and the Company street cleanly and thoroughly policed. Thus the time was spent until ten o'clock when the assembly sounded, and the Regiment formed line on the upper parade ground for inspection. An hour was spent by the Colonel and staff in inspecting the arms, equipments and general appearance of the men, after which the arms of each company were stacked in the various streets, in

Stereoview of Union soldiers in front of the Relay House and station, 1861 (editor's collection).

a neat and uniform manner, and the entire Regiment proceeded to the lawn in rear of Head Quarters, where we listened to an interesting and appropriate discourse, delivered by the Rev. Mr. Hepworth of Boston.[39] At twelve o'clock we returned to the parade and were dismissed.

The quarters of the men were then inspected by the Field and staff, with several invited guests among whom were Colonel Jones, commander of the Post and wife, Mrs. Hinks, and a number of other ladies. As they entered the Company street each member of the company stood at "attention," and I for one could not keep the affair of the 30th out of my head, as the Post Commander scrutinized the men, and their quarters, for 'tis said and with truth that "a guilty conscience needs no accuser," and it was but ten days since we burnt the dignified commander before us in effigy. The ladies were particularly delighted with the floral arrangements about the tents, and smiled charmingly upon us. Arriving at the last on the line, Colonel Hinks seemed to be highly pleased at the sight of his own name on the front, and said he felt highly honored with this expression of the good feeling that prevailed.[40] As the inspectors turned the corner of the street on their return, we were dismissed and at half past one fell in for dinner.

During the afternoon Commissioners arrived in camp from Massachusetts, for the purpose of examining into the condition of affairs. They too were highly pleased with the appearance of the Company street. At four o'clock we formed company and proceeded to a neighboring field on the village road, where we drilled for half an hour in the bayonet exercise and skirmishing. While here the assembly sounded and we returned and joined the Regiment for battalion drill, for the benefit of the Commissioners, who expressed great surprise at the rapid improvement of the Regiment since leaving the state. At half past five the companies were dismissed, and at six we fell in for supper. Retreat sounded at sundown, and the evening was spent in the usual manner, some writing and others singing until tattoo when roll was called and at taps most of us turned in.

Monday June 10th.

Reveille sounded at five o'clock and we were soon on the line for roll call. The morning was warm and sultry, and there was not so much as the faintest breeze to relieve the oppressiveness of the atmosphere. At seven o'clock "peas on a trencher" sounded, and we fell in for breakfast, but returned to our tents immediately afterward on account of the extreme heat of the sun. As the day progressed the temperature increased until it was by far the hottest day of the season thus far.[41]

At nine o'clock guard mounting took place and immediately after the assembly sounded and the line was formed, but after going through morning parade we were dismissed and returned to quarters. No further duty was required until late in the afternoon, and we endeavored to keep comfortable by laying about the tents in the easiest possible positions, but in vain for the sun poured down its heat upon the canvas, and the inside was like an oven.

During the forenoon Mrs. Devereux wife of the Captain, arrived in camp from Salem, intending to remain sometime with her husband, and we were all delighted to see her. We were also visited by Capt. E.H. Staten of the Mechanic Light Infantry, Fifth Regiment Mass., which Regiment was quartered at Alexandria, who also brought a friend with him and remained in camp a few hours with us.[42]

At half past five we formed company and were drilled for half an hour in skirmishing and load and fire lying, at the expiration of which we were dismissed and fell in for supper. At six o'clock the assembly sounded, and the line was formed but the after noon drill of the Regiment was omitted, and after going through with dress parade we were dismissed and returned to quarters. Retreat sounded at sundown.

During the evening considerable excitement was occasioned by the arrest of "Baltimore Joe" by Lieut. Brewster, Officer of the Guard. Baltimore Joe was the familiar title bestowed by the boys upon a jolly good natured chap from Baltimore, who had for some time kept a beer saloon within the line of sentries by permission of the Colonel. This saloon was liberally patronized by every company in the Regiment, but on the occasion referred to, Joe had not only overstepped the bounds of propriety but violated orders, in furnishing some of the men with whiskey. This offense was reported to the Lieutenant of the Guard, who with three men made a descent upon the bar of Joe, confiscating every drop of liquor on hand, and carrying Joe a prisoner to Head Quarters. After some investigation he was released and the beer returned, but the whiskey was retained, and Joe no doubt learned a lesson.

At ten o'clock tattoo sounded and roll was called, and at taps I turned in but not to sleep for it was a hot and uncomfortable night, and after turning and twisting for an hour, I got up and proceeded to the brook, took a bath, and returned to bed again, and was so much refreshed that I fell asleep without any difficulty and slept soundly.

Tuesday June 11th.

This was a morning which will be remembered by every member of the Company. The air at an early hour was much cooler than usual, and the Captain seized upon the opportunity to give us an extra drill before breakfast. Fortunately there had been a great change in the atmosphere during the night, otherwise we should have suffered intensely with the heat, during the double quick movements. Immediately after roll call at reveille we took our muskets formed company and were marched to the lawn in rear of Head

Quarters, where we were drilled principally in the wheelings for half an hour, after which we marched to the lower parade ground, near the rail road, and were put through the severest exercise for an hour and a half, such as wheeling, breaking into platoons and reforming company, and various other company movements all in double quick time. During the whole two hours drill at both places, we had but about ten minutes rest. It was surely the toughest drilling we had experienced since entering the service, and I for one was at a loss to know what had come over the spirit of the Captains dreams. Some of the boys thought it unfavorable to us for the Captain's wife to be in camp, for he had certainly resorted to unusually severe measures with us, since her arrival, but we finally came to the conclusion that there was nothing to be lost in a good long drill, and even if there was it was probably all the same, and if we didn't like it, all we could say or do would amount to nothing and we might as well make the best of it first as last. At about half past seven we were rejoiced to hear the order "break ranks," which was obeyed with a yell of satisfaction which might have been heard a mile, and we fell in for breakfast like so many hungry wolves.

After breakfast the detail for guard was made from the Company and no further duty was required of us until after supper. The sun was now scorching hot and it was with the greatest difficulty we could keep comfortable, though we did nothing but lay around the tents in our shirt sleeves. At about eleven o clock our friend Daniel H. Johnson Jr. returned from a short visit to Alexandria where a number of Massachusetts troops were on duty, and at four he took final leave of us, taking with him a number of letters for friends at home. He had been gone but a short time when Mr. Mark Lowd and Mr. Charles Odell of Salem, arrived from Alexandria, having been there on a visit to a son of Mr. Lowd in the "Mechanics."[43]

At six o'clock we fell in for supper and soon after the assembly sounded, and the line was formed for dress parade after which the Regiment proceeded to the lower parade ground, and were drilled by the Colonel for an hour and a half in battalion movements quick and double quick, chiefly the latter. The Company was detached as usual from the Regiment—for the Captain never would drill with the Regiment if he could possibly avoid it—and drilled near by in skirmishing. Of course Hill and myself were obliged to remain with the Regiment as markers, which was never satisfactory to me, for so far as the drilling was concerned, I had much rather remained with the Company, notwithstanding the severity of our Company drills sometimes. At about dusk we were marched to quarters and were dismissed.

During the evening, in accordance with a previous agreement, Lieut. Brewster, Sergt. Batchelder, Privates Hale and Dearborn, and myself met at the quarters of Lieut. Coe, in the Quarter Masters Department, then called on Lieut. Col. Ellwell at Head Quarters; by whom we were pleasantly entertained, with a number of other officers, and we sang for an hour or so until tattoo when we returned to our quarters to answer to roll call.

As soon as the camp had become a little quiet we returned again to Head Quarters and spent another half hour very pleasantly.

At half past ten we took our leave, having first procured the countersign, and adding half a dozen other good singers to our number, started out of camp on a serenade excursion, Lieut. Coe accompanying us with his flute. We proceeded under the escort of Lieut Putnam to the residence of Mr. LaTrobe, delightfully situated in a beautiful grove of pines about a mile from camp, and serenaded a lady friend of the Lieutenant by the name of Virginia.[44] The evening was quite cool and comfortable, and the sweet notes of Lieut. Coe's flute, floated on the still night air to a great distance, reverberating through the grove, and echoing back the sound with wonderful distinctness. We remained here about fifteen minutes only, then proceeded to the residence of Mr. Donaldson near by, and a distant relative of the Captain.[45] Here we likewise made a short stay and then wended our way slowly back to camp, enjoying a song at intervals as we went along, and arriving at about half past eleven.

Wednesday June 12th

At reveille we turned out and answered to roll call after which we marched to the lower parade ground, where we were drilled for an hour by the Captain in company movements. We were rather more fortunate than on the previous morning, for instead of the eternal double quick which caused us to steam with perspiration, the movements were executed in quick time only, making the drill much more interesting and comfortable. The morning air was not uncomfortably warm, but as the day advanced the sun made it very hot and sultry. At seven o clock we broke ranks and fell in for breakfast with a good appetite. At nine guard mounting took place and soon after, the assembly sounded and we fell in for morning parade. The line was formed under the trees near the lawn in rear of Head Quarters, in order to shield us from the burning hot sun as much as possible, and after the parade we were dismissed without the usual drill and returned again to quarters.

The forenoon passed in a quiet manner with nothing worthy of note, and at one o clock "roast beef" sounded and we fell in for dinner. The weather was now almost insufferable, and at about two o'clock at the suggestion of Odell, he, Mr. Loud and myself went down to the brook and took a bath, remaining in the water upwards of an hour, and enjoying it very much. Some of the boys had by damming up the stream at a certain point, converted it into a good sized pond in which the water was deep enough to swim, making it a desirable and frequent resort for the whole Regiment.

During the afternoon considerable excitement was created among the boys, by the circulation of a report that the proprietor of a small dwelling at the foot of the hill near the stream, had for some reason knocked down his wife, and severely bruised her by beating and kicking her. The report was soon found to be true, for the cries of the woman could be heard in camp. Although this was a matter entirely outside of military affairs, yet it aroused the indignation of all who heard it, and a number of us from the Company whose quarters were nearest repaired to the scene and on entering the house found the woman lying on the floor, evidently suffering a good deal of pain, while her brute of a husband walked leisurely about the yard, as unconcerned as if nothing had happened.

Lieutenant Brewster was sent for, who being also a surgeon examined the woman and pronounced her severely injured, and without enquiring into the particulars turned upon the rascal who had so maltreated her, and ordered him to be stripped intending to flog him. This was sport for the boys who were not slow in obeying the Lieutenants order and laid hold of him with violent hands. The culprit was of course now frightened half out of his wits, and the Lieutenant after giving him a good sound talking to procured a clothes line, tied one end around his neck and the other to a tree, and was about to string him up, (apparently) when a little daughter ran towards him from the house and begged for her pa-pa to be let alone, and after some deliberation the Lieutenant complied with her request and suffered him to be released. The affair was one in which we had no right to interfere, but some of the boys would have hung him with a will.

On returning to our quarters strange to say we met Lieut Lowe of the Gloucester Company (who was known among the boys as Lieut. "Straw") with a dozen men coming towards us. He entered the house <u>fearlessly</u> and arresting the man, carried him a prisoner into camp. The boys looked on in silence until they discovered his intentions, when they set up a hooting and hissing which the bold and fearless (?) Lieut. will long remember. No doubt he inwardly congratulated himself upon his bravery, in thus arresting with a dozen men a single unarmed civilian, for an offense with which he had no right to meddle. He <u>may</u> have been acting under orders, but if he was the boys did not hesitate to give an open expression of their opinion of his action.

At about four o clock clouds began to appear and soon stretched over the entire heavens, and soon heavy peals of thunder were followed by a pall of rain which continued in torrents without cessation for half an hour at the end of which the sun appeared, and the clouds gradually dispersed again. The shower was productive of much benefit, for the air was decidedly cooler after it.

At six o clock we fell in for supper immediately after which the assembly sounded and the line was formed for dress parade with the exception of

Capt. Martin's Company and our own, which had been previously detailed for picket. Hill and myself were obliged to remain on duty with the Regiment, but if I could have had my choice, I should much preferred to have gone on picket with the Company. After going through with dress parade we wheeled into column by platoons, and took a short march up the railroad, and over the turnpike to the distance of a mile, returning by the Relay House to camp. It was a very uncomfortable march, for the rain of the afternoon had made the roads quite muddy and the traveling was difficult. On arriving at the upper parade ground we formed square in four ranks, and a telegraphic despatch was read to us by the Colonel, to the effect that Butler had achieved great success at Big Bethel, Virginia. The despatch stated that we had captured a Rebel battery and one thousand prisoners. At this news the boys were exceedingly jubilant and tossing their hats into the air gave three rousing cheers for Butler. We had hardly finished when Maj. Poore arrived in camp with news that the report was untrue but Butler had received our cheers and we couldn't very well recall them.[46] We now deployed column, were dismissed and returned to quarters. The Company had already left camp for picket duty, and I spent the evening very pleasantly with Odell until tattoo when I tendered him the hospitality of the N.C.O. tent and we turned in.

Thursday June 13th.

It was another pleasant morning, and when we turned out for reveille roll call, the air was quite comfortable and none too warm for drill. After the roll was called we marched to the lower parade ground, where an hour was spent advantageously in company movements under our faithful drill master — the Captain. As the hours passed by it grew warmer, and soon it was hot and sultry, continuing so most of the day. At about half past six we received orders to rest, and spreading ourselves on the green grass, remained in this position until "peas on a trencher" sounded, when we returned and fell in for breakfast. At nine o'clock guard mounting took place and at half past nine the assembly sounded and the line was formed with the exception of the two companies which had but a short time previous returned from picket. But Hill and myself whose posts of duty were with the Regiment, went on to line with the rest. As soon as the line was formed, details were made by the Colonel from each company for a temporary company of Sappers and Miners, after which we were dismissed.

At about ten o'clock Messrs Lowd and Odell took leave of us and returned home, taking with them several letters for many of the boys. They had made quite a pleasant stay with us for a couple of days, and had become quite initiated into the habits and customs of camp life.

During the forenoon one of those amusing scenes so frequently witnessed in southern precincts, took place in camp. A couple of darkies who had been cutting wood in the vicinity of our quarters, were brought in by some of the boys bent on a good time, and placed upon a large box around which a crowd soon gathered to see the fun. The darkies each in turn took their stand in the centre of the box, and give repeated exhibitions of their skill in jig dancing, and sundry comical feats "on de heel and toe," while the other patted time on his knee. A good deal of sport was created, and the crowd kept up a continual roar at their fantastic maneuvres. The darkies enjoyed it as well as the rest and showed their ivory continually. The excitement was kept alive for considerable time by the occasional tossing into the ring of a few pennies, which the darkies eagerly picked up and stowed away in their pockets.

It being the day on which the election in Baltimore was to take place, and trouble being anticipated at the polls, Col Jones with the Battery and the Sixth Regiment marched into the city, and took a position to enforce order and quiet, leaving the Eighth to garrison the Post alone. The boys

Stereoview of Union soldiers in front of the Relay House and station, 1861 (editor's collection).

(who were always on the qui vive for any excitement or important duty,) expressed a desire to accompany them, and many were quite indignant at the selection of the Sixth, but they soon got over this. The time passed in a quiet manner, and all day long the arrival of the trains was anxiously looked for, for news from the Sixth, and some conflict momentarily expected with the citizens, but the troops in the city had the desired effect, and the election passed off very quietly.[47]

During the day several boxes from their homes arrived for different members of the Company, the contents of which, chiefly luxuries, were distributed with a generous hand in accordance with the usual custom, and I doubt if a more generous, open hearted or liberal crowd, could have been found.

At six o'clock we fell in for supper, after which the line was formed and the Regiment proceeded to the lower parade ground, where we were drilled by the Colonel in battalion movements for an hour, the Company drilling close by in company movements. At dusk we returned to quarters and were dismissed, dress parade being omitted.

Nothing of interest transpired during the evening, and at tattoo we fell in for roll call, immediately after which I turned in.

Friday June 14th.

At five o'clock reveille sounded and the companies turned out with the usual promptness for roll call. The morning was delightful, the sun shone with its usual brilliancy and the atmosphere was cool and comfortable. It was an elegant morning for work and at six o'clock we formed company and enjoyed an hour's drill in company movements on the upper parade ground. The cool air stimulated us to more than the usual energy and the boys seemed to take hold with determination and zeal, the result of which was an interesting and profitable drill. At seven o clock we returned to quarters and at "peas on a trencher" fell in for breakfast. Immediately after, the detail for guard was made by the Orderly, and the time passed quietly until nine o'clock when guard mounting took place.

At about half past nine the assembly sounded and the Regimental line was formed in rear of Head Quarters. We immediately formed hollow square and prayer was offered by the Chaplain, after which an hour was spent in battalion movements, at the end of which we were dismissed.

Many of the boys of the Company remained on the ground, and practiced the bayonet exercise, load and fire lying &c. in squads by themselves, and I joined the "pony squad" for this purpose. We had been engaged thus about half an hour, when an ambrotype artist, who had for some time been putting up a saloon within the line of sentries in hopes of securing a liberal patronage from the soldiers, came up to us and invited us to "sit" by way of experiment. We (the pony squad) of course made no objection, and adjourned to his establishment where after one or two trials he succeeded in getting a fine picture of us in the position of <u>ready</u>, in load and fire kneeling, which was so life-like that we agreed to take a copy each.[48] At about half past eleven we returned to quarters and spent the time in a leisure manner until "roast beef" when we fell in for dinner.

Nothing of interest transpired in the camp until about four o'clock when preparations were made by the Company, for having photographs taken of the different tents. Our artist who had been seen for soon arrived with his apparatus and the different squads arranged themselves in groups in front of their respective tents, but the sun reflected with such dazzling brightness on the new white canvass, that it proved difficult to get anything like a good negative, and after one or two unsuccessful attempts in [it] was postponed until some future day.

At six o clock we fell in for supper and soon after the assembly again sounded and the line was formed on the upper parade ground. We at once wheeled into column by companies, and proceeded via the rail road to the residence of the Colonel about half a mile from camp, who since the arrival of his wife had been boarding with her in the village, and who was then at home on account of some indisposition. Here we went through with dress parade, immediately after which we again wheeled into column and returned to camp, where an hour was spent in battalion movements, under the supervision of Lieut. Col. Ellwell, with the exception of the Company, who occupied a space by themselves as usual, and were drilled by the Captain in the bayonet exercise and skirmishing. At about eight o'clock we were dismissed and retreat was beaten by the musicians.

During the evening a lively time occurred in front of the Company quarters. A couple of men who had been enjoying themselves on the front of the parade, one with a violin and the other with a base viol, were prevailed upon to adjourn to the Company street which they immediately did. Here setts were formed and cotillions and contras were danced for an hour, after which a procession was formed and we visited every company street in the encampment, stopping at intervals to indulge in a serenade. We also visited the Sixth who had returned during the forenoon from Baltimore. The moon shone beautifully and considerable sport was kept up. At about half past nine we returned to the quarters of the Company, where a collation consisting of lemonade, pastry &c. &c. (a good supply of the latter having recently arrived in the boxes from home) was served up by Tent No. 3 under the supervision of Private Dearborn. We "pitched in" generally under interrupted by tattoo when all hands dispersed to quarters and fell in for roll call, after giving three rousing cheers for the music. At taps all was quiet and I turned in.

Saturday June 15th.
At reveille we turned out and answered to roll call. It was another beautiful clear morning, and immediately after the calling of the roll the recruits (or as the Orderly called them, "re-cruits) were divided into squads and placed under the charge of drill masters detailed for the purpose, by whom they were drilled in the bayonet exercise until breakfast. These movements being altogether new to them (the recruits were always dismissed when the Company drilled in the bayonet exercise) were of course very awkward at first, but many expressed a desire to attain a degree of efficiency equal to that of the more experienced members of the Company and took hold well. At seven o'clock they were dismissed and the Company fell in for breakfast, after which we had a couple of hours to ourselves.

At nine o clock guard mounting took place and soon after the line was formed on the lawn and morning parade was gone through with, after which we formed hollow square, and Major Poore stepped in the centre, leading by the hand the infant son of the Colonel, a bright little fellow of four years, and dressed in a neat little full-dress-uniform of blue with brass buttons, and sword sash and belt complete. Upon motion of the Major he was unanimously chosen a member of the Regiment and styled Corporal of the Regiment and received with hearty cheers. An hour's drill in battalion movements then followed, at the end of which we were dismissed, but the musicians remained upon the ground to practice, and Private Hill and myself remained with them occasionally trying our skill with the drumstick.

I had often listened with considerable interest to the famous French Beat (said to be) composed by that world renowned drummer Dan Simpson of Boston, and performed by him at the annual muster of the militia in Massachusetts, with a wonderful degree of accuracy and skill, and by a little practice at various times had become so familiar with it, as to be able to execute it on the drum after a style of my own.[49] I accordingly ventured to try my hand at it at this time, and quite elicited the attention of the musicians who desired to learn it, and asked my assistance to enable them to do so. This was asking a good deal of me for I was no drummer and probably had but a poor idea of the art. But as they seemed to be favorably impressed with the beat and were determined not to let me off, I gave them all the aid in my power, and with their knowledge and practice, they put together from my efforts a very desirable beat which afterward became quite popular with the Regiment, and was performed by them at dress parade daily for some time. A couple of men, one with a violin and the other with a base viol now came up on the lawn to practice (for music was getting to be quite the rage in the Regiment when the men were off duty) and we spent some time listening to them, then returned to quarters.

The sun was by this time almost insufferable and we sought the most comfortable way of passing the time until half past twelve when "roast beef" sounded and we fell in for dinner. We had no duty to perform during the afternoon, with the exception of about a half an hour's sweltering drill which the Company had to encounter for the accommodation of some friends of the Captain who came into the camp to see him and expressed a "desire to see the Zouaves drill." Of course in compliance with such desire we had to be "exhibited."

At six o'clock the line was formed and we drilled for an hour in battalion movements on the lower parade ground. At seven we were dismissed, returned to quarters and fell in for supper. The evening which was one of the most beautiful on record was passed in a lively manner under the "sweet silver light of the moon." At about eight o'clock a procession of men from the Sixth, visited our encampment, escorted by a band of musicians with sundry numerous stringed instruments, and after passing through every company street proceeded to Head Quarters, and the musicians serenaded the Colonel who come forth and responded in a few appropriate remarks.[50] He was followed by Lieut. Col. Elwell and Surgeon Breed, the latter delivering quite an able speech. Major Poore was then called upon and some sensation was visible through the crowd, for the Major was always full of wit and fun was expected. But in this we were disappointed for he had evidently "smelt a rat" and was nowhere to be found. Cheers were then given for the Colonel, Lieut. Col. Elwell, Surgeon Breed, The Union, The Flag, The Bay-state, The Eighth &c. It was now about ten o'clock, and clouds rapidly appeared completely obscuring the moon and a few drops of rain fell. Tattoo soon sounded and we dispersed to our quarters and fell in for roll call and at taps all was quiet.

Sunday June 16th.

At five o'clock we turned out and after answering to roll call a half a dozen of the Company myself among the number, procured passes from the Captain and proceeded to a favorite resort on the banks of the Patapsco a mile or so from camp, for the purpose of taking a swim. It was a beautiful June morning. The blue canopy of heaven was unspotted by even the smallest cloud, and the atmosphere enlivened by a slight breeze from the south-west, was comfortable and bracing. Arriving at our destination on the river, we were not slow in divesting ourselves of our clothing and plunging headlong into the stream. The temperature of the water was delightful, but the current was unusually strong and we at times discovered ourselves some distance down stream. Swimming against it was impossible, and we invariably had to strike out for the shore and walk back. We enjoyed some excellent aquatic sports for half an hour at the end of which we "donned our regimentals' and returned to camp with appetites greatly sharpened by this delightful exercise.

By this time the breeze had died away and the almost scorching sun's rays poured down upon the camp as usual. At seven o'clock "peas on a trencher" sounded and we fell in for breakfast, after which active preparations were made for the Sunday morning inspection. At nine o'clock guard mounting took place and soon after the line was formed on the lawn, immediately after which we formed hollow square and prayer was offered by the chaplain. We then reduced square, deployed column, wheeled into column by companies, and each company was minutely inspected by its commanding officer, under the supervision of the Colonel and the other Regimental officers. Each company as it was inspected was dismissed with the exception of the Zouaves, who had been previously detailed to escort the colors to Head Quarters. As soon as the last company had left the ground we formed with the music for this purpose, but before we reached Head Quarters rain commenced falling in large scattering drops. We had no sooner safely deposited the colors, than it came down in torrents and we returned double quick to quarters, or flew rather, and sought shelter in the tents. The shower continued with violence, the rain falling in perfect sheets. At the expiration of half an hour it gradually began to hold up and soon the sun made its appearance.

The time now passed with nothing worthy of note until half past twelve when "roast beef" sounded and we fell in for dinner. At half past four the assembly sounded and the line was formed without arms. We at once proceeded to the lawn to attend divine service and the Sixth soon joined us. The exercises were conducted by a tall, thin, meager looking individual whose name I did not learn, but who ran on in a style evidently original with himself, without any perceptible purport and devoid of the slightest meaning. Of course his <u>manner</u> denoted him an imposter, though he may have been a member of the clerical persuasion. At any rate his remarks utterly failed to attract attention. At half past five he concluded his attempts and we returned to quarters, where after receiving orders to fall in in full uniform at reveille in the morning, we broke ranks and fell in for supper.

Retreat was beaten at sundown.

The evening was pleasant and delightful, the moon shone in all her elegance, and the time was passed in a becoming manner. Tattoo sounded at the customary hour of ten, roll was called at the same time and at taps most of us turned in.

Monday June 17th.

This being a memorable day in the history of the country, the anniversary of the battle of Bunker Hill, it was duly observed with appropriate ceremonies. In obedience to the Captain's order of the previous night, we turned out in full uniform at reveille, as likewise did the rest of the companies, and after calling of the roll blank cartridges were distributed, thirteen rounds to a man, for the purpose of firing salute. It was a very comfortable morning the air being rather cool, and the sun hid by a veil of clouds.

Ammunition having been furnished to all the companies, the line was formed at about half past five, and the Regiment descended to the lower parade ground, where we remained about half an hour waiting for the Colonel, during which time we were drilled in battalion movements by Lieut. Col. Ellwell. The Colonel soon arrived from his quarters in the village, and we returned to the upper parade ground and formed line on the brow of the hill, with orders to load at will. A salute of thirteen was then fired by the whole line simultaneously. The first three rounds I am sorry to say, were poorly executed on account of inattention on the part of some of the members of our own company, but the rest were delivered with good precision and promptness. After the salute was fired we returned to quarte[r]s and fell in for breakfast. The clouds now disappeared and the sun made its appearance but was not so warm as usual, and the balance of the day was cool and comfortable.

At half past eight the companies were ordered to fall in for inspection, preparatory to a grand review of all the troops of the garrison, and which until now we had not received the slightest intimation of. The spot chosen for this review was the large field on the Washington pike, where we were accustomed to drill. At exactly nine o'clock the line was formed and after some little delay, we proceeded with the Sixth and the Battery to the field referred to, where three hours were occupied in the review by Maj. Gen. Morse which was tedious work and we were heartily glad when it was over.[51] At about half past one we returned to camp to find dinner awaiting us, and we fell in for this meal with good appetites.

The afternoon passed very quietly until about four o'clock when it was reported that the First Massachusetts, Col. Cowdin were on the cars at the Relay House, and the report was soon ascertained to be correct. The line was therefore hastily formed and we proceeded to the junction to meet them. They were a fine looking regiment and numbered over a thousand men, among whom we recognized a number of familiar faces. But we had a few moments only to converse with them for they were on their way to Washington and the train started soon after our arrival. We exchanged hasty congratulations, following along some distance with the train, until it became too dangerous to approach near the cars, when we sent three rousing cheers and a "seven" after them and returned to camp.

During our absence the Company had been detailed by the Adjutant for picket, and at about half past seven they left camp for this duty, Hill and myself remaining behind in camp. They had been gone about half an hour when loud strains of music broke upon our ears, coming from the direction of Head Quarters, and we repaired thither to find that a band of musicians had arrived from the village near the nail-factory. They were not musicians of the first class, though they exerted themselves a good deal for the occasion, for a great time appeared to be on foot at Head Quarters. The officers of the Sixth came up and soon a collation was served up in the mess tent of the Field and Staff, where speeches were made and toasts were drank until a late hour, with music and songs interspersed. Major Poore was as usual on such occasions "in his glory," and all present seemed to enjoy themselves in the highest possible manner.

Among the rank and file of the Regiment the occasion was equally as lively. Bonfires burned in many places, mottoes were burned on the ground in powder trains, and songs floated upon the air from every quarter. A procession was also formed which marched to and fro through every company street while loud cheers rent the air at every turn. Tattoo was omitted and the scene was prolonged until midnight when one by one the boys dropped into their quarters and the camp was soon quiet.

Tuesday June 18th.
This prolonged excitement had the effect to make me more drowsy than usual in the morning, and I was in no hurry to turn out, roll call being

"Sand-bag Battery" (Cook's Massachusetts Battery), commanding the road to Harpers Ferry, near the Relay House, *Harper's Weekly*, June 1, 1861.

omitted on account of the Company having just returned from picket. Reveille however sounded at the usual hour and the rest of the companies turned out promptly. The morning was quite pleasant and clear, and the atmosphere was cool and comfortable. We fell in for breakfast at eight o'clock and at nine guard mounting took place.

At half past nine the assembly sounded and the line was formed on the lawn, where after morning prayer by the chaplain, the entire Regiment was drilled in load and fire and Battalion movements for an hour, at the expiration of which we were dismissed and the time was spent in an unimportant manner until half past twelve, when we fell in for dinner.

No duty was required until late in the afternoon and most of the boys remained under cover, shielding themselves from the sun which had now heated the atmosphere to the usual high and uncomfortable temperature.

At half past one I procured a pass from the Captain, and in company with a friend from the Gloucester Company, took a stroll along the banks of the Patapsco to the nail-factory which curiosity prompted us to enter. We

A section of Cook's Massachusetts Battery, guarding the Baltimore and Ohio to Harpers Ferry, *Frank Leslie's Illustrated Newspaper*, May 18, 1861.

were cordially welcomed by one of the workmen who took pains to show us over the manufactory, and who described to us the different parts of the machinery and explained to us their uses. We spent an hour very agreeably, watching with no little interest the various processes through which the iron passed before it was converted into the nail.

In the first place large masses of the raw material were separated into convenient parts for working, and were thrown into smelting furnaces were they were subjected to almost white heat and each piece as it became sufficiently heated was taken out and passed between heavy rollers to render it solid and compact. From these it was passed between other rollers by which it was transformed into flat strips about a foot wide ten feet in length and of a thickness corresponding to the size of the nails into which it was to be cut. A third sett of rollers with knives between them, separated it into narrow strips the width of which corresponded with the lengths of the nail, and a fourth turned up or thickened one edge of each strip in such a manner as when cut to from the head of the nail. All this was but the work of a few moments, yet the different changes had sufficiently cooled the iron, and rendered it hard and brittle enough to cut. The last operation was now at hand. The stripes were placed under cutters, and one by one the nails were cut from the ends, dropped into kegs placed to receive them and were now ready for the market. Thus all day long huge masses of red hot material were passed and repassed with all the ease imaginable between the great heavy rollers, with great rapidity and in quick succession, attended with no fire or accidents to the workmen thus far.

After rendering us every attention in the factory, our friend invited us to his residence a short distance farther up the river, where we spent another half hour very pleasantly.

It was now about four o'clock and we took leave of the family returning over the rail road to camp where we arrived just in season to go on duty with the Regiment. The line was formed on the upper parade ground and we descended the hill towards the rail road where we were drilled an hour in battalion movements. At half past five we returned to quarters and at six fell in for supper. At eight o clock dress parade took place after which we were dismissed.

It was another beautiful moonlight evening, and various sports were participated in, in different parts of the camp until tattoo, when roll was called and at taps I turned in.

Wednesday Jun 19th.

At reveille we turned out and after the roll was called each non commissioned officer was assigned to the command of a squad of recruits, to drill them in the manual and bayonet exercise, while the balance of the Company were drilled by Lieut. Putnam in the manual. The atmosphere was warmer than usual in the morning, and in a short time grew to be quite hot and sultry continuing so all day. At about half past six we formed company and returned to quarters to breakfast.

Since our departure from Massachusetts many of the companies had received recruits at different times which together swelled the aggregate of the Regiment considerably. These men however had never been mustered into the service, and accordingly at eight o'clock all men of this class were ordered to report to Head Quarters for this purpose. The oath of allegiance was duly administered, and they were mustered in for the unexpired term of the Regiment.

At nine o'clock guard mounting took place, which was all the duty performed till after dinner. At about ten o'clock we were visited by an old friend who had just arrived from Salem, and one who was greatly interested in the welfare of the Company wherever we might be. This friend was no other than ex-General Devereux, and father of our worthy Captain. He brought with him letters and packages for many of the boys, also a number of uniforms which were unfinished when the balance of our grey suit was forwarded, some time since. Of course he was cordially welcomed by every member of the Company, and a general desire to converse with him was manifested.

During the forenoon four new drums were issued in addition to those already in use, and the musicians were increased to eight in number, the other four being detailed from the companies other than our own. We now had a drum corps of eight performers, and a little practice only was necessary to make them efficient in their duties.

A large and splendid storm flag was also received at Head Quarters, and preparations were at once made for raising it, in place of the little one which had heretofore floated from the top of a slender pole, fastened to the top of a great tree in front of Head Quarters, and which had become rather the worse for wear, the stripes having so faded as to become almost invisible. The first thing to be done was to procure a larger pole, the one in use being by far too slender and weak for the great flag which had just arrived. Accordingly a detail of men was made who at once started into the woods, and after a search of half an hour pitched upon a fine young oak, cut it down and brought it into camp, where it was soon trimmed and manufactured with little difficulty into quite a respectable flag pole, forty eight feet in length, and ten inches in diameter at the base. In a few moments, everything was ready for raising it into its place, which with a stout rope and two or three men was speedily accomplished, and we now had in place of the slender pole, a staff measuring seventy five feet in height from the ground to the truck.

It was now about one o'clock and the boys dispersed from their work and fell in for dinner. The afternoon was spent in a quiet manner until four o'clock when the assembly sounded and we formed Regimental line on the lawn. Without delay we wheeled into column by companies, proceeded to Head Quarters and formed into close column by division, after which the new flag was thrown to the breeze with appropriate ceremonies as follows. The Colonel addressed us in a few remarks adapted to the occasion, after which the singers of the Regiment were requested to take the right of the line. He then seized the halliards and raised the flag still folded in a loop of the rope, to the top, and with one hand still grasping the halliards, and lifting his hat with the other, gave a slight jerk and the new color was unfurled to the breeze. The singers received it with "The Star spangled Banner" and the musicians struck up "to the color" on the drums. Three rousing cheers were then given and we proceeded to the lower parade ground, where an hour was devoted to battalion movements, at the expiration of which we were dismissed, returned to quarters and fell in for supper.

During the evening another of those comical and exciting scenes came off in our Company street. A couple of darkies who had strolled into camp were seized upon by some of the boys and an old barn door procured from some of the neighboring premises. A violinist was soon found who was very willing to contribute his services. A ring was then formed around the door, on which the darkies took their stand, each in turn keeping the crowd in a roar by their "essence of ole Virginny." We had among the recruits of the Company two or three good jig dancers, who after the darkies had exhausted their efforts also added to the mirth of the occasion, by giving specimens of their skill, in which Private Shaw seemed to take the palm. All the while the moon shone beautifully and the sport was kept up until we were interrupted by tattoo which obliged us to discontinue and we fell in for roll call. The darkies now took their leave and at taps I turned in.

Thursday June 20th.

This was an eventful day with us, and one which there is no doubt will long be remembered by every member of the Regiment, wrought as it was with pleasant and festive occasions, such as are seldom witnessed in camp life. To commence with it was a beautiful morning, with an atmosphere of moderate temperature, cool and comfortable. A couple of hours later however it was as warm as ever and we found it difficult to keep comfortable excepting in our quarters. Reveille sounded promptly at the appointed hour, and after roll call the time was spent leisurely until "peas on a trencher" when we fell in for breakfast, and at nine o'clock guard mounting took place.

Soon after nine the assembly sounded and the line was formed on the lawn, where after the customary morning prayer by the Chaplain, an interesting ceremony took place in the presentation of a magnificent silk flag to the Regiment, in behalf of the lady friends of the New York Seventh. It will be remembered that during the time we were on detached service conducting the Constitution to the Brooklyn Navy Yard, the balance of the Regiment were engaged in rebuilding the rail road between Annapolis and Washington which had been destroyed by the Rebels. The Seventh New York were also with them, and between the two a strong feeling of attachment was formed, a natural consequence of being engaged in mutual occupations, and thrown together in similar situations. When the Eighth Mass. went ashore at Annapolis from the Maryland, they were without rations and had suffered not a little for want of them, but the Seventh were bountifully supplied and on learning the condition of our men, they generously emptied the contents of their haversacks and canteens for the benefit of the Eighth, which were thankfully received, an act truly commendable on their part, and productive of good feeling ever afterward. But to return to my subject, the color was the handsomest I had ever seen, being made of the heaviest silk of the rarest shades. In the centre of the union, a magnificent spread eagle was embroidered with silk in the most natural colors and surrounded with white silk embroidered stars. The summit of the staff was surmounted with a heavy spread eagle of white metal, perched upon a round ball of burnished silver, from which hung two large exquisite silver tassels suspended by silver cords.

This splendid emblem of national glory was placed in the hands of the Color Sergeant by the Colonel, who made some excellent remarks appropriate to the occasion. It was accompanied with an expressive letter of presentation from the ladies, alluding to the many pleasant associations of the two Regiments, and of the mutual good feeling existing between them, which letter was read to us by the Adjutant. At the conclusion of the reading of this letter, we were formed into hollow square when nine deafening cheers were given for the ladies and the Seventh.

A letter from General Butler, to whose charge the flag had been consigned at Fortress Monroe and by whom it was forwarded to the Regiment, was then read, in which he congratulated the Regiment on their good fortune, and alluded in high terms of praise to their valuable services at Annapolis, with the Seventh New York, while under his command. He closed with good wishes, and the hope of a speedy return home. This was followed by three rousing cheers for General Butler. Another letter from Governor Andrew was also read, who also alluded to the conduct and duties of the Regiment since its entry into service. The letter also contained sentiments of pride and honor from the Bay State and was listened to with much interest.[52] At its close three rousing cheers were proposed by the Colonel for Governor Andrew, which were given with a will.

We now deployed column and were drilled in battalion movements for an hour. At eleven o'clock we were dismissed and returned to quarters. After depositing our arms in the tents, the Company were ordered to fall in again immediately, and we descended to the cottage-yard on the hill next to our quarters, and here another pleasant time awaited us. The inclosure presented a gay and attractive appearance. In the centre stood a good sized table spread with a clean white cloth, and in the centre of which sat a large heavily ornamented loaf of wedding cake, surrounded with numerous boquets of natural flowers. A number of ladies were also present, including Mrs Hinks and Mrs Devereux, with a number of other invited guests and officers of the Regiment, among the latter of whom were Colonel Hinks, Pay Master Usher, Surgeon Breed, and Quarter Master Ingalls.[53] Ex-General Devereux also graced the company with his presence. The Company filed around the table, occupying the space in rear of the guests who were already seated. The Captain then stepped forward and explained to us the nature of the occasion.

It appeared that Miss Mary Silsbee of Salem had recently taken the eventful step in life, and among her other numerous relatives and friends had extended the hospitalities of the occasion to the Salem Light Infantry, (with which some of the male members of the family had formerly been connected), in the shape of a huge large loaf of cake, which was brought to its destination by the father of the Captain (who if I am not mistaken was a relative) and now sat before us on the table. With this introductory he turned to the Colonel and extended to him the honor of "carving" which the latter readily accepted, and while he was thus engaged the General arose and took the liberty as he said to make a few remarks relative to the present occasion. In the course of his remarks he alluded to the position of the old Infantry on southern soil, and said that he was proud of the honor of having once shouldered a musket in its ranks. (The General was an ex-member of our corps and at one time commander.) He also spoke of our sudden departure from home and friends, and of the promptness with which the Company sprang to arms, on receipt of the news of the fall of Fort Sumter, and dwelt at considerable length on the glorious cause in which we were engaged, closing with words of encouragement and cheer.

The cake was now ready for distribution and the Orderly officiated with good grace as waiter. (I hope he will not be offended should he ever read this.) Lemonade in good quality and quantity was also furnished, and after partaking largely of these luxuries, a number of the boys joined in "Vive la America," which was followed by a number of other patriotic songs. A rousing "Seven" was then given for the bride, the General, the Colonel, and the ladies and we took our leave and returned to quarters, while the ladies and the other guests adjourned to the cottage and took dinner. Thus an hour and a half was spent in the pleasantest possible manner.

It was now about one o'clock and "roast beef" sounded for dinner. This followed rather close to the "banquet scene" we had just left, and our camp dinner though plentiful and good was hardly touched.

The afternoon passed very quietly, no duty save guard being required on account of the excessive heat. About half an hour was spent by Sergeant Batchelder and myself in the woods adjoining cutting poles for the purpose of adjusting our tent. At six o clock we fell in for supper and at seven the line was formed for dress parade, after which the companies were drilled for half an hour in company movements. The evening which was delightfully pleasant, passed quietly, and at tattoo we fell in for roll call, immediately after which I turned in.

Friday June 21st.

At five oclock reveille sounded and we were soon on the line for roll call. The morning was a pleasant one, neither warm nor cool but of a good temperature for exercise without suffering with the heat. In a short time however it seemed to grow more uncomfortable and the atmosphere was soon close and muggy, growing more and more sultry with the progress of the day. After roll call we had an opportunity for bathing, and some half a dozen of us proceeded to the brook where we spent half an hour in the water, feeling greatly refreshed on coming out. At about six o'clock the Company was ordered to fall in, and the old members proceeded to the lawn and were drilled by the Captain in load and fire lying. The recruits were detached for the time being, and were drilled in the bayonet exercise by the Orderly. At seven o clock we reformed company, returned to quarters and were dismissed, and at "peas on a trencher" we fell in for breakfast.

It now became my misfortune to be detailed for a duty, anything but pleasant in its nature, and from which I would have gladly escaped if I could. From a careful review of things thus far it will readily be seen that the Captain was an unusually good disciplinarian, and one remarkable characteristic with him was, he never allowed an offense of any kind to go unpunished, however trivial in its nature. To look at this in the proper light, this was as it should be, and had all the Captains followed his example, there is no questioning that their Companies would have been in all respects quite as efficient as our own, which it must be admitted was far from being the case at this time. I do not intend by this to convey praise to my own Company nor censure to the others, but I think I may say and correctly that for any and every kind of duty, the right flank Company could always be relied upon.

But to resume. Slight offenses such as inattention in the ranks or absence at roll call were often attended with the penalty of an hour's extra drill, and in cases of a more aggravated nature the offenders were obliged

Stereoview of Cook's Massachusetts Battery at Camp Essex, Elkridge Heights, overlooking the Thomas Viaduct (editor's collection).

to drill with the knapsack on. Such was the case this morning. Some half a dozen of the recruits had an extra drill to encounter on account of some slight offense of the previous day, and I was detailed as drill master for the occasion, and I must say the punishment was about as severe on the drill master, as on those for whom alone it was intended, for the sun was scorching hot and the perspiration rolled from us in great drops. We however weathered through it, and soon after eight I dismissed my fellow sufferers and returned to quarters, where I endeavored in vain to seek a half an hour's comfort in my tent before the hour for the line to be formed should arrive.

At nine o'clock guard mounting took place and at half past nine the assembly sounded and the line was formed on the lawn, where we formed square in four ranks and listened to a prayer from the Chaplain, after which an hour was spent in battalion movements and we were dismissed.

No further duty was required of us until late in the afternoon. The sun

Cook's Massachusetts Battery, overlooking the Thomas Viaduct, *Frank Leslie's Illustrated Newspaper*, May 25, 1861.

was scorching hot and we found it difficult to keep comfortable even in the tents. We threw up the sod cloths to get a little fresh air, but in vain for not a breath was stirring, and it was impossible to enjoy with any sort of comfort, reading, writing or sleeping. At about four o'clock another visitor arrived in camp from Salem — Capt. Silver — and again many of the boys were made the recipients of letters, papers &c. from home, and we found an interesting way of passing the time until half past five when we fell in for supper.[54] At about six o'clock the assembly again sounded and the line was

Cook's Massachusetts Battery, overlooking the Thomas Viaduct, *Harper's Weekly*, June 1, 1861.

formed on the upper parade ground where an hour was spent in battalion movements, terminating in dress parade, at the conclusion of which we were dismissed.

 The evening was made delightfully pleasant by the beautiful moon, and at intervals songs floated upon the air from various squads of men gathered in different parts of the encampment. For my part I spread my blanket on the ground in front of my tent, and throwing myself upon it, found considerable enjoyment in watching the silvery clouds as they hurried past, at times obscuring the moon, and revolving in my mind the various scenes through which we had passed since our departure from home on the Seventeenth of April, amid the cheers and good wishes of patriotic citizens, and the God speeds of relatives and friends. I thought of the boisterous enthusiasm which everywhere greeted us on the route to Washington, particularly in Philadelphia; of the seizure of the Maryland at Havre de Grace, and the trip down the Chesapeake with the circumstances connected with our arrival at the Constitution in Annapolis harbor; of the withdrawal of the frigate from her dangerous situation; and here [her] safe removal to the

6. Relay House

Battery commanding the approach to Washington, on the heights of Elk Ridge, near the Relay House, *Frank Leslie's Illustrated Newspaper*, May 25, 1861.

Brooklyn Navy Yard in charge of the Company and the Sappers and Miners of the Regiment; of our pleasant sojourn in New York afterward while quartered at the Astor, awaiting orders; of our return to join the Regiment at Washington by water, and the various scenes which occurred on board the Roanoke during the voyage; of our arrival at the Washington Navy Yard and the march to the Capitol; of the many attractions which had met our eye while quartered there, and of the responsible duties which had fell to a portion of us as drill masters; of the removal of the Regiment to our present camp, and the various duties and innumerable pastimes we had experienced since our settlement for the first time in camp; all of which combined together presented more the aspect of a pleasure excursion or mammoth pic-nic, than a military campaign during the period of actual warfare. True, we had encountered many hardships, and had been the victims of many unpleasant predicaments, particularly in the matter of rations, yet taking all things into consideration, the two months of service thus far was productive of little to cause complaint or dissatisfaction.

All this and many other things suggested themselves to my muse, until my reverie was brought to a close by the loud beating of the tattoo when I sprang to my feet, tossed my blanket into my tent and fell in with the Company for roll call. Soon after taps we were favored in the tent of the N.C.O.

with a call from Capt. Martin of the adjoining company, and a lively conversation was kept up until a late hour.

Saturday June 22d.

I did not wake until reveille had sounded, for I had turned in unusually late and even then I was somewhat loth to turn out in obedience to the Orderly's familiar "fall in form company." But well knowing the penalty which befel absentees, I rather reluctantly obeyed. It was a dull cloudy morning made more disagreeable by a close muggy atmosphere. The company street presented anything but an inviting appearance, being very muddy, the effects of rain during the night. I made up my mind from all appearances, that it had sat in for a rainy day, but in the course of half an hour was happily disappointed, in seeing the clouds begin to break asunder, and shortly after the sun made its appearance as bright as ever. At six o'clock the Company were again ordered to fall in, and after a second roll call were drilled for nearly an hour by the Captain in the manual. At seven o clock we broke ranks and at "peas on a trencher" fell in for breakfast, after which I occupied considerable time writing, being interrupted by the assembly which sounded soon after nine o clock, when I repaired to the Adjutant's tent for duty as marker.

The line was formed on the lawn, and after forming hollow square and listening to the morning prayer by the Chaplain, an hour was occupied in battalion movements. At about ten o'clock we were dismissed and returned to quarters. The balance of the forenoon passed quietly and at one oclock we fell in for lunch.

I say lunch, for it was decided by the Company to postpone the dinner hour until five o'clock during the hot weather, partaking of a lunch only at noon. Now I do not wish to convey the idea that the boys were insubordinate, or that they ever <u>intended</u> wilfully to disobey orders, though it might appear so from a review of the effigy affair of May 30th, yet I must say that we had a remarkable way of doing things often times to suit our own convenience, the Army Regulations and General Orders to the contrary notwithstanding. In fact a more independent organization of citizen soldiery was never mustered into the United States service. We also professed to know our duties as well, and I think I may assert with propriety that we were entitled to the credit of performing them generally with promptitude and zeal, if we did overstep the bounds of propriety in outside matters occasionally. The changing of the dinner hour was in direct violation of the camp regulations recently published, but the proposed change met the approbation of the majority and was therefore readily adopted.

The afternoon was melting hot, but we "braved it well" and for a time some of the boys were engaged in reading, others in writing while many could be found employed in sundry domestic affairs. Soon after two I called at the Captain's tent, and while here indulged in a nap on Lieut. Brewster's bed. How long I remained under the influence of Morpheus I know not, but I was awakened by loud cries in the Company street, and pulled aside the front of the marquee just in season to see Sergeant Gray landed sprawling from tent No. 3 into the company street, much to the amusement of the inmates who immediately set up a roar of laughter.

I have before mentioned that each tent or squad was placed under the charge of a non commissioned officer, who was held responsible for its cleanliness, and the discipline of its occupants. The inmates of tent No. 3 who were under the charge of Sergeant Gray had styled themselves the "Plug Uglies," after the famous organization of that name in Baltimore, and caused considerable sport at times by the burlesque exhibitions of their authority and fighting propensities, about the camp. In like manner tent No. 5 had adopted the title of "Blood Tubs," and the two cliques, between whom a rivalry soon existed, often came in collision with each other, when a struggle would invariably ensue for the championship.

On the occasion referred to, the Sergeant had occasion to enter the tent under his charge, for what reason I know not, but a tustle ensued and he was quickly ejected as before described. Like a brave fellow he did not relinquish the idea of accomplishing his purpose, so summoning the Orderly and Sergeant Batchelder to his aid, the three entered the tent with the evident intention of "cleaning it out." The entire posse of Plugs was at once centered upon the three non com's, and a severe scuffle ensued. The Blood Tubs seeing the fun came en masse to the scene of the fracas and were soon "in." No sooner had they become engaged in the fuss, than the attention of the Plugs was diverted from the Sergeants who took advantage of the opportunity to "slide out," leaving the action to continue between the Plugs and Blood Tubs. By this time a crowd had collected from the other companies and a general desire was manifested to see who would come out ahead. But it was undecided for one chap was suddenly hurled against the tent pole, knocking it out of place and letting down the tent, which buried the whole crowd and put an end to the scene amid a tremendous roar of laughter. The crowd gradually dispersed and my attention was attracted by strains of music coming from the direction of the lawn and I resorted thither to find a complete quadrille band consisting of two violins, a bass viol, guitar, banjo, triangle and bones. The members were all amateur performers, and members of the Regiment. They had come here to practice and performed finely. Quite a crowd was collected about them, in the midst of whom a number of chaps were giving exhibitions of their skill in jig dancing, and who executed quite a number of flourishes and pigeon wings with all the grace of professionals. I spent an hour here enjoying the sport with the rest, and returned to quarters just in season to fall in for dinner with the company at five o'clock.

At six o clock the assembly sounded and the line was formed on the upper parade ground. The Company were excused having been detailed for picket, and left camp for this duty at about eight o'clock. Immediately after the line was formed we were marched to the level ground at the foot of the hill where we drilled about an hour in battalion movements, after which we returned to the upper parade ground and reformed for dress parade. Among the orders which were read by the Adjutant, was one to the effect that the line officers of the Regiment would hereafter be required to take command during the drill, commencing on Monday, first acting as Colonel then Lieut. Colonel, the Field officers substituting themselves for the time being, for the officers so detailed.

Here was indeed a fine chance for the company commanders to accustom themselves to the duties of field officer, a matter absolutely necessary, (though seldom thought of by Regimental commanders) since we could not tell what might at any time befal the field officers of the Regiment, and one which showed the desire of the Colonel to have the officers efficient in their duties as well as the rank and file. Considerable sensation was created among the men at this order, for it was well know that there were some among the officers referred to, who would make a fine show in command of the Regiment. At the conclusion of the publishing of orders we were dismissed and returned to quarters.

The evening passed quietly. The moon at times shown sweetly, and at times was hid by floating clouds. The air was close and uncomfortable. At about nine o'clock I proceeded to the stream with Private Hall and had a delightful swim, by which I felt very much refreshed. At ten o'clock tattoo sounded, and at taps I turned in.

Sunday June 23d

At five o'clock reveille sounded and the companies turned out promptly for roll call, but as the Company did not return from picket until half past five I availed myself of the opportunity to indulge in an extra nap, and did not turn out until half past six but when I did I was impressed with the almost enchanting scene about me. The morning was extremely pleasant. The atmosphere was delightfully cool and undisturbed by even the faintest breeze. The adjoining woods echoed and re-echoed with the songs of innumerable birds singing their maker's praise. Not a leaf moved and all nature was motionless and calm. The King of Day was far up in his daily path, and shed his rays upon the camp with a dazzling brightness seldom witnessed. It was indeed fitting weather for the Sabbath, and such as would at home be truly and deeply appreciated, but unfortunately with us it made but little difference, for the observance of the Sabbath in the service, is necessarily slight at best.

6. Relay House 167

The camp presented a lively appearance and everywhere might be seen groups of men, some with their muskets taken apart for cleaning, others sweating under the operation of blacking equipments and shoes, scrubbing buttons and brasses, brushing clothes &c. while others still were busily engaged folding blankets, packing knapsacks, policing the grounds and attending to various other matters too numerous to mention, all of which usually precede an inspection.

At seven o'clock everything was dropped for "peas on a trencher" sounded and we fell in for breakfast. The two hours immediately following passed quietly, some of the boys resumed their scrubbing while others engaged in reading writing &c. At nine o'clock guard mounting took place and soon after those of us who were not before summoned to go on guard, were now interrupted by the assembly, and fell in with our respective companies. The line was formed on the lawn, and without delay we wheeled into column by companies, opened ranks and each company, commencing on the right, was carefully inspected by its commanding officer under the supervision of the Colonel and staff officers, and immediately after was dismissed and returned to its quarters, with the exception of me, detailed to escort the colors to Head Quarters, which on this occasion was Company "C" Captain Martin. The arms were then stacked in the Company streets in a neat and uniform manner, there to remain until after the inspection of quarters, and we then broke ranks.

At about half past ten a number of us procured passes for the purpose of attending worship at the Episcopal church, about half a mile distant in the village. It was a small church well attended, and the services were of a highly interesting character. Our uniforms attracted some attention as we entered, and every body seemed not only willing but desirous of extending to us the favor of a seat. This was a more favorable reception than we were accustomed to receive from the inhabitants of this section of the country, for the greater portion of the community if not Rebels, were in tender sympathy with the enemies of the Union, and were inclined to treat the national uniform in a different manner. But we were glad to meet a single exception to the general rule.

At half past twelve we returned to camp, just in season to fall in with the Company for lunch.

No duty was required of us during the afternoon and most of the boys spent the time in the tents, shielded from the intense heat of the sun. For my own part I spent considerable time writing but was nearly roasted all the time. At five o'clock the assembly sounded and the line was formed without arms on the upper parade ground, from which place we proceeded to the lawn to attend divine service. The Sixth were in advance of us and were waiting when we arrived. A number of ladies were also seated on the Dr's

(Hall's) piazza, from which the Chaplain held forth, and their presence added much to the interest of the occasion. The services commenced immediately on our arrival, with the singing of a hymn by a choir selected from the two Regiments, which was followed by prayer. An interesting discourse was then delivered by the Chaplain of about an hour's duration. This was followed by another hymn, prayer and benediction, after which all the companies returned to quarters with the exception of <u>our</u> ill-fated heroes; who were detained for the purpose of entertaining our lady visitors with a half hour's drill in load and fire, and skirmishing.

At a few minutes before seven we were dismissed, returned to quarters and fell in for dinner. At eight o'clock dress parade wound up the duties of the day, and the evening passed quietly. I spent a half an hour very pleasantly in conversation with ex-General Devereux on the steps of the cottage on the hill, and at tattoo fell in with the Company for roll call, and soon after turned in.

Monday June 24th.

At five o clock reveille sounded and we turned out at once for roll call. It was another pleasant morning, the air being cool with a gentle breeze from the south west. It was another favorable morning for drill, and we fell in for this purpose at six o'clock. We were getting tired of this eternal drilling before breakfast but the monotony which characterized the drill was varied on this occasion by dividing the Company into squads each of which was placed under the charge of a commissioned or non commissioned officer, the recruits constituting one squad by themselves. We made the best use of the time until seven o'clock, when we broke ranks and fell in for breakfast, after which the time passed quietly until nine o clock when guard mounting took place.

At half past nine the assembly sounded and the line was formed on the lawn for battalion drill. The first thing in order was prayer and for this purpose we formed hollow square the better to accommodate the chaplain. An hour was then devoted to battalion movements, at the expiration of which we returned to quarters and were dismissed.

By this time it had reached the usual scorching temperature, the refreshing breeze of the morning had completely died away, and the atmosphere was very close and sultry. Nothing like a comfortable place could be found anywhere in our portion of the encampment. The sod cloths were thrown up, and boys might be seen lawling about in every conceivable attitude, with their hats and jackets thrown off, barefooted, and engaged in reading writing &c. I endeavored to write myself, but finding it impossible to do so with any comfort in my own tent, I proceeded to the quarters of Lieut Coe where I found it much more comfortable. Lieut. Coe was a clerk in the

Quarter Masters Department, and as a matter of course was amply supplied with writing materials, and I spent an hour with him to good advantage, writing in my journal. At half past twelve I returned and fell in with the Company for lunch, after which I resumed my writing, and succeeded in accomplishing a great deal.

At about four o clock we were very agreeably surprised by the arrival of the Rev. Mr. Wildes of Salem, who was cordially welcomed by every member of the Company. His presence called to mind the many kind attentions bestowed on us by him, and the fervent prayer he offered in our behalf in the armory, before our departure from home. He it [sic] was who first instructed us in the manner of packing and slinging the knapsack, in the Doric Hall, State House, Boston when they were first issued to us, and who also put into our heads many valuable ideas concerning the habits and duties of the soldier, gathered from his travels among the armies of the East, during the Crimean war, all of which we had had more than one opportunity of putting into practice since our entry into service.

Upon his approach to the quarters of the Company, he was surrounded by squads of men in turn all of whom were only too glad to take him once more by the hand. Congratulations were rapidly exchanged and a hundred questions were asked and answered, and thus the time passed until five o clock when the Company fell in for dinner.

In half an hour after, the line was formed on the upper parade ground, and wheeling into column by companies we left camp, taking up our line of march over the railroad and turnpike to the large field a mile distant. Here the order which created so much mirth when read at dress parade on Saturday, was first carried into effect by the detailing of Lieut. Col. Elwell as Colonel of the Regiment pro tem. Capt. Martin as Lieut Colonel, while Col. Hicks substituted himself as commandant of "C" Company in place of Capt. Martin. Lieut. Col Elwell handled the Regiment very well, and Capt. Martin did himself credit in his new capacity. We remained on the field an hour during which time we went through various movements, the most prominent among which was "form square in four ranks" which every member of the old Eighth will remember, was a kind of a stereotype movement with the Lieutenant Colonel.

At seven o'clock we returned to camp and after going through with dress parade, were dismissed and we dispersed to quarters.

During the evening we had an exceedingly pleasant time in company with ex-General Devereux and Mr. Wildes, the latter interesting us with accounts of his travels and experience in Europe during the Crimean war. He also spoke to us of the duties before us in the defence of the country, and gave us much encouragement and good instruction. He expressed himself highly pleased with the moral and physical condition of the boys, and of their efficiency in discipline and drill, and said he was proud to take back with him to old Salem, such good reports in every respect. At ten o'clock we were interrupted by tattoo and at once fell in for roll call, and at taps half an hour after most of us turned in.

Tuesday June 25th.

At reveille we turned out promptly and fell in for roll call after which we passed an hour very quietly. At six the recruits of the Company were divided into squads, each of which was placed under the charge of one of the drilled members, by whom they were exercised in various movements in the "School of the Soldier" until breakfast. It was another delightful morning for drill, with a pleasant sun, and a cool and comfortable atmosphere which continued through the day. This was indeed a treat, for although the mornings were frequently cool, by ten o'clock in the forenoon it would almost invariably be so hot and sultry, that we could hardly move without starting the perspiration from every pore and we were forced to the brook to bathe, or to divest ourselves almost entirely of clothing, to enjoy the least possible comfort. At seven o'clock we fell in for breakfast and as we marched down the hill to the cookhouse, the cry of "Hacker" was heard simultaneously from various quarters of the encampment, and was immediately taken up by nearly every member of the Company.

The history of "Hacker" forms a memorable part in the campaign of the old Eighth, and is certainly worth of mention. Hacker was the name of a cook in the Marblehead or in one of the Lynn companies, who though a very clever fellow, was the victim of an exceedingly irritable disposition which often got the better of his discretion. He also possessed a remarkably strong voice, which could be heard far above that of any member of the Regiment. To prove this it was only necessary for a body to enter the prescribed limits of the culinary department under his charge, particularly at or near meal time, no matter how good his reason for so doing, and he was sure to be received with a shower of epithets and expostulations, which he was only too glad to escape by retreating his steps immediately. Hacker was always in trouble, nothing went right with him, and he was eternally in a stew, as the saying is, from morning till night. This failing was seized upon by some merciless members of his company as a pretext for sport, and no sooner would he raise his voice, than half a dozen who always stood ready to harass him, would prey upon his sensitive nature by yelling "Hacker" to the top of their voice, whereupon Hacker would immediately "let himself out." This soon attracted the notice of the whole Regiment, and "Hacker" became a familiar bye-word used on any and all occasions, appropriate or inappropriate.

After breakfast the time passed quietly until nine o'clock when guard mounting took place, and at half past nine the assembly sounded and the line was formed on the lawn, where after morning prayer by the Chaplain, an hour was occupied in battalion movements. At about eleven o clock we returned to quarters and were dismissed. Nothing of importance transpired during the balance of the forenoon, and at half past twelve we fell in for lunch.

While thus engaged our attention was directed towards a most deafening clatter of tin ware near by us, among the Lynn Companies. The tables of these companies were built on the crest of the hill, and on this occasion they had either taken their seats at the table a little prematurely, or their dinner was a little behind hand, and as they sat waiting for it one of their men struck up the "Anvil chorus" in a loud voice, substituting his tin plate and dipper for the anvil and hammer. "Satan finds mischief for idle hands to do" and it was but a few moments before the efforts of the whole company were devoted to the tin dipper accompaniment, which was rendered in a style which completely eclipsed the brightest star in the burlesque firmament, and loud enough to be heard a mile. This performance was encored by the boys, and they kept it up until their dinner arrived which put an end to the racket.

No duty was required of us during the afternoon and I spent most of the time writing in my journal. The majority of the Regiment occupied themselves in reading, writing and other quiet vocations about the camp until six o clock when the assembly sounded and we fell in again for the afternoon drill. The line was formed on the upper parade ground, and we descended to the lower ground near the rail road, and Capt Devereux took command of the Regiment, Col. Hinks filling his place in command of the Company. Lieut. Austin was absent from the drill and the Colonel donned his uniform, and appeared in the grey coat and pants of the Lieutenant, which caused considerable mirth among the men. He handled the Company very well and acted the Zouave to a "T." The drill was both interesting and amusing, for the Captain appeared to be rather better versed in the Tactics than most of the officers of the Regiment, and caught most of them in their weak points, and not only cornered all of the line officers, but actually exposed the Colonel, who at the command "column against Cavalry" from the Captain, stood eyeing him like the rest for an explanation. Poor Colonel was completely nonplussed, and the Captain after indulging in a laugh at his expense and giving him a significant look, went on to explain the movement which was executed solely under his supervision.

While we were maneuvering, another visitor arrived in camp — Mr. James A. Gillis of Salem, and after the drill we had an opportunity of exchanging congratulations with him, learning the news from home &c. At seven oclock the Company fell in for dinner. The evening passed quietly, nothing of interest transpired and at tattoo I answered to my name at roll call and turned in.

7

Baltimore

Wednesday June 26th

Reveille was beaten at five o'clock and the Orderly was soon on hand with orders for us to fall in which order was promptly obeyed by the Company and after roll call we were dismissed. The weather of the morning was extremely uncomfortable again, contrasting greatly with that of the last two or three mornings, it being hot and sultry with not a breath of air stirring. Fortunately for us the usual morning drill was omitted and we had nothing to do but to seek comfort, and protection from the heat.

Various rumors were circulated through the camp at an early hour, the purport of which was that we were about to move, but no one seemed to know where or for what purpose, and little confidence was therefore placed in it.

At seven o'clock "peas on a trencher" sounded and we fell in for breakfast. Nothing of interest transpired during the forenoon, guard mounting took place at the usual hour, and at nine o'clock the line was formed on the lawn, where we drilled for an hour in battalion movements. The balance of the forenoon passed quietly, some of the boys started on a bathing excursion to the brook, while others the better to enjoy this exercise procured passes and resorted to the favorite banks of the Patapsco. At half past twelve we fell in for lunch and while thus engaged an amusing scene transpired.

We had no sooner reached the cook house than we were unceremoniously visited by sundry fragments, which were hurled among us with considerable force from the tables of the Lynn company, among which soft boiled potatoes formed a prominent part, and which flew about our heads in quick succession. This challenge was immediately accepted by some of our boys, who replied with junks of "salt hoss," hard tack &c. until the commissioned officers, who were interrupted by some of the missiles dancing about their heads and over the table in front of them, interfered and put an end to the disturbance.

Lunch over I sat down in my tent to write in my journal, but had been engaged in this way but a few moments, when the order came to pack up and be ready to move at a moments notice. Notwithstanding the report of the morning this order burst upon us rather suddenly as such orders always do, and in a moment all was hub-bub, and confusion. Men passed rapidly in and out of the tents, like so many bees about the hive, gathering their effects and taking them outside in order to get more room to work. Clouds of dust filled the air as blankets were shook and haversacks and knapsacks were emptied, and in an incredibly short time the camp, which had heretofore been kept as clean as brush brooms three times a day could make it, looked more like a pig-sty than the "thoroughly policed" grounds required by the Regulations. Cigar boxes, packs of cards, old song books, ink bottles, magazines and scraps of paper, lay strewn in every direction. And when we take into consideration the fact that the Company at least, possessed two distinct uniforms and havelocks innumerable, and that nearly every member had been the recipient of bundles, boxes and in some cases even barrels of sundries from home since our arrival in camp, it will readily be seen that our reduction of baggage, was anything but small.

At the expiration of half an hour, the Company were ordered to fall in with haversacks and canteens, and we proceeded to the cook house where we were furnished with such rations as could be procured, filled the canteens with fresh water and in a few instances with coffee. As we returned to quarters we noticed thick black clouds, which rapidly extended over the whole firmament, and which indicated that wherever we might be going, there was a prospect of a wet time for us. At two o clock the assembly sounded and we formed line on the ground in front of the encampment, and I now learned that the right wing of the Regiment only had received marching orders. This gave us reason to believe that our absence would be but temporary and that we should again return to camp, which was indeed encouraging, to me at any rate.

We had hardly taken our places on the line, when our attention was directed towards a group of familiar faces, hastily making their way up from the rail road. These were Mr. Curwen, Mr. Frank Lee, Mr. George B. Phippen and Mr. Charles H. Bates all of Salem. The latter two were members of the Company, who were prevented by business from entering the service with us, and Bates was a member of the pony squad. We were rejoiced to see them particularly the latter and would gladly have rushed forward to meet them, but unfortunately we were in a position which we could not leave without orders, and might not have an opportunity of speaking to them.

By this time it had grown quite dark and suddenly rain commenced falling. Much to our surprise and joy, the order "break ranks" was immediately given, which was followed by a simultaneous yell from the whole line, and we returned double quick to quarters, and I spent a delightful time in company with our friends. It rained torrents for an hour and we were in hopes the expedition might be given up for the day at least, but at about four o'clock the line was reformed and we went on board a train of cars which had been waiting on us a couple of hours at the foot of the hill, and in a few minutes were on the road to Baltimore. As yet we knew nothing of the cause which had called us from the camp though various rumors were circulated through the train, but in about three quarters of an hour we reached Baltimore, and leaving the cars proceeded to a level spot on the outskirts of the city known as Mt. Clare. Here we stacked arms, divested ourselves of our luggage and rested quietly awaiting orders.

Some of us procured passes to go outside of the line of sentinels and visited a lager beer saloon near by where we procured refreshments. Others took a stroll into the city. At the usual hour tattoo was beaten and we returned to make preparations for bivouacking. The ground was very wet and we had a decidedly uncomfortable bed, which was made doubly disagreeable by a heavy fall of rain during the night and in consequence of which we got wet to the skin. Altogether it was a pretty tough time for us, and we were fatigued somewhat by the trip, having worn our knapsacks for the first time since our arrival in camp, and therefore slept soundly until morning.

Thursday June 27th.

We turned out at reveille which sounded at five oclock, and answered to roll call. The scene about us was quite different from the comfortable camp we had just left, everything was soaked through, knapsacks, blankets and even the clothing on our backs, but we were favored with a beautiful sun, the clouds having entirely disappeared leaving a clear and spotless sky, with every prospect of a pleasant day. The first thing we did was to spread our blankets, and explore the contents of our knapsacks to day. We then seated ourselves to breakfast on the contents of our haversacks which had also suffered more or less from the rain, and which was somewhat adverse to the tastes of many of the boys, who resorted to a saloon near by to obtain something more substantial.

The sun was now getting insufferably hot, and we were without the slightest shelter whatever. There was not a tree or building of any sort on the ground and we turned our attention to the building of huts with the facilities at hand, and which we soon accomplished by first driving a couple of muskets into the ground up to the shanks of their bayonets, and fastening between the hammer and nipple of each, the corners of two woolen blankets.

We next drove the rammers into the ground opposite the muskets and fastened the other corners of the blankets to them, so that they sloped in either direction like a common roof. Thus in a very few minutes the ground was covered with a number of good sized huts, serving the double purpose of shielding us from the hot sun, and drying the blankets.

At about half past seven some little excitement was occasioned in the Company by the announcement that Private Cobb had been suddenly taken quite ill, and the Surgeon was sent for, who upon his arrival resorted to bleeding the patient from the radial artery. The blood which spirted from the opening was of a thick black ink-like consistency, which so much relieved Cobb that he was enabled to accompany us when we moved.

At eight o clock we received orders to pack up, and soon after removed to a shady grove of large oaks belonging to a fine residence on West Baltimore St. said to be the property of General Stuart, of the celebrated Stuart's Cavalry (Rebel).[1] It was a delightful place, the grass was nearly two feet high and as yet clean and untrampled. Here we stacked arms divested ourselves of our equipments and lay down in the shade to rest. Orders were issued for no man to leave the grounds, but a squad of us procured permission to visit the Brooklyn Thirteenth, Colonel Smith, who were encamped opposite in Rullman's Bellevue Gardens, which previous to the war, was a famous German resort.[2] Although the tents of the Thirteenth filled up the greater portion of the grounds there yet remained traces of a once fashionable spot. The main building was of brick, three stories high and contained many of the modern improvements and conveniences of a fine hotel. Directly in front of this building, was a large hexagonal stand for musicians, about five feet from the ground, roofed over and provided with settees and stands for the music. The grounds were laid out with a view to the ease and comfort of the visitors, and here and there were neat lattice work shelters each of which was furnished with a rustic table and seats, around which had sat many times no doubt the happy German and his frau to enjoy their lager and pretzel. Many other features too numerous to mention, presented themselves to our notice, all of which bore indications of scenes of pleasure and festivity. At about noon we returned to our quarters and partook of a scanty dinner.

During the afternoon the Sixth came in from camp, and occupied the ground with us. The balance of the day passed quietly with nothing worthy of mention, and at tattoo which was beaten at the customary hour, we spread our blankets and turned in.

Friday June 28th.

Another fine morning. At reveille we turned out and answered to roll call, and at eight o'clock partook of a scanty breakfast on the contents of our haversacks. There being no prospect of moving at present, some half a dozen of us procured passes and took a stroll into the city. Among other places we paid a lengthy visit to the Washington monument.

"This noble structure, erected by the State of Maryland in honor of Washington, is the object of first and greatest attraction to visitors to the city. It stands in the centre of a small square at the intersection of Monument and Charles streets, in the fashionable quarter of the city, one hundred and fifty feet above tide water. It is composed of a base of white marble, fifty feet square and twenty feet in height, with a Doric column twenty feet in diameter at the base, and one hundred and sixty feet in height, gradually tapering upward to a handsomely formed capital. Upon the top is a statue of Washington by Causici, sixteen feet in height, representing the chief in the act of resigning his Commission as commander-in-chief of the American forces. It cost sixteen thousand dollars, and is reached by a winding staircase on the interior. The ground on which the monument stands, was given for the purpose by John Eagre Howard the "hero of the cowpens." The corner stone of the monument was laid on the fourth of July 1815, with imposing ceremonies." The inscriptions on the base are as follows: On the east front,

>To George Washington
>by the State of Maryland.
>Born 22d. February 1732,
>Died 14th. December 1799.

West front,

>To George Washington
>Trenton, 25th. December 1776,
>Yorktown, 19th. October 1781.

North front,

>To George Washington
>Commander in chief of the American Armies,
>15th. June 1775,
>Commission resigned at Annapolis,
>23d. December 1783.

South front,

>To George Washington
>President of the United States
>4th. March 1789,
>Returned to Mount Vernon
>4th March 1797.

After a careful examination of the exterior of this beautiful obelisk, we ascended the winding stair case and from the top obtained a beautiful panoramic view of the city and its environs. At the expiration of a half hour we descended and as we did so we met three gentlemen who proved to be from the Keystone State on a pleasure trip. They questioned us closely concerning

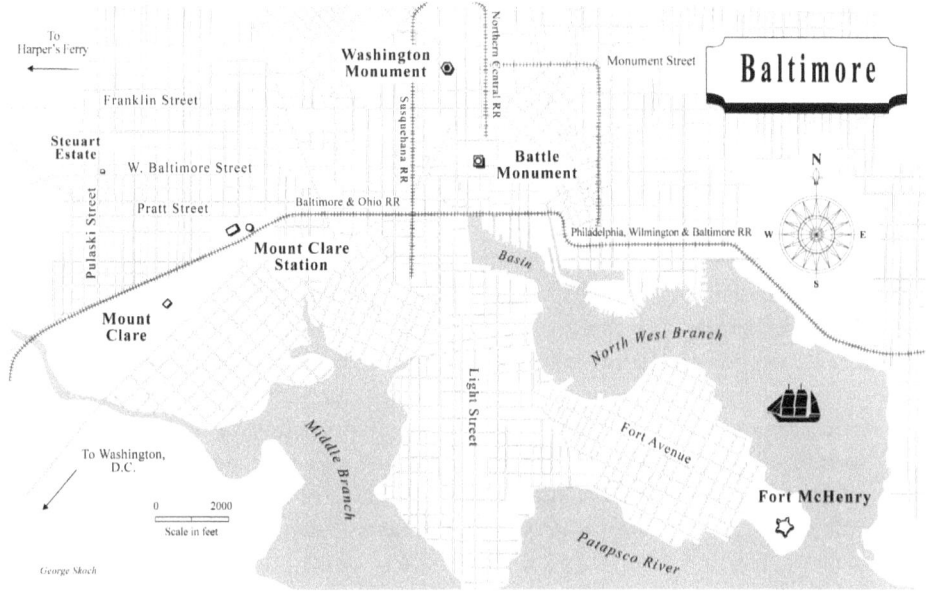

Map of Baltimore, 1861.

our military experience and appeared to take a great interest in us. They were on their way to Fort McHenry and invited us to accompany them, which invitation was accepted by all excepting myself, and I took leave of the boys and returned to camp.

Upon my arrival I found the companies drilling by themselves, but as my pass had not expired I did not fall in. Nothing of importance transpired during the balance of the day, save a drill in skirmishing by the Company at about seven o'clock. During the evening clouds made their appearance and we set ourselves to work to erect the best quarters we could with sticks and blankets. At tattoo we answered to roll call and immediately after I turned in. Rain fell during the night but I did not get wet.

Saturday June 29th.

At the usual hour reveille sounded and we turned out for roll call. The morning was a pleasant one but the camp was quite wet from the rain which had fallen during the night. Though we escaped a ducking ourselves, our blankets which had so well protected us, contained considerable water, and we spread them to dry while awaiting breakfast which we took at seven o clock. At nine oclock we again received orders to pack up and be ready to move and in a short time the assembly was beaten and we formed line, where we remained about an hour awaiting orders. As usual at such times all sorts of speculations were indulged in, concerning the cause of our being again placed under marching orders, and some conjectured one thing and some another. The prevailing idea was that we were to return to camp and no one would have regretted it, had such been the case. Our hopes however were soon dashed to the ground, for at ten o'clock we left our bivouac and took a short march into the city, while the Sixth started somewhere, I know not where, in the opposite direction.

This was our first appearance among the citizens en masse, though the Sixth had often times visited the city, and passed unmolested through many of the principal thoroughfares, since the memorable 19th of April. But as we proceeded through the aristocratic locality, it was easy to discern the feeling of hostility towards Union troops, depicted in the countenances of these people, and some unpleasant remarks reached our ears. This was almost too much for some of the boys, who would have left the ranks and retaliated with blows, had not the Captain restrained them and forced obedience to duty. Although the Federal authority had become fully established in this humiliated city, we rarely met with the emblem of national honor and glory — the Star spangled Banner, and when we did it seemed to be exhibited with great reluctance, and it was well that it was unconscious of the disgrace and shame it had been subjected to, at the hands of the traitors whose houses it ornamented. The insignia of Rebellion would without doubt have been produced from many a concealed corner, had the once bold and defiant Rebels so dared. In fact one of the boys did claim that he saw one on West Fayette St. but I am inclined to think it existed only in his imagination, for had one of their secesh rags been visible, it certainly could not have escaped either our eyes or our clutches. Few of the Company to say nothing of the rest of the Regiment, would have allowed such an ignominious thing to remain in existence after they had passed.

At about half past eleven we returned to camp, somewhat exhausted from the heat, and tramping over the cobble stone pavements with our heavily laden knapsacks, and were not slow in throwing off our loads, and sprawling ourselves on the ground to enjoy a short rest. We lay here until twelve o'clock when we fell in for dinner. During the afternoon no duty was required of us, and we sought relief from the fatigues of the morning in sleep. All over the ground which we occupied, lay the victims of Morpheus stretched in every conceivable attitude upon their blankets, and lost for a time to all the soldier's troubles and vexations. Nothing of interest transpired during the evening, and at tattoo we answered to our names at roll call and turned in.

Sunday June 30th.

Reveille sounded at five o clock and we at once turned out for roll call. The morning was cloudy and damp, and the atmosphere close and uncomfortable.

Rain had fallen during the night and at about half past five it commenced again in good earnest, and we began to think our exposed condition not the best for such weather. It was very evident that if we didn't do something and that immediately, we might get a good soaking. Accordingly we commenced a series of raids on the various fences in the vicinity, and particularly the one which enclosed our bivouac, which being composed of substantial boards, presented a tempting appearance. In less than half an hour this fence was reduced to a complete skeleton, and the boards used in the manufacture of numerous huts, irregularly scattered over the ground like so many wigwams. In these huts we found comfortable shelter, and spent the forenoon in a quiet manner.

At about one oclock the companies of the Eighth received orders to pack up, and we removed to an unoccupied building one square to the westward on _____ street, leaving the Sixth undisputed occupants of the bivouac. In this building we were assigned quarters, and having divested ourselves of our knapsacks and equipments, we proceeded in squads to explore the interior and reconnoitre the surrounding premises.

The rooms were large and convenient and in good condition, but had been visited by soldiers before us, and all over the otherwise clean white walls, many a volunteer had inscribed in lead pencil "his rude memorial and his name." Portraits and caricatures met our eyes at every turn, giving additional evidence of the peculiar desire of the soldier, thus to perpetuate his memory. The parlor on the first floor was appropriated to the Colonel as his Head Quarters, adjoining which was a piazza with steps leading down to the street. From the upper rooms we had a fine view of the city. From the conveniences and hotel appurtenaces which yet remained undisturbed, the building was without doubt a hotel or tavern. The grounds belonging to it were laid out in good taste, and fruit trees were plenty. Settees, swings and flowered walks <u>had</u> existed here, but were now mostly destroyed by the troops who had been there before us.

The comfort of the guests had evidently been studied by the proprietors, and many attractions outside had been added to the natural facilities for enjoyment. Among these was a shooting gallery, consisting of a small open building or shelter in which still remained the rest for a rifle or pistol, and fifty paces distant the place for a target against the end of a brick stable. To prevent the balls from entering, or glancing from the bricks, a double wall formed of sawed oak blocks, reaching to the height of ten or twelve feet and as many wide, was placed against the building, and was litterally full of bullets that had missed their mark. Some of the boys pulled down these blocks and amused themselves digging out the bullets for curiosities.

We spent the afternoon in this way until about six o'clock when the "first part of the troop" sounded, for the men who had been previously detailed for guard. ["First part of the troop"* is the name of the signal given by the drummer for the guard details to fall in preparatory to mounting the Guard] to fall in, and guard mounting took place under the trees in rear of the building.³ It fell to my lot to be detailed as one of the corporals, and I was placed in charge of the second relief. During the evening some of the boys got up considerable excitement wrestling &c. and made good sport. At tattoo roll was called and at taps most of us turned in.

At one o clock a.m I went on duty with my relief, and had just got through with posting the sentinels, when we were startled by a volley of musketry coming from the direction of the city, which sounded on the still night air very near to us, giving us a very vivid idea of the "deafening roar of battle." Of course such an occurrence did not fail to alarm the Companies and the line was formed in silence. Col. Hinks and the Captain rode into the city on horseback, and we afterward learned the firing to be the Twenty third New York Regiment discharging their muskets into the air. It was reported that one of their men was shot through the head by some carelessness, killing him instantly.⁴ The Companies of the Eighth did not leave their quarters, but the Sixth went into the city, and it was reported that they made some arrests, taking their prisoners to Fort McHenry.

Monday July 1st.
At five oclock reveille sounded and we turned out for roll call. The alarm during the night together with my tour of guard duty, caused me to be more tired than usual in the morning, and it was with some reluctance that I obeyed the order to fall in for roll call. It was a disagreeable morning the atmosphere was quite cool, and a slight drizzly rain fell which continued most of the day. As a natural consequence the day passed quietly with us, and most of the men confined themselves to the building. I continued on duty as Corporal of the Guard, posting my relief at the proper hours, and when off duty remained in the building with the rest.

It was now the fifth day of our absence from camp, and as yet we were entirely ignorant of the cause which had called us into the city. Neither could we ascertain how long we were to remain in our present situation, or what was the destiny before us. The fact that the Sixth had joined us led us to believe that preparations were being made for an expedition of some importance, but what it was, none of us could find out. Had we credited all the rumors which had been circulated since we had started, we might have been all over the country in the imagination and returned again. It was singular to me that one wing only of our own Regiment should have been selected for the duty before us, and the balance of the force required made up by the addition of the entire Sixth, if that was what they were here for. Whether it was or not I did not know but the Officers in command doubtless knew what they were about, and it was only necessary for us to await future developments, for the gratification of our curiosity.

During the afternoon the clouds several times exhibited signs of breaking away, and the sun was partially visible, but the expected fair weather did not visit us. At about six oclock guard mounting took place and I was relieved. During the evening the "Plugs" kicked up a considerable rumpus in the room in which I was quartered, having become tired of card playing and other monotonous pursuits occasioned by being pent un [up] in the house, and were boisterous and noisy. At eight o clock rain fell in torrents accompanied with high winds which continued without cessation for an hour. At the early hour of half past nine tattoo sounded, and we answered to our names and turned in.

Tuesday July 2d.

We were again favored with pleasant weather, and the morning was by far the most delightful we had enjoyed for some time. The sun arose in all its splendor, and with the exception of a few small white clouds the blue sky was entirely clear, a cool south westerly breeze also added much to the charms of the morning. I turned out at about six oclock, and in company with a squad of some twenty of the boys, proceeded to a street pump half a mile distant in the direction of the depot, for the purpose of a wash there being no facilities for this purpose about the premises, and after as thorough an ablution as the circumstances would permit, we returned again to our quarters just in season to fall in with the Company for breakfast. At about eight o clock I procured a pass from the Colonel, and in company with another of the boys started for the camp at the Relay House, just as the assembly was sounding for the Companies to fall in for drill.

The Campden station from which we were to take the cars was over a mile distant, and though we walked with hurried steps we did not arrive in season to catch the train, and were obliged to wait three quarters of an hour for the next. During this time we witnessed the morning parade of a Pennsylvania regiment who were quartered in the vicinity. Judging from the length of the regimental line they must have numbered not less than twelve hundred men, and were as fine a body of men for soldiers, as we had ever seen. They were generally speaking men of unusual size large, stout and robust looking, and physically speaking would have presented as strong a regimental front to the enemy, as could be found.

As we stood watching the maneuvres of the Key-Stone boys, our attention was attracted in another direction, by the loud distinct blasts of the familiar horn which heralded the approach of the cars from the upper depot, and which now rounded the corner of an adjacent street. Although the rail road track runs through some of the principal streets of the city, connecting the Philadelphia, Wilmington & Baltimore with the Baltimore and Ohio road, it is forbidden to run the locomotive through the streets. Upon the arrival of the cars, therefore, at the P.W. & B. depot, situated at the upper end of the city, the train is unshackled and such cars as contain passengers going farther south, are drawn through to the lower or Campden station by horses six to each car. Each driver is furnished with a horn which he blows continually to "clear the way." At the Campden station the train is again made up, another locomotive is hitched on, and a new conductor takes the train through to Washington.

At a quarter past nine we took our seats in the cars, and in a few minutes were on the road to the Relay which we reached in safety after a pleasant trip of about three quarters of an hour. Disembarking from the train we strolled leisurely along over the viaduct to camp where we arrived soon after ten oclock. We found the few boys of the Company which had been left behind, quietly engaged in cleaning their muskets or attending to some little domestic affair. They were glad to see us and asked many questions concerning our whereabouts, condition and future destiny, all of which we answered to the best of our ability. After a short rest I proceeded to the brook and indulged in a swim and change of clothing, which was indeed a luxury. At about twelve o clock I took dinner with the boys after which I sat down in my tent and spent an hour writing in my journal.

At about three oclock we started on our return in company with two or three members of some of the other companies who had been left behind, and taking with us several articles which had been sent for by some of the boys, and some few things from the Commissary department. We took the four o clock train from the Relay House and arrived in Baltimore at about quarter before five. As we rounded a curve in the road on the outskirts of the city, the train slackened its speed so much as to allow us to alight with our baggage which we did with safety, thereby saving a long journey on foot, which we should have had to encounter by continuing on to the depot. This was a lucky thought, for as we passed Mount Clare where we bivouacked the first night of our arrival in the city, we noticed the Sixth drawn up in marching order. Suspecting something new had transpired during our absence we quickened our pace to our quarters, where we found the companies of our Regiment also in line with knapsacks, haversacks and canteens ready to move immediately having been under orders since two o'clock. We were just in season to join them, and dropping our luggage, we hastily slung our knapsacks and fell in. Among other things which we had brought from camp, was a quantity of blackberry pies which we had purchased of a huckster on the road, a good sized ham and a quantity of molasses for mush. Such as could be was readily distributed among the men by the Captain and placed in the haversacks.

7. Baltimore

At about five oclock we received orders to march, and leaving our quarters proceeded up West Fayette and West Baltimore streets to South, down South to a pier on Light street near Federal hill and without delay went aboard the steamer Hugh Jenkins.[5] As we crossed West Pratt street on emerging from South, the scene of the attack on the Sixth by the mob on the 19th of April arose in our minds and without slacking our pace at all the order "fix bayonets" was given in loud tones by the Captain. It is possible we might have been assailed with a stray brick bat or two, but if any ideas of this kind were entertained by evil disposed persons, they were promptly dispelled by this precaution, for we saw no evidence of the slightest desire to molest us.

Having got on board the steamer we divested ourselves of our equipments and baggage, and sat down to view the scene about us and contemplate the nature of our expedition. The wharves were almost entirely destitute of shipping, and formed a striking contrast to the numerous steam and sailing vessels, which until within a few weeks only, the thrifty commerce of Baltimore had called into requisition. Business and store houses were closed, and the piers formerly continually laden with freight were vacant and deserted. In place of life, tumult and commotion, stagnation, quiet and desolation bowed obeisance to the throne of "grim visaged war."

As yet we were unable to conjecture anything concerning the true state of affairs. Various speculations were entered into as to the duties before us, and some were foolish enough to believe we had really embarked for New York again on the home trip. However much we might have indulged in this hope, it was soon dashed to the ground by the Captain, who in answer to a question put to him by one of the boys, coolly remarked that we might expect some sport before morning. The <u>sport</u> alluded to, conveyed its meaning without further explanation, and we asked no further questions.

Night was now rapidly approaching, and the Company were fortunate enough to have the saloon assigned to them as quarters. At half past eight o'clock we left the pier and steaming leisurely down the harbor were in a short time once more upon the broad Chesapeake, after two months of monotonous camp life. As we left the city a thousand lights shone behind, increasing in brilliancy as the darkness thickened around us, but gradually disappearing again until they were entirely lost in the distance. We now steamed along at the rate of about ten miles per hour, the waves dashing against either side of the sharp bows, as the boat cut through them. Some of the boys turned in at an early hour, others gathering in a group on the deck outside of the saloon, indulged in many a song until a late hour. At midnight all was quiet on the boat save the jarring and rattling of her machinery, and the short splash of the paddle wheels as they came in contact with the water.

Wednesday July 3d

We were aroused at the early hour of two oclock in the morning and fell quickly and quietly into our places, and as soon as the Company was formed we were ordered to load at will. We lay at anchor off Wye Point in Wye river, three or four hundred yards from the beach, it being impossible to approach nearer on account of the shallowness of the water, and preparations were at once made for going ashore, which was attended with some difficulty and much delay. A boat capable of holding some twenty or thirty, which we had picked up at the village of St. Michael during the night, was hauled alongside, and the disembarkation commenced with our own Company. As soon as the boat was filled we pushed off, but grounded a hundred yards from the shore, and were obliged to use still another boat, not more than half as large as the one we were at present in, before reaching the shore. In this way three quarters of an hour was consumed before the first company was landed, but when finally accomplished we pushed forward without waiting, leaving the rest of the companies to follow with all possible speed.

I now learned for the first time that we were to proceed to the residence of one Tilghman who was suspected of being engaged in furnishing recruits to the Rebel army, and supplying them with arms and ammunition. Our object so far as I could ascertain was to arrest Tilghman, search the premises for muskets and equipments supposed to be concealed somewhere in the vicinity, and gather all the information in our power concerning prominent Rebels in that locality. Two detectives accompanied us also two other persons as guides.[6]

We travelled I should think something over a mile by a round-a-bout road to escape observation, and over exceedingly rough and uneven ground, approaching the residence of Tilghman through a field of rye as high as our shoulders. As we near the house, a number of hounds attracted by the rustling in the rye field, set up an unearthly howling and sprang towards us, which only caused us to increase our speed to the double quick, lest the inmates whom we sought should become aroused, and suspecting the nature of our nocturnal visit, make good their escape. The first platoon took a direction in single file towards one side of the house, and the second in like manner towards the opposite, and thus deployed as skirmishers, as soon as the right had passed the house, we closed the flanks together forming a complete circle around it with orders to allow no one to approach or leave it. This done Col. Hinks, Capt. Devereux and the Acting Adjutant (Lieut Chandler of the Lynn Light Infantry,) leisurely ascended the steps of the front entrance and gave a loud knock. After waiting some time in vain for an answer to this summons they descended again and proceeded round to the rear entrance.

In a few moments a light in the second story, gave notice that the sleepers were aroused, and the summons of the Colonel was answered, who with the two officers before mentioned were admitted into the house. While we were waiting with some interest the result of their admission, a female raised a window on the side were [where] I was stationed, and deliberately pointed a revolver at us, at the same time uttering some expressions which I did not catch. In an instant half a dozen muskets were levelled at her, though we had no idea of firing, and she dodged back without firing. What went on inside I cannot tell, but in a few moments the Captain came out, and selecting about a dozen of the Company returned with them to make a careful search of the interior. Squads were also detailed to search the other buildings on the premises, but nothing in the shape of arms nor of ammunition could be found. While the search was going on, skirmishers made up from the other companies as they arrived, were thrown out in various directions to the distance of half a mile or more, to give notice of the approach of anyone, and thus prevent surprise.

After a careful search of all the buildings, about a dozen of us were called together by the Captain, who signified his intention to cross the river and search the neighboring premises. For this purpose a sail boat which lay at anchor several feet from the shore, was with some difficulty procured (the water being knee deep and obliging us to wade out to her,) and we got aboard and sailed across to the opposite shore. On ascending the bank we hailed a laborer who was engaged in a barley field, and took him with us as a guide to the residence of one Bryan a mile distant. We also observed two other suspicious looking persons as we landed, and a couple of the boys were detailed to remain behind and watch them. Arriving at the residence of Bryan we proceeded as with Tilghman, by first surrounding the house then making a thorough and careful search of all the buildings on the premises, but the search here was as fruitless as in the first instance, and having by this time become a little tired, and very hungry, we sat down to a lunch consisting of biscuits corn cake and bacon, which was furnished us by some of the negroes on the plantation, and which was duly relished.[7] At about half past seven we returned to our boat and recrossed the river, taking Bryan with us.

During our absence the Colonel and Tilghman had a lengthy interview, during which the latter is reported to have provokingly remarked to the Colonel, that the men under his command were the poorest material for soldiers he ever saw; that he "had a company of men whom Bryan was one, numbering only sixty who could clean out a hundred and twenty five of 'em." This was indeed a flattering compliment to the sons of the old Bay State and the Colonel of course resented it, but it is said he coolly replied by saying to Tilghman that if he felt disposed to summon his sixty chivalric heroes, he would place thirty "of those boys" (meaning the Zouaves) against them.

At about half past eight the companies were called together and we returned to the beach where we first landed, taking Tilghman and Bryan with us prisoners. With the exception of these, the only fruits of this expedition were a couple of old flint lock muskets bearing the date of 1817, one of which was secured by the Acting Adjutant as a trophy, and the other by one of the men of the Lynn company, unless I include a fine hound which Lieut Brewster brought with him as a <u>gift from some one</u>. Arriving at the beach we were furnished with a scanty breakfast consisting of dry bread and coffee, prepared by the cooks who had previously been sent back for this purpose. While thus engaged our attention was drawn towards a team rapidly driving towards us, and which contained a couple of individuals, one of whom a corpulent red faced fellow, desired an interview with the prisoner Tilghman which was granted, after which they returned in the same direction which the [they] came.

Breakfast over we gathered up our utensils and prepared to return to the steamer and at about eleven o clock we steamed down the river to the Chesapeake. At twelve o clock we stopped at the village of St. Michael and returned the boat which we had taken during the night. We remained here about an hour during which time preparations were made for dinner, which however was not served out to us until sometime after we had started again. We now steamed rapidly up the Chesapeake enjoying the return trip very much, for the air was clear and cool and hardly a cloud was visible above us. At half past two we passed Annapolis in the distance, which with the scenery around us called to mind the old Constitution, and our trip to New York on board of her.

At about four oclock we passed Fort Carroll in process of erection near Baltimore, and soon after the spires and towers of the city one by one became gradually visible as we steamed up the harbor.[8] At five o'clock we put in to the pier at Fort McHenry and turned over our prisoners to the Commander. While we lay here the Steamer Adelaide also came alongside and took aboard a couple of small guns from the Fort.[9] She was from Baltimore <u>en route</u> to Fortress Munroe, and had on board a guard of twenty five men from the Lynn City Guards, under the command of Capt. Hudson.

In about half an hour we left the pier and steamed up to the city arriving at the landing at six oclock precisely. As soon as possible we left the boat, and proceeded to our bivouac on West Baltimore St. opposite the Brooklyn camp where we found the left wing of the Regiment, and all of our tents and camp equipage. By this we understood at once that the camp at the Relay House was broken up and in future we were to be located here, and we afterwards learned that we were to remain here during the residue of our term of service. Upon our arrival we were received with hearty cheers by the Left, which we responded to with a will, after which we were dismissed. Some of the boys commenced to pitch their tents, but the majority of us were too tired for this and turned in at an early hour. We had been engaged in fatiguing duties during the twenty four hours which had elapsed since we left in the steamer, and many of us were sound asleep long before tattoo.

Thursday July 4th.
Of all the days in our Country's history which may be considered of any significance, the one before us should receive the earnest thought and attention of every one. The eighty-fifth anniversary of the framing of that noble instrument, the Declaration of Independence, proclaiming liberty and equality to all mankind, was upon us. After eighty-five years of success and prosperity unequaled in the history of nations, the 4th of July 1861 arrived to find the great principles upon which our government was founded, put to the severest test, and the eyes of the world were upon us for a final demonstration of this the great problem of self government. Thousands of traitors had at a given signal struck deep at the Nation's heart, with a fixed determination to overthrow the glorious free institutions left us by our fathers.
No country was ever less prepared to decide by war, the grave questions at issue, but the people were aroused by a conviction of right and duty, and volunteers from every occupation and pursuit, thronged to the country's support, and here we were, a squad of mere boys mustered into service to perform our part in the great drama yet to be enacted. Two months of this service had already expired, and though we had not as yet smelt the enemy's gunpowder, we had performed good service, and were fully able to appreciate and respect, the present anniversary. Though I cannot record any formal celebration, yet a number of scenes transpired among and around us, which served to impress upon our minds the fact that the day was not forgotten.

We were now established in a new camp. At five o'clock reveille sounded and we turned out for roll call. A heavy dew had fallen during the night and the tents were wet and heavy, but it was a beautiful morning, not a breath of air could be felt and unusual quiet seemed to prevail. The music of a hundred birds, echoing and re-echoing their makers praise through the trees with which the camp was interspersed, was indeed a fit anthem to accompany the approach of the golden sun, which now gradually appeared above the horizon, and stole through the trees into our new camp. We spent the couple of hours preceding breakfast in a quiet manner, for I may say we had as yet not fully recovered from the fatigue occasioned by the duties of the last two days. At seven o clock "peas on a trencher" sounded and we fell in for breakfast, after which the only formal observance of the day was the omission of the daily drill until late in the afternoon.

At about eleven o clock the Manchester N.H. Brass Band, with which we had previously entered into an agreement to furnish music for us during the balance of our term of service, arrived in camp from Washington, having accompanied a New Hampshire regiment to the Capital. Of course it was a unanimous desire that they should be placed on duty immediately, and for a half an hour they entertained us with some of their selections, in a style equal to the celebrated Gilmore's Band of Boston. In fact they performed as well as any band I ever heard, and nearly every member of the Regiment considered them excellent musicians. With this exception the afternoon passed quietly with us.

The day in the city was observed in various ways, business houses were closed, and several organizations paraded with music and banners. During the forenoon the boys of the House of Refuge passed the camp in uniform, escorted by a band of twenty pieces. They were juveniles, musicians and all, varying in age from ten to fifteen years, and occasioned much curiosity and excitement.[10] The boys of the Brooklyn Thirteenth on one side of the street, and those of our own Regiment on the other, crowded the fences within the respective lines of sentries, and, finally prevailed upon the little fellows to stop. Their band then favored us with "Red White & Blue" and several other patriotic airs, which elicited much applause from both regiments, and they moved on again.

The sun was now very hot, and we looped up the sod cloths of the tents to obtain if possible a good circulation of air, but it proved impossible to accomplish this, and we were obliged to make the best of it. At one clock we fell in for dinner after which I spent considerable time writing.

During the afternoon an appropriate incident took place in camp. The flag pole which had been used at Camp Essex (Relay House) and which was transferred here with the regimental baggage, was raised to the top of a large tree in front of the Colonel's marquee, and the Star spangled Banner was waved over our new encamp[m]ent, from its usual position at the top, being raised by the hand of the Colonel.

At six oclock the line was formed for battalion drill, but the Company was drilled by the Captain in the bayonet exercise and skirmishing. From the beating of the assembly visitors continued to arrive in camp, until it was literally crowded with the elite and fashion of the city, leaving us scarcely room enough to maneuvre.[11] The majority of the crowed seemed to centre around the Company, the light infantry movements attracting more attention than the more monotonous movements of the rest of the Regiment. As a matter of course the Captain "spread himself," and the great drops of perspiration rolled from under our fiery red caps in quick succession. We drilled for an hour and a half, during which time we were allowed a rest of about fifteen minutes, which interval was filled by the Band with some fine pieces, for the gratification of our visitors. At about eight o'clock the line was formed for dress parade, during which we more than ever appreciated the good qualities of our Band. Dress parade over we were dismissed, and the visitors gradually dispersed.

During the evening a number of bonfires were kindled about the camp, and some of the boys "celebrated" with punch, which was freely distributed without however any bad effects. At about nine o clock I took a stroll into the city, a short distance from camp, and spent a half an hour watching the different colored fireworks as the[y] shot into the air from several parts of the city. At ten oclock tattoo was beaten, but it was a long time before the camp was quiet.[12]

Friday July 5th.

At five o clock reveille sounded and we turned out for roll call. For my part I had much rather remained rolled up in my blanket, for I was one of many who had "kept 4th." until a late hour, and did not feel any too much like rising early. It was useless however to indulge in any such phantasies, for the failure to attend roll call in our company was a grave offense, which never failed to meet its penalty.

The morning was pleasant and comfortable, but the temperature of the atmosphere increased with the progress of the day until it was hot and sultry. At seven o clock we fell in for breakfast after which we engaged in quiet pursuits until nine oclock when guard mounting took place. At half past nine the assembly sounded, and the line was formed in front of the tents, which was immediately followed by battalion drill which lasted an hour. Nothing of interest transpired during the heat of the day and at one oclock "roast beef" sounded and we fell in for dinner, after which the different members of the Regiment occupied the time in reading, writing and sleeping, the majority preferring the latter. During the afternoon I made a visit to the camp of the Brooklyn Thirteenth and enjoyed a sociable game of euchre.

At four oclock the line was formed again and we took a short march into the city, accompanied by our band who performed some excellent pieces, and attracted a good deal of attention. Capt. Devereux insisted upon holding his usual position, on the march as well as in line, that is on the extreme right, the music intervening between us and the balance of the Regiment. Some objection was raised to this, but the Captain would not give up to it and we therefore led the column. The Company were always noted for taking an unusually long step in marching, termed by us the zouave step the length of which was thirty three inches. By these long strides we invariably gained distance leading the Regiment by several yards, and causing a gap between us and the music. So it was on this occasion, we found ourselves often times a long distance in the advance, and several times were obliged to halt to allow the Regiment to come up. For one I never could see the use or sense in such rapid marching, particularly when there was no need of it, and the balance of the Regiment did not appreciate it. It was particularly hard upon the musicians, and mighty inconvenient for us of the left flank also. I say us for it was my misfortune to be one of the shortest men in the Company, and my position was next to Sergt. Batchelder who held the extreme left as left guide. This step like everything else which we did was carried to an extreme, and christened "Zouave," for oddity.

We passed through some of the principal thoroughfares of the city, meeting with no molestation, and for a wonder no unpleasant taunts were offered to us, at least I heard none. At the expiration of an hour we returned to camp, reformed for dress parade and at the close of this were dismissed. At six o clock we fell in for supper, and at seven retreat was beaten.

During the evening the Band favored us with some of their selections, among which were a number of popular operatic airs. After they had finished many of the boys gathered in groups, and enjoyed themselves singing until ten o clock, when tattoo sounded and we fell into line for roll call, and at taps I turned in.

Saturday July 6th.

It was a dull cloudy morning, and the atmosphere was close and uncomfortable, but more agreeable during the forenoon. Reveille sounded at the usual hour and the companies fell into line for roll call, after which we passed the time in an easy and quiet manner until seven oclock when "peas on a trencher" sounded and we fell in for breakfast. Some change was adopted in the hours for the different camp calls, and guard mounting took place at the early hour of seven and three quarters o'clock. At nine o clock the assembly sounded and the line was formed. Immediately we formed hollow square and the Chaplain stepping into the centre offered prayer for the first time since our change of station. The square was then reduced, we deployed column, and the companies were dismissed to the charge of their several commanders for company drill, which occupied the next hour.

The drilled members of our own company were dismissed, but the Captain took the recruits by themselves, and put them through a severe test, to ascertain what progress they had made in different movements, and how many were in his judgement sufficiently will [well] versed to be classed with the drilled members of the Company. This drill lasted for an hour, and out of the entire number some thirty men, two only, Privates Nichols and Driver were considered proficient enough to be admitted to the number of drilled members.

The balance of the forenoon passed quietly, and at one o clock "roast beef" sounded and we fell in for dinner. Soon after dinner the clouds began to grow thicker and heavier, and in half an hour or more rain commenced falling continuing for an hour. Of course we confined ourselves to the tents, but they afforded us poor protection and the water poured through them as through sieves. At about four o'clock the rain ceased, and the clouds bore appearances of clearing away. On emerging from the tents, we were agreeably surprised to notice visitors whose faces were familiar to us coming into camp. These were Stephen B. Ives, Dr. Perkins and Daniel Perkins, all of Salem. When visitors arrived from old Salem we were accustomed to look for letters, papers, small packages &c and we soon discovered that <u>they</u> had not arrived minus these welcome comforts. They remained with us but an hour or so, being on their way to Washington, but what time they were with us was passed in the usual pleasant manner.

At five o'clock Orderly Sergeant Devereux and Private Upton returned from furlough, and also brought sundry <u>et ceteras</u> for many of the boys. At half past five we fell in for supper. The sun now shone beautifully, and at seven oclock the assembly again sounded and dress parade took place after which the Company were drilled for a short time in the manual, but the rest of the Regiment were dismissed. At half past seven retreat was beaten and the Band favored us with some excellent music for an hour, drawing around them a large crowd of both citizens and soldiers. Among other favorite pieces, they rendered the world renowed "Wood up" in a manner which drew forth loud bursts of applause.

During the evening a number of singers congregated in the Chaplain's tent, with some of the musicians, and a choir was organized who practiced sacred music with instrumental accompaniment. At ten o'clock tattoo sounded and after roll call I turned in.

Sunday July 7th.

At five oclock we responded to reveille, by turning out and answering to roll call. The morning air was cool and comfortable, and very desirable for the work before us, for it was inspection morning. We spent the time in a leisure manner until seven o'clock when we fell in for breakfast, after which fatigue details were made from each company for general police, who set to work with brush brooms to put the parade in a condition for inspection, while the rest of the members of the different companies were employed packing their knapsacks, cleaning their muskets, sweeping the tents and company streets and attending to numerous other matters pertaining to the Sunday Morning inspection. The cool air of early morning was now converted into almost insupportable heat, and the perspiration oozed from every pore.

At eight oclock guard mounting took place and at nine the assembly sounded and the Regimental line was formed for inspection. Without delay we were wheeled into column by companies ranks were opened, and the inspection commenced with the Company on the right, each company as it was inspected being marched to their quarters and dismissed. As soon as we were through with, we returned to our quarters and leaving our jackets in the tents, formed Company again and proceeded to a lot half a mile or so from the camp to the southwest, where we in turn discharged our muskets which had been loaded since our Tilghman adventure, at a mark set up for the purpose and some very good shots were made, one in particular by Sergeant Gray. We then returned to camp and some of the boys proceeded to the Patapsco to bathe, while others busied themselves writing &c.

At about eleven o clock a meeting of the Company was called in the Captain's tent, to consider the subject of new uniform, which for a number of days had been discussed by several members of the Company. The matter seemed to meet with favor among the old members of the Company, but the recruits were almost unanimously opposed to it. After considerable discussion on both sides in which the Orderly took an active part a vote was taken, and it was decided to adopt a new zouave uniform complete, and a committee of five were chosen to take full charge of the matter, select the style, ascertain the expense &c. and report at a future meeting. The meeting then adjourned and at half past twelve we fell in for dinner.

It was now scorching hot and by far the hottest day of the season. At about two oclock some little excitement was occasioned by the accidental discharge of a musket belonging to a member of Co. "A." It appeared that the musket had been lying in the sun for some time, until the barrel had become so heated as to cause an explosion of the charge. Fortunately no one was injured, but the sleepers in the vicinity were aroused very suddenly.

At half past five we fell in for supper and at six the assembly was beaten and the line was formed for divine service which was held in a shady portion of the encampment selected for the purpose. The services were conducted by the Chaplain, and the band and choir furnished excellent music and singing. The instrumental music of the Band attracted a number of visitors to the camp many of whom were ladies, and after the services were over the line was reformed and companies were dismissed for company drills under the supervision of their respective commanders. Our time was now come, but the Captain was a little considerate and ordered us to throw off our jackets which we did. We then "pitched in" for nearly an hour for the accommodation of our visitors, and returned to quarters wet to the skin with perspiration.

The evening passed quietly, nothing of importance transpired and at tattoo we fell in for roll call and soon after turned in. It was an unusually hot night, and I found it next to impossible to sleep.

7. Baltimore

Monday July 8th.

The morning was much more comfortable than usual, the air being cool with a light breeze from the westward. We turned out at reveille and answered to roll call, after which an hour [was] spent in various uninteresting ways, occupied the time until breakfast which we took at seven oclock. Guard mounting took place regularly at eight o clock and at nine the assembly sounded and the line was formed on the parade. We at once proceeded to the upper portion of the camp under the shade of some large trees, where we formed hollow square and prayer was offered by the chaplain. The Regiment with the exception of our own company were then drilled for considerable time in battalion movements by Lieut. Col. Elwell, Col. Hinks being absent.

The Company occupied a portion of the camp by themselves, and drilled for an hour and a half in our shirt sleeves and without arms, in company movements by the Captain. This was a change from the usual drill and much easier, and it was almost a wonder that we did not have to go through with the same thing every day, for from the manner in which we maneuvred there seemed to be great need of it. At half past eleven we were dismissed and returned to quarters, and most of the boys endeavored to refresh themselves as much as it was possible to do under the hot sun, which was now as uncomfortable as ever.

At half past twelve we fell in for dinner and immediately after I procured a pass with some half a dozen of the boys, and we proceeded a couple of miles from camp, to a most delightful place on the Patapsco called Franklin falls, for the purpose of a swim. These falls were a succession of regular steps, formed by the crumbling away of pieces of the rock which formed the bed of the river at this point, from time to time by the action of the water. Over these steps three or four in number, the waters of the Patapsco fell gracefully, hurrying along to a collection of irregular masses of rock, which with the exception of a gorge or channel between them nearly blockaded the river. Through this gorge the river swept with great force, in a smooth stream several feet deep, and we found considerable sport in swimming out into the middle of the river some distance above, and allowing the current to sweep us through to the more tranquil waters a hundred feet beyond. We also stretched ourselves flat upon the steps of the falls, and were greatly refreshed by the cool water falling gently over us. We found amusement in a number of other aquatic sports, and remained in the water an hour or more, after which we rambled a mile or two into the woods and returned to camp, where we arrived after an absence of about two hours and a half.

The balance of the afternoon passed quietly, there being no duty to perform except guard. At about half past four a friend from the Engineer corps, attached to the Brooklyn Thirteenth came over to see me, and I spent a half an hour very pleasantly with him until five o'clock when we fell in for supper. At about six the line was formed and the Regiment proceeded under the command of Major Poore, to an adjoining lot northwest of the encampment, where we were reviewed by Colonel Hinks. After the review the Company returned to camp and after divesting ourselves of our jackets, we were drilled by the Captain for nearly two hours in all the different branches of the Tactics, before an immense crowd of spectators who thronged the camp, and among whom were a number of distinguished ladies. This was about the toughest drill we had experienced at any time since our entry into service, and we were almost melted when we had finished. At eight o clock we were dismissed, and I spent the evening in company with my friend of the Thirteenth. At ten oclock tattoo sounded, roll was called and at taps most of us turned in.

Tuesday July 9th
Another quiet day with us, with little or no change from the daily monotony, unless it be that less transpired than usual. At five oclock reveille sounded and we obeyed its summons promptly by turning out for roll call. It was another beautiful morning with a clear serene sky, and a refreshing northwest breeze. The sun which had just passed the horizon, sent his golden streaks through the trees into the encampment with less warmth than usual, and a hundred birds welcomed him with their songs of praise. Nothing of interest transpired during the first two hours of the day, and at seven o clock we fell in breakfast. Guard mounting took place at eight o clock and at nine the assembly sounded and we formed Regimental line, then hollow square and listened to prayer from the Chaplain. The two hours following was devoted to battalion drill, but the Company were dismissed altogether and a meeting of the committee on uniforms was held in the marquee. I spent most of the day manufacturing a gunrack of a circular form to fit the rear tent pole of our tent, and large enough to hold the muskets of the seven non commissioned officers. At half past twelve "roast beef" sounded and we fell in for dinner.

The afternoon was more quiet than usual, not so much as the afternoon drill being required, and the time was spent in a hundred unimportant ways. At five o'clock clouds suddenly made their appearance, and rain commenced falling gradually increasing to a heavy thunder shower which lasted for a half hour, at the end of which the sun again appeared as bright as ever; but not to continue for heavier clouds followed those which were rapidly disappearing, and in a few minutes it rained harder than ever, falling in sheets and with great force.

If the tents had leaked before, they were comparatively tight to their present condition, for now they afforded us no protection whatever, and the rain poured through them as freely as if great holes were cut in the canvass, and the inmates were obliged to seek shelter as best they might. We scattered in various directions and for one I took my blanket to preserve it from the wet, and made for the large hospital tent, which for a wonder proved to be water tight. Many others followed my example until the tent was pressed to its utmost capacity for accommodation, and a lively time was kept up in here, by the refugees from the wet. In some of the other tents the boys amused themselves by jumping up and down on the tent floors, and besmearing their comrades with mud and water, who though wet to the skin were in good spirits and enjoyed the joke (?) with the rest.

The rain continued all the evening and the camp was flooded with water, in consequence of which dress parade was omitted. The drum heads had also become so soaked and stretched that it was impossible to beat retreat, tattoo or taps, a circumstance quite acceptable to the drummers. Tattoo roll call was also omitted in all the companies, and I remained in the hospital tent all night. Though I turned in at an early hour with the rest, we found it impossible to sleep until a late hour, for we were kept in a continual roar of laughter, by the string of yarns which was spun first by one and then another, until we were lulled to sleep in spite of ourselves.

Wednesday July 10th.

At reveille we turned out for roll call to find pleasant weather once more. The sky was very clear, and the air was cool and comfortable. As the sun gradually appeared, it grew to be warmer very fast and it was but a short time before we were enveloped in the usual hardly endurable heat. As we entered our various quarters from the hospital tent, we found the tents completely soaked through and puddles of water standing on the tent floors of many of them. The first thing we did on being dismissed from roll call, was to brush out as much of the water as we could, then loop up the sod clothes and allow the sun to penetrate and dry up the balance. The whole camp was also interspersed with puddles, or more correctly speaking small ponds of water, with patches of mud between them, but the hot sun commenced its work immediately, and in a few hours only the camp was comparatively dry again.

At seven o clock "peas on a trencher" sounded and we fell in for breakfast, and soon after the detail for guard from the Company was made by the Orderly, including myself as one of the Corporals, and to our surprise was double the usual number. There was one reason in particular why we felt somewhat interested in this matter, for it increased our chances of coming on duty to twice as often as heretofore, and as guard duty in the service was ever an unpleasant one, it was natural for us all to evade it as much as possible, consistent with our position as a soldier. We did not understand it but at eight o clock guard mounting took place, and as I marched on to line with the Company detail, I noticed that the details from the other companies were all fully as large as our own, so that the guard when formed consisted of one hundred and eighty men, an average of eighteen from each company, which when divided into three reliefs, gave us the large number of sixty men to a relief. This with the guard about to be relieved, (and who would be excused from duty during the forenoon) of course greatly reduced the number for Regimental or Company drills, and as I mentioned before, we did not understand it. Bu the secret was soon explained.

A number of men from different companies had been reported to the Colonel as having forced the guard on the previous day, and several complaints were received from citizens, who substantiated the fact that the men had committed various depredations upon their property, had become intoxicated and insulting, and otherwise conducted themselves in an unsoldierly manner. These offenses detrimental to the interests of the citizens, and particularly so to the good reputation of the Regiment which we had heretofore been fortunate enough to enjoy, were promptly punished by the Colonel, and to prevent their future occurrence, the police guard was increased to double its usual strength, and we were now reduced to the humiliating position, of having a sentinel at every ten feet around the camp. The strictest vigilance was also enjoined upon the officer and non commissioned officers of the guard, particularly at night.

At nine o clock the line was formed and after prayer by the Chaplain the Regiment were drilled for a short time only in battalion movements, with the exception of the Company who were for some reason dismissed. The balance of the forenoon passed with nothing worthy of note, and at half past twelve "roast beef" sounded and we fell in for dinner. No duty was required until late in the afternoon, and the time passed as quietly as possible. At four o'clock the assembly sounded again, and as soon as the line was formed the Regiment proceeded to an adjoining field west of the encampment, where they were drilled by the Colonel, finishing with dress parade. During this time, the Company were drilled by the Captain under the trees at the upper end of the encampment, but before they had finished maneuvring black clouds made their appearance at the westward and soon overspread the entire firmament, accompanied with violent gusts of wind which several times nearly levelled the tents to the ground. In a few minutes rain fell and the boys were dismissed and scattered double quick to quarters. The rain continued incessant for an hour, at the end of which the sun made its appearance but only for a few moments, for it clouded up a second time and rain again fell, continuing most of the night.

At about five o clock a procession of beautiful ladies, dressed in white and decorated with flowers, passed the encampment bearing a magnificent silk banner which was intended as a present to the Brooklyn Thirteenth.

7. Baltimore

The ceremonies of the presentation had actually commenced, but were interrupted and afterward postponed, by the sudden appearance and continuance of the rain. The evening which was rather cool, was spent by most of the boys in the tents. Retreat, tattoo and taps were all omitted and a majority turned in at an early hour. I was summoned at the proper hours during the night, and went on duty with my relief.

It was a habit among some men when on post at night, to improve every chance they could get to go to sleep, thereby not only neglecting their duties, but laying themselves liable to be court martialled and perhaps suffer severe punishment. The non commissioned officers were therefore instructed to visit their reliefs frequently while on duty, and if any of the sentinels were found asleep, their muskets were to be taken from them and deposited with the officer of the guard, and they were then to be left to wake up at their own convenience, and afterward to be arrested and charges preferred against them. I regret to add that a number were found guilty of this grave offense in each and every relief. Of course the first idea of a victim on waking from his slumbers was to feel for his musket and on finding it gone it did not take him long to realize his unpleasant predicament, and it was of course impossible for him to hide his shame, at being thus found by the officer of the guard, walking his beat unarmed. He might have left his post altogether and escaped meeting the officer at all, which after all would have been no worse than leaving it and journeying to the land of dreams, since in either case the man was absent, but none had courage to commit a second offense so soon, by leaving before being regularly relieved. It was indeed a poor soldier who would be caught a second time in this situation, yet such cases did occur.

It was amusing as well as provoking, the measures some of the sentinels would employ, to indulge in a snooze without detection. Some would stand their musket against a tree, then sit down and lean their back against it, so that it was next to impossible to take it from them without waking them. But we had a case in our own Company which eclipsed anything in the Regiment. One of the recruits whose name I will not mention (but who will readily be recognized by members of the Company, particularly the Captain, from the fact that he was such a nervous, excitable and troublesome individual,) almost invariably went to sleep on his post, and the manner in which he worked it, was this. In the first place there was a large stump on his beat about two feet in height, and making a very convenient and comfortable seat the top being perfectly flat. On this stump he would seat himself, then twisting the corner of his blanket firmly around his musket, would wrap the blanket around his shoulders, fold his arms and hug his musket firmly, inwardly congratulating himself that no one could take his musket away. In a few minutes his head would droop, and once or twice he was detected in this position by the Corporal of his relief, but sprang to his feet before the

Corporal could reach him, and commenced walking his beat as unconcerned as if nothing had happened. He however did not escape the quick eye of the Corporal, who said nothing, but passed on and reported his case to the officer of the guard, who was determined to catch C--- himself if possible. In about half an hour therefore he visited the relief with the Corporal and as he came to the beat of C--- he approached very stealthily, and as he expected found C--- quietly seated on the stump, his musket firmly clasped in his folded arms, his head drooped upon his breast, and snoring loud enough to be heard a great distance. Dreaming perhaps that the relief wouldn't possibly be visited again. The Lieutenant advanced quickly, siezed the musket of the delinquent sentinel, and attempted by a violent jerk to wrest it from him, but it was so twisted up in the blanket which encircled the waist and shoulders of its unworthy master, that he was unsuccessful. Of course C--- was nearly prostrated, but quickly recovering himself he sprang nervously to his feet and exclaimed in a confused and hurried manner, "No you don't --- I --- Who comes there? --- I ain't asleep." The Lieutenant paid no notice either to the challenge or the protestations of innocence of the guilty sentinel, but gave orders to the Corporal to march him off to the guard house, and supply his place by a more reliable man.

Thursday July 11th

It was a cloudy morning, though once or twice the sun shone for a moment or two through openings, as the clouds occasionally separated. The rain during the night had produced a desirable change in the atmosphere, and it was quite cool. At five o clock reveille sounded, and the companies turned out for roll call, but I remained an hour later in my "virtuous couch," with others who had been on duty during the night. At six o clock I was summoned by the Corporal of the relief on duty, and turned out to muster my relief to relieve them. The time was occupied in sundry unimportant ways, until "peas on a trencher" at seven o clock, when the companies fell in for breakfast, and I swallowed mine with as much haste as possible, and returned to my post at the guard house. At eight o clock we (the guard) were rejoiced to hear the "first part of the troop," and soon after guard mounting took place and we were relieved.

At nine oclock the assembly sounded, and as the Company formed, I remained in my tent as usual after coming off guard, but was soon visited by the Orderly, who was sent by the Captain with orders for all of the old guard detail, to fall in with the rest of the Company. Of course there was nothing for us to do but to obey, but we who were interested thought it hardly fair, and were forced to think still harder of it, from the fact that immediately after the morning prayer, which took place as soon as the line

7. Baltimore

was formed, the balance of the Regiment were dismissed and returned to their quarters.

The drill however was a short and light one, for we proceeded to the cool shade under the trees at the upper end of the encampment, divested ourselves of both jacket and equipments, and were drilled for half an hour only in deployments and the formation of squads, for the benefit of the recruits, this being their first lesson in skirmishing with the rest of the Company. After the drill we indulged in a social rest, stretched out in groups on the grass, and the subject of bathing was proposed by Lieut Brewster, who might well be called a perfect water dog. Most of the boys reciprocated this desire, and the Captain being also "in," marched us to quarters, after which all who felt so disposed proceeded in a squad with towels swinging, to the favorite resort on the Patapsco for this purpose.

I remained behind with a number of others, and during the absence of the boys spent the time writing in my journal. All was quiet with the rest of the Regiment until half past twelve, when "roast beef" sounded and we went to dinner. As I approached the Company tables, I was, like all the rest, surprised and pleased to find thereon some fresh vegetables consisting of boiled cabbage and new potatoes. Where they came from we didn't know, certainly not from the commissary. There had either been a foraging expedition, or the cooks had made good use of the slop fund. The latter was probably the case, as every company who was fortunate enough to have good cooks, could always have on hand something of a fund, with which to purchase delicacies not furnished by the commissary department, if they were careful to save the grease and slops, for which there was always a ready market. While the former was highly improbable if not impossible, for situated as we were, in the very heart of a great and loyal (?) community, foraging with any success, was attended with great difficulty and a heavy penalty if discovered.

It was no time however to enter into speculations, as to the source from which the new vegetables were obtained, they were before us, and all were anxious to dip into so great and desirable a change from the customary salt bill of fare, and every one did justice to them.[13]

While we were thus engaged, the boys returned from bathing, and were not slow in taking their customary places around the festive board(s). They brought with them a good sized keg of lager, which they had obtained from a brewery on their route, which was placed in the Captains tent and generously distributed to all hands, who "put away" one glass after another, until the Captain thought it prudent to shut off the stream. Considering the intense heat of the noon day sun, the cool lager <u>worked</u> in admirably and was very refreshing. The only thing we had to regret was that the faucet didn't fly out when the Captain attempted to shut it off, for we all stood ready with our dippers.

The afternoon continued hot and sultry, and as no duty was required until four o clock, we occupied the time in as quiet a manner as possible, confining ourselves to the shady portions of the encampment, and abstaining from all exercise likely to cause perspiration, which by the way it was only necessary to move gently about, to induce. At four o clock the assembly sounded and as soon as the line was formed, the entire Regiment proceeded to an adjoining lot, where we passed in review, after which the Company withdrew and were drilled by the Captain for an hour, in deployments and other movements pertaining to the skirmish drill while the Regiment maneuvred in batallion movements. At about five o clock the line was reformed on the Regimental parade for dress parade, but rain suddenly commenced falling, clouds having come up while we were drilling, and we were dismissed and retreated into our quarters. The shower however was of short duration, and by half past five it was clear again.

At six o clock the ceremonies of the flag presentation, which were postponed on account of the rain yesterday, took place in the Brooklyn camp. A majority of the Regiment were allowed to attend, and our Band furnished the music. An immense crowd of spectators were present, a majority of whom were ladies, and the affair was of a highly interesting character. At about half past six we fell in for supper, and immediately after a lively scene transpired, and one which does not often occur in camp. Private Moody had a foot ball which he had obtained during the day, which was the cause of exciting sport for an hour. One or two were unfortunate in getting their shins kicked of course. Who ever heard of a foot ball scrape without such an occurrence? We should have kept it up much longer, but darkness over took us and we were obliged to desist. There was a new moon, but it was too young to "throw any light on the subject."

During the evening I caught a glimpse of a fine sword with a silver scabbard, which I was informed was presented to the Captain by a friend— Col. Bruce of Baltimore.[14] The particulars concerning, or the circumstances connected with the presentation, I did not learn. At ten o clock tattoo was beaten under the direction of the drummer of the Band, who it seemed had during the day introduced to the drum corps a new and lively beat, which was far more stirring and inspiriting than the dry, old fashioned, stereotyped beat as it were, which we had heretofore been accustomed to hear at this hour. At half past ten lights were extinguished in obedience to taps, and everything was soon quiet, save the feint tramp of the sentinels.

Friday July 12th.

At reveille which sounded at five o clock, we turned out and answered to roll call, after which their being no duty to attend to for some time, the

Company engaged in a lively game of foot ball. The morning was a most delightful one for this exercise, the air being uncommonly cool, in fact quite chilly. The sun was also obscured by heavy clouds, and we had the most joyful time on record. Every member of the Company was on hand, officers and all, and the crowd was soon swelled by a number from the other companies. Some comical scenes occurred, in which a chap would receive a slight bruise, causing momentary pain, and a good many kicked shins, both of which were productive of mirth and laughter, the customary sympathy for the latter in particular. In this way the time passed rapidly and before we were aware of it "peas on a trencher" cut short the sport, and we fell in for breakfast. At about half past seven the clouds cleared away, and we were visited by a bright clear sun, which for a wonder did not make it uncomfortably warm.

At eight o clock guard mounting took place, and at nine the assembly sounded and as soon as the line was formed we proceeded to the adjoining field, formed hollow square and prayer was offered by the Chaplain. The Regiment were then drilled in battalion movements, but we (the Company) were dismissed and returned to quarters, where I spent most of the forenoon writing. In an hour or so the Regiment were dismissed, and the time passed quietly until half past twelve, when "roast beef" sounded and we fell in for dinner.

Nothing transpired during the afternoon until four o'clock, when the assembly sounded and the line was formed. The Regiment resorted to the adjoining field for battalion drill, but the Captain took the Company to the shade at the upper portion of the camp, and after ordering us to throw off our jackets, we were drilled in skirmishing with the recruits. At the expiration of something like an hour, we sat down on the grass to enjoy a short rest, and while in this position a zouave stranger came towards us, dressed in full uniform, and soon became very sociable. His uniform consisted of a dark blue jacket with a superabundance of gaudy yellow trimming, red pants, leggins, sash &c. After a short acquaintance he took a musket from one of the boys, and shew [show] us a novel way of loading and firing sitting. He also went through a number of other fancy movements, in all of which he was very expert. Upon inquiry he proved to be a member of a Zouave organization, belonging to the Brooklyn Regiment opposite. This was the first I knew of another zouave company so near us.

Of course he soon became quite a favorite. Why shouldn't he, Wasn't he a Zouave? He was a jolly little fellow (particularly attractive to me on this account,) and invited the whole company to a beer store close by, to take a glass of beer. We were all "in" of course, officers and all, and after the beer was put away, la-petite zouave didn't like it because we wouldn't let him pay for it. We let one little dutch man (he was a dutchman and two thirds "beard") treat a crowd of sixty? Not much! Such noble generosity was worthy a --- bigger man. After settling the bill we <u>honored</u> him with a "seven," he responded with three cheers, solitary and alone, and we parted; he to return to his Regiment, while we went for our jackets and joined the Regiment for dress parade.

At half past six we fell in for supper, and immediately after spent an hour kicking foot ball. At half past seven retreat was beaten, and the Band stationed themselves on the parade, and favored us with some good music for half an hour, drawing a number of spectators into camp. The rest of the evening passed quietly, and at ten o'clock the new inspiriting tattoo was beaten and we fell in for roll call. At taps I turned in.

Saturday July 13th

It was not often that reveille was omitted in our camp, but such was the case this morning, and most of the Regiment took advantage of the opportunity to indulge in a morning snooze, and it was nearly seven oclock before any one was astir. Even the Orderly, who was always sure to be out before light, ready to yell "fall in—form company" as soon as the first tap of the reveille sounded, was on this occasion behind hand with the rest, to our great satisfaction. No one will deny that Charlie was a "tip top feller," but he did have a confounded bad habit of tumbling out too early in the morning, which we were in hopes he was beginning to correct. I have said it was seven o clock before we turned out and of course the first thing on the programme was breakfast, for which "peas on a trencher" had already sounded. It was a damp cool morning, and rain soon commenced falling which continued through the forenoon.

As it was a dull wet day, I expected to have a fine opportunity to write, and had already seated myself for this purpose when I was interrupted by the Orderly, who handed me my detail as Corporal of the guard, and as the "first part of the troop" had already sounded, I laid aside my writing, and had just time to prepare for guard mounting, which took place at eight o clock.

While this ceremony was taking place Pay Master Usher arrived in camp, but had not passed the line of sentries, before his arrival was telegraphed to every member of the Regiment, who turned out to greet him, and as he proceeded to Head Quarters the air was rent with deafening cheers of welcome. Orders were at once issued for the companies to fall in to be paid off, and all men of the guard not on duty at the time were ordered to join their respective commands. It was a lively scene that followed, delinquents and absentees appeared spontaneously, and all men who had received passes instinctively returned to camp, each company vieing with the rest to be the first in readiness. When our turn finally came we marched up to the pay table to the tune of "<u>twenty-seven dollars, ten for the uniform, and one for</u>

the band" which our boys will remember, these amounts being our assessment, for the new uniform and band.

No duty was required of the Regiment during the forenoon, and considerable excitement occurred around the huckster stands, to which places the men restored as soon as they received their money, and in a short time many a petty vendor "sold all out" and went for a new supply. Strict orders were issued to the guard, for the temptation to slip out was rapidly on the increase. Applications for passes were more numerous than ever, every one having some "pressing business" to attend to which they had been obliged to postpone until they were paid off, and which now must be attended to, more particularly since the clouds had cleared away and the weather was quite pleasant again, for it might rain tomorrow. Many were fortunate enough to receive this indulgence and started into the city. At half past twelve "roast beef" sounded and we fell in for dinner, but the tables were not so crowded as usual, many having satisfied their appetites before hand.

The formal ceremony of guard mounting, which forms such an important part of the daily routine in the service, and which is so explicitly laid down in the Army Regulations, was often slighted in the Regiment, and passed over in a very unsatisfactory manner, the Officer of the Day who alone was responsible for its faithful performance, generally manifested little or no desire that it should be otherwise. The review in particular was often shameful, yet was seldom corrected or criticised. Whether this neglect on the part of those whose duty it was to attend to it, was the result of ignorance or carelessness I cannot say, though the former was most probable. Be the reason what it may, it was not with the sanction or knowledge of the Colonel, for a more careful or thorough man in the instruction of his officers and men, never commanded a Regiment.

To day Capt. Devereux was Officer of the Day, and as the guard passed before him in review, I saw by that peculiar expression of his countenance, so well understood by every member of his company, that some things didn't suit him, and I felt sure that before the day was out [?] somebody would catch it. But as the Pay Master had already entered the camp, he (the Captain) was no doubt anxious to relieve the old guard as soon as possible, in order that they might rejoin their companies for payment, and therefore suffered us to pass on to the guard quarters, to be brought to account at another opportunity. Let the Captain alone for that. That opportunity was now come. The "first part of the troop" was sounded, the guard reassembled, and the whole ceremony of guard mounting was repeated. This was indeed commendable in the Captain, and it is perhaps needless to add that it was a great improvement over the original guard mounting.

The afternoon passed very quietly, and I spent considerable time cleaning my musket. At about five o clock it clouded up, but very soon cleared away again. At six o clock the assembly sounded and the line was formed for dress parade, after which the companies were dismissed and returned to their quarters. During the evening reports reached the Colonel that some of the men who had received passes, were abusing their privilege by disorderly proceedings in the city, and some were reported intoxicated. Each man as he returned was therefore required to report in person to Head Quarters, and such as could not give a satisfactory account of themselves, were lodged in the guard tent, and all who returned after tattoo, without the countersign, were treated in the same manner.[15]

At about eight o clock a pattern of the leggins belonging to the uniform which we were having manufactured were exhibited as a sample in the Captains tent, by the tailor who had the matter in charge, and most of the boys gave him their measure for them. At ten oclock tattoo was beaten and all was soon quiet.

Sunday July 14th

It was another cool morning and the sun was hid by a thick veil of clouds. At five oclock reveille sounded and the companies were prompt in turning out for roll call, after which the various preparations were commenced for the Sunday morning inspection, and the camp presented a lively, busy appearance. I remained at the guard quarters most of the time, for the guard tent was full of prisoners, who had straggled into camp at all hours of the night, and more than the usual vigilance was necessary to keep them within the canvass walls.

It was really amusing to note the various expressions and remarks of these victims, as one by one they peeped out on either side of the tentpole, to see where they were. Some who were just recovering from their nocturnal hallucinations, called for the Corporal of the guard to know what they were arrested for, what they had been doing &c. Others produced a pass as a justification of their being "out late," forgetting that all passes were void after retreat, and should be replaced by the countersign, while others "wasn't with 'em" &c. To all of which the poor Corporal, though powerless to act was obliged to listen and pass unheeded, much to the dissatisfaction of the unruly prisoners, who instead of giving him the credit for doing his duty, accused him of being "stuck up," "putt'n on airs" &c. and swore they'd break his head as soon as they <u>did</u> get out.

At seven o'clock "peas on a trencher" sounded, all work was suspended and the companies fell in for breakfast. At eight guard mounting took place and as soon as we were relieved, I commenced putting myself and accoutrements in condition for inspection—for not even the old guard escaped this important duty — which occupied us during the next hour. At ten o clock the assembly was beaten, and the line was formed on the parade, but we adjourned to the adjoining field which was more commodious, and the companies were each in turn subjected to a close and careful scrutiny of arms, equipments, knapsacks, clothing and general appearance, returning to quarters as soon as they were through with, excepting the company detailed to escort the colors, for which purpose the Band also remained on the ground.

After divesting myself of my luggage, I sat down in my tent to write, but had hardly commenced when the Orderly came out of the Captain's tent with orders to "fall in — form company" to be paid off, which he promulgated in a loud clear voice, placing that peculiar emphasis on the words <u>fall</u> and <u>form</u> so characteristic with him, and repeating it at every step he took. It need not have been repeated at all, for at its first utterance the boys sprang out of their tents, and the Company was formed in short order. The roll was called of course, but no one was absent, and without delay we were marched to the pay table, and were paid each one month's pay, and mileage from Boston to Washington, amounting in the aggregate to something over thirty dollars to each Private, those of higher grade receiving the difference in the pay proper, more. With the Company, the payment of the Regiment was completed, those companies who were not paid on the previous day, having been paid before us during the forenoon. Again the huckster and cake stands became the centre of attraction, and a good quantity of the "needful," found its way into the trousers pockets of these happy vendors. At half past twelve "roast beef" announced dinner, but not quite so much attention was paid to it as usual, most of the boys preferring to "dine out."

During the afternoon clouds appeared occasionally obscuring the sun and once or twice rain fell, but lasted only for a moment or two each time.

Fort McHenry, Baltimore, *Frank Leslie's Illustrated Newspaper*, June 1, 1861.

We had a great many visitors in camp, but nothing whatever occurred to attract attention. The time was passed in a quiet manner, the boys laying about the tents and enjoying such luxuries as could be obtained. Reading matter was in great demand, but the stores of the city were all closed and none could be had, for the hucksters didn't deal in the article. The Sunday service was omitted and dress parade also. At half past six we fell in for supper, and in an hour after retreat was beaten, immediately after which the Band played for nearly an hour on the parade, drawing around them the customary audience of citizens and soldiers.

During the evening the moon shone beautifully and I obtained permission from the Captain to be absent until tattoo, and in company with Private Smith ("Fred") called at the residence of the Methodist preacher, Dennis, on Rock St. where we spent the evening very pleasantly in the company of the two young and interesting daughters of Mr. D. with whom we had previously become acquainted.[16] At about half past nine we took our leave, sauntered leisurely back, and arrived in camp in season to attend tattoo roll call, after which I turned in.

End of Part second.

Monday July 15th.

Reveille sounded at five o'clock and the boys were soon on the line for roll call. It was another cloudy morning, but cool and comfortable and unusually still and quiet. Before the company was dismissed, orders were issued for every man to pack his knapsack, and be ready to move at a moments notice.

A small detail from the Regiment was made, sufficient to guard the camp during our absence, which would be but temporary.

We soon learned that we were to proceed to Fort McHenry, two miles from the city proper, and five from our present camp, where we were to be reviewed by the Dept. Commander, Maj. Genl. N.P. Banks.

Every care was exerted by the Officers and no pains spared by the men, to put everything into the best possible shape. The muskets received an extra rub, and the equipments an extra touch of blacking, while the knapsacks were packed, and the blankets rolled with even more than the usual care and precision. All this required but little time, for we were subjected to frequent and careful inspections, and it was impossible for anything to remain long out of place. Everything was ready so far as the company was concerned, long before breakfast, and we waited some time for "peas on a trencher," which sounded at seven o'clock.

At eight o'clock guard-mounting took place, and the old guard was soon in readiness, to join the Regiment.

At nine o'clock the assembly sounded, and the line was formed in full marching order, and it was really gratifying to see the Regiment together once more; the immense guard which for a number of days had been kept up, together with the old guard relieved each morning, and who were excused from duty, except on some such important occasion as the present, with the sick and those on pass, reduced the Regiment to half the number of its available force, but to day the line stretched out far beyond the reach of the Adjutant's voice, and the command "Guides Post" was only understood, by the Officers on the left, watching the movements of those on the right. The Colonel now appeared on his white horse, gave the order "in place rest," and we unslung knapsacks, seated ourselves upon them, and remained in this position for an hour awaiting orders.

At ten o'clock we left camp, marched up West Baltimore St. to the music of our superb band attracting attention from every quarter, and arrived at Fort McHenry at about twelve o'clock.

It was pretty tough work marching over the cobbles, but the sun was obscured, and the good condition of the roads, which were comparatively free from dust, made the march as comfortable as could be expected. The company were favored with frequent halts also, for the Captain always marched us in advance of the band, claiming it as proper for skirmishers, and our thirty-three inch step, shot us so far ahead of the Regiment that we were obliged to halt at intervals to allow them to catch up.

Arriving within the Fort, we stacked arms, unslung knapsacks and were allowed a half hours rest, which was most acceptable. At half past twelve we reformed, and proceeded to a level sandy area, just outside the walls of the Fort, where we were drawn up in open order and awaited the reviewing officer. He soon made his appearance from his headquarters close by, and came galloping towards us with his Staff clattering at his heels, reminding me of the militia musters, on Winter Island, Salem Harbor. "Attention Battalion" from the Colonel, was immediately followed by "Carry" and "Present Arms," and the General with his staff, clattered majestically down along our front and around our rear, the band playing "hail to the chief." Having taken up his position in front of our centre, we were marched in review in both common and quick time. Without unslinging knapsacks, the Regiment were drilled for an hour in Battalion movements, the Company at the same time drilling near by in skirmishing. The General remained on the ground expressing himself, highly pleased with the movements.[17]

It was now about half past two, we were nearly perished with hunger, and melted with hard work into the bargain. Returning to the Fort we stacked arms, pitched off our knapsacks, and took dinner. Many strolled outside and patronized the hucksters which were always numerous in our vicinity.

After dinner we had an hour to ourselves, and strolled about the Fort. Some snoozed on the grass, and others went in bathing. It was particularly interesting to me to gaze upon the water, and contemplate the glorious associations connected with these old walls of masonry. This then was the very work, which was subjected to such a terrific bombardment by the British fleet in 1814, but which so successfully resisted all attempts to capture it, and dashed the hopes of the British Commander, who had hoped to sail up to the piers of the monumental city. Surely we were on historical ground. The site of the Fort was most admirably selected for a defensive point, commanding the entrance to the harbor of Baltimore, the channel of which is extremely narrow, so narrow that on the occasion of the bombardment above referred to, two or three old sunken hulks only, were required to make the obstruction complete. The Fort consisted of five lunettes, or bastions of masonry, connected by a curtain, or wall of the same, in the form of a pentagon. The walls were surmounted by a neat turf embankment, over which protruded the guns in barbette, which constituted the chief armament. I was about to survey the internal construction, when I was interrupted by the familiar sound of the "assembly," and fell in with the company, preparatory to returning.[18]

At half past four we marched out of the Fort, and proceeded leisurely, halting occasionally to rest. As we passed the piers on Light St. a carriage drove up from one of them, around which gathered quite a concourse of people. The carriage contained Gov. Hicks of Maryland. Some curiosity was manifested to see the would-be Rebel, who while professing his loyalty to the Nation, used every means in his power to encourage the secession of his state, and endeavored to refuse the passage of troops through the State, on their way to the defense of the National capital. As we marched by, we caught a glimpse of him through his carriage window.[19]

At half past six we arrived in camp, and formed line on the parade. The Colonel made a short address, complimenting us on the success of the day, after which we were dismissed, divesting ourselves of our luggage, and fell in for supper with sharpened appetites.

At half past seven, retreat was beaten, but the band were used up like everybody else, and the music which we should otherwise have been favored with, was dispensed with.

During the evening our tailors arrived in camp from the city, and a number of the Company were measured for the new uniform.

At ten o'clock tattoo sounded roll was called, and immediately after every body turned in, pretty well tired out with the duty of the day.

Tuesday July 16th.

Reveille was again omitted by the drummers, and the sun was high in the heavens before the Regiment was astir. This was a good thing for us, for the duty of the previous day, was as tough as any we had encountered heretofore. To say that we were tired would not express it. Many were foot sore, and the feet in some cases, so swollen that it was impossible to get the shoes on. Others complained of galled shoulders, stiffness in the back and legs &c. The march to Fort McHenry, would hardly be called a long one, being about ten miles in all, but to troops unused to the march, the cobble stone pavements with the knapsacks, and the drill without unslinging them would be enough to use up most men, and we were no exception.

It was but a short time after we turned out, before "peas-on-a-trencher" sounded, and we fell in for breakfast.

The morning was delightful, the atmosphere being cool and comfortable from a north west breeze.

Guard mounting took place at eight o'clock, and was all the duty required during the forenoon. Most of the Regiment lay about the camp, under the trees, many in their bare feet, and all seeking general comfort.

During the forenoon, one of our new uniforms arrived in camp, the property of Sergt. Emmerton, and having been completed for a sample. Emmerton immediately put it on, and gave the company an opportunity to inspect it. It consisted of a short rounded zouave jacket, of blue-black flannel, cut very low in the neck, and trimmed all round with a scarlet worsted braid, half an inch wide, and having on each front near the lower corners, a figure resembling the letter "S" in narrower braid of the same kind and color. A double knot or scroll extending down the back from the neck, and three parralell rows around the sleeve, forming a cuff, of scarlet braid. The chevrons for non-com-officers of gilt braid, half an inch wide.

Vest of the same material, also cut low in the neck, and long enough to tuck into the pants, and fastened with a long row of small brass bell buttons, half an inch apart, with a row of small scarlet serpentine braid, running up and down on each side of the buttons, an inch and a half apart, between the braids.

Pants of the same material, cut full zouave pattern, being plaited at the waist to give the desired fullness, and very much like a pair of common meal bags, and having a stripe of scarlet worsted braid, three quarters of an inch wide, down the outside seam.

Leggins of thick white canvass or duck, slashed with a strong white cotton lacing, reaching up the leg, to within an inch of the knee joint. The pants were made full length, but were pulled up so that the bottoms extended about two inches below the top of the leggins on the inside, then fell over the same to about half way between the knee and ankle.

A scarlet woolen sash, about ten inches wide, with a fringe a foot long at either end, and long enough to go twice around the waist, and reach to the knee after being tied.

Considerable controversy arose concerning the red stripe on the pants, which, it appeared, was not included in the original pattern, but after discussion a vote was taken, and it was decided to adopt it.

The red cap we were at present wearing, was retained, and the uniform was considered complete.[20]

During the forenoon a dozen or more procured passes, and rode into the city, with no other object in view than to see what was going on, and make a few purchases.

Nothing of interest transpired during the afternoon until half past four. The boys continued to lay about the camp, reading, smoking, sleeping &c. Clouds appeared threatening a shower, but passed over.

At half past four the "assembly" sounded, the line was formed and proceeding to an adjacent field, the Regiment were drilled by the Colonel in Battalion movements. The Company proceeded to the ground in front of our quarters, stacked arms, and were drilled by Lieut Putnam in company movements without arms. Capt. Devereux being absent "Put" let up on us, and the light drill served to limber us up, and was a good panacea, for the ills contracted from the march to Fort McHenry. At five o'clock we were dismissed, and at half past six fell in for supper.

The evening was most beautiful, the moon shone in all its splendor. Squads rambled into the city, tattoo sounded at the usual hour and at taps the camp was quiet.

Wednesday July 17th.

Reveille sounded at the usual hour, but for some reason which I didn't learn, the company roll-call was omitted, and we were therefore not over anxious about turning out, though the other companies were on hand with the usual promptness. It was not so lively as usual in the company, until "peas-on-a-trencher" when the boys resumed their accustomed vivacity. It was a beautiful morning, bright and pleasant, and as comfortable as we could expect, with not a cloud to be seen.

When the Orderly received his detail for guard, it appeared that the entire company, with the Allen Guards, had been detailed for this duty. We seemed to have gone back again to the custom of detailing the guard by companies. For what reason I know not unless to gain more officers and non commissioned officers. It was a fact that it required a guard equal to two companies to keep the balance of the Regiment within the prescribed limits of camp. What with the Brooklyn Thirteenth, encamped in Rullman's Bellevue gardens across the street, and our close proximity to the bustle of the city, the temptations to "skin out" were many and great as the guard knew to their sorrow.

At eight o'clock guard-mounting took place, and I found myself, detailed as Corporal of the first relief, and of the guard at head quarters.

At nine o'clock the "assembly" sounded, the line was formed, and proceeding to the adjoining field, the colors were received with the formality prescribed in the Army Regulations, the first time the ceremony had taken place in our present camp. The ceremony over, the Regiment marched to Mont Clare, a mile distant, and were drilled by the Colonel in Battalion movements.

Nothing transpired in camp worthy of note. The sentinels were regularly relieved, at half past eleven the Regiment returned, and an hour after "roast beef" sounded for dinner.

It was now as hot as we had been accustomed to have it, and continued so 'til night.

During the afternoon, we had an unusual number of visitors in camp, including many of Baltimore's fair sex, and many a tete-a-tete was indulged in by the boys, who were never slow in making acquaintances.

At about four o'clock the line was again formed, and after a short drill in the manual, the Regiment with the band, took a short march into the city, taking a number of the visitors with them. Enough however were left behind, and the Company being on guard, those off duty had a gala time in the absence of the Regiment. At five o'clock the Regiment returned, and an hour after we fell in for supper.

At about quarter past seven retreat was beaten, and immediately after the band performed on the parade, eliciting frequent applause from the crowd which always assembled around them.

At eight o'clock the music ceased, the camp was cleared of spectators, and resumed its customary appearance.

The evening was delightfully pleasant, not a cloud to obstruct the brilliant moon, and groups of singers attested their appreciation of the situation in different parts of the camp.

Tattoo sounded at the usual hour, roll was called immediately after, and though taps followed in regular order, nobody thought of turning in, and the camp resounded with merry song, far into the night.

Thursday July 18th.

At three o'clock a.m. I was summoned by the Corporal of the relief then on duty, and proceeded to post my relief. It was very cold, and we were enveloped in a thick fog, which however burnt off with the sun and the day was as hot as usual. At five o'clock the second relief came on duty, and our relief proceeded to quarters while reveille was sounding through the camp. The Company did not turn out with the rest, not having been relieved as guard.

At seven o'clock "peas-on-a-trencher" sounded and the company were on hand with the rest, for breakfast. At eight o'clock guard-mounting took place and the Zouaves, and Allen Guards, were relieved by two other companies.

At nine o'clock the Regimental line was formed but the absence of four companies, two on guard duty, and two just relieved, was quite conspicuous. The six companies on line, were formed into a hollow square, prayer was offered by the Chaplain, after which they were dismissed.

At eleven o'clock, in company with a dozen others, I procured a pass, and we went to Franklin falls, for a swim in the Patapsco. "Roast beef" had sounded when we returned and we joined the company at dinner.

During our absence, orders had been received for a grand review of all the troops in the vicinity, and preparations had already commenced. At two o'clock the line was formed, in full marching order, none being excused except the guard, actually on post at the time. We remained here a half an hour awaiting orders, during which time the Brooklyn Thirteenth, marched out of their camp opposite, with over a thousand men, with knapsacks on, colors flying, and making a magnificent appearance in their splendid grey uniforms and double white crossbelts, as they formed their line dressing with unusual precision on the horse rail road track. As they wheeled into column by companies and started with their superb drum corps of juveniles, the crowd followed en masse. Soon after our own Regiment followed the Brooklyn boys, our band attracting the crowd, who dropped behind to allow us to come, up until the street was so packed we found it difficult to march, particularly we of the pony squad on the left.

The spot selected for the review, was a level plain beyond Mont Clare, on the other side of the rail road, and the road to it was dusty in the extreme so much so that when we arrived, we looked as if we had emerged from a grist mill on the outside, while we were nearly suffocated within. The ground was already occupied by a dense crowd of spectators, occasioning some delay in pressing them back by guards detailed for the purpose. The line was then formed with some difficulty, and consisted of the Eighth Mass. Col. Hinks on the right, Thirteenth Brooklyn, Col. Smith, Eighteenth Pennsylvania, Col. Lewis, Nineteenth Pennsylvania Col. Lisle, Twentieth Pennsylvania Col. Morehead, Twentieth New York Col. Pratt, and the Boston Light Artillery, Capt. Cook, numbering in all about 5,000 men.[21] The Sixth Regt. being still at the Relay House, were not included. At half past three the General made his appearance, galloped towards the right of the line, and down our front, the troops saluting and the bands in turn playing "hail to the chief." Half an hour was occupied in this ceremony, the General then galloped off towards his field-color, and the entire column were marched in review in both common and quick time.[22]

At about five o'clock, we started on our return to camp. The dust which before was bad enough, was now almost insufferable, and it was impossible to see any distance at all in advance of us. Arriving in camp we formed immediately for dress parade, after which we were dismissed, brushed up, and fell in for supper.

During the evening an animated discussion took place in the Captain's quarters, on the subject of appearing in our new uniform on our return home, at the expiration of our term of service. It appeared that a number of the boys had written home concerning the new uniform, and several letters had been received exhorting us to wear the old uniform, suggesting that rags indicated service, and were the more honorable from this fact. The boys were completely non-plussed at this. The uniform was ordered and nearly finished, and there seemed to be a doubt as to what we should do. The Officers argued that our friends had been very kind to us in many ways and we were in duty bound to respect their feelings, regardless of our own. Various attempts were made to find out how the matter had leaked out, which was intended as a surprise. No one knew any thing about it of course. One by one the boys yielded to the counsel of the officers, that it was better under the circumstances to wear home the old uniform.

During the evening clouds appeared, and later rain fell.

Tattoo sounded at ten, roll was called, and many turned in before taps.

Friday July 19th.

Reveille sounded at the usual hour, but as there was no roll-call in the company, the boys did not turn out until breakfast. Loose clouds hung about, and it was very damp and muggy. The camp was muddy, everything was wet, but the sun soon made its appearance, and dried things up.

At eight o'clock guard-mounting took place, and I stationed myself on the parade to hear the band which always attracted a crowd of listeners. The ceremony of guard-mounting, usually occupied about three quarters of an hour, and consisted of the verification of the details, by the Serg't. Major and Adjutant, an inspection of arms, equipments, and general appearance of the men by the Officer of the Guard, and a review of the whole by the Officer of the Day. The duties of the Band formed an important part of the ceremony, they being required to play the details on to line, perform during the inspection, beat down the line and back, and escort the Guard in review. When properly performed it is an interesting ceremony, and though of daily occurrence, was always witnessed by a majority of the Regiment, who generally had nothing else to do at this hour.

At nine o'clock the "assembly" sounded, Regimental line was formed, we then formed square in four ranks and prayer was offered by the Chaplain. Companies were then dismissed to the charge of the Captains for company drill and proceeding to the area in front of our quarters, we had our usual "Zouave" stent. At half past ten we were dismissed and nothing further transpired until dinner. In the N.C.O. we were favored with a call from a couple of the Brooklyn boys, with whom we had an interesting game of euchre. "Roast beef" sounded at twelve and we fell in for dinner, the Brooklyn boys accompanying us.

It was now as hot as usual, and no duty was required of us until towards night. We were visited by the usual throng of visitors from the city, and recognized many familiar faces of both sexes, some of whom informed us that they came to see the Zouaves drill. This was no new thing to us, for hardly a day passed without our being "exhibited," reminding us of the frog story. "Fun for you but death to us."

At six o'clock the assembly sounded for dress parade, which was witnessed by a tremendous crowd of spectators. After which the Regiment were dismissed, with the exception of our ill-fated selves, who proceeded to the area in front of our quarters, threw off our jackets, and waded in for a two hours drill in our shirt sleeves, in the bayonet exercise and skirmishing. The crowd were of course drawn around us, and if they didn't get their fill, it was no fault of the Captain's.

Retreat was beaten at half past seven, the Band followed with some good selections, drawing the crowd to the parade, much to our satisfaction, for our audience having dispersed we were dismissed.

The evening was again beautiful, except that occasional silvery clouds obscured the moon, and groups of singers might have been heard about the camp, until a late hour.

Tattoo sounded at ten, roll was called, and immediately after, about twenty of us were selected by the Captain and ordered to step one side. The balance of the Company were then dismissed. The squad thus selected, were instructed by the Captain to have their equipments ready to put on at a moments notice during the night, for some secret expedition, the nature of which was not divulged to us. We were then dismissed.

Taps sounded regularly, and we generally turned in, and soon after I heard the sweet strains of a clarionet, which sounded beautifully in the night air, and proved to belong to a string band from the city, serenading the Colonel at Head Quarters. I soon fell asleep under its charming influence.

Saturday July 20th

At five o'clock Reveille sounded and we turned out for roll-call.

The expedition contemplated, did not take place during the night, and for the very good reason that it rained in torrents, and the camp was a sea of mud and water. The wind was blowing fresh, and as overcoats and blankets were pretty wet, we spread them in the wind to dry. It was a dull and stupid morning, and we hung round generally, until "peas on-a-trencher" sounded when we fell in with a yell for breakfast and did unusual justice to our tin

7. Baltimore

dippers of hot coffee. The clouds soon began to disperse, and the sun made its appearance, making a decided change in the aspect of things.

Guard mounting took place at eight o'clock, and at nine the assembly sounded to form the line. After prayer by the Chaplain, the Regiment proceeded to the adjoining field for Battalion drill, the first morning drill of the Regiment, since the plan was adopted of doing guard duty by companies. Some little discussion took place between the Colonel and the Captain in regard to the Zouaves drilling by themselves, as was their custom instead of with the Regiment. There were but six companies on the line, two being on guard, and the two just relieved being excused from duty during the forenoon, leaving out the right flank company, there would be but five left, just two divisions and a half, making an awkward Battalion for drill, so the Company were retained to maneuvre with the other companies of the Regiment. This proved an unlucky thing for us, for after the Regiment were dismissed, we proceeded to our quarters, only to divest ourselves of our jackets, and immediately fell in again, for another hours drill in the manual and load and fire, being dismissed a few minutes only before "roast beef" sounded for dinner.

The afternoon was as hot as usual but the monotony was broken in the company street, by the following incident.

Lieut. Brewster was in the habit of indulging in a snooze on a hammock which he had rigged up under a large tree in the rear of his tent, and often slept there at night. One end of this hammock was fastened to a strip of wood nailed to the tree, and the other to a post set in the ground, supporting the foot by strings. A knot of a dozen got around the Lieut. as he lay asleep and some one conceived the idea of letting him down for a joke. One says "knock off the head strip" "No that might hurt him as he would come down head first." Another whispered "cut the strings." One offered a knife, but somehow the thing didn't work. "Why delay? It'll be a bully joke on the Lieut." Still the intrepid squad hung back. All the while the Lieut. slept on, and his faithful hound, which he had brought with him from Tilghman's lay on the ground under him, with his eyes constantly fastened on the squad, causing more terror than bullets, for the scheme was abandoned, and Brewster was never the wiser for his escape.

At five o'clock we formed company and were drilled for an hour by the Captain, and at six marched on to line with the Regiment for dress parade. At half past seven retreat was beaten, and the band performed on the parade. The moon was now at its full, the evening passed quietly, and tattoo and taps sounded at the regular hour. Soon after taps the squad selected the night before, were again instructed to be ready to fall in quietly when ordered during the night and the Orderly was instructed to call the Captain and muster us at three a.m.

Sunday July 21st

My first thought on waking was that I had been left behind during the night, but on looking round the tent found no one was absent. Each looked at the other when the Orderly broke the silence by saying "I expect Arthur (meaning the Captain) will break my head," for he had slept soundly all night, neglecting to wake the Captain or anybody else. Nothing daunted however he grabbed his roll book, and bouncing out of the tent yelled to the top of his voice "fall in-form company" in his usual inimitable style. As soon as he had finished calling his roll, the Captain yelled "Orderly!" from his tent. The Orderly immediately obeyed the summons, and presented himself before the Captain, whose voice was distinctly audible, and from whose tones we concluded the Orderly was "catching it."

It was an unusually beautiful sabbath morning, the sky was clear and spotless, and there was a lively breeze blowing. At seven "peas-on-a-trencher" sounded for breakfast, and at eight guard-mounting took place. The camp presented the usual appearance of a sunday morning inspection and knots of men were scattered about cleaning their guns and equipments and everybody generally was busy, putting things to rights.

Immediately after guard-mounting, the select squad were called together for the third time (which the proverb says never fails) and we started from camp. It appeared that we were going to a small place called Calverton, about six or eight miles from camp to the westward, in search of concealed weapons, said to be in charge of a secessionist at that place, whose name I did not learn.[23] The journey was a disagreeable one, through stock yards, across creeks, up and down hill, while the sun had got melting hot and the dust was almost suffocating. In a couple of hours we reached our destination, approached the premises in two ranks Sergt. Batchelder being instructed to take charge of one rank, and myself the other, for the purpose of surrounding the place. The lady of the house who was on the piazza manifested some fright at our sudden approach and movements and ran towards us to know what was the matter, but we could answer none of the questions. The circle of sentinels being complete, and instructions having been issued to allow no one to enter or leave the place, the Captain approached the lady and asked for the master of the house. He then with two or three men, myself among the number, commenced a thorough and careful search of the premises, but nothing could be found. We entered the carriage house, and here our efforts were rewarded. Behind a board nailed up between a couple of joists near the door, which Corpl Reynolds readily pryed off with his bayonet, we discovered a couple of brand new U.S. muskets,* with two full setts of equipments. The gentleman was questioned but professed to know nothing about them. This discovery led to renewed efforts. The hay-loft was ransacked, the hay turned over, but nothing further was discovered.[24]

*1 Harpers Ferry 1860, 1 Springfield 1855

During the search we had a good opportunity to examine the surroundings. It was a beautiful place. Fruit and shade trees were abundant, and various attractions existed to make life pleasant here. A dairy was frequently visited by the boys, who got several draughts of cool fresh milk. There were young ladies in the family who conversed freely with the boys, and fresh bread, pears and milk were generally distributed, making altogether a very pleasant time of it. At eleven o clock we took our leave, bringing with us the muskets. No arrests were made. When we reached camp the Regiment were engaged in divine service, and we proceeded at once to dinner.

There was no duty required during the afternoon, and I spent most of the time writing. The camp was very quiet, until the daily crowd of visitors began to pour in, when the boys were again on the qui-vive as usual.

At half past six the assembly sounded for dress parade, after which we were dismissed and fell in for supper. At seven o'clock the band commenced playing on the parade, after which retreat was beaten.

At about eight o'clock, news reached headquarters of the terrible battle of Bull Run, fought during the day. A telegram had been received in Baltimore but a short time before and it was communicated with lightning rapidity, to all the troops in the vicinity, and was the occasion of the wildest excitement we had witnessed at any time during our term of service. Despatches conflicted, but the general news was most excellent, announcing the complete success of the Federal troops. It was the general impression that the War was over. The most wild and vociferous cheering was kept up. The Brooklyn boys perched themselves on the fence surrounding their encampment, cheered, tossed up their hats, which the guard were kept busy picking up for them, and everybody gave themselves up to the wildest manifestations of joy.

At ten o'clock tattoo sounded roll was called, and at taps we turned in with orders to be ready to move at a moments notice.

Monday July 22d.

At the sound of Reveille those who had not already turned out leaped from their tents. After the roll was called everybody was on the qui-vive for a morning paper. The Bull Run battle was every where discussed, and the greatest excitement prevailed. A yell and a rush now proclaimed the arrival of the newsboy, who was nearly trampled under foot by the boys, in their eager desire to procure a paper. I was fortunate to secure a "Clipper," which contained a long account of the "First battle of the War," the substance of which was, that the Union army were victorious everywhere. Masked batteries were captured one after another, and the Rebels driven back in confusion. Peace was predicted and everybody was in the highest spirits, not minding the rain which fell quite fast.

At seven o'clock "peas-on-a-trencher" sounded and we fell in for breakfast, and at eight guard-mounting took place. At nine the line was formed and a most impressive prayer was offered by the Chaplain, in which he alluded to the recent bloody battle and returned thanks for the victory bestowed on our arms. At the close of the morning service we were dismissed. The forenoon passed quietly, most of the boys confined themselves to their tents, discussing the late events.

At half past twelve "roast-beef" sounded, and we fell in for dinner.

During the afternoon no duty was required, and the rain having held up, a number of us engaged in a game of base ball in which the Captain joined. This sport was soon cut short by circumstances which the boys will never forget. News reached the camp, contradicting the previous accounts of the battle, and changing the whole from victory to defeat. Of course no one believed it, but the Colonel soon came down to the Captains tent corroborating the report, and saying it would result in a three years bloody War. The afternoon papers were waited for in anxiety. At four o'clock they came, and the news boy was charged on by the Regiment. The accounts in them were far more deplorable than any thing we had yet heard. Our troops were routed everywhere, and reported fearfully cut up. Many Regiments were reduced to skeletons and badly demoralized. It was reported that Ellsworth's Zouaves went into the fight with eleven hundred men, and came out with two hundred.[25] Our troops were flying in all directions, and came one by one into the hotels in Washington, falling on the floor form shear exhaustion. The whole army was reported to be retreating on Washington, throwing away their arms to precipitate their flight. The road to Centreville was said to be strewn with arms equipments and knapsacks. The account was horrible to read, and the future sickening to contemplate. The term of service of the Regiment, had nearly expired, and the first battle of the War had just been fought, with a disastrous result. The opinion was expressed that we should be ordered to the front immediately. The Fifth Mass. were engaged, but we could learn nothing concerning the Mechanic Light Infantry, or City Guards, both of whom must have been in the fight. In the city considerable trouble and almost a riot, grew out of the latter accounts of the battle, but no damage was done to persons or property, probably on account of the presence of so many troops in the vicinity.

At six o'clock we fell in for supper, after which the time passed in a dull and gloomy manner. During the evening a vote was taken in the several companies, upon the subject of remaining in service fifteen days after our term had expired, should the emergency require it. One company alone voted to remain.[26] At ten o'clock the Capt. returned from a trip into the city bringing the report that the Federal troops were retreating in good order which was the occasion of vociferous cheering through the camp.

7. Baltimore 219

Tattoo now sounded, roll was called, and without waiting for taps most of us turned in, it being still wet and disagreeable.

Tuesday July 23d.
At five o'clock we turned out at the sound of reveille, but for one I should have preferred to lay, the night had been cold, and our blankets and overcoats were none too comfortable. It was more like September than midsummer, with a cool northerly wind blowing as we fell into line. At seven "peas-on-a-trencher" sounded and the hot coffee went to the spot.

Soon after breakfast the new Zouave uniform arrived in camp in charge of the tailors, at whose expense we had a hearty laugh, in consequence of some irregularities in the matter of chevrons. For instance, for the Orderly, he had two chevrons and a lozenge, making a new rank of Orderly Corporal. Some other matters were equally comical, which we noticed of course, being soldiers in regular service. The tailor promised to have them all remedied and the Captain ordered us to put them on at once.[27]

At eight o'clock, guard-mounting took place, and at nine the "assembly" sounded. As we marched on to line, some little surprise was manifested, by the other companies, who seemed in doubt as to who we were. After prayer by the Chaplain, the Regiment proceeded to the adjoining field for Battalion drill, and the Company remained on the ground and were drilled by the Captain in the manual, load and fire lying &c, and the new uniform was pretty well broken in. At half past ten all were dismissed, returned to quarters, and the time passed quietly until dinner.

During the forenoon we were visited by one Ellsworth, brother of the lamented Colonel, who was a member of a Battery encamped near by.[28] A number of the Officers of the 4th Wisconsin, which had just arrived, and were in camp near Mount Clare, also visited our camp.

At half past twelve we fell in for dinner, Ellsworth accompanying us.

Nothing transpired during the afternoon, until four o'clock, when the line was formed, and the Regiment marched into the city. Being indisposed I got excused and remained in camp. A number of visitors came into camp as usual among them a Major Blanchard, who proved to be a native of Salem, and with whom I had a pleasant chat.[29] He belonged to the Fifth Maryland. At six o'clock the Regiment not having returned, I visit-[ed] the Brooklyn Camp, to see the dress parade of the Thirteenth. It was a grand sight, the line numbering nearly twelve hundred men. The hour for the beating of retreat had arrived and still the Regiment did not return. I began to think something was up. At eight o'clock I heard the familiar strains of our band in the distance, and the Regiment soon filed into Camp. They had taken a march to Druid Hill Park, some five miles from the city, and were pretty well tired out. Dress parade was dispensed with and supper was the first thing in order.

The evening was quiet enough, many turned in early but were obliged to turn out again and answer to roll-call at tattoo, or be marked absent.

Wednesday July 24th

Reveille sounded at the usual hour and roll was called. The morning was delightful, cool with a westerly breeze. The boys complained of their feet, and lay about generally until ordered to fall in for breakfast at seven o'clock. At eight guard mounting took place, and at nine the "assembly" sounded and line was formed. After prayer by the Chaplain, the Regiment were drilled in Battalion movements by the Colonel, and the Company proceeded to the shade at the upper end of the camp, and were drilled in Company movements and skirmishing, by the Captain. At half past ten we were dismissed, and the boys sought generally comfort, from the fatigues of yesterday's march, until "roast beef" sounded for dinner. I never knew sore feet to keep our boys from answering the summons to fall in for grub.

During the afternoon another pleasant ceremony took place in our camp, in the presentation to the Regiment of another silk standard, by the loyal citizens of Baltimore. An occasion which proved to us that we had made friends among the citizens, in whose midst we were encamped. All through the afternoon, visitors continued to pour into camp, and at four o'clock the flag itself arrived in charge of the committee entrusted with the presentation. The "assembly" was at once sounded, the line was formed, and the Regiment proceeded to the shade at the upper end of the camp, and formed a hollow square around a temporary stand, which had been erected during the forenoon. The spectators arranged themselves, promiscuously in rear of the Regt. and presently the Brooklyn Thirteenth, to whom an invitation had been extended, marched in, to the music of their splendid drum corps, and formed square in rear of the spectators. They appeared in full ranks, and completely surrounded the whole. The order was given "order arms," "parade rest," and the Colonel took his place on the stand. The handsome standard was then unfurled, and presented to the Colonel, on behalf of the loyal citizens of Baltimore, by Mr. R.R. Lovejoy, in a neat address, full of loyalty to the Union, and friendship to the Regiment.[30]

The Colonel responded in a lengthy and eloquent manner, and the band followed with the "Star Spangled banner" which was loudly applauded.

The ceremonies wound up by a comic song, appropriate to the times, by a Soldier whose name I did not learn, but which made a decided hit, and was the cause of a good deal of laughter and applause.[31]

The Regiment was then dismissed, the crowd dispersed, and the Company, at the request of some of the visitors present, marched into the city, and gave an exhibition drill, on West Fayette St., in front of their residences. This was a fashionable quarter of the city, and we had no sooner arrived, than the crowd which had followed us from camp, and augmented on the way, pressed so close to us that it was impossible to maneuvre at all. Deploying in line however with bayonets fixed we soon cleared the space, and entertained our friends with an hour's drill in the load and fire, manual, skirmishing and bayonet exercise. The windows of the residences were full of ladies, who waved their handkerchiefs frequently, while the crowd on the steps and sidewalks, gave us several rounds of hearty applause. At seven o'clock we stacked arms on the side-walk, and accepted an invitation to tea from the residents, who seemed to vie with each other in their attentions to us. The Company were divided into groups, and distributed among a half dozen residences. The pony squad were entertained at Mr. Lloyds, and a very pleasant evening we had of it. We were dined and wined and entertained with music on the piano, and singing by several young ladies present. Major Brown of the Fourth Wisconsin, a veteran of the Mexican War, with the Adjutant of the same Regiment, were among the Company at Mr. Lloyds.[32] The Major was rising six feet tall, and loomed up far above the pony squad when he stood up. He entertained us with reminiscences of his experience, and though, as he said, he was pretty well "up," he waived all distinctions in presence of our boys, whose drilling he had never seen anything like in all his experience. This occasion will long be remembered by our boys, and was by far the pleasantest evening we had spent since leaving home.

At about half past nine the pleasures were cut short by the Orderly, whose infernal "fall in, form company" rent the air outside.

We fell in at once, gave a rousing "seven" for our friends and marched back to camp.

Tattoo had sounded and at taps all was quiet.

Thursday July 25th

Reveille sounded at five, and we turned out to roll call. The weather of the morning was still delightful, and there was a good breeze blowing. "Peas-on-a-trencher" sounded at seven, and at eight guard mounting took place, but was prolonged on account of some irregularity which I did not learn so that the guard had not left the parade when the "assembly" sounded to form the Regimental line.

The line was formed however without delay, and though the Chaplain was present, the morning prayer was offered by a young man whose name I did not learn. Some new domine probably. The Regiment was then dismissed for Company drills, and we were drilled in the manual and Company movements until eleven o'clock.

During the forenoon, among the visitors I came across a couple of gentlemen, whom we had met at Mr. Lloyds the evening before, one of whom invited the pony squad to spend the evening with him at his residence. I promised him if nothing prevented, the pony squad would certainly accept, and he left us quite pleased.

At half past twelve, "roast beef["] sounded and we fell in for dinner.

The afternoon was hot and sultry and there was no duty required until five o'clock, when the "assembly" sounded and the line was formed for Battalion drill. The Company left camp under the command of the Capt. and we proceeded to the camp of the Fourth Wisconsin, where we drilled for an hour and a half in all the different branches of our drill. This was done at the request of Col. Payne of the Fourth, whose Regiment was entirely unacquainted with Hardee, which was being adopted by the different Regiments as fast as possible after their muster into service. The Colonel had heard of us through Major Brown, who was present with us at Mr. Lloyds, and was desirous of procuring drill masters for his Regiment.[33] After the drill we had a short rest, which was spent in pleasant intercourse with the officers and men of the Wisconsin Regiment.

At half past seven we formed company, and returned to camp, with the band of the Wisconsin Regiment, which the Colonel kindly tendered us. We at once marched to supper with sharpened appetites, and the evening which was delightfully pleasant passed without anything worthy of note. Our trip to the Wisconsin camp, interfered with the pony squads invitation, and we probably lost a good time.

Tattoo and taps sounded at the usual hour.

Monument Square, Baltimore, *Frank Leslie's Illustrated Newspaper*, July 13, 1861.

7. Baltimore

Friday July 26th.

Reveille sounded at five o'clock, and roll was called.

The weather continued to be pleasant and cool in the morning, but grew hot and sultry as the day advanced, varying but little in this respect from day to day.

Soon after breakfast, which took place at the usual hour, I was notified that I had been detailed, in company with Sergt. Gray, Sergt. Batchelder, Corporal Evans, and Private Hill, for duty as drill masters to the Fourth Wisconsin Reg't. and we repaired at once to the Wisconsin camp for this duty. We were cordially received by both Officers and men, who were anxious to become acquainted with the new drill as soon as possible. Their line was formed at once, & divided into subdivisions, to each of which a drill master was assigned. Under instructions from the Captain, we drilled in the old Scott manual, for what reason I knew not, unless it was to ascertain if the Wisconsin men were acquainted at all with the use of the musket. We found them well versed in Scott, and had reason to expect good progress in taking up Hardee. At half past ten ranks were broken, and after a pleasant chat with the Officers, Sergt. Batchelder, Hill and myself, rode into the city, went to Barnum's Hotel in Battle monument square, had a bath which was a luxury indeed, and read the papers. Our uniforms attracted a good deal of attention, and we met with a good many frowns from Secessionists, a number of whom could always be found at this house.[34]

While here we had a good opportunity to examine the monument in the square erected at a cost of sixty thousand dollars in 1815, in memory of those who fell at the battle of North Point, and at the bombardment of Fort McHenry. And as this journal is kept for my own reference in future, I give a full description of it as a work of art, interesting to myself, from an account by another writer:

"The monument is of pure white marble, and rests upon a square plinth or terrace, of the same material, forty feet square and four feet high, at each angle of which is placed erect, a brass cannon, having a ball apparently issuing from its mouth. Between the cannon and along the verge of the platform, extends a railing of brass-headed spears, the beauty and effect of which, are much heightened, by the disposal at equal distances, of eight fasces, forming a part of, and supporting the railing. These fasces, are composed of corresponding spears, bound with iron fillets. The whole protected by massive chains in festoons, suspended from posts of granite, enclosing a walk of four or five feet on every front."

"From the platform rises a square Egyptian basement, entirely rusticated to indicate strength. It is composed of eighteen layers of stone, to signify the number of States, which formed the Republic, at the period of the event which the monument commemorates. It is surmounted by a cornice, each of the four angles of which is surmounted by a griffin with an eagle's head, as an emblem of the eagle of the Union. A winged globe adorns each centre of the Egyptian cornice, symbolical of eternity and the flight of time. On each of the four fronts of the basement, is a false door, in the antique style, closed with a single tablet of black marble, imparting the character of a cenotaph, with the remains of the dead deposited therein. Three steps to ascend to these doors, are intended to indicate the three years of the War."

"The column which surmounts the cenotaph, represents a high fasces (symbolical of the Union) the rods of which are bound by a fillet, with the names of the honored dead inscribed thereon in letters of bronze. Around the top of this fasces are bound a wreath of laurel, and a wreath of cypress, the first expressive of glory, the other sepulchral and mourning. Between these wreaths in letters of bronze, are inscribed the names of the officers who perished at the shrine of glory." Three in number.

"The names of the non commissioned officers and privates, are inscribed on the fillet binding the fasces." Thirty-six in number.

"The lower part of the fasces is ornamented with two basso relievos, the one on the south front representing the battle of North Point and the death of General Ross, the other on the north front representing a battery of Fort McHenry at the time of the bombardment. On the east and west fronts are lachrymal urns, emblematical of regret and sorrow. On the south part of the square base is this inscription in letters of bronze.

"Battle of North Point 12th September A.D., 1814 And the independence of the United States the thirty-ninth."

"On the north front, beneath the basso relievo on that side, is the following inscription, also in letters of bronze." "Bombardment of Fort McHenry 13th September A.D., 1814 And of the independence of the United States the thirty-ninth."

"The basement and fasces, form together a column thirty nine feet in height, to show that it was founded in the thirty-ninth year of the independence of the United states."

"The colossal, but exqui[si]tely beautiful statue, which surmounts the fasces, is a female figure, representing the city of Baltimore. Upon the head is a mural crown emblematic of cities. In one hand she holds an antique rudder symbolic of navigation, and in the other she raises a crown of laurel, as with a graceful inclination of the head, she looks towards the theatre of the conflict. At her feet on the right is an eagle, and near it a bombshell, commemorative of the bombardment."

"The height of the monument including the statue is fifty two feet, two inches."

"The monument, in its conception and execution, is worthy of the event it is designed to commemorate, and a gratifying evidence of the rapid advancement of the arts in this country."[35]

After sufficiently admiring this work of art, we went into the Gilmore house, of more Union sentiment, and took dinner. At about two o'clock we returned to our own camp. Nothing more than the ordinary routine had transpired, principally camp calls, on account of the heat.

At four o'clock the "assembly" sounded, the line was formed, and the Regiment with the band marched to Mont Clare, to greet the 12th Mass. Reg't. Colonel Fletcher Webster, which was expected to pass through on its way to Washington. After waiting an hour or more, the Captain gave orders for the drill masters to proceed to their duties in the Wisconsin camp, which we obeyed at once. Their companies were formed on our arrival and we drilled for a couple of hours in Hardee, then remained to witness their dress parade. We took tea with the Wisconsin Officers returning to our own camp at about nine o'clock.

The Regiment saluted the Twelfth as they passed through then marched back to camp.

Tattoo and taps sounded at the regular hour.

Saturday July 27th.

Reveille sounded at the usual hour, and after roll call I proceeded with the rest of the drill masters, to attend to our duties in the Wisconsin camp. My narrative is now liable to be of a more personal nature, since I was away from the Regiment each day. On arriving at the Wisconsin camp, the companies were already formed, and we went to work at once. In my company I took up the load and fire, drilling by the numbers. It was necessary to do this but little, for the Wisconsin boys, (or rather men, for most of them were six-footers) were apt scholars, and made rapid progress in the drill.

At seven o'clock we broke ranks and went to breakfast, the drill masters being entertained at the Officers mess. I speak of this, because being enlisted men, it was an unusual thing to be so honored, the Regulations being explicit in the matter of the relations of Officers to enlisted men. This mess, was a large and sociable one, consisting of the Field Staff and Line officers of the Regiment. The cooks and waiters were wives of men in the Regiment, and the Caterer well understood his business. It was a happy, genial, home-like circle, and we enjoyed it much.

At nine o'clock we reformed the companies, and drilled for another hour, after which we returned to our own camp.

At noon I dined with the Wisconsin Regiment, having become a frequent visitor.

The afternoon was perhaps more interesting to myself, than to any other reader of these jottings. I called on some lady friends in the city and had a pleasant time. While here a little circumstance transpired, in the pinning of a rosette on the breast of my uniform jacket. I note it here for this reason. It was quite a common custom among ladies of Baltimore, if they can be so called, to manifest their sympathies with Secession and the South, by wearing upon their persons, as adornment, pins, girdles and other flagrant ornaments, representing the insignia of Rebellion, and as an offset, ladies of Union sentiments decorated themselves with roseattes and other ornaments, displaying the red white and blue. Many a soldier in the various Regiments encamped within the city limits, wore upon his breast, one of these roseattes, placed there by the fair hand of some lady friend. It was indeed sport to watch the countenances of fair secession sympathizers as they encountered these evidences of female loyalty on the soldiers uniform. Some of them would indignantly cross the street, rather than meet them.

At five o'clock I took leave of my lady friends, with an invitation to dine with them next day, and returned to the Wisconsin camp and took supper. An hours drill followed, and after witnessing their dress parade, the drill masters returned to their own camp.

Nothing of interest transpired in our own Regiment during the day. The usual daily routine took place, and the camp calls were beaten at the appointed hour. The Company had their usual dose at drill, witnessed with satisfaction by the usual crowd of visitors, whom the band also entertained after retreat on the parade.

At ten o'clock tattoo sounded taps following in regular order.

Sunday July 28th.

Reveille sounded at five o'clock, and after roll call, the drill masters started for the Wisconsin camp. An hour was spent in drill, after which we broke ranks for breakfast and the next hour was spent in a social manner in the large mess tent. At eight o'clock the drilling was resumed. It is fair to record of the Fourth Wisconsin Regiment, that they took hold of the drill with wonderful zeal, and during the few days we had been at work with them wonderful progress was made. Officers and men were alike interested, and our duty with them was made pleasant and agreeable. At about ten o'clock we broke ranks and the next half hour I spent with the Officers of Company "I" which was the Company I had been drilling. Much regret was expressed by them, at the prospect of losing so soon, as they inevitably must, the services of the drill masters from our company. Those who were fortunate enough to be detailed in this capacity, will remember their intercourse with the Wisconsin Regiment, as one of the brightest spots in their term of service.

In our own Regiment, the usual Sunday morning inspection took place, and divine service was held.

At about twelve o'clock, having previously procured a pass, I rode into the city with Private Fred Smith, to dine with our lady friends by appointment the previous day. We spent several hours very agreeably in their society, bidding them when we left a lasting farewell, not expecting another opportunity to visit them, as our term of service was rapidly drawing to a close. The afternoon was exceedingly hot, and we returned to camp, to find no duty required.

The boys could think or talk of nothing but returning home. A rumor spread through the camp that orders had already been received. During the day the Third and Fourth New York Vols. arrived in the city, the latter taking up their quarters on the ground at the upper end of our camp, evidently to relieve us.

The Brooklyn Thirteenth were already in receipt of marching orders, and it was a lively time with them. I called over to shake the hands of my friends once more, but should hardly have recognized their quarters. All traces of their familiar camp had disappeared, and all was dire confusion. The tents were struck, disclosing the naked features of Rullman's Bellevue Gardens once more, though in place of once beautiful green swards, were the regular patches, each surrounded by a trench, showing where the tents had stood, rusty and thread-bare. Straw, boxes, barrels, sutler's cans, old paper, covered the ground, in marked contrast to the well policed quarters of the Regiment. Amid all the confusion and rubbish, the Brooklyn boys were flying about with merry faces and light hearts. At about half past five I took leave of my friends, and resorted to the Wisconsin camp[,] the companies were soon formed and we commenced drilling.

For an hour previous heavy clouds had begun to appear, and we had scarcely commenced drilling, when rain began to fall, increasing to a heavy shower, cutting short the drill, and causing us to retreat double quick under cover.

As soon as it held up we returned to our camp. The evening passed quietly, the boys confining themselves to the tents on account of the wet.

Tattoo and taps sounded at the regular hour. The night was cold, and at times rain fell.

8

The Return Home

Monday July 29th.

At five o'clock Reveille sounded, and the companies fell into line for roll call. The weather was clear, and the rain during the night had laid the dust without making it muddy. The drill masters duties in the Wisconsin camp were ended, and the general theme of conversation was our return home to be mustered out, orders for which were momentarily expected. The boys chatted merrily over the prospects until "peas-on-a-trencher" sounded for breakfast.

At eight o'clock, guard-mounting took place, after which no further duty was required until the afternoon.

At about ten o'clock our attention was attracted towards an immense concourse of people, pouring out of the Brooklyn camp, and soon after the gallant Thirteenth, filed out of their quarters for the last time, fully equipped and formed line in the street to await orders. They were indeed a fine looking body of men, as they stood there in full marching order. Every man was present with his entire luggage, numbering in all fourteen hundred men — the largest Regiment we had met any where in the service. They were in high spirits—every eye beamed with delight, and every countenance was lighted with a joyous expression, at the thoughts of returning home. In half an hours time they wheeled into column by companies, filling the street from curb to curb, and started up West Baltimore St on their homeward march, their full drum corps beating with a vigor drawn from the surrounding enthusiasm. The start was the signal for tremendous cheering by our Regiment, who had assembled to see them off, the crowd of civilians joining, and the ladies waving their handkerchiefs all seeming to delight in giving the Brooklyn boys a good send off. We watched them out of sight and returned to quarters afterward with hopes that we might soon follow them.

8. The Return Home

At half past twelve "roast beef" sounded, and we fell in for dinner.

During the afternoon the Sixth arrived in Baltimore, en route to Massachusetts, and a little later orders reached the Colonel of our own Regiment for the same purpose. This news spread like lightning through the camp and was received with loud and continued cheering, and now commenced a lively time with us. Many hasty visits were made to friends in the city, who in turn came into camp to bid us farewell. The Regiment had made many friends among the citizens of Baltimore, and had acquired a good reputation during their encampment within the city limits. The good opinion of the citizens, was manifested in many ways toward the Regiment, and its individual members, of which the recent flag presentation was a good illustration. Company "F"—the Lynn City Guards, were also presented with a handsome silk standard, by the "Native Americans" of Baltimore, a circumstance I have neglected to record before. Our own Company had also much to boast of, in the way of attentions and favors from the citizens, and our Officers made many and warm friends. These things made our stay in Baltimore, immeasurably pleasant, and proved to us that we were quite mistaken in the reception we should receive, when we moved our camp from the Relay House to its present location. All this was now to end. The necessary reduction of baggage and packing up, occupied the rest of the afternoon. At four o'clock the tents were struck, and the camp of the Eighth Massachusetts was no more. Some difficulty was encountered in getting transportation, which we finally had to hire, to get our camp equipage to the depot.[1]

At the usual hour we fell in for supper, and our last meal in camp. Retreat was beaten at half past seven, and the band favored us with spirited and appropriate airs.

The teams did not arrive until late at night, and while waiting for them, we collected all the rubbish from the Cook house and Commissary together with our camp furniture, manufactured from barrels boxes and the like, into one hugh [?] pile, and set fire to them. The fire loomed up in the darkness, and might have caused an alarm, but nobody would have cared if it did, for everybody was elated. This was a good thing so far as personal comfort was concerned, for the night air was cool, and we were quite chilly standing round waiting for orders.

At about ten o'clock the teams arrived, and details were at once made to load them. At midnight the assembly sounded, the line was formed in full marching order, and we left our camp for the last time. The city was buried in slumber and our departure was hardly known, though our band and drum corps, thundered louder than ever. Some friends of the Captain's were waiting with lighted parlors, and saluted us as we passed their residence.

Arriving at the Philadelphia Wilmington and Baltimore depot we made a short halt only while the train was making up. We soon filed aboard, threw off our luggage, and were soon curled up on the seats, snoring in the arms of morpheus.

Tuesday July 30th

We slept soundly, for the day had been a fatiguing one, and it was late in the morning before many of the boys were awake. When I opened my eyes we were some miles from Baltimore, which we did not leave until daylight, the small hours having been occupied in getting the horses and baggage aboard with other delays, the nature of which I did not learn.

The weather was exceedingly fine, and many rode outside on the platforms and tops of the cars. The train was heavily loaded and proceeded very slow, frequently coming to a full stop. Upon either side of the railroad through Delaware and Maryland, blackberries grew in profusion, and as they were mostly dead ripe, many of us took advantage of these stoppages, to get off and feast on them. The snails pace at which we journeyed along, finally grew tedious, and Private Ross introduced a diversion, bringing forth his untrained animals of Ross' Menagerie, and afforded much amusement by his boisterous and humorous descriptions, of their peculiarities. His animals were no other than the platoon of recruits, who not being up to the standard of the drilled members, he had distinguished by the comical title of untrained animals.

As we passed through the various towns and villages on the route, we were greeted with smiling faces, cheers and the waving of handkerchiefs. At Burlington New Jersey, which we reached at sunset the train stopped for a half hour or more, at a point of the road, running lengthwise of the street, with residences the entire length; and while here we received many attentions from the people living therein. Ladies flocked towards the train, waving their handkerchiefs, and the boys engaged them in lively conversation from the windows, many showing their gallantry by disembarking altogether. Hot coffee and other refreshments were freely distributed along the train by these patriotic citizens, which were very welcome, for we had subsisted during the day, chiefly on the rations issued to us before leaving camp. We left Burlington and its ladies, with boisterous cheers, which were acknowledged by the waving of a hundred handkerchiefs, and journeyed slowly towards New York. Darkness soon overtook us, and one after another curled themselves up on the seats. It was however difficult to sleep, for the ever comical Private Ross, and some others, kept the boys astir and often in a roar, with his yell of "New York"! precisely as he did when we left Boston on the memorable Eighteenth of April.

At midnight we were aroused by the order to fall in with "knapsacks, haversacks and canteens," and peering out into the darkness I found we had reached Jersey City. We disembarked from the train, spread our blankets on the floor of the station, and passed the balance of the night. Orders were issued for no one to leave the station, but the proximity to New York was too much for some of the more restless, and the usual stragglers, found their way out, to whom sleep was of little consequence under the circumstances.

Wednesday July 31st.

At an early hour, one by one we turned out, and squads proceeded in various directions in search of breakfast. Long before anything could be got in readiness the hotels and saloons of Jersey City were thronged with the boys of the Regiment, who could not wait for the regular Commissary accommodations.

At about seven o'clock the "assembly" sounded, and as soon as the Regiment could be got together, which was accomplished with some difficulty, we filed aboard the ferry-boat and were soon, once more in the bustling city of New York. At the landing foot of Courtland St. we were met by a Committee of the "Sons of Massachusetts," and by them escorted to the Park Barracks, where we stacked arms, and were furnished with a substantial breakfast, the officers being entertained at the same time at the Astor.[2]

Orders were issued for no one to leave the Park, and there was little or no desire manifested to disobey them, for the arrival of the Regiment was heralded over the city, the mention of the Eighth Mass. and Salem Zouaves, being sufficient to draw an immense concourse of people to our temporary quarters, giving us abundant enjoyment in the search of friends among them, in which we were more than successful.

At about nine o'clock our attention was attracted by music coming down Broadway, which we soon learned to be the New York Seventh, who had turned out to escort us through the city. They marched into the Park, formed line, stacked arms and were dismissed for a short time, to indulge in a fraternal intercourse with our Regiment. The utmost good feeling existed between the two Regiments, growing out of their service together at Annapolis, and every member of one Regiment seemed to be personally acquainted with every member of the other. Thus a couple of hours passed in the pleasantest possible manner.[3]

At about eleven o'clock the respective "assemblies" sounded, and the members of both Regiments fell quickly into line. Soon after eleven the column left the Park, the escort consisting of the "Sons of Massachusetts," Seventh New York, Col. Marshall Lefferts, and the First Chasseurs, Lieut. Col. Alexander Shaler, the whole escorted by a detachment of the Metropolitan police.[4] The windows and balconies of Broadway were crammed with people, and crowds lined the sidewalks and tops of the buildings. The march up Broadway was a perfect and continuous ovation, and we were greeted with the clapping of hands, the waving of handkerchiefs, and other demonstrations of enthusiasm. Arriving at Madison Square the column halted for a couple of hours, during which time we partook of refreshments at the Fifth Avenue, and wandered about in the crowd meeting friends and acquaintances at every turn.

At about three o'clock the "assembly" sounded and the entire column were soon under arms again. We passed down Twenty-third street, and marched directly aboard one of the Fall River boats which was awaiting us at the pier, the escort being drawn up in line on either side at present arms, as we marched through, on to the pier. On board the boat we divested ourselves of our luggage, and collected on the side nearest the pier to salute our escort who had so kindly honored us, and cheer after cheer from them rent the air in return. At about five o'clock the boat steamed slowly out into the river, which was the signal for a final interchange of cheering, soon after which the escort formed and we watched them until they were out of sight.

The sail down the Hudson, rounding the Battery and up the East River through Hell-gate into the Sound, is always delightful, particularly so was it to us on this occasion, for every turn of the wheels of our boat, brought us so much nearer home. We coursed along at moderate speed, leaving New York enveloped in the twilight, and chatting merrily over the subject of our arrival until darkness overtook us, when we spread our blankets and turned in.

Thursday Aug. 1st

At daylight we were routed by the Orderly, and immediately went aboard the cars at Fall River, and were soon on the road to Boston in the highest spirits. At ten o'clock we arrived at the Old Colony Depot, where the Boston Tigers and New England Guards with Gilmore's Band, were drawn up in line to receive us.[5] It was the work of but a short time to alight from the cars and take our place in the column. No sooner was this done than we were completely overwhelmed by crowds of friends, who shook us so violently, as to almost divest us of our luggage, causing a regular clattering of the tin ware, which we carried slung to our knapsacks, creating a good deal of attraction and amusement.[6] At about half past ten we took up our line of march through South, Summer, and a number of the principal streets to the Parade ground on the Common, where after a short rest, we partook of a bountiful collation which was spread for us on long tables, under the trees on the mall. The inner man having been refreshed, we re-formed, and were marched in review, the "Tigers" and New England Guards performing guard duty. The hill adjoining the parade ground was covered with people, who frequently applauded our movements. Gov. Andrew was not present on account of ill health but sent the following letter to Col. Hinks:

Commonwealth of Massachusetts
Executive Department
Boston, Aug. 1, 1861

To Col. Hinks, Commander
of the Eighth Mass. Vol. Militia
Colonel: —

    I regret exceedingly that the condition of my health prohibits me absolutely from meeting you and your gallant Regiment personally to-day, and expressing to you and them, my congratulations upon their return after a period of such efficient service. I can only beg you in my behalf to express how highly I appreciate their invariable good conduct, their varied capacity, and the honor they have done to the Commonwealth."

    "I look to the return of such of them as may again proceed to the field for a longer term of service, as one of the surest means of promoting the efficiency of our volunteer regiments, and of maintaining the military reputation of Massachusetts, which they have already done so much to establish.

    I am faithfully and sincerely yours
John A. Andrew

Immediately after the review the Regiment were drilled for a short time in Battalion movements the principal feature of which, was the formation of squares in double quick time, which was done with such rapidity and correctness, as to draw forth loud applause. The Company were also drilled in all the different branches of Company movements, the skirmish drill and bayonet exercise eliciting loud manifestations of approval. At the close of the drill, hollow square was formed once more, and we were formally mustered out of service by the following order:

"Head Quarters Boston Aug 1, 1861
Special Order
No. 381

The Eighth Regiment of Massachusetts Volunteer Militia, Col. Hinks, after three months of active service has returned to Massachusetts. Instantaneously it responded to the call of the Commander-in-Chief to proceed South to protect the Government from threatened attack."

"It represents the extreme sections of the Commonwealth — the sea shore and the mountains — Berkshire and Essex. Its service ever will be regarded with proud satisfaction, and will add lustre to the history of the State.

"The Regiment is now dismissed until further orders.

By Command of his Excellency
John A. Andrew
Governor and Comdr-in-chief
William Schouler
Adjutant General."[7]

The Colonel then delivered an affecting farewell address, and after taking leave of the old Eighth he concluded by addressing the two flank companies which had been assigned to it. Our own from the old Seventh, and the Allen Guards of the old First Battalion. Turning to Capt. Devereux he said:

"But I have yet a duty to perform. Company "J" our right flanking company, has now been mustered from the service of the United States. I know, and you know, that if we had gone into the field of battle, they would have done all their duty. They were worthy to be the right hand company of the old Eighth; were they not? (Cheers and cries of–"that they were.") Captain Devereux there is my hand – it is the hand of a truly fraternal fellowship. Let me convey to you, Sir, and your command, our united assurances that we respect your characters and attainments, your moral strength as we do your physical bravery. You have been mustered out of the United States service, and I dismiss you with all the honor and reputation my voice can confer upon you. God bless you all!"

Here the company gave a rousing cheer, a "seven" and a "Hacker" for the Colonel, who after acknowledging it, turned to Capt Richardson of the left flank company and resumed thus:

"There is yet another command, which I must in justice specially notice. That is the left flanking company, which joined us after we arrived at the Capital. To Captain Richardson and his noble and brave command, I would convey my personal thanks for the strict propriety of conduct which has always characterized them; and also the thanks of the Regiment, every man of whom will bear testimony that the company has never been delinquent in anything. You have been mustered out of the service, and I dismiss you Captain Richardson, and your command, with the assurance that you have nobly earned the character of soldiers, and with the wish that Heaven may bless you all." He then shook Capt. Richardson warmly by the hand, and the Regiment gave several hearty cheers, in which the spectators joined.

Some instructions were then given to the Officers of the different companies, relative to the final muster for pay, after which the Company took leave of the Regiment and proceeded to the Eastern depot, leaving for Salem, at exactly three o'clock. Many friends had come to Boston to meet us, and the train was crowded with curious spectators and anxious relatives. The train stopped at the foot of Hancock St. at about quarter of four, and with beating hearts we alighted from the train. We were once more in dear old Salem, and as our feet pressed her soil, the ringing of bells and the firing of cannon foretold the reception that was in store for us. Hancock street was crowded with people, but the masses that thronged Lafayette street, as far as the eye could reach, gave evidence that our return had been awaited by a whole city.

The company was hastily formed, and preceded by the Manchester

Cornet Band which we had brought with us, we moved up Hancock to La Fayette where the Home Guard, Genl. Geo. H. Devereux, father of the Captain, and the Zouave Drill Club, Capt. Isaiah Woodbury, were drawn up in line to receive us.[8] We took our places in the line at once, and without delay the column started down La Fayette St. marching through Central, Essex, Pleasant, Brown, Church, Washington, Essex, and Central streets to the armory.

Dense crowds lined the streets, salutations were exchanged, and boquets were thrown among the boys from fair hands, at various points along the route. In front of the residence of Eleazer Austin Esq. father of the Lieutenant, a large number of lady friends of the boys were gathered with bouquets, which were thrown in a shower among us as we appeared. On the arrival at the armory the congratulations were hearty, and a more joyful gathering is seldom seen.

We were in old Phoenix Hall again. What hours of toil, with closed doors, we had spent in that familiar room, the previous winter, little dreaming of the grand achievements, we were to accomplish, and which were now to us a living reality. A flood of recollections crowded upon us, but were as [s]peedily made to give way, to the more engrossing scenes of the present. As soon as the first paroxysms of joy, at meeting friends, relatives and dear ones was over, the Captain's voice rang through the hall in that peculiar command "Attention!" carrying us back, to the same familiar echo, in that same place, four months previous, and sounding more natural than ever. Silence at once reigned. We were instructed to appear at the armory at ten o'clock the next forenoon in full uniform, with "knapsacks, haversacks and canteens" to participate in the formal reception, for which great preparations had been made, the programme of which was also announced. We were then dismissed, and with a "seven" for Capt Devereux our officers, our friends and ourselves, we left the armory one by one, to be snatched by warm hearted friends, and wended our way, to the dear old homes.

Friday Aug. 2d.

It was a most beautiful morning the sun arose in all its splendor, and it was generally remarked that it was real Infantry weather, not too warm, thus rendering more complete the prospects of a thorough enjoyment of the festive programme of the day. For we expected to be shown off and there was without doubt a march before us, with a "zouave drill" after it.

The company began to assemble at the appointed hour of ten o'clock, and every man was present. At eleven the escort, consisting of the past members of the Salem Light Infantry, under command of S. Endicott Peabody, and the Zouave Drill Club, under Capt. Isaiah Woodbury, with Gilmore's Band, left the armory, under a salute from Capt. Manning's Battery of

Artillery, and the ringing of bells, escorting the Company with the Manchester Cornet Band, through Lafayette, Central, Essex, St. Peter, Church and Washington streets to the City Hall, where the Mayor, and other invited guests were formally received, and assigned a place in the line.[9] The march was then resumed, the Company marching at "route step" through Essex, Summer, Chestnut, Third, Warren, Pine, Essex, Boston, Federal, Munroe, Essex, Pleasant Brown and Newbury streets to Washington Square, more familiarly known as the Common, where we were greeted by another salute from the Battery. After a short rest, a hollow square was formed, the Company in the centre, and Genl. Devereux stepping to the front, welcomed the return of the boys, in a most admirable and impressive speech, betraying some emotion on his own part, and causing the eyes of many to moisten. I regret very much that I cannot give a verbatim copy of it in these records. The General concluded by introducing the Mayor of the city, Hon. Stephen P. Webb, a past member of the Corps.

Mayor Webb, spoke as follows:

"Mr. Commander of the Old Guard:"

Being here among friends, I am going to make to you, a frank and honest confession. I was asked by you, Sir, to say a few words of welcome in behalf of the City, to these our young friends, of whom we are so proud, and so fond on the joyous occasion, of their return from service in the field. But really after what has been so eloquently and touchingly said by you, I find myself very much in the condition of the Sergeant of Light Artillery in Captain Braggs Battery, in one of the battles of Mexico. A great General, then of the United States, now of the Confederate Army, whose head is as soft as his name, Genl. Pillow, rode up in the midst of the engagement, exclaiming at the top of his voice, "The crisis has come Captain Bragg, for God's sake open fire." Whereupon Captain Bragg instantly gave the word "Fire!" The Sergeant in utter amazement said "What shall I fire at, Captain Bragg there is nothing in front." "I don't know" said Bragg, "the General says the crisis has come, fire at the crisis."[10] Now, Sir, my crisis has come, you have left nothing before me, and now tell me to fire away (Laughter). But it shall never be said that an old Guard, couldn't find a kind word to utter in behalf of the city, to the gallant, dashing, renowned young Light Infantry men, late of Baltimore, now of Salem. Mr. Commander, Officers and Men of the Salem Light Infantry: It has been considered proper that I should in behalf of the City, extend to you a sincere and hearty welcome home. We devoutly thank God, my young friends, that having taken up arms so promptly at your country's call, in her hour of sore distress and peril, having so zealously and energetically met every requirement of duty, whether by sea or land, and having gloriously illustrated the name of Massachusetts Volunteer by a discipline and perfection of drill, usually expected only of members of a standing army, He has in His good Providence, returned you to us in safety and high health.[11]

"It has seldom, indeed, that so joyful and proud an occasion is so entirely free from any reflection which could by possibility lessen its triumph, or mar its pleasure. No shot or shell has torn your ranks. No skulking traitor has foully done to death, an unsuspicious sentry of yours. No disease or accident has thinned your numbers, or reduced your strength. You are returned to us, with no word of disgrace, or stain of dishonor, more to be mourned by friends than death itself, adhering to your name or fame. But here to day, in presence of your admiring fellow citizens, you stand proudly conscious that your record is fair, that you have the full approval of your own consciences, the hearty testimony to your gallant conduct, and valuable services, of the Officers under whom you have served, and the crowning glory of a vote of thanks by the Congress of the United States, for eminent service, to your and the other Companies composing the gallant Eighth Regiment of Massachusetts Volunteers."

"What more now could you ask, that ear and eye supply? For you, to day, the streets of your native city are crowded with rejoicing people. Their shouts ring through the air. For you from every tower, blithe bells are pealing forth, their merry tones. In your honor, peacefully bellow the brazen dogs of War. From neighboring towns and hamlets flow the jocund thousands intent to hail you, with kind impetuosity, your march impeding."

"Honor has justly crowned desert, and relatives and friends, the City and the citizens, have joined to give you emphasis, to the cry of Welcome! Welcome home!"

"After the address of the Mayor, Captain Devereux of the Zouaves in a most modest, sensible and attractive speech, related a few of the experiences and services of the Company, on the route to Washington. He disclaimed for himself and his men any credit other than that of having endeavored to discharge their duty faithfully when suddenly called into active service, not for the acquisition of fame, though if fame had followed anything which they had done he was glad of it, but simply because the necessities of the country demanded, as he thought, the services of every man. In alluding to the probability of his not appearing again at the head of his company, he made a very affecting allusion to their readiness on all occasions, to their subordination and gentlemanly character and deportment. The speech was all that it should be, and gave the greatest satisfaction to the friends of the company, and the great number of the citizens present.

"At its close, Capt. Devereux and his Company were most enthusiastically cheered. The escort and Zouaves then broke ranks, and partook with their numerous friends of a bountiful collation in their tents, and a couple of hours were passed in pleasant intercourse. At three o'clock the Zouaves mustered, and in presence of an immense concourse of spectators, were for several hours submitted to a drill of wonderful exactness and beauty, which constantly elicited the warmest applause, manifested by a general clapping of hands and expressions of delight. The city may well be proud of such a splendid exhibition of the soldiership of her young men."[12]

"After a fine dress parade, the three companies took up their line of march through the principal streets to the armory of the Salem Light Infantry (and by the by, we hope the old name endeared by so many tender ties and pleasant memories may never be given up)."

Here we were instructed by the Captain to meet at the same place at one o'clock the next day, after which we were dismissed to make preparations for the evening.

The festivities of the day closed by a levee in old Hamilton Hall, so dear to the minds of the old Infantry, and the place of all others, for such a gathering as the day called forth.

One after another the boys in company with their parents, and fair lady friends, began to assemble, and the hall was soon filled with an immense crowd of smiling faces of both sexes.

The hall was tastefully decorated with patriotic emblems and mottoes, among them an eagle bearing the words, "my wings have been over you," and a large motto at the east end of the hall, "welcome to our boys," while the sides of the room bore the names, "Perryville," "Annapolis," "Washington," "Constitution," "Relay House" "Baltimore" "Salem."

Among the assemblage of invited guests were Adjutant General Schouler, Col. Hinks, Officers of the Charlestown City Guards, and many others; also among the civilians, the Rev. Mr. Leeds of Philadelphia, formerly rector of St. Peters Church, in this city.[13] I looked for our friend the Rev. Mr. Wildes of Grace Church but on inquiry learned that he was absent from the city.

The music was furnished by Wyatt and Parsons Quadrille Band, and dancing was kept up until a late hour. It was a most brilliant assemblage, the toilettes of the ladies were superb and attractive, and the whole affair, both day and evening was a grand success, with nothing to mar its complete enjoyment, doing credit to our past members, and lasting honor to the boys, who will never forget it.[14]

Saturday Aug. 3d.

The day was spent generally in quiet, naturally, from the fatigues of the formal reception, and its surfeit of enjoyment, being the first real release from the excitement attending our return, and the first opportunity to enjoy the social intercourse of family and friends.

The only circumstance which calls for an entry in these records, being that the company met at the armory at one o'clock, where we were paid off, and the last obligation of the Government so far as the company was concerned was thereby fulfilled.[15]

On the Sunday following the Company attended divine service at Grace Church (Episcopal) by invitation of our friend the Rector, Mr. Wildes, which was the last time the Salem Zouaves appeared in uniform.

As I close these records, what a flood of recollections crowd upon my mind. Some months before, a couple of dozen boys, having the interest of the S.L.I. at heart, started out upon a new plan of action. We bound ourselves by the strictest code of bye-laws, drilled for months with closed doors, two evenings a week from seven o'clock until eleven, with crackers and coffee at ten, in old Phoenix Hall. What glorious times they were? We run our own machine, pledging ourselves never to run in debt. For this purpose we gave private theatricals, building our own stage, painting our own scenery, furnishing our own actors. We were more than successful. Events followed rapidly. Ellsworths famous Zouaves came to Salem, and we received them, yes, drilled with them, our "load and fire by file" being pronounced superior, by Ellsworth himself. We gave an exhibition drill before the Governor at Mechanic Hall, astonishing his Excellency with our movements. War came upon our happy country we volunteered, at once, were accepted, and now came the test, and crowning glory, of those hours, weeks and months of hard continuous drill, when our knees ached at "guard," our elbows at the "perries" and "thrusts," and our whole bodies reeked with perspiration. Now we were off for the seat of War, head and shoulders in advance of Militia or Regulars in Hardee's tactics, triumphant in ourselves, "the observed of all observers." Three great cities, New York, Philadelphia and Baltimore, lay their tributes of praise at our feet, individuals and organizations alike doing us honor.

The Government too discovered merit in us, and our boys were elevated to the rank of instructors for new Regiments arriving in service, while humbly serving as Privates themselves. What an experience for young men of twenty, fresh from homes and the walks of civil life! The three and one half months of service, imperfectly narrated in these records, was a marked event in their lives.

The continuous ovation attending our departure, passage through "New York!" and arrival at Philadelphia. Our quarters at the Girard and midnight alarm. "Double-quick forward" on the Rail Road track and seizure of the steamer Maryland. Capture of the Frigate Constitution, and the trip on her to New York, in the varied capacity of Soldiers and Sailors combined.

The "rest" at the Astor, will any of us, ever forget that week, notably that banquet at Mr. Wards, and the route-step-tangle-foot return march to the Astor. Passage on the steamer Roanoke, court-martial of "Du-dah" on board, and the terrific grandeur of a thunder storm at — sea." The trip up the Potomac river, being the last vessel to reach Washington, the Company being ordered below, to keep out of sight of the Rebels. Our quarters at the Capitol—"all marble!" Our camp at the Relay House with its picket duty, night alarms, stereotyped cry of "Baltimore!" from without, and "Hacker!" from within, together with the flag presentation, numerous expeditions, and all the innocent (?) deviltry of camp life, such as hanging a Brigade Commander in effigy. And those drills on Dr Halls green in general, and the one on the morning after the arrival of the Captain's wife in particular. "Sh--- here comes Harper with his d--- old Ferry. Blood Tubs and Plug Uglies- Bouse out here!" The expedition to Tilghman's down Wye river, occupying two days and a night being successful to the extent of two old flintlock muskets, and a hound, a musket for each day, and the "purp" for the night work. Our camp at Baltimore, and attentions from its citizens, including another flag presentation, banquet at Mr. Lloyds &c. giving "value received" in those exhibition drills with the thermometer among the nineties, the "untrained animals of Ross' Menagerie," being generally held in reserve—or the guard house. The march to Druid Hill Park, Review at Fort McHenry, and another at Mount Clare. Reconnoisance of the Company in search of concealed arms, being successful to the extent of two muskets, which "Put" and Private Hill re-captured as souvenirs. The excitement attending the battle of Bull Run. Our new uniforms contracted for by the terms of "twenty seven dollars, ten for the uniform and one for the band[.]" The farewell to camp life, excitement attending our return, and the magnificent reception given us on our arrival, eclipsing all previous ovations. All this with the thousand and one experiences, written and unwritten, combined to make the life we led, one of almost unalloyed pleasure and satisfaction. Though we did work hard at times and contended with some bitter experiences, for the Government Commissariat did not grow as rapidly as the demands that were made upon it. But the Zouaves were born of hard work, and obstacles faded before us like dreams. Thus the petrified "biscuit" and rusty water of the Constitution were supplemented by Du-dah's pigs, Luscombs lob skouse, and the beer barrels of "Baltimore Joe."

All honor to Capt. Devereux, who made such an experience possible. May he live long! and may the name of the Salem Zouaves, live while memory holds, in the minds of all its members.

These records would not be complete without the following, original Roll of Members

Captain	E.A.P. Brewster, 2d.	Geo. W. Batchelder, 2d.
Arthur F. Devereux	Geo. D. Putnam, 3d.	George C. Gray, 3d.
Lieuts.	Sergeants	Chas. S. Emmerton, 4th.
George F. Austin, 1st	Chas. U. Devereux, 1st.	

Corporals
Alvah A. Evans
Chas. F. Williams Jr.
John P. Reynolds Jr.

Privates
Archer George N.
Batchelder Charles J.
Brooks Joseph H.
Brown Albert W.
Brown Elbridge K.
Bruce Daniel Jr.
Carlton John W.
Chapple Wm. F.
Claflin Wm. H.
Cobb Leonard D.
Crowningshield E.O.
Dalrymple Simon O.
Dearborn Chas. A. Jr.
Derby Putnam T. Jr.
Devereux John F.
Dimon Chas. A.R.
Douglass Albt. C.

Driver William R.
Field Joseph W.
Fowler William T.
Hale Henry A.
Hall Edward A.
Hall Harry S.
Hitchings A.F.
Hill William A.
Hodges John Jr.
Howard Frank C.
Lake David G.
Lakeman John R.
Lewis Albert H.
Luscomb Chas. P.
Luscomb Geo. W.
Mansfield Chas. H.
Moody Convers
Nichols James W.
Osgood Edwd. T.
Palmer Wm. L.
Perkins Joseph A.
Plummer Frank

Pratt Edwin F.
Reeves Robert W.
Ross J. Perrin
Ross William H.
Shaw Cyrus P.
Shackley Moses
Smith Albert P.
Smith Fred W.
Smith Saml. H.
Stevens Edwd. P.
Stevens George O.
Stimpson Edwd. S.
Swasey Wm. R.
Sweetland Alonzo
Symonds Geo. B.
Symonds Henry
Thorndike Albert
Upton William B.
Ward J. Langdon
Wiley Sullivan J.
William F. Wiley
Whittredge Charles E.

Appendix

Copy of the letter accompanying the flag, presented to the 8th. Regt. by the lady friends of the N.Y. 7th Reg't.

"To Genl. Butler in charge, for the 8th. Regiment of Massachusetts."
"Sir: —

We, the lady friends of the 7th Reg't. of New York, take much pleasure in presenting to the 8th. Regiment of Massachusetts, the accompanying Flag, as an acknowledgement of the courtesy, the energy, the ability and the patriotism displayed at Annapolis, on the 24th. of April, when, in conjunction with the 7th. N.Y. they so fully developed by their fraternal action, that great principle, which, in the heart of the true patriot is above all consideration. Our Country first and last! One union indivisible! Our Government the popular voice! Our flag, the stars and stripes; now and forever. Believing for the sake of humanity, that this great Republic has not yet fulfilled its glorious destiny we place this banner in their charge, knowing it will be nobly defended, and that it can find no safer resting place, than in the hands of the gallant Soldiers of the Massachusetts 8th.
New York May 28, 1861"

Copy of Genl. Butlers letter, forwarding the flag to the Reg't. from Fortress Munroe.

"Head Quarters
Department of Virginia
Fortress Munroe
June 17th. 1861

To
Col. Hinks
Commanding 8th. Reg't. M.V.M.
Sir:
    I send herewith a flag, presented by the lady friends of the New York 7th. Reg't. to your Corps, with the accompanying note of presentation of them. The gift will call up to your minds, the glorious reminiscences of your march from Annapolis to Washington, when you first opened a route from the loyal states to the National Capital. I cannot let the occasion pass, without putting on the records of your Regiment, my high appreciation of that fortitude and courage which bore privations without murmurs, faced dangers without flinching in an Enterprise which brought out to the knowledge of the country those high soldierly qualities which I know the Soldiers of Massachusetts to possess. And that ready adaptation of [?] the arts of peace to the operations of War, which has given a name and fame to your Regiment, to be striven for and envied by all. Renewing the assurances of the kindest regard and respect to yourself and each Soldier of your command, who suffered with us the privations of the Steamer Maryland, and the labors of the rescue of the Constitution, I am
Most Respectfully and truly Yours &c
Benj. F. Butler
Maj. Genl
Commanding"

Appendix

Letters of "G.W.B." (Sergeant George W. Batchelder),
Salem Light Infantry, Published in the
Salem Register and *Salem Gazette*

THE SALEM LIGHT INFANTRY'S RETURN TRIP.
ON BOARD PACKET SHIP ROANOKE, May 5, 1861.

  We are again on the ocean returning on the same track which we passed over in the Constitution, but under exceedingly different circumstances. We are now on a very large Packet ship, one of a line which formerly ran between New York and Richmond; but since the Virginia secession act, she has ceased making such trips, and is now chartered by the government, to carry stores and provisions to the troops at Fort Monroe and Washington. She is of 1200 tons burthen, and handsomely fitted up. Most of our fellows are provided with state rooms containing two or more very comfortable berths. We non commissioned officers have a small room with eight berths which render us very cosey and comfortable. At the stern is a small parlor, intended originally for a ladies' parlor, with a hanging lamp, and a marble topped table in the centre, upon which I am now writing. There is a plenty of good provisions on board, and ample accommodations exist for cooking, so that we have no such cause for complaint as on board the Constitution. We are sailing at a very fast rate so that we shall probably reach Washington some time to-morrow afternoon. We are to stop at Fort Monroe this afternoon and I will take notice enough of it to describe it to you. This morning, Sunday, after breakfast, extracts from the Army Regulations were read in accordance with the orders of the Regular Service, and after that was done, we had a Religious observance of the day. We have about a dozen very good singers with us, so that our choir was one which would not disgrace one of our churches. H.H., our Boston recruit, read the Episcopal service, and extracts from the Psalms and Proverbs. The fifth chapter of Matthew was then read, he reading one verse, and the company the next, thus alternating through the chapter. A gift of a number of Testaments, one for each man, which we received while in New York, now proved highly acceptable to us. They were given to us by the New York Bible Society. Last night was a hard one to most all of us. The sea was very rough, and in consequence we poor landsmen had to make our votive offering. I turned into my berth very early, and a good night's rest restored me to my usual comfortable state, and I am to day as well as ever.

Our stay in New York was made very pleasant to us by the constantly appearing Salem faces out of which beamed nothing but the kindest of hearts, and whose mouths spoke nothing but the most cheering of words. Mr. W., (L's father), in particular, did everything for us that he could think of. He supplied the Captain liberally with funds for the purchase of canteens, haversacks and shoes, which we did not get in Boston, and not content with this, he invited us to his house, where he gave us an entertainment of the nicest description. Capt. S., one of our past members, also entertained us at the Fifth Avenue Hotel. R.S., one of our Salem acquaintances, was with us several days, which made us very happy, you may be sure. We also made many friends in N.Y., all of whom had nothing but continued expressions of kindness for us; and taking these things, in connection with the repeated flattering notices of the N.Y. papers, we were in imminent danger of being spoiled. However, none of us regret to leave N.Y. and the comforts of the Astor House once more, in response to duty's call. God grant that we may all revisit it again when this unnatural strife is at an end, although I fear it cannot be, as we are to be ordered South under General Butler on our arrival — at least that is what we are led to expect. There is one of the N.Y. 7th Regiment with us who is going on to join his Regiment. There were an hundred others who would have liked to go with us also, but the orders of Maj. Gen'l. Sanford were against any more uniformed troops leaving N.Y. city, at present. There are now in and around New York city some 10,000 men who desire nothing more than permission to come on to the seat of war, and some of them, being most desperate characters, would prove most efficient fighters. I saw one of Major Cobb's new company of Flying Artillery from Boston, while we were in New York. He called on us at our quarters and posted us thoroughly on military matters in Boston. He came on with a friend to make the necessary purchases for equipping the company, and when I saw him again at 3 o'clock, Saturday, P.M., he told me that he had finished his business. By the way, one remark in the above sentence recalls to my mind something I have intended to say in every letter — that is, send a Salem newspaper when you get an opportunity, as they are of great interest to us at this distance, and, another thing, ask everybody to write to us. I should, for example, be much pleased to hear from the pastor of the Barton Square Congregational Church, and right speedily too. N.W. came on to N.Y. on Saturday morning and brought on three or four Boston papers, which, after reading an hour, made me forget where I was and almost fancy myself again in Boston. We saw Hon. Hannibal Hamlin frequently while in N.Y., as he stopped at the Astor House, and Hon. N.P. Banks also stopped there, purposely to see "his Massachusetts boys." I am swelling every day with pride for Massachusetts, and the position which she has taken in this struggle; and she won't be behind hand in what comes after, no matter how hard fighting there may be to be done.

We arrived at Fortress Monroe a few minutes after 9 o'clock on Sunday evening. It is a very beautiful place. The fort is built of stone, and from what I could make out from the ship, a distance of almost a mile and a half, it is nearly square. It extends completely across a narrow peninsula, almost half a mile wide. The walls are fifteen or twenty feet high, surmounted by a grassy embankment, and pierced for one row of guns only, although there were others *en barbette*, that is, on the top of the wall uncovered. Capt. D. and Lieut. P. went on shore. They represented the interior of the fort as being very beautifully laid out with gravelled walks like Boston Common. Beyond the fort on one side is a curving bench, about a mile in extent, with a number of houses and a light-house thereon. We also saw on the beach the celebrated large Columbiad, the range of which is said to be about five miles, and the muzzle is of so large a size that a man could crawl inside of it. There were many vessels around us when we came in, but not till morning did we make out what they were. One of them we were overjoyed to see was the Cambridge, and we were much pleased, the next morning, to receive a visit from all the Salem boys, who represented that they were having jolly times and capital accommodations. We hoped to be allowed to go on board of her, but were not permitted to do so.

The Cumberland, a jackass frigate, that is a man of war of about 32 guns, lay alongside of us, whose duty was to stop all vessels, as there is a strict blockade of Hampton Roads. In the morning, a band of music on board of her "discoursed sweet music," played National Airs and the irrepressible "Dixie," which sounded to us very pleasant. Later in the morning, a ship was coming in, and was hailed from the Cumberland, but gave no answer, and did not heave to, but continued on her course. She was, however, brought to, and dropped anchor at very short notice, by a shell, fired from one of the Cumberland's guns, which burst somewhere in her vicinity. It seems that she had just come in from the West Indies, and knowing nothing of the fact that Virginia hade seceded, supposing her still loyal, she was proceeding on her way to Norfolk when thus suddenly brought to. About seven o'clock in the morning, the Cambridge, which had been taking in guns and ammunition, started for Washington, to convoy us safely there. At about half after twelve we had passed her, and before half past one she was out of sight. Either she was very heavily laden or else is an inferior boat.

We sailed till about half after seven when we dropped anchor at the mouth of the Potomac, light-houses on the Maryland shore with the lights burning, but those on the Virginia shore unlighted. This seems to me a most barbarous and unchristian act, one not to be tolerated in any enlightened community — (no joke intended). A cold, drizzly rain set in, which lasted till about one o'clock. The whole company was divided into four watches, each relief to continue on three hours. I went on as sergeant of the guard at eleven o'clock, and it continued raining till about one, when it cleared up and was soon bright starlight. The morning was a delightful one, and at five o'clock we set out on our way to Washington. The river was about a couple of miles wide at its mouth, and the water was of a muddy brown color. After breakfast I went out to look around at the scenery, and saw a darkey driving a cow on the beach, which was the only thing of note on the Virginia shore for the first hour. Along the Maryland shore we saw several small villages and many negro huts. Plantations with busy blacks were not unfrequent. The scenery was magnificent, everything being green and growing, temperature mild, and everything combining to make our trip a pleasant one. The Cambridge accompanied us a short distance astern of us. At three o'clock we passed Mount Vernon, when the bell of the steamer was tolled every minute, which I hear is the custom of the steamers which pass up and down the river. I mounted the rigging so as to get a good view of the place. Above Mount Vernon on the opposite side is Fort Washington, situated on the top of a beautiful green hill, on a sort of a peninsula commanding a fine view up and down the river. There was a steamer lying at the wharf, the captain of which hailed us and told us that Alexandria was in the hands of the secessionists, and we might expect trouble. So we were immediately sent below with orders not to come up, until Alexandria was passed. I went down and as the dead light at the foot of my bunk looked out in the direction of Alexandria, I kept my eye fixed on that side. It is not a very large place and of rather a dingy description. Some said that they saw many secession flags, although "nary one saw I," however they may have been there. No attack as yet. We arrived at Washington about 5 P.M. On shore where we first arrived, a soldier waved his hand and cheered for Salem; who he was no one knew. After about an hour's steaming we came to the Navy Yard where we dropped anchor, and are now lying as I write. Capt. D. and Lieut. A. went ashore to find quarters for us, and at 8½ P.M., the present moment, have not yet returned. P. has been told by the Quartermaster, that we are to be quartered on Capitol Hill in two houses there by ourselves, which we shall enjoy very much. The N.Y. 71st Regiment are quartered at the Naval Barracks and tonight we are gratified by the sight of their Regiment drawn up for Dress Parade, and by hearing the music of their fine band. Three of the Mechanic Infantry also came into the yard, and exchanged greetings with us. They told us all about themselves; said they were having rather poor fare. Milk is 50 cents per gallon. We have fared well enough on board the Roanoke; plenty of fresh roast beef, although very tough.

P.S. Capt. D. has just come back and brings old letters and tells us that we are to be quartered in the Capitol, leaving to-morrow morning after breakfast. The Sappers and Miners will be disbanded and return to their own companies. We are still to be attached to the 8th Regiment. It is very warm here, quite sultry in fact. We are sitting with windows wide open, heads uncovered, bats and mosquitos being numerous. Capt. D. brought a copy of the New York Herald of Sunday, which contained a most ludicrously inaccurate account of our departure from New York.

I am now, at 1½ P.M., in the Capitol, in an entry just outside the Representatives' Hall, writing on a variegated slab. The floor is inland mosaic, and the door-ways are of black walnut and gilding — built in Gothic style. I will write again soon.

G.W.B. *Salem* (MA) *Register*, May 13, 1861

LETTERS FROM THE CAMP.
RELAY HOUSE, Elkridge Landing, May 16, 1861.

Here we are, at last, at the celebrated Relay House, and a very pleasant place it is. I wrote you last Saturday night in a hurry that we were to leave the Capitol at once for the Relay House, and thence were to go to Richmond. We were called up and ordered to put on knapsacks, haversacks and canteens, were supplied with rations of hard (that *means hard*) crackers, salt fish, raw potatoes, and cold water. We then were marched into an entry where we waited over two hours for orders from Gen. Scott. The time was passed pleasantly, songs and stories intermingling. At the end of that time we were sent back into quarters, where we slept fitfully for the rest of the night, every little while starting up at the sound of some one's voice, thinking it to be the order for march. But the order did not come till Tuesday morning. Our stay in Washington, though short, gave us plenty of hard work. Every morning and every afternoon, we went out upon parade, and drilled for a couple of hours, sometimes more. The second day we were there, orders were published before the Regiment, by which Captain D., Lieut. Putnam, myself and Sergeant Gray, Corporals Evans, and Reynolds, and Willy Hill, were detailed to act as drill officers. I had charge of the Lynn Light Infantry, and they made in three days very satisfactory progress. I am glad to have an opportunity to renew my acquaintance with the Lynn boys, and am more pleased that the pleasure seems mutual. They invited me, by special messenger, to come up to their quarters and pass the evening. I went up, and stopped about an hour, enjoying myself much.

Sunday was not spent much like a Sabbath. We had services, morning and evening, in the Representatives Hall, conducted by Mr. Haven, but they were short. Most of the day we were in the field drilling the Eighth Regiment, and hot work it was, too. The sun is well fired up here, thus early even, to a degree greater than we experience at home. We were well provided at Washington, three of our men acting as cooks. I passed outside of the Capitol yard but once, and stayed only a short time, not long enough to see any of the buildings of note.

We left Washington on Tuesday about 10 o'clock A.M. The streets were very muddy, and the heat was oppressive. These, combined with our heavy accoutrements, tried us harder than any thing we had yet undergone. We rode in the cars about an hour and a half, the whole of which time I devoted to cooling off. We passed sentinels at intervals of about a quarter of a mile, posted along the railroads, and sometimes parties of about a dozen, variously occupied, cooking, washing clothes, building huts, &c. After marching from the Depot up the steepest hill that I ever attempted to mount, and moistening the earth with the streams of perspiration which flowed freely from us all, we came to the camp of the Massachusetts 6th Reg't, and the New York 8th. Only small detachments of these Regiments are left here, the rest having gone on to Baltimore. At the summit of the highest hill was the celebrated Winans steam gun, which looks something like an Alligator's head on wheels. That is all the description I can yet give of it, as I have had no opportunity of examining it, not being allowed to pass the guard of the 6th. We had hardly arrived, when we were ordered to go down to the depot, and stop a baggage train; down we pitched at the rate of twelve miles an hour, and in three minutes were at the depot, and accomplished our duty. While waiting for a messenger whom Capt. Devereux had despatched to the Colonel to inform him that the train was stopped, I saw an officer whom I knew I had seen before, but could not think where. After cudgelling my brains for a few moments, however, I recollected that it was Lieut. Emery of Boston. I went up and claimed acquaintance with him, and he recognized me at once. From him I learned how he had faired; but as the Mass. 6th, with which he is connected, and deservedly well known, I need not relate to you his account.

We went back to the hill, and were marched down into a field at the foot of the hill, where we grounded arms and baggage, and lay down in the shade. After idling for an hour our men were ordered into ranks, and marched at the double quick (all our motions are made in double quick time, now,) to the other end of the field, where in a short time we constructed a rough shed under which to put the stores of the regiment. We then dug several holes, and constructed cooking ranges, over which our cooks were to preside. Meanwhile a party of ten from one of the companies of the regiment had constructed a dam across one of the many brooks that encircle the foot of the hill. By the time these things were done, our supply was ready, after partaking of which our company was detailed for guard. Three reliefs were formed, in the first of which were C. and myself. We went on at half past nine and stayed till 12, when we were relieved. While our guard was being posted, the sentinel on the upper hill, where the 6th Reg. was quartered, fired his gun, and shouted at the top of his voice the signal of alarm. Our regiment was soon formed and plunged up the hill into the darkness, at the double quick, of course. We were in suspense for about an hour as to what was the cause of the alarm. At the end of that time, the companies returned and we found that Ross Winans had been arrested, and as the curious crowd pressed around eagerly, the guard, fearing an attempt at rescue, fired his gun and shouted the word of alarm. We had no tents nor any huts built, so that we turned in, with nothing between the damp cold ground but our blankets, under the open sky. We built a large camp fire, and by "snuggling" up close to each other managed to keep pretty warm.

The next afternoon, however, we determined to build some huts. A rail fence near by, furnished us ridge poles and rafters ready to our hand, and the woods behind gave us plenty of branches and leaves for thatch and bedding. Soon after our party of six commenced their hut, others began to do the same, till after a while we had built eight or nine large huts, each of which could accommodate six sleepers. The example which we set was soon followed by the whole regiment, and many other similar huts soon crowned the hill. The view from these huts is splendid. We can see the smoke rising over the roofs of Baltimore nine miles distant, and in the country intervening, the greatest diversity of scenery imaginable. Rivers spanned by splendid bridges, scattered houses, with here and there a village, woods and plains, all combine to make the handsomest view I ever saw. I luxuriated in the thought that I could "lie at my ease in mine own 'ouse," and lazily take in life as it is at Elkridge Landing; but the arrival of a car load of tents dispelled the fond illusion. We were routed out of our comfortable quarters, and worked till night pitching our encampment on another hill.— The site for a camp is an excellent one. Everything needed for our comfort is within a few moments' walk.

This morning, after washing in the brook, I strolled with C. Emmerton through the woods, and picked some flowers, the ones most highly prized being a couple of violets, usually called, though why I know not, modest. I placed them on the table near which I am writing, intending to send them to you, but the wind has stolen them away from me. The woods are very beautiful around here, but I notice one thing, which is, that there are no evergreens, no undergrowth of consequence. The Sixth Regiment have built a dam in one of the brooks in the vicinity, which does much to add to the comfort of the troops.

On Thursday evening, at a meeting of the commissioned officers of the Regiment, Lieut. Col. Hinks was elected Colonel; Maj. Elwell was elected Lieut. Col., and Ben. Perley Poore, Major. The report about Capt. Devereux, though accredited here, turned out to be false. It caused, however, a great deal of consternation amongst us, and we were quite despondent for a few days.

On Friday forenoon, the Sixth and Eighth Regiments were marched a couple of miles out into the town, passing through a long covered bridge, and through most exquisite scenery, just to give Col. Jones a chance to review us, there being no field sufficiently large for the purpose nearer our camp. In the afternoon our Drill Masters were again called out to their posts, and did duty for an hour, after which came the evening parade.

In the evening, at 8 o'clock, we were detached to do duty as picket guard, and were thrown out in the direction of Harper's Ferry about five miles. The marching was of the hardest kind, over a railroad track, the bed of which was made of rough stones, whose sharp edges did more to tire us than any thing else. All but five of us, — Capt. Devereux, Lake, Cobb, Swasey and I — were posted at different intervals along the railroad. We went on about two miles in front of the outposts and halted. We sat down by the side of the track, and ate a couple of hard boiled eggs, salt fish and crackers. After this we retreated upon the outposts and arrived there at 2 o'clock. Here we turned in. I was very warm from walking, but when we awoke, at four in the morning, to return to camp, I was nearly frozen, and so were the rest, so that when challenged by our sentries, "Who comes there?" I answered at once, in the words of Grumio, "A lump of ice — A lump of ice!"

At a point near the Relay House, commanding the track so as to prevent trains passing unchallenged, the Boston Light Artillery have erected a battery for two pieces. They have wooden shanties designed for sleeping places and seem to be quite comfortable. We were sent out on this expedition because an attack was expected from Harper's Ferry, and we were to give the earliest notice of it. This was our first experience in this kind of duty, and I like it very much. When reading old hunting stories, I always thought I should like camp fire life, but never expected I should ever see any of it. Nor did I, for we had no fire, but everything else. To-day (Saturday) we have had nothing to do in the line of duty, but in the afternoon we were sworn in for three months from the first of May. All took the oath with the exception of two, who made some demur at enlisting for more than three months, but they afterwards changed their minds and determined to see it out.

Our Havelocks came this morning, and were much liked. I have worn mine all day, and I can assure you they are very useful articles. Indeed I had worn my pocket handkerchief for the same purpose, and am glad to devote it to its legitimate use again. Can you make one more for me, and one for Moody, size 7¼, one of our men, who drilled all last winter with us, but went out West the week before our ball. He is a capital fellow, and we are much rejoiced to have him with us again. The pattern by which John Hodges's was made, is the one I wish you would use, as it is the best one I have seen. Moody got as far as Detroit, where he joined a Michigan company, with the intention of joining us when he came across us. Yesterday morning, when the 6th and 8th Regiments were on line together, I read the letters which Charles received and read that Charley Frye was with the Washington Light Guard. Accordingly as soon as a halt was made, I ran across and spoke to him. He was very glad to see all of us, and said he should have been glad to come with us had he known we were coming so soon. He is looking finely, although much sunburnt. Charles Whittredge has arrived. He passed through to Washington this afternoon, and will probably return in a day or two. Capt. D. has also gone to Washington. He went to find Moody and attend to other business, but Moody's arrival has rendered his journey almost unnecessary. Great numbers of troops are continually passing to Washington through this village. The Michigan and Ohio troops passed through yesterday, I am told, and since I have been writing here two long trains have passed having troops on board. While I am writing now the drums are beating for evening parade. I do not go out to-night as George Gray will take my place. We had religious services last night after parade, consisting of reading extracts from the Psalms, singing a hymn, and prayers. We have orders now to have every one at his quarters as we may be off in half an hour. But I have exhausted my writing faculties now, so that I must bid you good bye. G.W.B. *Salem* (MA) *Register*, May 23, 1861

LETTERS FROM THE ARMY.
ELK RIDGE LANDING, Relay House, Camp Essex June 5, '61.

Dear Friends: It is some time since I have written to you, but in the dearth of incident, at present weighing heavily upon us, it is difficult to find material with which to fill a sheet. I commenced a letter to one of the family last Sunday, but could not finish it, as we were obliged to prepare for Sunday morning inspection. It is our duty to pack our knapsacks neatly, and range them along the side of the tent, and fold our blankets, placing them in the left hand upper corner. A party of six is then detailed, whose duty it is to "police" the company street, as it is called; that is they are to clear up every scrap of paper and every stick, and make everything presentable. The muskets are all taken from the tents, and must be thoroughly cleaned of rust and dirt, and stacked in front of the several tents. After this, the company are formed in line, and taking their muskets march to the Regimental Parade Ground, where the muskets and equipments are inspected. If the former are not sufficiently clean, the men will be sent back to quarters to finish them. After this, comes the tent inspection. The Colonel and other officers march along the company street, just glancing into the tents to see if the regulations have been fulfilled. Our tent has a gunrack neatly built at the head of it, which we find rather preferable to the old arrangement, which was, to pile them up in one corner, where the chances were about even of their standing up, or falling over upon some of us when asleep. At the mouth of the tent stands a nondescript article, which we make the general depository of all our loose goods. It partakes of the nature of the genus bedstead, species crib, being a large box mounted on four legs. It serves as a bureau in pleasant, and a breakfast table in rainy weather. As it is raining quite hard this morning, it will be devoted, in all probability, to the latter purpose. It commenced drizzling yesterday, and a part of the day rained quite hard, but cleared up sufficiently for us to go out on evening parade at seven and a half. In the afternoon, Charles Frye and a friend of his, called on us, and soon after, a number of others of the 6th Regiment, and we managed to pass a very pleasant afternoon.

This morning I obtained a pass and went down into the village to get my shoes repaired, and bought a pail and coffee-pot. It was the first time I had been in the village when I had an opportunity to look around me. The place is terribly behind the age; there seems to be nothing done, but just enough to enable the inhabitants to live from hand to mouth. There is what is called a Furnace Iron Factory, but no signs of anything having been done there for a long time. This village has but about twenty-five houses, and of these seven at least are grocery stores. Almost every one of these has a bar-room, although they sell no liquor, having a holy horror of Col. Jones, by whose orders they stopped selling. After my business was completed, I walked down to see what was going on at the Depot. A train of cars arrived at the same time that I did, which was bound for Harper's Ferry. As soon as it stopped, a party of about a dozen soldiers marched up under command of Col. Jones, and one man was stationed at each flight of steps leading from the cars, in order to prevent any person from leaving them. Col. Jones, accompanied by another officer and a couple of soldiers, entered the cars and searched them thoroughly, in order to find a secessionist, whose description had been forwarded to him from Baltimore by telegraph. He was for a long time unsuccessful, on account of the man having changed his dress, but at length discovered him, after searching the Relay House and adjacent buildings, in one of the cars through which he had already passed. He was arrested, and his baggage seized and searched. On opening his trunk the first object which met the view was an American flag. Under this, some packages, which being opened, were found to contain percussion caps to the number of *two millions*, a very important seizure in view of the fact that the article is more needed by us now than any other except shoes.

This is only one instance of what might be done, if we could throw our pickets farther from camp than they now are; and it was, with a desire to take possession of some ammunition which was to be transported from Baltimore to Harper's Ferry, that our picket guard started under Capt's. Devereux and Martin about three o'clock one afternoon, and marched through a thick dust, under a fiery sun, for about 15 miles from camp. On our return Capt's. D. and M. were arrested, as you have seen by the Boston papers. As all sorts of stories have been circulated in relation to the affair, I will give you an account of it here, from facts which I *know to be correct*. On the night of picket which preceded the one of which I speak, one outer picket met on the Harper Ferry railroad two of the 6th Regiment, who said they had been to Ellicott's Mills, a town about 12 miles from the Camp. They said that they had been told several times by different persons that ammunition had been carried nightly by road to a town a short distance above Ellicott's Mills, and from thence transported by railroad to Harper's Ferry. The next day, information was received from two persons, that six cannon were concealed at some place near Baltimore, which were to be transported when occasion offered to Harper's Ferry. One of those persons was the same who brought intelligence which led to the capture of the Winan's Steam Gun. This person offered to conduct the party to the place where the guns were concealed. Desirous of seizing them, Capt. Devereux, with Lieuts. Brewster and Palmer went on horseback the same afternoon, to reconnoitre the place. A night or two afterwards, our Company and Capt. Martin's were detailed for picket guard, and acting on information, which was considered reliable, that a quantity of powder was that night to be conveyed to Harper's Ferry over the Liberty Road, we stared at about 3 o'clock in the afternoon, with our overcoats and blankets slung on our backs, and our canteens and haversacks filled with rations for a whole day. We left camp by the back route, and went through the country by a round-about way of three miles, till we struck the straight road about half a mile from camp. There were about 50 of our Company, and about 40 of Capt. Martin's. The desire on the part of men to go was so great, that every man who was not allowed to do so, considered himself personally aggrieved. Every one of our sixty-seven men would have gone had he been allowed, and the same is true of Capt. Martin's company. A part of our way lay through a gentleman's private grounds which were laid out very beautifully. When we again struck the high road, we came upon a view, which is far beyond anything I have yet seen. We were on elevated ground, from which we had an uninterrupted view of Baltimore at a distance of about four miles over hill and dale, rivers and villages, till the sight ended in Chesapeake Bay.

About half a mile from the road is a large, unfinished, and as far as it goes, handsome building, intended for a Lunatic Asylum, where the First Pennsylvania Regiment is now quartered. Shortly after, we came to a party of about a dozen, who turned out to be the first picket of the Pennsylvania Regiment. They supposed us to be Secessionists at first, and considered themselves little better than prisoners, so that you may judge how glad they were, to find that we were Massachusetts boys. We came upon three or four more of their pickets, and the last one was posted at the very point for which we started. They had been posted for about three quarters of an hour, and not twenty minutes before we arrived, had seized the very ammunition which was the object of our expedition. This, coupled with the fact, that the driver confessed this ammunition came from a storehouse which contained 2000 kegs of powder, which would be sent forward, as occasion offered, clearly shows the necessity of just such an expedition as ours. We proceeded over a tiring road about four miles further, till we came to a place where four roads meet, when we encamped for the night. We slept, very cold, till four, when we started on again, and marched about four miles further, when we came to the Harper's Ferry railroad, after marching up the steepest hill out of Essex County, and waited a couple of hours, which we occupied in firing at a target with revolvers. At the expiration of this time, the regular passenger train from Frederick came along, and as there was no room for us, the conductor sent back a train of dirt cars for us, into which we climbed, and rode back to camp through a region luxuriant with patriotism and Star Spangled Banners. We passed through Ellicott's Mills, a miniature Lowell, where flags were flying on almost every building. The scenery on this road, is, as you know, celebrated for its beauty; and its entire difference from anything we see in the vicinity of home, is its chief charm.

When we returned to camp, the two Captains were put under arrest, and delivered up their swords at headquarters. Being thus deprived of their command, the members of the two companies took the readiest way of expressing their feelings, by marching to the Colonels' quarters with their Captains; after which they placed their muskets in a pile in front of the Colonel's quarters, and returned without them, subsequently resuming them at the request of Col. Hinks. In the evening the Captains were taken before Colonel Jones and examined, after which their swords were returned from Col. Hinks's tent, where they had been hanging all day, wreathed with flowers. This is the correct version of the whole affair, without gloss or prejudice.

But I must stop now, promising you another letter in two or three days. Both of us are well. We have received our new uniforms and the underclothing from Salem, and are much pleased with them, particularly the underclothing. What our boys have done to deserve so much kindness as has been shown us, none of us know, but if occasion offers, we will show that we know how to deserve it. Capt. Devereux has received from a lady in Beverly, a sprig of laurel, which she sent, she says, in token of her appreciation of the services of the S.L.I., with a request that he should wear it in his button hole. This request he will comply with on the first pleasant day, if we ever have one, of which there is no favorable prospect just now. Good bye, God bless you all.

Your affectionate son and brother, G.W.B.

Salem (MA) *Gazette*, June 14, 1861

LETTER FROM THE CAMP.
RELAY HOUSE, ELK-RIDGE LANDING, June 13, 1861.

Dear J: I have received two or three letters from you lately, and to repay you for your tired little fingers, for such they must have been, the least I can do is to write you a letter in return. It was very kind in you, little tot, to remember so kindly your absent brothers, and we are both much obliged to you. It seems to me very much as if we must be in Salem, so many familiar faces are constantly appearing to us. Dan'l Johnson came here last week, Thursday, and returned last Tuesday. He did not stay with us all of this time, but went to Alexandria to see the other Salem boys. His stay was very pleasant to us, and I hope, so to him. He put on one of our uniforms, and went out on line with us two or three times, and on picket guard, Friday night. He seemed to enter with hearty gusto into all our duties, and he did them as well as the best of us. We wished him to stay with us till the end of our three months, and I think he would have liked it much, but his business engagements would not allow of it. He is, as you know, a Cadetman, and he found in our ranks with our uniforms on, two of the men with whom he has marched shoulder to shoulder in that splendid corps. There has been a strong rivalry, and perhaps some jealousy between our two corps in time past, but the generous way in which they tendered to us an escort, the morning of our departure from Salem, proved that they had buried the hatchet, and we, I assure you, will never dig it up again. Their kindness to us throughout demands, and has received oft and again our hearty thanks. If we ever get home, we will show them that we are not unmindful of their attentions and know how to repay them. I can conceive how impatient they are to be ordered into service, from what Johnson has told me, and the kindest wish to them, I think, that I can offer, is, that they were here with us in this beautiful spot. I know they would do their duty.

Mrs. Devereux arrived here last Tuesday and was, as you can conceive, a most welcome visitor. It did us good to see the kind face of her who did so much last winter to sustain and benefit the corps. She is stopping at a house in the village, where Mrs. Col. Hinks makes her head-quarters, I suppose I may call it.

Day before yesterday, Charles Odell and Mr. Mark Lowd, both of Salem, came into camp. We were told some time before, that they had passed through this place on the way to Alexandria, and we expected them some days before. From Odell, I got the largest piece of wood which I sent you. It is a piece of the flag staff on which was flying the Secession flag which Col. Ellsworth pulled down. The small piece is from the stair, with a small portion of painted oil cloth which covered the stair, on which Col. Ellsworth stood when shot. Please take good care of them for me till I return. The two gentlemen stopped with us a couple of days, and told us much about our Salem friends now in Alexandria. The stories they told us of stuffed furniture and piano fortes, which the Fire Zouaves now have for every day use, made us rather envious of their good luck in being the first to be ordered into Virginia. We are, to be sure, very comfortably situated at the Relay, but this constant state of inaction, only varied by a hard and sharp two hours drill in the hot sun, makes us envious of anybody who can have something to do, no matter how difficult or dangerous.

The Sixth Regiment went yesterday morning to Baltimore and returned this morning, not having done anything of any moment. They went in order to be ready in case there were any riot, but the election passed off very quietly, more than usually so, in fact. We were disposed yesterday to growl at our hard luck in being left behind, but the event showed that we were just as well at home. Some of the boys who have been at different times to Baltimore, come back with stories of having been taunted and insulted in the streets, while others say that the city is as well conducted and orderly as could be desired. We went out on picket duty the night before last, but saw and heard nothing out of the way. In the afternoon of that day we had "a right smort" shower, and the woods, as we went through them just at twilight, were very beautiful. Flowers were on every hand, charming to the eye, and fragrant in perfume. Such a variety of flowers as I never conceived of at home, but too perishable to transmit any of them home, so that they may retain any of their beauty or fragrance. The most abundant flower in our woods is the laurel which occupies every space which Nature has chanced to leave unoccupied by other growth. The blossoms are just now in perfection, and the boys know how to appreciate them. Last Sunday morning we were ordered to prepare for the customary inspection, and not content with cleaning the company street, and the tents as clean as a dairy milk pan, the boys commenced beautifying and decorating the latter with laurel, roses, geraniums, oak leaves, and any flowers they could come across. It appeared to be a sort of contagion, for before ten o'clock every company but one had their tents more or less decorated. Some of their attempts at decoration were highly successful, and the Colonel was so much pleased with the appearance of the entire camp, that he invited a number of ladies and gentlemen to visit and inspect it. Among them were Col. Jones and his wife. Col. Jones remarked when passing through our company street, (which, by-the-by, a sign posted on one of the tents, informs the visitor is Ellsworth's Av.-enue,) that he thought he should suggest to Col. Watson, now commanding the 6th, that he should march his entire regiment through our camp in order to take pattern of so cleanly an example. In the afternoon, I suppose in accordance with this thought of his, he rode through the camp with Col. Watson, and next Sunday, I suppose, will show some appearance of the same sort in the 6th Regiment camp. Their case is different, however, from ours. The horses of the artillery and the heavy gun carriages passing over their encampment, render it impossible to keep it in very good condition, and on this account I think we are better situated than they.

Rev. Mr. Hepworth of Boston preached a patriotic sermon last Sunday morning, and was I believe universally liked. The sermons of Mr. Quint and

Mr. Atwood I have read, and thank heartily the lady who sent them. I shall pass them round to all who I think would like to read them.

I believe we have now received everything which has been sent us. The box from home came about a week ago, and the contents were very acceptable. The boys to whom the spoons were sent, are thankful, much. Moody forwards acknowledgements for his 'avelock. The things which had been sent to Fort Monroe got here to-day, and the letters, though dated "May 21," were not less welcome. I regret to hear the sad news about one of our old friends, and am more sorry that he should have been so maimed in support of such a cause. But one can hardly blame a man for adhering to the faith he was born in, and I have no doubt that he consoles himself for his misfortune, in the thought that he incurred it in his country's defence. Would to God this war could end, and all traces of division be swept away. But I wish it not, till some settlement can be had with those *traitors* who have misguided and deceived a once well meaning, loyal and chivalrous people. The papers tell us daily, that the Union cause gathers strength every day, but I am afraid that the disastrous bungle at Big Bethel will throw us back to where we stood a fortnight ago. But Gen. Butler is at Fort Monroe still, and he will soon regain the prestige we have lost, I have confident assurance. That things are fast coming to some issue or other, is very evident from the fact of the rapid concentration of troops at two or three points. Half a dozen regiments have passed from Washington through this post on their way to Chambersburg, which seems to indicate an attack on Harper's Ferry. In that event, I hope we shall be ordered there too, as the papers say we shall be, but no one can tell. Rumor is still in the ascendant, and scandal flies. Last night we got news that Gen. Butler had taken the Big Bethel Battery, and this morning it is contradicted.

To-night we are off on picket duty again, and the cooks are preparing a day's rations for us to take with us. No one but "those in authority" knows our course. Our boys are now in capital health. Out of the seventy men whom we have in camp at this date, 69 can do duty, and the other is disabled only by a sore hand. If that does not show an alarming state of good health, then I am no judge. In the absence of Dr. Breed, Brewster has been officiating as surgeon, and has had not a case from our company except the man with the sore hand. But I must stop now. Give love to all, from your affectionate brother.

G.W.B.   *Salem* (MA) *Register*, June 20, 1861

Letter of Captain Arthur Devereux to "My Dear George," on "The Clarke Automatic Steam Valve Co. Cincinnati" stationary, dated June 22, 1886

March of Zouaves and Knott Martin's Marbleheaders. Not withstanding Butler had placed Baltimore again under Federal Authority, the City was largely in sympathy with the rebel cause and many neglected no opportunity to send substantial aid. Arms and ammunition were constantly being run through our lines to the upper Potomac and thence sent across. With the small force at command of Butler it was impossible to stop all the rat holes. Information more or less reliable was constantly coming to the ears of officers. It came to my knowledge that two pieces of cannon would be run out at night to be secreted during next day and next night hurried on to Frederick City which at that time was substantially inside the Rebel lines.

A forced march of 20 miles, to be accomplished in late afternoon and early evening, placing a small body of troops in light marching order at a given spot would be likely to intercept the convoy. Two or three hours sleep would sufficiently rest active men and another forced march bring them back to Camp with the trophies by morning.

I communicated with Knott Martin. The very suggestion to the fiery old fellow was enough. He and his boys would go any where with the Zous. Keeping our own counsel we applied to our own Col (Hinks) for permission to be absent. As usual Hinks was ready for anything that looked like doing something. He was hampered however by a something which had self appointed itself a "Brigadier" on the strength of being the ranking Col of the two Regts stationed at Relay House. Application in that direction only elicited a preemptory refusal. Consultation over the matter discovered that Companies were allowed to pass Camp lines for purposes of drill. If their zeal for instruction should lead them inadvertently beyond the usual distance from Camp, it was their business to find their way back to their quarters after discovering their error.

Sure enough the Zous and Marbleheaders found themselves at the "gloaming" of that day just 20 miles from Camp and they found another thing besides. Probably some ten minutes before they reached this point a Regt from Pennsylvania which had been marched down to Baltimore had just run across and seized the coveted prize.

This was notice enough, of course that our party was as far from Camp as there was any need to be.

After some hours sleep in bivouac we started back. But if in the night march through a strange country daylight found us at Ellicotts Mills instead of Relay House it was not a matter to be much surprised at. Besides we might run across some other contraband; any how we could get some idea how near the enemies' lines were to us along the B&O road which we nightly picketed some mile or two out from the viaduct at Relay. I now asked Knott Martin if he thought we mistook our road that night and if he ever thought so he has ever since kept the reflection to himself.

It was after Guard mount when the two companies reappeared in Camp and their arrival was the signal for an outpouring of curiosity excited comrades from both Regts winding up with the immediate arrest of the two company commanders for absenting themselves from Camp without leave with their commands.

On the announcement of the arrest every man in each of the two companies marched up to Regt Hd Quarters and laid his musket down in front of the Col's tent.

Here was a pretty "how de do." Two captains in arrest and two companies refusing duty whilst their commanders were in duress. The "Brigadier" was furious. The Captains didn't appear to be much disturbed and the rest of the Camp enjoying the fun.

All the persuasion in the world on the part of the superior officers and all the threats of the "Brigadier" failed to move a single Zou or Marbleheader. They weren't going to stand to see their Captains put in arrest for hard work in the interest of the service. Thus matters stood all day even Major Ben Perley Poore's knowledge of military law backed with his great powers of urban diplomacy and capacity to be "damned polite" couldn't mitigate the wrath of the "Brigadier."

Suddenly the news came that Capts Devereux and Martin were released from arrest "by order of Genl Winfield Scott commander in chief" who complimented them on their exhibition of zeal against the enemy.

This let the prisoners out in triumph though they never got that distance from camp again through any inadvertence.

We always laid it to Perley Poore, that knowing a thing or two, he had supplemented ineffectual importunity at "Brigadier" Hd Qrs, with a quiet bit of information purposely put in the direction of higher authority.

Notes

Introduction

1. James L. Bowen, *Massachusetts in the War, 1861–1865* (Springfield, MA: Clark W. Bryan & Co., 1889), 7.
2. *The Boston Herald*, April 15, 1861.
3. *Private and Official Correspondence of Gen. Benjamin F. Butler, During the Period of the Civil War*, 5 vols. (Norwood, MA: The Plimpton Press, 1917), I: 89–90. Hereafter cited as *Private and Official Correspondence*.
4. U.S. War Department, *The War of the Rebellion: A Compilation of the Official Records of the Union and Confederate Armies*, 128 vols. (Washington, D.C.: Government Printing Office, 1880–1901), Series III, Vol. 1, 67. Hereafter cited as *Official Records*, followed by the series, volume and page number.
5. *Boston Daily Advertiser*, April 16, 1861. The state's officials were no less determined to oppose secession. Massachusetts Speaker of the House John A. Goodwin noted, "Massachusetts sacrificed much to establish the Union…. She is ready to sacrifice more," while Adjutant General William Schouler believed, "We have no boasts to make; history tells what the men of Massachusetts have done, and they will never disgrace that history." Bowen, *Massachusetts in the War*, 2–3.
6. *The Boston Herald*, April 15, 1861.
7. *The Boston Journal*, April 17, 1861, as quoted in Mary A. Hedrick, *Incidents of the Civil War* (Lowell, MA: Vox Populi Press, 1888), 22–23.
8. *The Boston Herald*, April 18, 1861.
9. *Boston Daily Advertiser*, April 16, 1861; April 19, 1861.
10. D. Hamilton Hurd, *History of Essex County, Massachusetts*, 2 vols. (Philadelphia: J.W. Lewis & Co., 1888), I: 200.
11. P.C. Headley, *Massachusetts in the Rebellion* (Boston: Walker, Fuller, and Co., 1866), 119–20; Charles S. Osgood and H.M. Batchelder, *Historical Sketch of Salem, 1626–1879* (Salem: Essex Institute, 1897), 65.
12. *Boston Daily Advertiser*, April 16, 1861. Although Secretary of War Simon Cameron required Massachusetts to furnish two regiments (74 officers and 1,486 men, a total of 1,560), the state actually provided 3,736 soldiers. *Official Records*, ser. 3, 1: 69.
13. Bowen, *Massachusetts in the War*, 6–7; Federal Publishing Co., *The Union Army*, 8 vols. (Madison, WI: Federal Publishing Co., 1908), I: 137–140. The Salem Company was originally Company A, Seventh Regiment, Massachusetts Volunteer Militia, but was detached to the Eighth Massachusetts for the 1861 campaign. George M. Whipple, *History of the Salem Light Infantry from 1805 to 1890* (Salem, MA: Essex Institute, 1890), 128.
14. *Private and Official Correspondence*, 23.
15. William Schouler, *A History of Massachusetts in the Civil War*, 2 vols. (Boston: E.P. Dutton & Co., 1868), I: 52.
16. Bowen, *Massachusetts in the War*, 6–7; Federal Publishing Co., *The Union Army*, I: 1 37–140; Robert F. McGraw, "Minutemen of '61: The Pre–Civil War Massachusetts Militia," *Civil War History*, vol. XV, No. 2 (June 1969), 101–115.
17. *Official Records*, ser. 3, 1: 66–67.
18. *Boston Daily Globe*, April 17, 1911. In another instance, Knott V. Martin, captain of Company C, Eighth Massachusetts, was ready to dress a pig when a mounted messenger rode up and handed him a message. Knife in hand, he read the message, which called him to bring his company to Boston. Martin threw down his knife and hurried to put on his uniform. "What

will you do with the pig?" his wife asked. "— — the pig," Martin replied. Charles Carleton Coffin, *Drum-Beat of the Nation* (New York: Harper & Brothers, 1899), 50–51. In another version of this tale, regimental adjutant Edward Hinks delivered the message to Martin, who "uttered an exclamation," threw down his knife, went immediately to notify his orderly sergeant, then returned to his butchering. John D. Billings, *Hardtack and Coffee, Or the Unwritten Story of Army Life* (Boston: George M. Smith & Co., 1888), 29–30.

19. Reynolds appears in the 1860 Census with his father, a master mason, his mother and four sisters in the city's second ward. Curiously, the Arthur F. Devereux who led the Salem company appears with his father, another male relative (perhaps an uncle), seven siblings and two servants in Salem's sixth ward, while another Arthur F. Devereux, clerk, age 24 appears in the household of John F. Putnam, master mariner. National Archives and Records Administration, *Eighth Census of the United States*, 1860, Microcopy 653, Roll 497, Massachusetts, Essex, Ward 2 Salem, p. 1052; Essex, Ward 6 Salem, p. 211; Ward 5 Salem, pp. 1152–53. According to the 1861 Salem Directory, the clerk Devereux was still a boarder with Captain Putnam at 82 Lafayette Street but working in Boston, and John Reynolds Sr. lived at 13 Northey Street, but John P. Reynolds Jr. does not appear in either the Salem or Boston directory. Adams, Sampson, and Co., *The Salem Directory, Containing the Names of the Citizens, City Officers, A Business Directory, and an Almanac for 1861* (Salem: G.M. Whipple and A.A. Smith, 1861), 75, 152.

20. Ellsworth and Captain Devereux had met several years before, when Devereux ran a patent-soliciting business in Chicago and employed Ellsworth as an office clerk. According to one source, both were members of the city's National Guard Cadets militia company, while another source relates that Ellsworth had enlisted a number of young men, known as the Chicago Cadets, who wished to join the National Guard, and they were admitted on the condition that Devereux serve as their drill instructor. Devereux supposedly instructed Ellsworth in military matters in their back office on Sunday afternoons. After the business failed, Devereux returned to Salem. Ruth Painter Randall, *Colonel Elmer Ellsworth: A Biography of Lincoln's friend and first hero of the Civil War* (Boston: Little, Brown and Co., 1960), 34–39, 188–89; George W. Nason, *History and Complete Roster of the Massachusetts Regiments, Minute Men of '61* (Boston: Smith and McCance, 1910), 250. According to Charles A. Ingraham's *Elmer E. Ellsworth and the Zouaves of '61* (Chicago: University Press of Chicago, 1925), however, Ellsworth took no active part in military affairs while in Devereux's employ, as he could not afford to belong to any group in the city. Ingraham's work contains an extensive account of Ellsworth's visit to Salem. Deveruex was obviously a talented drillmaster, for in 1856 he was presented with "a very handsome sword" by the members of the National Guard Cadets for his services as company drill instructor. *Chicago Daily Tribune*, August 15, 1856.

21. Whipple, *History of the Salem Light Infantry*, 63. Originally formed in the 1830s by the French Army from native North African troops, by the time of the Civil War the French Zouaves were non-natives. Their distinctive uniform included a short jacket, baggy trousers, sash, gaiters and a fez with turban. Their bravery in combat in the Crimea and later in Italy thrilled the American public and led to the formation of many Zouave companies in this country. Ellsworth's men drew inspiration from, but did not directly copy the uniform of these Frenchmen. A newspaper reporter noted the Chicago Zouaves had loose-fitting uniforms that allowed for freedom of movement, training in the use of bayonet, and loading and firing in every possible position, with evolutions performed mostly on the run in "a splendid gymnastic exercise." Ingraham, *Elmer E. Ellsworth*, 31; Michael J. McAfee, *Zouaves: The First and the Bravest* (Gettysburg, PA: Thomas Publications, 1991), 14–15, 20–21, 25–26.

22. *Salem Register*, April 11, 1861; Whipple, *History of the Salem Light Infantry*, 61–64, 128–129.

23. *Private and Official Correspondence*, 15–16.

24. Benjamin F. Butler, *Autobiography and Personal Reminiscences of Major-General Ben. F. Butler, Butler's Book* (Boston: A.M. Thayer & Co., 1892), 170–173; *Private and Official Correspondence*, 15–16. Benjamin Franklin Butler (1818–1893), was born in Deerfield, New Hampshire. A successful lawyer, he won election as a Democrat to the Massachusetts House of Representatives and Senate in the 1850s. By 1861, Butler was a brigadier general in the state militia. Appointed the first volunteer major general of the war, his military career was marked by numerous successes and failures. His loss at the Big Bethel, Virginia skirmish in June 1861, the stagnation of his forces at Bermuda Hundred near Richmond and his failure to capture Fort Fisher, North Carolina in 1864 were balanced by his capture of Hatteras Inlet in August 1861 and his relatively successful administration of New Orleans in 1862. Following the war, he served in Congress, first as a Republican and later as a member of the Greenback Party, and as governor of Massachusetts. Ezra J. Warner, *Generals in Blue: Lives of the Union Commanders* (Baton

Rouge: Louisiana State University Press, 1964), 60–61. A number of biographies of Benjamin Butler detail this period in his life. Examples include *Stormy Petrel: The Life and Times of General Benjamin F. Butler, 1818–1893* (Rutherford: Fairleigh Dickinson University Press, 1969); James Parton, *History of the Administration of the Department of the Gulf in the Year 1862* (Boston: Fields, Osgood, & Co., 1871); Robert S. Holzman, *Stormy Ben Butler* (New York: The Macmillan Co., 1954) and Chester G. Hearn, *When the Devil Came Down to Dixie: Ben Butler in New Orleans* (Baton Rouge: Louisiana State University Press, 1997).

25. Edward W. Hincks (Hinks), *Extracts from Speech by General Edward W. Hincks, of Cambridge, at Peabody, November 5th, 1883* (Cambridge, MA: William H. Wheeler, 1883), 11. According to John Reynolds, Captain Devereux asked Governor Andrew to request the Salem company as soon as troops were called, and supposedly the Salem company was one of the first called out. *Boston Daily Advertiser*, October 21, 1897.

26. Hedrick, *Incidents of the Civil War*, 25.

27. Nason, *History and Complete Roster of the Massachusetts Regiments, Minute Men of '61*, 231. Some period documents refer to the Salem Zouaves as Company "J," and John Reynolds claimed that his company was the only one designated as "J" during the war. According to him, while en route from Boston to Washington, General Ben Butler discovered that both his Salem and Newburyport companies were designated Company "A," so when asked to name a new letter for the Salem organization, he quickly replied, "'Call it J.'" Since the more standard Company "I" also appears in period documents to designate the Salem Zouaves, it will be used here. Adjutant General of Massachusetts, *Annual Report of the Adjutant-General of the Commonwealth of Massachusetts for the year ending December 31, 1861* (Boston: William White, 1861), 16. In addition, Reynolds claimed that the company was referred to as the "Salem Zouaves" for the first time when the unit arrived in Boston on April 18 and gave an exhibition drill at the State House. *Boston Daily Advertiser*, October 21, 1897.

28. *The Boston Herald*, April 18, 1861.

29. Hedrick, *Incidents of the Civil War*, 27.

30. Henry Greenleaf Pearson, *The Life of John A. Andrew*, 2 vols. (Boston: Houghton, Mifflin & Co., 1904), I: 186; *The Boston Herald*, April 18, 1861.

31. *Boston Daily Advertiser*, April 19, 1861.

32. Headley, *Massachusetts in the Rebellion*, 119–20.

33. *Boston Daily Advertiser*, April 19, 1861

34. McGraw, "Minutemen of '61," 101–115.

35. *The Salem Register*, June 6, 1861. The regiment included the "Cushing Guards" (Company A, Newburyport); the "Lafayette Guard" (Company B, Marblehead); the "Sutton Light Infantry" (Company C, Marblehead); the "Light Infantry" (Company D, Lynn); the "Light Infantry" (Company E, Beverly); the "City Guards" (Company F, Lynn); the "American Guard" (Company G, Gloucester); the "Glover Light Guard" (Company H, Marblehead); the "Light Infantry" (Company I, Salem) and the "Allen Guard" (Company K, Pittsfield). Schouler, *A History of Massachusetts in the Civil War*, 74–75.

36. *Berkshire County Eagle*, May 2, 1861.

37. *The New York Illustrated News*, May 4, 1861.

38. Henry Wyckoff Belknap, *Simon Forrester of Salem and His Descendants* (Salem, MA: Essex Institute Historical Collections, 1935), 46.

39. Schouler, *A History of Massachusetts in the Civil War*, 77.

40. *Berkshire County Eagle*, April 25, 1861.

41. *Private and Official Correspondence*, 23.

42. *Berkshire County Eagle*, May 2, 1861.

43. Hedrick, *Incidents of the Civil War*, 32.

44. *The New York Illustrated News*, May 4, 1861. The "hardy" men, "just arrived from the sacred precincts of Bunker Hill," gave nine cheers for the new banner. *Salem Register*, April 22, 1861.

45. *Berkshire County Eagle*, April 25, 1861.

46. *Berkshire County Eagle*, May 2, 1861.

47. For more on the "Pratt Street Riot," see George William Brown, *Baltimore and the Nineteenth of April, 1861: A Study of the War* (Baltimore: N. Murray, 1887).

48. *Private and Official Correspondence*, 16–17.

49. Thomas Holliday Hicks, born in Maryland in 1798, was a career politician who served as a member of the state legislature, governor's council, county sheriff and state constitutional convention before his election to governor in 1857. Elected to fill a vacancy in the U.S. Senate, Hicks served there as a Unionist from December 1862 until his death in February 1865.

50. Brown, *Baltimore and the Nineteenth of April*, 58–59. For more biographical details about Hicks, see United States, 38th Congress, 2nd Session, *Addresses on the Death of Hon. T.H. Hicks* (Washington, D.C.: Government Printing Office, 1865). For more on the governor's defense of his actions in the bridge burning incident, see Frank Moore, *The Rebellion Record*, 11 vols. (New York: G.P. Putnam and D. Van Nostrand, 1861–68), 2: 181–84. One historian who examined the issue concluded, "there can be little doubt but that Hicks gave that night some form of authorization for the burning of the bridges." George L.P. Radcliffe, *Governor Thomas*

H. Hicks of Maryland and the Civil War (Baltimore: The Johns Hopkins Press, November-December 1901), 57.

51. Isaac R. Trimble (later a Confederate general) led 160 men to destroy the Harris Creek Bridge (within the city limits of Baltimore). Although intending to destroy additional bridges and the steamer *Maryland*, Trimble and his men abandoned the latter mission, but were able to burn the Bush River and Gunpowder bridges. They also unsuccessfully attempted to destroy the Back River Bridge. William Bender Wilson, *History of the Pennsylvania Railroad Company*, 2 vols. (Philadelphia: Henry T. Coats & Co., 1895), I: 318–20. The bridges at Cockeysville, Relay and Melvale were also destroyed.

52. *St. Louis Globe-Democrat*, February 23, 1883.

53. Schouler, *A History of Massachusetts in the Civil War*, I; 101–03. Felton's message to Captain Galloway regarding the use of his steamer by Union troops included the instructions to "give them every attention, and promote their comfort in all ways possible. They are our mainstay now, and God speed them." *Private and Official Correspondence*, 17. Others later disputed Felton's version of events. Captain R.B. Forbes claimed that he went with his brother John M. Forbes to Governor Andrew and suggested that troops be sent through Annapolis, and Andrew sent a message to Butler or the railroad officers. *Boston Daily Globe*, September 12, 1886. At least one source claims that Captain Arthur Devereux of the Salem Zouaves was present for the meeting between Butler and Felton. *Boston Daily Advertiser*, October 21, 1897.

54. *Official Records*, ser. 1, 2: 582–86; Emmons Clark, *History of the Seventh Regiment of New York, 1806–1889* (New York: By the Seventh Regiment, 1890), I: 476–77.

55. *Private and Official Correspondence*, 18–20.

56. Clark, *History of the Seventh Regiment*, I: 479–81.

57. Emmons Clark, *History of the Second Company of the Seventh Regiment* (National Guard), N.Y.S. Militia (New York: James G. Gregory, 1864), 299, 293–95.

58. *Private and Official Correspondence*, 20.

59. Hedrick, *Incidents of the Civil War*, 35, 52. "Leatherstocking," a member of the Allen Guards, reported that "we took each comrade's hand, and some of us concluded for the last time on earth." Stuart Murray, *A Time of War: A Northern Chronicle of the Civil War* (Lee, MA: Berkshire House Publishers, 2001), 35.

60. *Private and Official Correspondence*, 44.

61. Belknap, *Simon Forrester of Salem and His Descendants*, 46.

62. *Autobiography and Personal Reminiscences of Major-General Ben. F. Butler, Butler's Book*, 188–89.

63. *Private and Official Correspondence*, 45.

64. *New York Daily Tribune*, April 25, 1861.

65. *Private and Official Correspondence*, 45.

66. *Autobiography and Personal Reminiscences of Major-General Ben. F. Butler, Butler's Book*, 181–97; *Boston Daily Advertiser*, October 21, 1897. Tyrone Martin relates a different version of the events. In his narrative history of U.S.S. *Constitution*, he explains that Captain George Washington Rodgers threatened to open fire on the Maryland, but was stopped by the voice of the Naval Academy's chaplain. The officer was returning from leave in the North and had happened upon Butler's men at Havre de Grace, Maryland. Tyrone G. Martin, *A Most Fortunate Ship: A Narrative History of Old Ironsides*, revised edition (Annapolis: Naval Institute Press, 1997), 315–16.

67. George S. Blake enjoyed an active and varied career in the U.S. Navy. Born in Worcester, Massachusetts, in 1803 and appointed a navy midshipman in 1818, Blake first saw combat three years later when his ship captured a Portuguese vessel. Commissioned lieutenant in 1827, he commanded the brig *Perry* when it was damaged in a hurricane off the Florida coast in 1846. Promoted to commander in 1847 and to captain in 1855, Blake became commandant of the Naval Academy two years later and led that institution until 1865. Promoted to commodore in 1862, Blake served as a lighthouse inspector after he left the Naval Academy, and died in Longwood, Massachusetts, in 1871. James T. White & Co., *The National Cyclopedia of American Biography*, 63 vols. (New York: James T. White & Co., 1906), 13: 422.

68. United States Naval War Records Office, *Official Records of the Union and Confederate Navies in the War of the Rebellion*, 31 vols. (Washington, D.C.: U.S. Government Printing Office, 1894–1927), ser. 1, 4: 269–72, 315.

69. *Autobiography and Personal Reminiscences of Major-General Ben. F. Butler, Butler's Book*, 192; *Private and Official Correspondence*, 33.

70. *Official Records*, ser. 1, 51 (1): 1273–75.

71. *Private and Official Correspondence*, 46; *Autobiography and Personal Reminiscences of Major-General Ben. F. Butler, Butler's Book*, 192

72. *Official Records*, ser. 1, 2: 586–89.

73. *Official Records of the Union and Confederate Navies in the War of the Rebellion*, ser. 1, 4: 398; *Boston Daily Advertiser*, October 21, 1897. Martin puts the total number of Massachusetts men aboard at 107. Martin, *A Most Fortunate Ship*, 316. Butler claimed that a Marblehead company was placed on board to help sail the ship, but Reynolds states in both his diary and his 1897 article that the "Salem Zouaves," "Allen

Guards" and Sappers and Miners were the only troops detailed to "Old Ironsides."

74. Charles E. Clark, *My Fifty Years in the Navy* (Boston: Little, Brown and Co., 1917), 18–19; *Boston Daily Advertiser*, October 21, 1897.

75. Anonymous, "Secession at the Naval School," *United States Service Magazine*, Vol. I, No. 4 (New York: Charles B. Richardson, 1864), 388–394.

76. Anonymous, "How Marblehead Fishermen Saved the Constitution," *The Sailors' Magazine and Seamen's Friend*, Vol. LII, No. 3 (March 1880), 80–81.

77. George Washington Rodgers (1822–1863), son of a U.S. Navy commodore and nephew of naval heroes Oliver Hazard and Matthew C. Perry, became a midshipman in 1836. He served in the West Indies, the Mediterranean and the Gulf of Mexico before being promoted to lieutenant in 1850. After further duty both at sea and ashore, he took command of U.S.S. *Constitution* in September 1860. Following that ship's successful transfer to New York, Rodgers was promoted to commander. In April 1863, he commanded the monitor U.S.S. *Catskill* during a U.S. Navy attack on Fort Sumter in Charleston Harbor. That August, when the *Catskill* participated in another assault on the fort, Rodgers fell to Confederate artillery fire. Dumas Malone, ed., *Dictionary of American Biography*, 22 vols. (New York: Charles Scribner's Sons, 1935), 16: 74.

78. Anonymous, "Secession at the Naval School," 388–394.

79. *New York Times*, April 29, 1861; *New York Daily Tribune*, April 25, 1861. The need to remove the *Constitution's* guns might strike some modern readers as unnecessary, but in the fall of 1860, Captain Blake noted that the ship's great draft prevented her from leaving Annapolis Harbor easily, thus necessitating the removal of the guns in April 1861. Mark C. Hunter, *A Society of Gentlemen: Midshipmen at the U.S. Naval Academy, 1845–1861* (Annapolis: Naval Institute Press, 2010), 144. In fact, in order to enter the harbor in the fall of 1860, stores and equipment had to be unloaded and her water tanks pumped. The armament of the ship at that time consisted of sixteen 32-pounders. Martin, *A Most Fortunate Ship*, 312.

80. *The New York Herald*, May 1, 1861.

81. Hedrick, *Incidents of the Civil War*, 58.

82. Theodore Winthrop, *Life in the Open Air, and Other Papers* (Boston: Ticknor and Fields, 1863), 229.

83. Hedrick, *Incidents of the Civil War*, 74; *Boston Daily Advertiser*, October 21, 1897; Winthrop, *Life in the Open Air*, 227. Those on board the *Maryland* fared no better. According to one officer, the Massachusetts men on that ship were given rations transferred from the U.S.S. *Constitution*, including pilot-bread "stamped '1848,' the year it was made, and salt pork bearing the same brand, which the men were obliged to eat raw. Salt water only could be procured: this was eagerly drank by some, making them more thirsty than ever." Schouler, *A History of Massachusetts in the Civil War*, 104.

84. Hedrick, *Incidents of the Civil War*, 58.

85. *Official Records*, ser. 1, 2: 589–91.

86. *Autobiography and Personal Reminiscences of Major-General Ben. F. Butler, Butler's Book*, 181–97.

87. Winthrop, *Life in the Open Air*, 230–31.

88. *Berkshire County Eagle*, May 2, 1861. Many years after the war, one Massachusetts man told the fantastic story of a young man "with the olive complexion and dark eyes of Italy," carrying a monkey and hand organ, who appeared before General-in-Chief Winfield Scott's headquarters in Washington, D.C. When the man began to grind out a tune, the general's orderly came to order him away, but the "Italian" insisted on seeing General Scott. He saluted the general and gave his name and rank in the Regular Army. The imitation Italian was really a young Massachusetts officer who had been sent by Butler to report that the Eighth Massachusetts had landed at Annapolis. The officer had dyed his complexion with walnut juice, and Butler had purchased the elaborate disguise. The Treasury Department hesitated to pay the bill until the ruse was fully explained. No other evidence has been found to corroborate this tale, although in May 1861 Butler also sent Captain Peter Haggerty into Baltimore "by ruse" to spy on secessionist activity. *The National Tribune*, March 24, 1887; *Autobiography and Personal Reminiscences of Major-General Ben. F. Butler, Butler's Book*, 226.

89. Anonymous, "How Marblehead Fishermen Saved the Constitution," 80–81; Winthrop, *Life in the Open Air*, 230–31.

90. Clark, *History of the Seventh Regiment*, I: 486. Union officer Carl Schurz wrote that when he visited Butler about this time, he was "clothed in a gorgeous militia uniform adorned with rich gold embroidery. His rotund form, his squinting eye, and the peculiar puff of his cheeks made him look a little grotesque." Butler "thoroughly enjoyed his position of power, which, of course, was new to him, and that he keenly appreciated its theatrical possibilities." The general received officers with an "air of high authority," and a "tone of curt peremptoriness peculiar to the military commander on the stage, with which he expressed his satisfaction or discontent, and with which he gave his instructions. And, after every such scene, he looked around with a sort of triumphant gaze, as if to assure himself that

the bystanders were duly impressed. But he did expedite business, and, no doubt, he got over his theatrical fancies as the novelty of the situation wore off." Carl Schurz, *The Reminiscences of Carl Schurz*, 3 vols., 1907–09 (New York: The McClure Company, 1908), 2: 225–26.

91. Clark, *History of the Seventh Regiment*, I: 487–88; *Private and Official Correspondence*, 22–23.

92. William Swinton, *History of the Seventh Regiment, National Guard, State of New York, During the War of the Rebellion* (New York: Charles T. Dillingham, 1886), 89–93; Clark, *History of the Seventh Regiment*, I: 487–88. Author William J. Roehrenbeck believed that two messengers arrived to meet with Lefferts. The first was Frederick W. Lander, who had been sent by General-in-Chief Winfield Scott to determine the status of the two regiments, and urged Lefferts to march to Washington at any cost. A second, unnamed messenger that he believed was Captain Morris S. Miller (the Army's assistant quartermaster) then arrived and recommended the troops use the railroad route to Annapolis Junction. William J. Roehrenbeck, *The Regiment That Saved the Capital* (New York: Thomas Yoseloff, 1961), 102–04.

93. *Private and Official Correspondence*, 32.

94. *Official Records*, ser. 1, II: 589–91.

95. Hedrick, *Incidents of the Civil War*, 55.

96. Winthrop, *Life in the Open Air*, 233.

97. *Boston Daily Advertiser*, October 21, 1897.

98. *Official Records*, ser. 1, II: 589–91. A member of the Eighth Massachusetts pointed out that if U.S.S. *Constitution* had been seized, Annapolis harbor would have been blocked to U.S. vessels and the only practical route to Washington eliminated. *Berkshire County Eagle*, May 2, 1861. Captain R.B. Forbes, on the other hand, claimed that Commodore Christopher Rodgers told him that U.S.S. *Constitution* was never in danger, and that he had more than enough men to repel any attack. *Boston Daily Globe*, September 12, 1886.

99. Headley, *Massachusetts in the Rebellion*, 128.

100. *The New York Herald*, May 2, 1861; Belknap, *Simon Forrester of Salem and His Descendants*, 46.

101. *The New York Herald*, May 1, 1861.

102. United States Naval War Records Office, *Official Records of the Union and Confederate Navies in the War of the Rebellion*, ser. 1, 4: 315; *Boston Daily Globe*, September 12, 1886.

103. Belknap, *Simon Forrester of Salem and His Descendants*, 46.

104. United States Naval War Records Office, *Official Records of the Union and Confederate Navies in the War of the Rebellion*, ser. 1, 4: 398–99.

105. Clark, *History of the Seventh Regiment*, I: 488–491; Clark, *History of the Second Company*, 302–305; Hincks, *Extracts from Speech*, 14–23.

106. Headley, *Massachusetts in the Rebellion*, 129.

107. Hedrick, *Incidents of the Civil War*, 63. Colonel Hinks of the Eighth carried hard cash, and was able to persuade one local resident to provide some eatables by the "pleasant jingly of silver." Roehrenbeck, *The Regiment That Saved the Capital*, 110.

108. Clark, *History of the Seventh Regiment*, I: 491–98; Swinton, *History of the Seventh Regiment*, 100.

109. Hincks, *Extracts from Speech*, 15–20. According to Hinks, General Benjamin Butler labeled the young subordinate's exploit "the most gallant act of this or any other war." Nason, *History and Complete Roster of the Massachusetts Regiments, Minute Men of '61*, preface.

110. Hedrick, *Incidents of the Civil War*, 59.

111. *Salem Register*, May 6, 1861.

112. *Salem Observer*, May 18, 1861.

113. Historians disagree about the seriousness of the Confederate threat to Washington in mid–April 1861, and about whether the nation's capital was truly under siege during the early days of the war. It is clear that the city's residents feared an enemy attack and suffered through several anxious days until Union reinforcements (such as the Eighth Massachusetts) arrived. It is also clear, however, that the secessionists seemed content with merely destroying telegraph and railroad lines and did not oppose the march of Union troops to the city or block the Potomac River. In addition, neither Confederate President Jefferson Davis nor General P.G.T. Beauregard, the hero of Fort Sumter, planned to capture Washington. For another view of this period in Washington's history, see John and Charles Lockwood's *The Siege of Washington*, published in 2011.

114. Winthrop, *Life in the Open Air*, 234–35, 226–27.

115. Swinton, *History of the Seventh Regiment*, 122.

116. Hedrick, *Incidents of the Civil War*, 64.

117. Clark, *History of the Seventh Regiment of New York, 1806–1889*, II: 8. A Massachusetts man wrote that the Seventh "immortalized itself" by providing about twenty casks of beer, several barrels of boiled eggs, bread, oranges and lemons. *Salem Register*, May 6, 1861.

118. Moore, *Rebellion Record*, I: 319.

119. Hedrick, *Incidents of the Civil War*, 64. Despite the friendship between members of the two regiments, there was some resentment as well, because the Seventh New York reached Washington before the Eighth Massachusetts

and by doing so received a great amount of publicity. In 1924, Constant R. Marks of Company K, Eighth Massachusetts hinted that this was because "[Major Theodore] Winthrop in his history of the Seventh got into print first," but that "The 7th Reg. [sic] did not even serve three months, but were allowed to return to New York." *The National Tribune*, November 27, 1924.

120. Bowen, *Massachusetts in the War*, 181–83.

121. *New York Times*, May 11, 1861; *Berkshire County Eagle*, May 30, 1861. General Butler occupied the Relay House on May 5 and soon had a force of 1,700 men there. *Official Records*, ser. 1, 2: 623.

122. Anonymous, "Camp Life at the Relay," *Harper's New Monthly Magazine*, Vol. XXIV, No. CXLIII, April 1862, 628. In May 1830, the first section of the Baltimore and Ohio Railroad opened from Baltimore to Ellicott's Mills. In the early days, before steam-powered locomotives, horse drawn cars were pulled along the tracks. Because a single team could not make the entire thirteen-mile journey, they stopped mid-way in order to be replaced by a fresh team. The point where the change was made became known as "Relay." Daniel Carroll Toomey, *A History of Relay, Maryland, and the Thomas Viaduct* (Baltimore: Toomey Press rev. 3rd ed., 1995), 8–11. The Relay House was a three-story frame structure containing 32 rooms, and a place where passengers could enjoy food and lodging. It burned to the ground in December 1897. *Baltimore Sun*, December 25, 1897.

123. *Private and Official Correspondence*, 71.
124. *Boston Daily Advertiser*, June 17, 1861
125. *The Boston Herald*, June 13, 1861.
126. "Camp Life at the Relay," 629.
127. *Private and Official Correspondence*, 76.
128. *Boston Daily Advertiser*, June 17, 1861.
129. "Camp Life at the Relay," 630.
130. *The Boston Herald*, June 4, 1861.
131. *Salem Gazette*, June 11, 1861.
132. *Berkshire County Eagle*, June 13, July 11, 1861.
133. *Berkshire County Eagle*, June 6, June 13, July 11, 1861.
134. *Berkshire County Eagle*, June 13, June 6, July 11, June 27, 1861.
135. *Berkshire County Eagle*, June 6, 1861.
136. *Salem Register*, June 20, 1861.
137. *Berkshire County Eagle*, July 11, 1861. Patrick Sarsfield Gilmore (1829–1892), an Irish immigrant, was one of the most famous bandleaders in America. In 1858, he founded Gilmore's Band. On September 16, 1861, only a few weeks after he performed for the Massachusetts men, Gilmore enlisted in the 24th Massachusetts Infantry, and became leader of the regimental band. Massachusetts Adjutant General, *Massachusetts Soldiers, Sailors and Marines in the Civil War*, 8 vols. (Norwood, MA: Norwood Press, 1931), II: 777; Bruce C. Kelley and Mark A. Snell, *Bugle Resounding: Music and Musicians of the Civil War Era* (Columbia: University of Missouri Press, 2004), 196–98.

138. *Berkshire County Eagle*, June 6, July 11, 1861.
139. *Private and Official Correspondence*, 83.
140. *Baltimore Sun*, May 16, 1861.
141. James G. Hollandsworth, Jr., *Pretense of Glory: The Life of General Nathaniel P. Banks* (Baton Rouge: Louisiana State University Press, 1998), 46–48; Fred Harvey Harrington, *Fighting Politician: Major General N.P. Banks* (Philadelphia: University of Pennsylvania Press, 1948), 56–59.

142. National Archives, *Letters Received by the Office of the Adjutant General (Main Series), 1861–1870*, Microcopy 619, Roll 2, Frames 353–54.

143. For an interesting newspaper editorial on the supposed efforts by Union "sensationists" to frighten the government into subjugating Baltimore, see *Baltimore Sun*, May 28, 1861.

144. *Official Records*, ser. 1, 2: 138–143.
145. Roy P. Basler, ed., *The Collected Works of Abraham Lincoln*, 9 vols. (New Brunswick: Rutgers University Press, 1953), IV: 457.

146. Although the Steuart family referred to the home as "Maryland Square," the area around it became known as Steuart Hill. After the Civil War, the home was used as a boys' school and was referred to as Steuart Hall. *Baltimore Sun*, February 10, 1963. Major General John A. Dix noted that the Steuart Mansion was an important military position, close to the Baltimore and Ohio Railroad and its Mount Clare depot, "as well as from the relation it holds to the direction from which the city is most likely to be assailed from without." *Official Records*, ser. 1, 5: 566.

147. Morgan Dix, *Memoirs of John Adams Dix*, 2 vols. (New York: Harper & Brothers, 1883), II: 24–27.

148. *Official Records*, ser. 1, 5: 558–59.
149. *Berkshire County Eagle*, August 1, 1861.
150. *The Boston Herald*, August 1, 1861.
151. *Berkshire County Eagle*, August 8, 1861.
152. *Salem Gazette*, June 21, 1861.
153. *Journal of the House of Representatives of the United States: Being the First Session of the Thirty-seventh Congress; Begun and held at the City of Washington, July 4, 1861* (Washington, D.C.: Government Printing Office, 1861), 182.

154. *Salem Register*, July 11, 1861.
155. *The Boston Herald*, August 1, August 2, 1861.
156. Hedrick, *Incidents of the Civil War*, 84.

157. Massachusetts Adjutant General, *Record of the Massachusetts Volunteers, 1861–1865*, 2 vols. (Boston: Wright & Potter, 1868), I: 45–47.
158. *Salem Register*, August 5, 1861.
159. *Salem Observer*, August 3, 1861.
160. Hinks believed that 463 members of the regiment re-enlisted for three years service. Hincks, *Extracts from Speech*, 11. Of the seventy-two members of the Salem Zouaves, fifty-five re-enlisted in the Union Army. Of that number, thirty-four received officers' commissions.
161. *Boston Daily Globe*, October 21, 1897; April 20, 1911; *Boston Daily Globe*, April 19, 1918.

John Perkins Reynolds, Jr.: A Biographical Sketch

1. *Salem Observer*, August 31, 1861.
2. For Reynolds' account of his role in the Battle of Antietam, see Charles Carleton Coffin, ed., *Stories of Our Soldiers: War Reminiscences, by "Carleton" and by Soldiers of New England*, published by The Journal Newspaper Company in Boston in 1893, Volume I, 140–45. According to the Nineteenth's regimental history, Lieutenant Colonel Devereux ordered Reynolds to the rear after he received his ankle wound. Reynolds hobbled back to his company, however, and received his elbow wound. Devereux jokingly said that it "served him just right" for disobeying his commander. Ernest Linden Waitt, *History of the Nineteenth Regiment Massachusetts Volunteer Infantry 1861–1865* (Salem: The Salem Press Co., 1906), 141.
3. The design for a work of art described as a "Military or Naval Emblem" was intended to commemorate "the successive stages of army service," with room for the veteran's rank, units, etc. His patent is Design Number 3,103, dated July 14, 1868, and is part of the United States Patent and Trademark Office website (http://www.uspto.gov/index.jsp), accessed 27 March 2010. Some of the company's business records are in the collection of the Rutherford B. Hayes Presidential Center in Fremont, Ohio. Reynolds also worked as a clerk in the auditor's office of the Massachusetts State House. National Archives and Records Administration, *Tenth Census of the United States*, 1880, T9C, Roll 532, Massachusetts, Essex, Salem, p. 629.
4. Undated copy of Reynolds obituary. Reynolds was educated in the Salem public schools and was a member of the twenty-sixth class of the old Salem English High School, graduating in 1855. *Military Order of the Loyal Legion of the United States, Register of the Commandery of the State of Massachusetts* (Cambridge: The University Press, 1912), 366; *Boston Journal*, February 1, 1893; Massachusetts Adjutant General, *Massachusetts Soldiers, Sailors and Marines in the Civil War*, II (1931), 439; VII (1933), 249; Nason, *History and Complete Roster of the Massachusetts Regiments, Minute Men of '61*, 258–59; *Boston Daily Globe*, June 21, 1919.

Arthur Forrester Devereux: A Biographical Sketch

1. John P. Reynolds Reminiscences, 1861–1862, Manuscript S-7, Massachusetts Historical Society, Boston.
2. Nason, *History and Complete Roster of the Massachusetts Regiments, Minute Men of '61*, 250–52; Perley Derby and Dr. Frank A. Gardner, "Elisha Story of Boston and some of his Descendants," in *The Essex Institute Historical Collections*, Vol. L, No. 4 (October 1914), 311–12; Roger D. Hunt and Jack R. Brown, *Brevet Brigadier Generals in Blue* (Gaithersburg, MD: Olde Soldier Books, 1997), 159; *The [Cincinnati] Enquirer*, February 14, February 16, 1906; Harrison Ellery and Charles Pickering Bowditch, *The Pickering Genealogy*, 3 vols. (Cambridge: University Press, 1897), II: 747–49; Bowen, *Massachusetts in the War*, 915–16; *Boston Daily Globe*, April 23, 1905; Massachusetts Adjutant General, *Massachusetts Soldiers, Sailors and Marines in the Civil War*, II: 411. For Devereux's account of his role in Pickett's Charge, see "Some Account of Pickett's Charge at Gettysburg," in the *Magazine of American History*, Vol. XVIII, No. 1, July 1887, 13–19.

1. Off to War

1. Chandler and Company is listed in the 1861 Boston Directory as "John Chandler, E[dward] W. Capen, W.F. Nichols, and E. Wyman jr.), dry goods, 6 and 8 Summer." Adams, Sampson and Co., *The Boston Directory, Embracing the City Record, a General Directory of the Citizens, and a Business Directory*. (Boston: Adams, Sampson, and Company, 1861), 87.
2. The Salem Light Infantry's armory was located in the Phoenix Building on Lafayette Street. Adams, Sampson, and Co., *The Salem Directory*, 236, 40.
3. Edward W. Capen of Chandler and Co. Dry Goods boarded at 17 East Newton Street in Boston in 1861. Adams, Sampson and Co., *The Boston Directory*, 80.
4. Although impossible to identify with any certainty, this person may be Mrs. Harriet Cut-

ler, who lived at 13 Washington Street. Adams, Sampson, and Co., *The Salem Directory*, 71.

5. Henry Appleton Hale, also a member of the Salem company, lived at 12 Northey Street. Adams, Sampson, and Co., *The Salem Directory*, 98.

6. The *Salem Register* of April 22, 1861, described the demonstrations associated with the departure of the Zouaves as "such as have never been surpassed here." The Salem band accompanied the troops to the depot to the tune of "Yankee Doodle." "God bless our patriotic volunteers and return them all in safety to their friends!" the paper prayed. "The city was a unit in its enthusiasm," claimed one county history, "and while there was plenty of 'gush,' if the word may be pardoned, and an exaltation of sentiment greater than our national temperament has been usually given to, the occasion justified it, and it was hearty and genuine to the last degree." The Rev. Dr. George Dudley Wildes was the pastor of Salem's Grace Episcopal Church (organized in 1858) from 1859–1867. He died in Riverdale, New York, in 1898. D. Hamilton Hurd, *History of Essex County, Massachusetts*, 2 vols. (Philadelphia: J.W. Lewis & Co.1888), I: 200, 61; *The New York Times*, June 5, 1898.

7. Although most members of the company were wearing the Zouave uniform, many needed to be issued equipment in Boston. *Salem Register*, April 22, 1861. The drill at the State House was "loudly applauded," and three cheers were given for the company. Reynolds believed that this was the first occasion that the appellation "Salem Zouaves" was used, "and it was heralded in its movements from this time on and referred to in the papers as the Salem Zouaves." *Boston Daily Advertiser*, October 21, 1897.

8. Reynolds failed to note that the Zouave squad gave "a specimen of their drill," and "were greatly cheered." Each of the company's officers was presented with a fine revolver. *Salem Register*, April 22, 1861.

9. According to one source, fully five thousand people greeted the regiment in Springfield, including military and fire companies, with the late night ringing of bells, blazing bonfires, band music and cannon firing. Nason, *History and Complete Roster of the Massachusetts Regiments, Minute Men of '61*, 231.

2. New York and Philadelphia

1. As the regiment marched down Broadway, the "Bunker Hill boys, the flower of Essex County, the Bay State lads" were greeted by cheering men and women waving handkerchiefs. Perhaps the most demonstrative portion of the crowd consisted of a group of natives of the Bay State, including 76-year-old Massachusetts General James Appleton, who remarked as the Eighth passed by that "Those boys won't run," as he had "commanded a regiment of them in the last war." The Zouaves gave their "peculiar cheering salute" as they passed Major Robert Anderson of Fort Sumter fame. The "hardy" men, "just arrived from the sacred precincts of Bunker Hill," vowed solemnly to defend the new flag with "their lives and honor." *Salem Register*, April 22, 1861.

2. Reynolds wrote, "for we have no canals east," but marked it out.

3. The chief of police and 300 policemen escorted the regiment to the Girard House. *The Press* (Philadelphia) reported that the Eighth did not "present so fine a military appearance" as the Sixth Massachusetts, but the Eighth's companies contained "a fair proportion of soldierly-looking men, stout-limbed, and no doubt strong hearted." Because the men were fatigued, they were not kept to strict military discipline. The fact that the companies were not "sized" according to height and that many men lacked caps and other uniform items gave them a rather incongruous look. Nevertheless, the spectators "looked with interest to the manly appearance of the volunteers" and found them a "hardy-looking set of men." *The Press* (Philadelphia), April 20, 1861.

4. While the Massachusetts soldiers enjoyed the hospitality of Philadelphia, General Butler telegraphed Governor Andrew, consulted with the Navy Yard commander and the president of the Philadelphia and Baltimore Railroad, and poured over maps and gazetteers. He then called his officers together and explained his plan to occupy Annapolis and march from there to Washington. Butler's brother, serving as his aide, scoured the town for pickaxes, shovels, tinware and provisions. Parton, *History of the Administration of the Department of the Gulf in the Year 1862*, 71–72.

5. In a letter written on April 23, Captain Devereux derisively wrote that the "*bully Seventh* backed down," for "'twas too much risk," but the Salem men were willing to take such a dangerous, even a desperate, service." Headley, *Massachusetts in the Rebellion*, 128.

6. Lieutenant Colonel Edward Hinks recalled that nearly a hundred men immediately volunteered for the "Sappers and Miners," but about 40 were selected. The men were supplied with axes, picks, crowbars, shovels and other equipment to remove barricades and other obstructions if found in the streets of Baltimore. Hincks, *Extracts from Speech*, 12.

7. The *Berkshire County Eagle* described the scene: "You may well imagine that some hands were not so steady as usual and that some men

who at home were quite familiar with firearms exhibited under the inspection of the staff officer unusual awkwardness.... [I]t may be considered a fair test of the pluck of man for the first time called to contemplate the immediate dangers of an assault with the bayonet." The captain of the Allen Guards proposed to lead the assault carrying a musket, and asked for a volunteer to give up his weapon and remain behind. Not one man offered, so the captain ordered one of his men to hand over his musket. The unlucky private burst into tears and begged the captain to allow him to keep his firearm and take part in the action. *Berkshire County Eagle*, May 2, 1861.

8. Not all accounts agree with Reynolds. One writer wrote that the men were "packed as close as negroes in the steerage of a slave ship." Parton, *History of the Administration of the Department of the Gulf in the Year 1862*, 75.

3. Old Ironsides

1. According to one dramatic account, the U.S.S. *Constitution*'s gunners had lanyards in hand, and Captain George Rodgers was about to hail the *Maryland* before giving the order for his men to open fire, when a voice came from the *Maryland*, and after a short exchange, Rodgers became convinced that the Eighth Massachusetts had come to their rescue. James Russell Soley, *The Sailor Boys of '61* (Boston: Estes and Lauriat, 1888), 45–55.

2. Reynolds remembered the guns were piled aboard the *Maryland* "like so much cordwood." *Boston Daily Advertiser*, October 21, 1897.

3. Reynolds reported that the men spent an hour in trying to extricate the *Constitution*. During these attempts, one of the hawsers snapped, injuring one of the *Constitution*'s sailors—the first casualty of the operation. *Boston Daily Advertiser*, October 21, 1897.

4. The *Maryland* was a railroad ferryboat connecting the two rail lines, which transferred cars from one road to the other. *Boston Daily Advertiser*, October 21, 1897. According to one story, when the troops could not push the cars overboard, Butler had all his drummer boys beat their drums to excite the men, but that had no effect. The general then pulled off his coat, took a drum and began to beat it, and soon broke the drumhead. In a like manner, he broke every drum. The drummer boys began to cry, but the cars were rolled overboard, and each boy received a new drum. An eyewitness disputed the story, stating that pushing the car off was an easy matter and took only a small part of the regiment, and that while Butler beat the drum to try to get the ship free, there was only one drum head broken, as Butler grabbed the drum from the drummer, "and with a blow or two broke in the head." *National Tribune*, February 20, 1890, March 13, 1890. Others claim that Butler "double-quicked" up and down the deck with the men as he beat the drum, and even helped throw the car overboard. Charles Carleton Coffin, *Stories of Our Soldiers* (Boston: The Journal Newspaper Co., 1893), II: 14.

5. Fred Smith of the Pittsfield company agreed, noting that the Massachusetts men wanted to lynch the pilot, as "he is an old pilot, and understands every foot of the harbor." *Berkshire County Eagle*, May 2, 1861.

6. Although, as Reynolds explained, "soldiers aboard ship were like cats in a strange garret," Captain Rodgers' threat "had a good effect." *Boston Daily Advertiser*, October 21, 1897.

7. Reynolds wrote but then struck out the words, "and Revolutionary fame."

8. Some members of the regiment became far more emotional about "Old Ironsides." "Leatherstocking" of the Allen Guards, for instance, noted that a friend in the ranks had tears in his eyes when he exclaimed, "'I love that old noble ship!,'" and further explained that securing her from the secessionists "is of more glory to us than the fighting and winning of a battle!" Murray, *A Time of War*, 36.

9. One source claimed that both the hard bread and salt pork were stamped "1848, the year they were purchased. The salt pork had to be eaten raw or not at all, as there was no means of cooking it." The hard bread had to be soaked in water until it was soft enough to eat. Nason, *History and Complete Roster of the Massachusetts Regiments, Minute Men of '61*, 233. The men laughingly recalled the breakfast they had received on the morning they left Philadelphia, when Continental Hotel owner and Massachusetts native Paran Stephens gave his countrymen a proper meal. Now "it was a well-worn joke, to call for delicate and ludicrously impossible dishes, which were remembered as figuring in the Continental's bill of fare; the demand being gravely answered by the allowance of a biscuit, an inch of salt pork, and a tin cup half full of water." Parton, *History of the Administration of the Department of the Gulf in the Year 1862*, 82.

10. Reynolds noted that a few of the Zouaves had some nautical experience. The capstan bars came about breast high, so the boatswain began a lively air on his fife, and the men marched around the circle with the music until two short "toots" gave the signal to "avast heaving." *Boston Daily Advertiser*, October 21, 1897.

11. The U.S. Quartermaster's Department chartered the steamship *Ariel* in October 1861

from C. Vanderbilt, while the steamship *Baltic* was chartered on April 8, 1861, from the North Atlantic Steamship Company. 37th Congress, 2nd Session, Senate Executive Document No. 37, *Letter of the Secretary of War, in answer to a resolution of the Senate of the 30th day of January, in relation to the vessels purchased or chartered for the use of the War Department since the 1st day of April last*, 2,4. The *Harriet Lane*, built in 1857, was a two-masted brigantine and the only steam vessel in the U.S. Revenue Cutter Service in 1861. Transferred to the U.S. Navy in March 1861, *Harriet Lane* attempted to relieve Fort Sumter and fired the first shot by a Navy vessel in the Civil War. Confederate forces in Galveston, Texas captured the ship on January 1, 1863. Paul H. Silverstone, *Warships of the Civil War Navies* (Annapolis: Naval Institute Press, 1989), 82.

12. A reference to Daniel Defoe's *Robinson Crusoe*. The shipwrecked Crusoe had little use for money and considered it worthless ("The money I had by me lay as despicable dross, which I would freely have given for a gross of tobacco pipes, or a hand-mill to grind my corn").

13. The Mechanic Light Infantry became Company A, Fifth Massachusetts Infantry; the City Guards became Company F of the Eighth Massachusetts Infantry.

14. John Henry Upshur (1823–1917), a native of Virginia, became a midshipman in 1841. He saw service with the Mediterranean, East India and African Squadrons, in addition to shore duty, before becoming an instructor at the Naval Academy in 1859. Promoted to lieutenant in 1855, Upshur retired from the Navy in 1885 as a rear admiral. William B. Cogar, *Dictionary of Admirals of the U.S. Navy, Volume I, 1862–1900* (Annapolis: Naval Institute Press, 1989), 198–99.

15. One midshipman thought the Bay State men were "a disorganized mob," and a "noisy, dirty crowd," but also admitted that these raw militiamen eventually became the equals, if not the superiors, of any soldiers in the world. John C. Pegram, "Recollections of the United States Naval Academy," in *Personal Narratives of Events in the War of the Rebellion, being papers read before the Rhode Island Soldiers and Sailors Historical Society*, 4th series, No. 11 (Providence: By the Society, 1891), 28–29. Hammocks had been distributed to the Massachusetts men, which the midshipmen claimed when they arrived aboard. "Something more than the gold lace and haughty airs of the midshipmen ... was needed to make them give the hammocks up," Reynolds reported. "One or two knockdowns took place" before the officers interfered and the hammocks were restored to the midshipmen. Both the Bay Staters and sailors "soon came to a better understanding" and "lived in harmony" during the trip to New York. *Boston Daily Advertiser*, October 21, 1897.

16. The U.S. Quartermaster's Department chartered the steamer *Josephine* on April 20, 1861, from the Philadelphia Steam Propeller Company. 37th Congress, 2nd Session, Executive Document No. 37, *Letter of the Secretary of War, in answer to a resolution of the Senate of the 30th day of January, in relation to the vessels purchased or chartered for the use of the War Department since the 1st day of April last*, 2. According to Pittsfield company member Fred Allen, some of the men were pleased to leave the ship, while others regretted it, "but generally I think they are pleased to get on shore once more where they stand a chance to get something to eat, besides salt horse and hard bread rations." *Berkshire County Eagle*, May 2, 1861.

17. The *National Intelligencer* newspaper marveled that the Eighth could "reconstruct a steam engine, lay a railroad track, and bend the sails of a man-of-war." *Salem Register*, May 2, 1861. Supposedly, a delegation of Washington ladies offered to sew and bake bread for the Bay State men, but was told that tailors and bakers could be found in their ranks. "The Massachusetts men are nearly all mechanics," wrote the *Washington Chronicle*, and their numbers embrace artizans [sic] in almost every department of mechanical skill." *Salem Register*, May 6, 1861. Private Simon O. Dalrymple, for instance, took a block in his teeth, crawled along the underside of the yardarm, and made it fast to the weather earing, "a feat few old sailors would care to attempt." *Boston Daily Advertiser*, October 21, 1897.

18. The U.S. Navy chartered the *Monticello* from April to July 1861, from H.B. Cromwell and Company of New York. Report of the Secretary of the Navy, in 37th Congress, 2nd Session, Senate Executive Document No. 1, *Message of the President of the United States to the Two Houses of Congress*, 3 vols. (Washington, D.C.: Government Printing Office, 1861), III: 144.

19. Here Reynolds later inserted the note, "Many years afterward I learned that one of these two was Geo. S. Dewey, the hero of Manila Bay, and who died in 1917 as Admiral of the Navy. And is buried in Arlington."

20. The steam frigate *Niagara*, launched in 1855, helped lay the first transatlantic cable and delivered the first diplomatic mission to Japan. Returning to Boston on April 23, 1861, the ship soon headed south for blockade duty. U.S. Navy Department, Naval History Division, *Dictionary of American Naval Fighting Ships*, 8 vols. (Washington, D.C.: U.S. Government Printing Office, 1970), V: 81.

4. Return to New York

1. The U.S. Navy Department purchased the steam tug *Oliver M. Pettit* from R. Coffin and Company in New York in August 1861. Report of the Secretary of the Navy, in 37th Congress, 2nd Session, Senate Executive Document No. 1, *Message of the President of the United States to the Two Houses of Congress*, 3 vols. (Washington, D.C.: Government Printing Office, 1861), III: 127, 140. Built by Lawrence and Foulkes for Messrs. Palmer and Crary of New York, the 100-ton tug *James A. Stevens* was launched in November 1856. *The U.S. Nautical Magazine, and Naval Journal* (New York: Oliver W. Griffiths, 1856), 384.

2. How the company came to be quartered at the luxurious Astor House "was a mystery to the rank and file, who, of course, 'obeyed orders' just the same." In fact, Charles Stetson, its proprietor, was an old member of the company, and at the suggestion of W.R.L. Ward, the men were quartered at the hotel for $4 per day per man. This posed a problem, in that the army regulations provided one ration (thirty cents) per day, but the Salem men had not been mustered into service and were ineligible to receive even that rate. Thanks to General Butler's order, the "faith and credit" of Massachusetts was pledged to the Salem company, and when the account was settled, Stetson submitted a bill for only $450 for 110 men for five days (the Salem company plus thirty-eight sappers and miners)—less than $1 per day per man, a discount of more than 75%. *Boston Daily Advertiser*, October 21, 1897.

3. Ellsworth's Eleventh New York Volunteer Infantry (First New York Fire Zouaves) traveled to Annapolis and were mustered into service in Washington on May 7, 1861. The regiment's field officers and captains were all fire company officers or firemen. The two flank companies of the regiment were issued the Model 1855 rifle with saber bayonet (probably the soldiers Reynolds saw), with the others were given the Sharps rifle with saber bayonet. Richard Warren and Roger Sturcke, "11th New York Volunteer Infantry, (Ellsworth's First New York Fire Zouaves, 1861–1862), in *Military Collector and Historian* 39 (Winter 1987), 174–77.

4. Laura Keene (1826–1873) was born in England but immigrated to the United States and began her acting career in the early 1850s. She managed Laura Keene's New Theater in New York from 1855 to 1863. Despite her successful acting career, she is perhaps most famous for being present at Ford's Theater when Lincoln was assassinated in 1865. David S. and Jeanne T. Heidler, *Encyclopedia of the American Civil War* (New York: W.W. Norton, 2000), 1107–08.

5. The famous gallery of Henry William Mathew Meade (his brother died in 1858 but the name "Meade Brothers" was retained) was located at 233 Broadway.

6. Taylor's, at the corner of Broadway and Franklin, opened in the early 1850s. Described as "finished in a gorgeous manner," the "immensely popular" establishment became "one of the institutions of Broadway" until it closed in 1866. *New York Times*, July 31, 1866.

7. Mrs. John Wood came to America from England in 1854, and in 1863 became manager of the Olympic Theater in New York. Comedian Joseph Jefferson became famous for his role as "Rip Van Winkle." Arthur Hornblow, *A History of the Theatre in America From Its Beginnings to the Present Time*, 2 vols. (Philadelphia: J.B. Lippincott Co., 1919), 2: 113, 217.

8. Phineas Taylor Barnum's celebrated "American Museum" operated from 1841 until it was destroyed by fire in 1865. For Barnum's detailed account of the operation of his museum, see *Life of P.T. Barnum, Written by Himself*, published in Buffalo by the Courier Company in 1888.

9. A native of Williamsburg, Massachusetts, Erastus Titus worked as a mercantile house clerk before he came to New York in 1825. He worked for about 20 years for Ephraim Tredwell, a wholesale ship's bread and cracker baker, but then established his own business on Washington Street. Titus retired about 1870 and died on November 28, 1890. *New York Times*, November 29, 1890.

10. W.R.L. Ward was a prominent merchant, former member of the company, and the father of Private J. Langdon Ward. "Mr. Savory" was George Savory. *Boston Daily Advertiser*, October 21, 1897.

11. From the English Order of the Garter, meaning "Shame be to him who thinks evil of it."

12. Probably the Twentieth Regiment, New York State Militia, otherwise known as the "Ulster Guard."

13. One member of the company noted that due to the kindness of the company's many friends in New York and the flattering notices in the New York papers, "we were in imminent danger of being spoiled," but that no man regretted leaving New York in response to "duty's call." *Salem Register*, May 13, 1861.

14. *The New York Herald* labeled the Zouave's cheer "peculiar," but their drill "much admired." *The New York Herald*, May 5, 1861. A member of the Eighth described the *Roanoke* as a "very large Packet ship" of 1,200 tons," handsomely fitted up," part of a line that had formerly operated between New York and Richmond, but since the outbreak of war had been chartered by the government to carry stores and provisions

Notes—Chapter 5

to Federal troops at Fort Monroe and Washington. The company's non-commissioned officers enjoyed a small room with eight berths, "very cosey [sic] and comfortable," along with ample provisions. *Salem Register*, May 13, 1861.

15. One member of the Eighth wrote, "As a company we were all much pleased to get away from New York.... With the most of them, they lived too high at 'the Astor,' as was proved by the sea-sick ones on passing Sandy Hook." *Salem Observer*, May 18, 1861.

16. Another member of the company noted the rough weather, and that "we poor landsmen had to make our votive offering." *Salem Register*, May 13, 1861.

17. Extracts from the U.S. Army Regulations were read first, and then Hall, a Boston recruit, conducted the service. Because of the presence of about a dozen very good singers, "our choir was one which would not disgrace one of our churches," and the testaments given each man in New York by the New York Bible Society were put to good use. *Salem Register*, May 13, 1861. "With deeper feelings than I can express," wrote one Zouave, "the first religious service since leaving home was deeply appreciated." "All seemed impressed with that same inexpressible awe and thankfulness to Him, who held us then even 'in the hollow of His hand,' and who had so kindly guarded us and kept us from the many dangers with which we had been encompassed," a soldier believed, "and from every heart went out the silent plea for guidance through the dangers we were hourly approaching, and with each plea an earnest prayer for a continuance of that inspiration which has been with us all, and which would transform the terrors of death into a glorious privilege." *Salem Observer*, May 18, 1861.

18. U.S.S. *Cumberland*, a frigate launched in 1842, saw service in the Gulf of Mexico during the Mexican War. In the late 1850s, the *Cumberland* was the flagship of the African Squadron, but when the Civil War began was at Norfolk Navy Yard. On April 20, 1861, when the yard was in danger of capture by Confederate forces, many ships there were scuttled, but *Cumberland* was towed away and survived. The following March the ship was destroyed in combat with the CSS *Virginia* in the action that preceded Virginia's duel with U.S.S. *Monitor*. U.S. Navy Department, Naval History Division, *Dictionary of American Naval Fighting Ships*, (1963), II: 214–15. A member of the Salem company described the *Cumberland* as a "jackass frigate" of about thirty-two guns. The *Cumberland*'s band serenaded the Massachusetts men with several national airs and "Dixie." *Salem Register*, May 13, 1861.

19. The U.S. Navy Department purchased the screw steamer *Cambridge* in Boston on July 30, 1861. Report of the Secretary of the Navy, in 37th Congress, 2nd Session, Senate Executive Document No. 1, *Message of the President of the United States to the Two Houses of Congress*, 3 vols. (Washington, D.C.: Government Printing Office, 1861), III: 127. Reynolds included a list of the Coast Guard members on a separate sheet of paper inserted in his diary. The note reads, "Mass. Coast Guard on the Cambridge off Fortress Monroe Apr. 1861," and lists the names John Dove, sergeant, Charles J. Lee, corporal, and Charles Phillips, William Huntington, Albert Upton, Frank Pope, Andrew J. Millett, James H. Turner, Thomas A. Arnold, William Henry, Benjamin C. Nichols, Nathan Cutler, and Charles E. Pond.

20. Another member of the Eighth believed that the merchantman was coming from the West Indies, did not know of Virginia's secession, and was proceeding to Norfolk. *Salem Register*, May 13, 1861.

21. One member of the company reported that "never will any of us forget that night," as the rain fell "in perfect torrents," and the night was black as ink, except when a "bright, fierce flash" of lightning would "make objects apparent for miles around." *Salem Observer*, May 18, 1861.

5. Washington

1. Other soldiers were far more eloquent in their description of Mount Vernon. "It may be, and I suppose it is, imagination, but the hazy atmosphere laden with the fragrance of the sugar and corn fields, seems to collect in all its glory over that sacred place. With unutterable feelings, which were only displayed in tears, did we all uncover as we passed that shore," wrote one Zouave. "I feel as if I had received there, anew, a charge from the fountainhead of patriotism, which spurs me on, quickens me, and now I know I am right, and am more than ever, ready to give up my life to that country upon whose altar that great man laid all that was dear to him and when we look from that sacred place and trace back the career of our dear fore-fathers ... it does seem to me that we grumble too much." *Salem Observer*, May 18, 1861.

2. Its garrison destroyed the first Fort Washington during the British invasion of Washington in 1814. The second fort was completed in 1824.

3. Company A, Fifth Massachusetts Infantry was also known as the "Mechanic Light Infantry."

4. Construction on two extensions of the Capitol was started in 1851 but still not finished when the Civil War began. On May 15, 1861,

Montgomery Meigs, the supervising engineer of the Capitol, suspended construction on the building. Work was not renewed until April 1862. Despite the order, work continued on the Capitol dome. On December 2, 1863, the statue of Freedom was completed atop the two massive iron shells. The dome was entirely finished in 1866, the extensions in 1867. William C. Allen, *History of the United States Capitol: A Chronicle of Design, Construction, and Politics* (Washington, D.C.: U.S. Government Printing Office, 2001), 314, 318, 325, 340–42.

5. Colonel Edward Ward Hinks was born in Bucksport, Maine, on May 30, 1830. By the mid–1850s, he had moved to Boston and was a member of the Massachusetts legislature. A printer by trade, he established a printing and publishing business and studied law. In 1859, he became adjutant of the Eighth Massachusetts Infantry, and on December 18, 1860, wrote to Major Robert Anderson at Fort Moultrie in Charleston, South Carolina, offering his services in case the Federal garrison was attacked. Anderson replied to his "gallant" offer, stating that if they were attacked, "there is scarcely a possibility of our being able to hold out long enough to enable our friends to come to our succor." In early March 1861, Hinks applied to Secretary of War Simon Cameron for a commission in the Regular Army. Assured of a commission as a lieutenant, Hinks was arranging his affairs in order to accept the commission when the bombardment of Fort Sumter took place. Still an officer in the Massachusetts Volunteer Militia, he went with the Eighth Massachusetts to Washington, where he learned that he had in fact been appointed a second lieutenant in the Second U.S. Cavalry, and had orders to report to that unit. General Benjamin Butler requested a leave of absence of 15 days for Hinks, but at the conclusion of that period Hinks requested an indefinite leave of absence from the Regular Army. The Adjutant General informed Hinks that further leave would not be granted, and the only way for him to retain his commission in the Eighth Massachusetts would be to resign his commission with the Regulars. He reluctantly resigned from the Second Cavalry on June 4, 1861. Following his service with the Eighth Massachusetts, at whose head he had achieved "an enviable reputation," Hinks was appointed colonel of the Nineteenth Massachusetts Infantry on August 3, 1861. He led the regiment at the Battle of Ball's Bluff, the siege of Yorktown, the Battle of Fair Oaks and other actions. Hinks was wounded twice during the Peninsula Campaign's Battle of Glendale (once severely in the ankle, and again through the upper part of his right thigh). He was wounded twice at the Battle of Antietam as well (in the abdomen, the bullet passing "through body in the bowels perforating colon," and a second bullet that fractured the bone in his right arm). Appointed a brigadier general of volunteers on March 4, 1863, Hinks briefly commanded the Point Lookout, Maryland, prisoner of war camp, then led an African-American division at the Siege of Petersburg. He was named a brevet major general of volunteers before his resignation from the army on June 30, 1865. Given a commission again in the Regular Army in 1866, Hinks served until his retirement in 1870, then became commandant of the U.S. Soldiers' Home in Hampton, Virginia, and moved to the Milwaukee branch and served there until 1880. He died in Cambridge, Massachusetts on February 14, 1894. In 1871, Hinks changed his middle name to Winslow and his surname to "Hincks." Harrison Ellery and Charles Pickering Bowditch, *The Pickering Genealogy*, 3 vols. (Cambridge: University Press, 1897), III: 933–35; *Appletons' Annual Cyclopedia and Register of Important Events of the Year 1894*, New Series Vol. XIX, Whole Series Vol. XXXIV (New York: D. Appleton & Co., 1895), 581–82; National Archives, *U.S. Army Generals' Reports of Civil War Service, 1864–1887*, M1098, Roll 1, Vol. 2, pgs. 341–69; Warner, *Generals in Blue*, 229–30; *Milwaukee Daily Sentinel*, July 10, 1879; Francis B. Heitman, *Historical Register and Dictionary of the United States Army*, 2 vols. (Washington, D.C.: Government Printing Office, 1903), I: 532; Massachusetts Adjutant General, *Massachusetts Soldiers, Sailors and Marines in the Civil War*, II: 411; VI: 765; Hurd, *History of Essex County*, I: 362–65; Waitt, *History of the Nineteenth Regiment Massachusetts Volunteer Infantry*, 3.

6. On the morning of May 9, Colonel Ellsworth was asked for assistance to put out a fire near the Willard Hotel. Nearly the entire regiment of Zouaves battled the blaze for two hours and prevented the Willard from catching fire, earning the praise of local citizens. Randall, *Colonel Elmer Ellsworth*, 241–42. The incident was front-page news for *Harper's Weekly*, which featured the prowess of Ellsworth's men in its May 25, 1861 issue.

7. Winfield Scott's three-volume *Infantry-Tactics* (for use by the Regular Army) appeared in numerous editions between 1835 and 1861. In addition, a version of Scott's work for use by the militia first appeared in 1830 and was republished in several additions as well. Grady McWhiney and Perry D. Jamieson, *Attack and Die: Civil War Military Tactics and the Southern Heritage* (University, AL: University of Alabama Press, 1982), 31.

8. During breaks from their drill sessions, members of the Seventh New York lounged on the grass and amused themselves by watching the drill of their "friends" from Massachusetts.

"They, too, like ourselves, were going through the transformations," wrote Theodore Winthrop. "These sturdy fellows were then in a rough enough chrysalis of uniform," he noted. "That shed, they would look worthy of themselves." Winthrop, *Life in the Open Air*, 260. According to one newspaper account, any member of the Salem company who chose to remain in Washington to drill recruits received an offer of the princely sum of $100 per month. Not one volunteered. *The Boston Herald*, August 1, 1861.

9. Probably U.S. Army Quartermaster Major Michael M. Clark, a Virginia native and West Point graduate who died in Baltimore on May 10. His funeral was held in Washington at 3 P.M. on May 11 with full military honors. (Washington, D.C.) *Daily National Intelligencer*, May 11, 1861.

10. A member of the Lynn Light Infantry (Company D, Eighth Massachusetts) reported to his hometown newspaper that the weight of his musket, knapsack, haversack, cartridge and cap boxes and ammunition made it "no easy thing to march," while his heavy overcoat and three woolen shirts were "awful warm and uncomfortable." "We are the homeliest set of mortals you ever saw, with our United States uniform on," he believed. After an issue of hard bread and salt fish, this unfortunate soldier threw away some clothes, as he could not carry them all, and then waited to leave the Capitol, with everything "in readiness for a hard fight." Despite rumors that "the rebels were shooting the [Union] troops like dogs, and our men must be reinforced as soon as possible," the order to march never came. After spending the night on the marble floor, wearing his equipment and using his knapsack for a pillow, the Lynn soldier agreed, "the men did not like the idea of not going, after all the fuss, but complaints are of no use here." *Daily Evening Item* (Lynn, MA), May 13, 1911.

11. Lutheran Rev. Dr. John George Butler, born in Cumberland, Maryland, in 1826, attended the Theological Seminary in Gettysburg, Pennsylvania, but in 1849 became minister at St. Paul's Church in Washington, D.C. He served as a Union Army chaplain during the Civil War. The Rev. J.C. Jensson, *American Lutheran Biographies* (Milwaukee: Houtkamp, 1890), 129–31.

12. Although Reynolds enjoyed his visit to the Senate Chamber, one of his comrades had a far less agreeable experience there. Soon after the regiment's arrival at the Capitol, a stack of muskets fell down, one discharged, and a bullet struck the foot of Lieutenant Moses S. Herrick of Beverly. He was carried to the old Senate Chamber, then occupied by the Supreme Court, where his foot was amputated. He remained there until he could be removed, and in fact other members of the regiment were housed there in a makeshift hospital. Members of the Massachusetts Relief Society waited on the patients. *National Tribune*, March 24, 1887. The members of the Seventh New York raised the sum of $500 for the wounded Herrick. Roehrenbeck, *The Regiment That Saved the Capital*, 134.

13. John B. Floyd, James Buchanan's secretary of war from 1857 to 1860, was accused by Northerners of having transferred thousands of weapons from Northern to Southern arsenals in anticipation of war. A Congressional investigative committee returned no verdict, although its chairman exonerated Floyd. Reynolds is quite likely referring to the U.S. Model 1816/22 .69 caliber smoothbore musket, converted from its original flint to the percussion ignition system, manufactured at the Springfield and Harpers Ferry Armories and issued in large numbers to Union volunteer units early in the war.

14. Reynolds is incorrect. Lieutenant Roger Jones set fire to the Harpers Ferry Arsenal buildings on the night of April 18, 1861, nearly a month before this event.

6. Relay House

1. Colonel Edward Franc Jones became colonel of the Sixth Massachusetts Regiment in 1858. He led the regiment to Washington following the "Pratt Street Riot" in Baltimore, and ended the Civil War as a brevet brigadier general of volunteers. The Boston Light Artillery (Major Asa M. Cook commanding), consisting of six 6-pounder guns, left Boston on April 21 and arrived in Annapolis three days later. They arrived at the Relay House on May 5. The battery returned to Boston on August 3 in order to be mustered out. Nason, *History and Complete Roster of the Massachusetts Regiments, Minute Men of '61*, 221, 287.

2. According to one participant, the combination of mud, heat and heavy accoutrements "tried us harder than any thing we had yet undergone." *Salem Register*, May 23, 1861.

3. The viaduct referred to is the Thomas Viaduct, the longest bridge in the United States (700 feet) at the time of its construction, and the second longest in the world.

4. Only a few days before, General Butler had discovered that, "to his disgust and horror," a private in the Sixth Massachusetts had been poisoned by strychnine-laced food sold by a peddler. The soldier survived, but Butler was compelled to temporarily "cut off all purchases from unauthorized persons." Butler labeled such people "insane enemies," and cautioned that any similar attempts would be "followed by the

Notes — Chapter 6

swiftest, surest, and most condign punishment." Moore, *Rebellion Record*, I, 209. In mid–June, after a row originated around a beer table, Colonel Jones of the Sixth Massachusetts ordered all "pea-nut and pasty stands" off the camp grounds. "Their absence will be much felt by the troops," wrote one member of the regiment. *Berkshire County Eagle*, June 27, 1861. The same soldier noted later that the refreshment stands were nearly all gone, but would reappear when the men were paid. *Berkshire County Eagle*, July 11, 1861.

5. Joseph Short of Salem patented his knapsack on November 12, 1861. U.S. House of Representatives, 37th Congress, 2nd Session, Executive Document 53, *Patent Office Report for the Year 1861-Mechanical*, 98.

6. An illustration of the Baltimore Steam Gun or Steam Battery, invented by Charles S. Dickinson, appeared in the May 18, 1861 issue of *Frank Leslie's Illustrated Newspaper*, the May 25, 1861 issue of *Harper's Weekly* and the May 25, 1861 issue of *Scientific American*. Dickinson's prediction that the gun would be "generally adopted" by the powers of the Old and New Worlds and would "prove the means and medium of peace" proved premature. One member of the Eighth believed that the gun "looks something like an Alligator's head on wheels." *Salem Register*, May 23, 1861. Reynolds was quite correct in his belief that railroad inventor and Baltimore manufacturer Ross Winans was incorrectly named as its inventor, and merely repaired the gun, but General Butler inaccurately described Winans as "a gray-haired old man of more than three score and ten, a bitter rebel, and reputed to be worth $15,000,000," and "builder of ... a very much relied upon instrument of warfare or assassination." *Autobiography and Personal Reminiscences of Major-General Ben. F. Butler, Butler's Book*, 227. The gun was held by the Massachusetts men until May 22, when it was shipped under guard to Annapolis, then to Fortress Monroe, and finally to Boston. *Berkshire County Eagle*, May 30, 1861. For a thorough history of this unusual weapon, see John W. Lamb's *A Strange Engine of War: The "Winans" Steam Gun and the Civil War in Maryland*, published by the Chesapeake Book Company in 2011.

7. A fellow member of the Eighth reported that the guard who arrested Winans had become alarmed by the curious crowd that pressed around them, and fearing his rescue, had fired his weapon and shouted the alarm. *Salem Register*, May 23, 1861. Federal authorities accused Winans of a number of disloyal acts, but he was soon released from custody upon the intervention of Secretary of State William Seward. *Autobiography and Personal Reminiscences of Major-General Ben. F. Butler, Butler's Book*, 234; Lamb, *A Strange Engine of War*, 38–40.

8. Another member of the regiment described using the rail fence nearby for ridgepoles and rafters, with the woods providing branches and leaves for thatch and bedding. The "huts" could accommodate six sleepers. *Salem Register*, May 23, 1861.

9. A member of the Eighth described being able to see the smoke rising from roofs in Baltimore nine miles away, and in between was "the greatest diversity of scenery imaginable," with rivers, bridges, houses, villages, woods and plains all combining to make "the handsomest view I ever saw." *Salem Register*, May 23, 1861.

10. The Federals were encamped in a fashionable part of Elkridge Landing known as "Lawyers' Hill," so named because Judge George W. Dobbin, Thomas Donaldson and John H.B. Latrobe, all attorneys, were the first to build homes in the area. Dobbin's home was known as "The Lawn," Donaldson's as "Edgewood" and Latrobe's as "Fairy Knowe." The area was divided politically, with Donaldson a Republican, while most of the Latrobes and all of the Dobbins were Democrats. The three families had a pact never to discuss politics with each other, although the Dobbin family supposedly helped Confederate recruits on their way south, and Donaldson used his influence to protect his neighbors from Union foragers. *The Sun* (Baltimore), February 21, 1909; April 4, 1937.

11. Albert C. Douglas was born in Salem in 1842. Although described as "physically delicate," Douglas re-enlisted in the Nineteenth Massachusetts Infantry and rose to the rank of sergeant major. He served for the remainder of the war and died in Sacramento, California, in 1905. Nason, *History and Complete Roster of the Massachusetts Regiments, Minute Men of '61*, 268.

12. Members of the Eighth reported varied encounters with the civilians of Baltimore, ranging from displays of open hostility to enthusiastic pro–Union sentiments. In early May, a member of the Pittsfield company walked through downtown Baltimore and was treated "in the most gentlemanly manner" with one exception. *Berkshire County Eagle*, May 23, 1861. In late June, another soldier wrote that the city appeared "as strongly bent to defy the Federal Government" as when the Baltimore riot took place. *Berkshire County Eagle*, July 11, 1861. At the same time, some members of the Salem Zouaves reported being "taunted and insulted" in the city, while others thought the city "well conducted and orderly." *Salem Register*, June 20, 1861. Pittsfield soldier Fred Smith wrote on July 5 that the Massachusetts men did not receive a solitary cheer during their march through the city, though Union flags were displayed in con-

siderable numbers and occasionally a youngster would yell, "I am a Union man." He complained that so slight a demonstration from a city that claimed to be Union was "an idle farce." When most of the regiment paraded through the city in late July, the Eighth's men received gifts of handkerchiefs and flags from Union ladies. *Berkshire County Eagle*, July 25, August 1, 1861. Understandably, Baltimore visitors who made the lengthy trip to Camp Essex were quite friendly. On May 15, visitors from Baltimore were "quite social and the troops have enjoyed their society much." *Berkshire County Eagle*, May 30, 1861. On another occasion, two little girls came into camp dressed in Union costume. *Berkshire County Eagle*, July 11, 1861.

13. In his resignation letter submitted to Governor Andrew, Monroe cited his thirty years of service in the Massachusetts Militia, noting that he was now "more than threescore years of age" and wished that a younger officer would take command of the regiment. General Benjamin Butler noted that "no suspicion of unworthy or improper motives can by possibility attach to his application," and Governor Andrew paid tribute to Monroe's "long and meritorious services." *Salem Register*, May 20, 1861. The regiment's officers met on May 22 and offered resolutions stating that with Monroe's resignation they were deprived of the services of "a meritorious officer," and an "agreeable and respected gentleman," and hoped he would not forget his old command. *Daily National Intelligencer* (Washington, D.C.), May 27, 1861.

14. Benjamin Perley Poore was born on November 2, 1820 in Newburyport, Massachusetts. Although educated for the law, he spent much of his pre–Civil War life as a newspaper editor or correspondent. After his service with the Eighth, he served as clerk of printing records of the United States Senate, edited the Congressional Directory and Congressional Record and published many books, including his reminiscences, the year before his death. Poore was personally acquainted with every president from John Quincy Adams to Grover Cleveland, and "made a reputation as a raconteur." He died in Washington, D.C., on May 30, 1887. John J. Currier, *Ould Newbury: Historical and Biographical Sketches* (Boston: Damrell and Upham, 1896), 351–55; *Bangor* (ME) *Daily Whig and Courier*, May 31, 1887. For Poore's recollections of the first few weeks of the war in Washington, D.C., see *National Tribune*, March 24, 1887.

15. Fred Smith of the Pittsfield company described the forenoon drill as "one of the most severe drills that we have experienced," part of the "Hardee tactics, which is now adopted in the U.S. Army. It comes rather hard upon the boys." *Berkshire County Eagle*, May 30, 1861.

16. The men were so cold that on their return trip to camp, when challenged by sentries with the cry "Who goes there?" one wag answered, "A lump of ice!" Nevertheless, the same soldier admitted, "I like it [this duty] very much. When reading old hunting stories, I always thought I should like camp fire life, but never expected I should ever see any of it." *Salem Register*, May 23, 1861.

17. According to the *Baltimore Sun*, ten members of the regiment ("but not the original members") refused to take the oath, one claiming to have been intimidated, the remainder because Colonel Monroe had added thirteen days to their service. *Baltimore Sun*, May 21, 1861.

18. Singing relieved "the monotony of solider life, and remind us of pleasures and associations which we have left behind us." *Berkshire County Eagle*, July 11, 1861.

19. Salem native Charles Babbidge graduated from Harvard and the Divinity School and was ordained in 1833. He left his Pepperell, Massachusetts, congregation to serve as chaplain of the Sixth Massachusetts Infantry, and was a veteran of the "Pratt Street Riot" in Baltimore. He died in 1898. *The Year-Book of the Unitarian Congregational Churches for 1899* (Boston: American Unitarian Association, 1899), 7.

20. Because of a "special arrangement" made between the federal government and New York's governor, the Seventh was mustered in for only thirty days rather than the three-month period required of other Union units serving at this time. Roehrenbeck, *The Regiment That Saved the Capital*, 130–31.

21. Another participant in the expedition recalled, "the desire on the part of men to go was so great, that every man who was not allowed to do so, considered himself personally aggrieved." *Salem Gazette*, June 14, 1861.

22. A participant in the expedition described Ellicott's Mills as "a miniature Lowell, where flags were flying on almost every building." *Salem Gazette*, June 14, 1861.

23. A Salem newspaper reported that the both public and private reports about the affair were "anything but creditable" to Massachusetts, and believed "the quicker the matter is thoroughly investigated and the trouble removed, the better." The paper also noted that Captain Devereux was one of the most popular officers in the regiment. *Salem Gazette*, June 7, 1861.

24. Mary Reynolds appears in the 1860 Census as 16 years old, born in Massachusetts. National Archives and Records Administration, *Eighth Census of the United States*, 1860, Microcopy 653, Roll 497, Massachusetts, Essex, Ward 2 Salem, p. 1052.

25. Not every man in the regiment was pleased

with the $5.50 payment. Many expected to receive and believed they were entitled to the amount usually paid by the state when militiamen were called out for special service, but received only the regular army pay. *Berkshire County Eagle*, June 6, 1861.

26. Although Captain Devereux had asked for ten recruits, nearly twice that number volunteered to join the company. Reynolds refers to William T. Fowler of 40 Mill Street, Salem. Several hundred citizens who "cheered them lustily as the train left" had witnessed the departure of the recruits. *Salem Observer*, May 25, 1861.

27. One member of the regiment estimated that 150 men were tried. He guessed that their punishment would be extra drill or imprisonment in the guard tent with only bread and water. He noted that the latter was no punishment, "as this is the standard bill of fare throughout the regiment." *Berkshire County Eagle*, June 6, 1861.

28. A member of the Allen Guards thought the sham battle "was very well conducted, and seemed quite like war to witness a whole regiment rushing on at double quick time, and charge bayonets," with the artillery battery defending itself "in a soldierly manner." *Berkshire County Eagle*, June 6, 1861.

29. The officers of the regiment voted to suspend drills on Sunday, a move that pleased the men, as it allowed them "one unbroken day" to clean up their tents, bathe, etc. *Berkshire County Eagle*, June 13, 1861.

30. In a letter home, a member of the regiment detailed the preparations for Sunday inspections: "It is our duty to pack our knapsacks neatly, and range them along the side of the tent, and fold our blankets, placing them in the left hand upper corner. A party of six is then detailed, whose duty it is to 'police' the company street, as it is called; that is they are to clear up every scrap of paper and every stick, and make everything presentable. The muskets are all taken from the tents, and must be thoroughly cleaned of rust and dirt, and stacked in front of the several tents. After this, the company are formed in line, and taking their muskets march to the Regimental Parade Ground, where the muskets and equipments are inspected. If the former are not sufficiently clean, the men will be sent back to quarters to finish them. After this, comes the tent inspection. The Colonel and other officers march along the company street, just glancing into the tents to see if the regulations have been fulfilled." The soldier also described his tent: "Our tent has a gunrack neatly built at the head of it, which we find rather preferable to the old arrangement, which was, to pile them up in one corner, where the chances were about even of their standing up, or falling over upon some of us when asleep. At the mouth of the tent stands a nondescript article, which we make the general depository of all our loose goods. It partakes of the nature of the genus bedstead, species crib, being a large box mounted on four legs. It serves as a bureau in pleasant, and a breakfast table in rainy weather." *Salem Gazette*, June 14, 1861.

31. The nearby village was described as "terribly behind the age," with inhabitants living hand to mouth, about twenty-five houses (of which at least seven were grocery stores), almost all of those containing bar rooms (but no liquor for sale, per orders from the Federal commander), and a defunct "Furnace Iron Factory." *Salem Gazette*, June 14, 1861.

32. This officer could not be identified.

33. Although the Massachusetts men probably read anything available, the *Atlantic Monthly* magazine seemed to be quite popular. The "reading and writing regiment" enjoyed perusing the *Atlantic* "with evident pleasure and satisfaction." At one point thirty copies of the magazine were distributed to each company, so that every other man in the regiment received a copy. *Salem Gazette*, June 11, 1861.

34. Fred Smith agreed, writing that the country had lost a powerful man, "and one whose fidelity to the Union was of the strongest material." *Berkshire County Eagle*, June 13, 1861.

35. Regimental punishments included confinement in the stocks, a log and chain attached to the leg, and fatigue duty. *Berkshire County Eagle*, July 25, 1861. In this particular instance, two men were sentenced to chop wood and draw water for three companies for one week; another to drill two hours per day for ten days while wearing a knapsack; and one to forfeit ten dollars, "or his month's pay." These punishments were inflicted for running the guard, being absent from roll call, drunkenness, etc. *Berkshire County Eagle*, June 13, 1861.

36. According to one eyewitness, it rained steadily for more than fifty hours. *Salem Gazette*, June 7, 1861.

37. Johnson also turned out for guard duty one evening. "He seemed to enter with hearty gusto," wrote one Salem man, "into all our duties, and he did them as well as the best of us," but "business engagements" would not allow him to enlist. *Salem Register*, June 20, 1861.

38. On June 5, Fred Smith wrote, "our quarters are in a miserable condition," reminding him of a "model pig pen." *Berkshire County Eagle*, June 13, 1861.

39. Boston native George Hughes Hepworth became the minister at the Church of the Unity in that city on a permanent basis in 1858. He later became a Union Army chaplain. Susan

Hayes Ward, *George H. Hepworth: Preacher, Journalist, Friend of the People* (New York: E.P. Dutton and Company, 1903), 66–67.

40. A member of the Pittsfield company wrote, "The boys say that Col. Hinks is a white man, and I think I can endorse their opinion." *Berkshire County Eagle*, July 25, 1861. He later wrote, "He is in every respect a gentleman, and is greatly beloved by the entire regiment." *Berkshire County Eagle*, June 13, 1861.

41. One observer reported the temperature to be "99 in the shade, and the sweat pours off of us as we lie under the trees." The men anticipated even hotter weather in July, and prayed, "we may not get moved further south." *Berkshire County Eagle*, June 20, 13, 1861.

42. Edward H. Staten was captain of Company A, Fifth Massachusetts Infantry.

43. Sergeant Albert J. Lowd of Salem was a member of Company A, Fifth Massachusetts Infantry.

44. "Fairy Knowe" was the year-round home of John H.B. Latrobe from 1857–1863. For a detailed description of the home, see John E. Semmes, *John H.B. Latrobe and his Times, 1803–1891* (Baltimore: The Norman, Remington Co., 1917), 453.

45. Thomas Donaldson, a civil engineer on the Baltimore and Ohio Railroad, married his cousin Mary Elizabeth Pickering Dorsey of Boston in 1838. He purchased land in Elkridge, Maryland, about 1843, and built "a comfortable house" he called Edgewood. George William Brown, *A Sketch of the Life of Thomas Donaldson* (Baltimore: Cushings and Bailey, 1881), 13. He was described as an "avowed Union man" during the Civil War. Ellery and Bowditch *Pickering Genealogy*, II: 456–58.

46. General Ben Butler, then at Fortress Monroe, ordered two Federal columns from Hampton and Newport News against Confederate earthworks near Big Bethel Church. On June 10, 1861, in the first land battle in Virginia, the Federals launched two uncoordinated assaults and were repulsed, suffering approximately 76 casualties, including Colonel Theodore Winthrop, the New York Infantry officer who had traveled with the Eighth Massachusetts from Annapolis to Washington. The Confederates suffered only a handful of casualties.

47. Marylanders went to the polls on June 13 to select six members of the U.S. House of Representatives for the special session of Congress scheduled to convene on July 4.

48. On June 3, Fred Smith of the Pittsfield company noted that "an ambrotype car" had wheeled up in front of the tents, and "a great rush for pictures" had occurred. *Berkshire County Eagle*, June 13, 1861.

49. Daniel Simpson was born in Maine in 1790. He began his career in military music at the age of ten when he became the drummer for a militia company. Simpson migrated to Boston in 1810 and served in the War of 1812, and while making a living as a businessman, continued to drum for military companies. He also organized his own band and became a drummer for the famous Ancient and Honorable Artillery Company. He died in 1886. *Boston Daily Globe*, July 29, 1886.

50. Fred Smith of Pittsfield noted that the Sixth came to the camp "leading an elephant, one of their own manufacture," accompanied by their regimental band. After the parade, Colonel Hinks spoke of the friendly relations between the Sixth and Eighth Massachusetts. Hinks offered 30 cents as a reward for the arrest of the "deserter" Major Poore. *Berkshire County Eagle*, June 20, 1861.

51. Augustus Morse was born in Worcester, Massachusetts, on May 16, 1817. In 1832, he went to Leominster as an apprentice to his brother in the "comb trade," and worked in partnership with him until the war broke out in 1861. His military career began at the age of eighteen, when he joined a local militia rifle company. Moving up through the ranks, he became major, then colonel of the Ninth Massachusetts, then brigadier general. He was chosen major general of the Third Division by the state legislature in 1856, an office he held until August 1861, when he resigned to become colonel of the Twenty-first Massachusetts Infantry. He retired from military service in the fall of 1863. Governor Andrew ordered him to take command of all troops arriving in Boston in April 1861. Morse died in Brooklyn, New York, on November 25, 1888. William A. Emerson, *Leominster, Massachusetts, Historical and Picturesque* (Gardner, MA: Lithotype Publishing Co., 1888), 156–58; *Boston Daily Advertiser*, February 13, 1856; November 28, 1888. Morse was supposedly "much pleased with the improvement which our regiment has made since leaving home," reported one soldier, "and remarked that he would never know that it was the same regiment which marched out of Faneuil Hall a few weeks since." *Berkshire County Eagle*, June 27, 1861.

52. Andrew's letter supposedly also noted that none of the new Massachusetts regiments would bear the same number as a regiment already in the field, a decree that pleased the Eighth's men, as "we prefer the new regiments should earn their own honors rather than take those which we have won and which justly belong to us alone." *Berkshire County Eagle*, June 27, 1861.

53. Officers not previously identified include three residents of Lynn, Massachusetts: Roland G. Usher, age 38, who left the Eighth Massachu-

setts to be commissioned as a paymaster in the U.S. Army on June 1, 1861; Bowman B. Breed, age 29, who served with the regiment for its entire service; and Ephraim Alfred Ingells, age 34, who also served until the regiment was mustered out in August 1861. *Massachusetts Soldiers, Sailors and Marines in the Civil War*, I: 517.

54. Possibly Captain Peter Silver, a Salem native and ship captain who made voyages throughout the world and retired just before the Civil War. He then served on the city's board of alderman and water board, and was president of the Salem Savings Bank when he died in 1883. *Boston Daily Advertiser*, October 8, 1883: Walton Advertising and Printing Company, *The One Hundred Years of the Salem Savings Bank* (Salem, MA: Salem Savings Bank, 1918), 33–35.

7. Baltimore

1. Reynolds is mistaken. George Hume Steuart (1828–1903) was born in Baltimore and graduated from West Point in 1848. After service on the frontier, Captain Steuart resigned in April 1861 and accepted a commission in the Confederate Army. He led the First Maryland Infantry at the Battle of First Manassas. Promoted to brigadier general the following March, Steuart commanded a brigade in the Shenandoah Valley Campaign in 1862, at Gettysburg in 1863, and during the Petersburg Campaign in 1864–65. William C. Davis, ed., *The Confederate General*, 6 vols. (Harrisburg, PA: National Historical Society, 1991), 6: 2–3. The Second Massachusetts Battery (Nims' Battery) arrived at the Steuart home just after the departure of the Eighth Massachusetts. An engraving of the area around the house is included in Caroline E. Whitcomb's *History of the Second Massachusetts Battery (Nims' Battery) of Light Artillery, 1861–1865* (Concord, N.H.: The Rumford Press, 1912).

2. The Bellevue Gardens was described as a twelve-acre plot with a view of Chesapeake Bay, the Patapsco River and the city, "stocked with shade trees of various kinds." The area was the scene of German-American celebrations, including the "Steuben Festival" honoring Baron von Steuben in 1858. *The [Baltimore] Sun*, September 3, 1858. William Rullman, the owner, was a native of Hesse-Darmstadt and appears in the 1860 U.S. Census as a "tavern keeper." National Archives and Records Administration, *Eighth Census of the United States*, 1860, Microcopy 653, Roll 465, Maryland, Baltimore, 18th Ward Baltimore City, p. 867. The 1860 city directory lists William Rullman at "Baltimore w[.] of Fulton. *Woods' Baltimore City Directory* (Baltimore: John W. Woods, 1860), 330.

3. Reynolds inserted the following after the asterisk: "'First part of the troop,' is the name of the signal given by the drummers for the guard details to fall in preparatory to mounting the Guard."

4. This was likely nineteen-year-old Private Edward Burge of Company I, Twenty-second New York Infantry, who was killed in Baltimore on June 30, 1861.

5. The steamer *Hugh Jenkins*, built in 1849, was purchased by the U.S. Quartermaster's Department from the Eastern Shore Steamboat Company on September 9, 1861. 37th Congress, 2nd Session, Senate Executive Document No. 37, *Letter of the Secretary of War, in answer to a resolution of the Senate of the 30th day of January, in relation to the vessels purchased or chartered for the use of the War Department since the 1st day of April last*, 12.

6. Colonel Samuel Ogle Tilghman was accused of "drilling a rebel company" and being "a noted secessionist and commander of a mixed battalion of infantry and cavalry." *Salem Register*, July 11, 1861; Nason, *History and Complete Roster of the Massachusetts Regiments, Minute Men of '61*, 235. The 40-year-old Maryland-born farmer was living in Queen Anne's County, Maryland, in 1860, with $8,000 in real estate and $6,000 in personal property. National Archives and Records Administration, *Eighth Census of the United States*, 1860, Microcopy 653, Roll 479, Maryland, Queen Anne's County, District No. 5, p. 743. On July 6, 1861, Tilghman stated that while at his home at Bennett's Point, Queen Anne's County, Maryland, he was disturbed by knocking at his front door. He found a party of armed men and "a person representing himself to be a Deputy of the United States Marshal" there to arrest him on the orders of Governor Thomas Hicks. Tilghman was placed aboard a steamer and taken to Fort McHenry. There he gave an oath that he would not commit any hostile acts against the United States government, and would, as soon as possible, surrender the arms furnished his company. National Archives, *Unfiled Papers and Slips Belonging in Confederate Compiled Service Records*, Microcopy 347, Roll 394. Sources differ as to the date of Tilghman's release. One source states that he was released on a parole of honor on July 16, 1861. Another source lists him as a political prisoner confined at Fort McHenry on July 3, 1861 and released on July 6. *Official Records*, series II, vol. 2, 36, 226. A third source claims that Tilghman was released on July 18. *The [Baltimore] Sun*, July 19, 1861. A member of the Pittsfield company noted that the Salem men "seemed highly elated at their success, as this is the third attempt which has been made to capture him." *Berkshire County Eagle*, July 11, 1861. The man named Bryan that Reynolds states was also taken prisoner is prob-

ably neighbor George L. Bryan, who may have been a witness against Tilghman. *The* [Baltimore] *Sun*, July 4, 1861.

7. Surprisingly, this is one of the few references Reynolds makes to slaves or slavery. Other members of the regiment were far more willing to make note of the contentious practice. "W.A.F," a member of the Eighth (perhaps William A. Fraser, the first sergeant of Company D, the Lynn Light Infantry) wrote to a Massachusetts paper that Maryland was "indeed a rich country; but alas! the 'institution' of slavery darkens and despoils this fair portion of 'our common heritage.'" The presence of New England farmers, he noted, would make it the "'garden of Eden.'" Murray, *A Time of War*, 40.

8. Following the War of 1812, the Army's Coastal Fortifications Board determined that Fort McHenry could no longer adequately defend the rapidly growing city of Baltimore against a naval bombardment, and urged the construction of another fort further southeast of the city. Construction began on Fort Carroll (named in honor of Charles Carroll, a signer of the Declaration of Independence) on Sollers Point Flats, about four miles from McHenry, in 1847. Engineer officer Robert E. Lee supervised the fort's construction from 1848 to 1852. Although capable of mounting 225 guns in four tiers, the fort was only partially finished in 1861, and in fact was never completed.

9. The U.S. Navy chartered the *Adelaide* from the Baltimore Steam Packet Company. Report of the Secretary of the Navy, in 37th Congress, 2nd Session, Senate Executive Document No. 1, *Message of the President of the United States to the Two Houses of Congress*, 3 vols. (Washington, D.C.: Government Printing Office, 1861), III: 144.

10. A Mr. Lincoln, a Massachusetts man formerly of the Westborough State Reform School, managed the City House of Refuge. *Berkshire County Eagle*, August 1, 1861. One eyewitness believed the house of refuge contingent numbered 120. *Berkshire County Eagle*, July 11, 1861.

11. The crowd of visitors did not include any African-Americans, who "swarmed" into the camp during the first few days after the regiment's arrival, but who were eventually refused entrance by order of the colonel, so that, according to one member of the regiment, "the character of our visitors" was "much improved." *Berkshire County Eagle*, July 25, 1861.

12. Fred Smith of the Pittsfield company wrote that their celebration of the Fourth was "not a very grand affair," but the festivities "have in a substantial manner assisted in perpetuating the existence of our flag and Constitution which this day commemorates." *Berkshire County Eagle*, July 11, 1861.

13. A member of the Pittsfield company noted that summer vegetables were quite plentiful in the city, and were making their appearance in camp. He visited the market and found an abundance of vegetables, "at prices comparing favorably with those of our northern cities," including potatoes from $3 to $3.75 per barrel, cabbages at $2 to $4 per hundred, and blackberries at 6 cents per quart. The Pittsfield company enjoyed new potatoes and cabbage, a "great treat," along with green peas, "great quantities of cherries" and strawberries at eight cents per quart. *Berkshire County Eagle*, July 25, 1861; July 11, 1861; June 13, 1861.

14. Possibly Lieutenant Colonel Robert Bruce of the Second Regiment, Maryland Infantry, Potomac Home Brigade.

15. On July 10, 1861, General Banks issued Special Orders Number 54, which allowed passes to be issued "for good cause," but instructed soldiers to leave their arms in camp "to avoid controversy or collision with citizens." Soldiers were urged to obey the laws of the city, while commanders were instructed to pay attention to the army regulation that encouraged "useful occupations and manly exercises and diversions" while repressing "dissipation and immortality." Soldiers who violated city ordinances were to be punished by civil tribunals according to Maryland law and denied further opportunities to visit the city. National Archives, *Letters Received by the Office of the Adjutant General (Main Series), 1861–1870*, Microcopy 619, Roll 2, Frames 494–495.

16. This individual could not be identified.

17. Massachusetts Major General Nathaniel Prentiss Banks and Regular Army Major W.W. Morris, the commander of Fort McHenry, reviewed the troops. Morris stated that the regiment's drill was "the best he ever saw executed by a volunteer organization in his life." *Berkshire County Eagle*, July 25, 1861.

18. Another member of the regiment found small trees and stout brush embedded in the ground 20 feet from the outer wall, pointed outward to delay attackers, palisades with loop holes covering the entrance to the gate and "two or three weak points," a large number of field pieces and "vast quantities of ammunition." Some soldiers found the fort's artesian well intriguing, while other men took note of the prisoners confined there, including the recently captured secessionist Tilghman, "a man of about 50 years of age" and "a determined character." *Berkshire County Eagle*, July 25, 1861.

19. Fred Smith of Pittsfield had a completely different view of the governor: "The satisfaction to us of being able to meet a man who has assumed so true a position for the Union, and that against so large a portion of the citizens of the

state over which he governed, was great. The threats which are frequently made to take his life do not seem to affect him, as he declares his position to be a true one, and one which he will never abandon." *Berkshire County Eagle*, June 20, 1861.

20. One of the Salem newspapers quoted a camp correspondent who noted that the uniform was "an elegant affair and reflects credit on the parties who have got it up." *Salem Register*, July 29, 1861.

21. Officers not previously identified include Colonel Abel Smith of the Thirteenth New York, Colonel William D. Lewis, Jr. of the Eighteenth Pennsylvania, Colonel Peter Lyle of the Nineteenth Pennsylvania, Colonel William H. Gray of the Twentieth Pennsylvania, and Colonel George W. Pratt of the Twentieth New York. Reynolds might be mistaking Lieutenant Colonel George Moore for Colonel Morehead of the Twentieth Pennsylvania.

22. Another member of the Eighth found the parade ground "fine," and the sight "grand." The reviewing officer was again General Nathaniel Banks. *Berkshire County Eagle*, July 25, 1861. An estimated 8,000 spectators, a large number of whom were women and children, witnessed the review of 5,468 soldiers. *The* [Baltimore] *Sun*, July 19, 1861.

23. In 1820, the 320-acre estate of D.A. Smith, known as Calverton, was offered for sale, and the village of Calverton arose on the spot. By the early 1880s, Calverton contained a population of 400. J. Thomas Scharf, *History of Baltimore City and County* (Philadelphia: Louis H. Everts, 1881), 840.

24. A brief account in a local newspaper claimed that after "a tiresome search" they recovered not modern firearms, but "two old muskets." *The* [Baltimore] *Sun*, July 22, 1861.

25. The Eleventh New York Infantry suffered 188 casualties at First Bull Run, including 48 killed, 75 wounded, and 65 missing. *Official Records*, ser. 1, 2: 405.

26. Some members of other companies seemed to vacillate in their decision to remain in the service. Fred Smith of the Pittsfield company wrote on July 20 that few men in his company would re-enlist for three years, "unless compelled so to do for want of employment," that they had done their duty by responding promptly to the first call, that others would sacrifice less by a three year stay in the army than they would, and the "veterans" would let the new recruits fill their places. Only a few days later, however, he believed that "if [the] government needs our services, and should make a formal request, I think all would stay without a murmur" and the regiment would "respond to a man" as they would "pursue such a course as will reflect nothing but honor upon the State and those of our friends who are watching our movements." *Berkshire County Eagle*, July 25, 1861; August 1, 1861.

27. A member of the Berkshire company described the Zouave uniforms as "tasty," "which takes well, and draws for them, in connection with their good drilling, considerable praise." Other less fortunate members of the regiment were still attired in either their original militia uniforms or the "ungainly but comfortable blues, furnished by the U.S." *Berkshire County Eagle*, July 25, August 1, 1861.

28. Reynolds is incorrect, as Ellsworth had no siblings that survived until 1861.

29. This officer could not be identified.

30. Reynolds most likely misidentified Professor Perley Ray Lovejoy. Born in Fayette, Missouri, Lovejoy moved to Baltimore in the 1840s, became principal of Newton University, and taught at Baltimore City College. He joined the six-month Ninth Maryland Infantry (U.S.) as a private in June 1863 but was soon promoted to captain. Wounded in battle in October 1863, Lovejoy was mustered out in February 1864 and returned to teaching at the City College. He worked as a lawyer and public school principal and died in 1889. Bernard C. Steiner, *History of Education in Maryland* (Washington, D.C.: U.S. Government Printing Office, 1894), 263.

31. The presentation speech was described by one eyewitness as "one of those fearless productions which characterizes all the Union speeches which are made here," saying that the march of the Eighth through Maryland to the capital "had saved Maryland from becoming the bloody battle field which the once happy Virginia is now experiencing." Colonel Hinks' response was "apt and patriotic," and the event "gave us all pleasure and satisfaction, to know that there were as true fearless Union men in the city of Baltimore as can be found in the country." *Berkshire County Eagle*, August 1, 1861.

32. Reynolds is mistaken. The major of the Fourth Wisconsin Infantry was Frederick A. Boardman of LaCrosse. He was killed in action with the regiment in 1864. Ohio-native Halbert Eleazar Paine was the colonel of the Fourth Wisconsin. Promoted to brigadier general in 1863, Paine survived the war. Michael J. Martin, *A History of the 4th Wisconsin Infantry and Cavalry in the Civil War* (New York: Savas Beatie, 2006), 428, 470.

33. William J. Hardee's *Rifle and Light Infantry Tactics*, a two-volume work, was first published in 1855. Used to train many Union regiments in the early part of the Civil War, it replaced Winfield Scott's *Infantry-Tactics*. McWhiney and Jamieson, *Attack and Die*, 49–54.

34. Barnum's City Hotel, on Fayette and Calvert Streets, was established in 1826. David Barnum died in 1844; by 1861, Andrew McLaughlin owned the hotel. Scharf, *History of Baltimore City and County*, 515–16. Another member of the regiment described Barnum's as comparable with the first-class New York hotels. The hotel occupied the greater portion of a square, and "is fitted up in first class style," including the first floor that contained 50 spacious rooms for the elderly and invalids who needed attention from waiters. *Berkshire County Eagle*, May 23, 1861.

35. This text is taken from *The Library of American History*, published by U.P. James of Cincinnati in 1855 (pages 202–03).

8. The Return Home

1. A member of the regiment described an earlier move, noting that when a camp was disassembled, it presented a "very distracted appearance, and reminds one of moving day, not the moving of one family, but rather that of a small city," with piles of tent poles, floor boards, trunks, carpet bags, cooking utensils and extra accoutrements in sundry piles. *Berkshire County Eagle*, July 11, 1861.

2. Constructed in April and May 1861, "on the truncated triangle forming the southern part of the City Hall park," Park Barracks was in constant use until it was demolished following the war in 1865. According to one source, the barracks could accommodate at least 1,000 men. Silas W. Burt, *My Memoirs of the Military History of the State of New York during the War for the Union, 1861–65* (Albany: J.B. Lyon Co., 1902), 155–56.

3. Fred Smith of the Pittsfield, Massachusetts company wrote that the Eighth Massachusetts and Seventh New York enjoyed "bands of friendship which will never be severed." *Berkshire County Eagle*, August 8, 1861.

4. The First Chasseurs was also known as the Sixty-fifth New York Infantry.

5. The Boston Light Infantry, or "Tigers," was organized in 1798, and the New England Guards in 1812.

6. One Boston newspaper noted the "almost impenetrable crowd," and the regiment's souvenirs, including muskets and other arms, secession flags, pets (chiefly cats and dogs carried in knapsacks and haversacks), and a number of former slaves who had followed the regiment home as officers servants. *Boston Daily Advertiser*, August 2, 1861. Not all escaped slaves were allowed to remain with the Federal troops. The slave of William Dorbacker, for example, was hired by some Massachusetts officers as a servant, and followed them to the Relay House.

Dorbacker sent a messenger to the camp to have the slave returned, but the messenger was "somewhat maltreated by the soldiers" and hastily left the camp. Another messenger, armed with an order from Baltimore's provost marshal Colonel John B. Kenly to surrender the slave, appeared at Sixth Massachusetts Colonel Edward Jones' headquarters. Jones said he did not recognize slaves as contraband, and gave up the man. *The Liberator*, July 19, 1861, Vol. XXXI, No. 29, Whole Number 1595, p. 115. Governor Thomas Hicks wrote General Butler on May 10, reporting that a prominent citizen of Annapolis had sent him a letter, reporting that several free blacks had gone to Annapolis with Butler's troops, and were "armed and insolent" and were "corrupting our slaves." Hicks informed Butler that such activity violated state statutes, and the federal government should not allow a violation of the state's laws by "permitting them to accompany its troops," and urged Butler to send them back. *Private and Official Correspondence*, 78.

7. William Schouler, born in Scotland in 1814, enjoyed a career as a newspaper publisher and state legislator before being appointed Massachusetts adjutant general in 1860. Schouler retired from that position in 1867 and was again elected to the state legislature. He died in October 1872. *New York Tribune*, October 25, 1872; *New York Times*, October 25, 1872.

8. The Manchester (NH) Cornet Band had accompanied the Second New Hampshire Infantry to the front, and had purchased a "fine Zouave uniform" in New York. The Eighth engaged the Manchester men, at their own expense, starting in July. When the band and its full drum corps marched through a portion of Baltimore, it presented a "very creditable appearance," and received many tokens of applause, with miniature national flags waved from windows by "fair hands." *Salem Register*, July 11, 1861; *The Boston Herald*, August 1, 1861.

9. Salem's Captain Charles H. Manning's artillery section, part of the Second Division of Massachusetts Militia, became the nucleus of the Fourth Massachusetts Battery. Schouler, *A History of Massachusetts in the Civil War*, 195.

10. The story is apocryphal.

11. *The Boston Herald* used similar language to pay tribute to the men of the Eighth Massachusetts: "All of them have laid their lives upon the altar of their country. All were exposed to the chances of war. The soldiers who have just returned to us were the first fruits of New England patriotism, the first offering we laid before the shrine of the Goddess of Liberty, which is the hope of all men who desire to be free anywhere in the world.... They have had the experience and discipline calculated to fit them to take part in this, the grandest and most momen-

tous conflict of modern times—a war which is fraught with interests of incalculable value to the whole human race. The regiments that have returned may form the nucleus of 'an army of the Lord' that will march on to victory." *The Boston Herald*, August 5, 1861.

12. According to a participant, the drill lasted three hours, in the hot sun, with the Zouaves giving an "exhibition of their proficiency and peculiar drill," which gave "great delight to thousands of assembled spectators." *Salem Register*, August 8, 1861.

13. The Rev. George Leeds resigned as rector of St. Peters Episcopal Church in Salem in April 1860. He died in Philadelphia in April 1885, while rector of Grace Protestant Episcopal Church in Baltimore. Hurd, *History of Essex County*, 46; *New York Tribune*, April 16, 1885.

14. "Thus ended a day not soon to be forgotten in Salem," wrote one newspaper, "and which must, we should think, have entirely satisfied the most inveterate Old Guard that ever lived in our midst." *Salem Register*, August 5, 1861.

15. According to one source, the Eighth Massachusetts was mistakenly paid twice (once by the state and once by the federal government) for their first fifteen days of service, which caused "some feeling among those who have received less." *Salem Gazette*, August 20, 1861.

Bibliography

Books and Articles

Adams, Sampson, and Co. *The Boston Directory, Embracing the City Record, a General Directory of the Citizens, and a Business Directory*. Boston: Adams, Sampson, and Company, 1861.

_____. *The Salem Directory, Containing the Names of the Citizens, City Officers, a Business Directory, and an Almanac for 1861*. Salem: G.M. Whipple and A.A. Smith, 1861.

Adjutant General of Massachusetts. *Annual Report of the Adjutant-General of the Commonwealth of Massachusetts for the year ending December 31, 1861*. Boston: William White, 1861.

_____. *Massachusetts Soldiers, Sailors and Marines in the Civil War*. 8 vols. Norwood, MA: Norwood Press, 1931.

_____. *Record of the Massachusetts Volunteers, 1861–1865*. 2 vols. Boston: Wright & Potter, 1868–1870.

Allen, William C. *History of the United States Capitol: A Chronicle of Design, Construction, and Politics*. Washington, D.C.: U.S. Government Printing Office, 2001.

Appletons' Annual Cyclopedia and Register of Important Events of the Year 1894, New Series Vol. XIX, Whole Series Vol. XXXIV. New York: D. Appleton & Co., 1895.

Barnum, Phineas Taylor. *Life of P.T. Barnum, Written by Himself*. Buffalo, NY: The Courier Company, 1888.

Basler, Roy P., ed. *The Collected Works of Abraham Lincoln*. 9 vols. New Brunswick, NJ: Rutgers University Press, 1953.

Belknap, Henry Wyckoff. *Simon Forrester of Salem and His Descendants*. Salem, MA: Essex Institute Historical Collections, 1935.

Billings, John D. *Hardtack and Coffee, or the Unwritten Story of Army Life*. Boston: George M. Smith & Co., 1888.

Bowen, James L. *Massachusetts in the War, 1861–1865*. Springfield, MA: Clark W. Bryan & Co., 1889.

Brown, George William. *Baltimore and the Nineteenth of April, 1861: A Study of the War*. Baltimore: N. Murray, 1887.

_____. *A Sketch of the Life of Thomas Donaldson*. Baltimore: Cushings and Bailey, 1881.

Burt, Silas W. *My Memoirs of the Military History of the State of New York during the War for the Union, 1861–65*. Albany, NY: J.B. Lyon Co., 1902.

Butler, Benjamin F. *Autobiography and Personal Reminiscences of Major-General Ben. F. Butler, Butler's Book*. Boston: A.M. Thayer & Co., 1892.

_____. *Private and Official Correspondence of Gen. Benjamin F. Butler, During the Period of the Civil War*. 5 vols. Norwood, MA: The Plimpton Press, 1917.

"Camp Life at the Relay." *Harper's New Monthly Magazine* 24 (April 1862): 628–633.

Clark, Charles E. *My Fifty Years in the Navy*. Boston: Little, Brown and Co., 1917.

Clark, Emmons. *History of the Second Company of the Seventh Regiment* (National Guard), N.Y.S. Militia. New York: James G. Gregory, 1864.

_____. *History of the Seventh Regiment of New York, 1806–1889*. New York: By the Seventh Regiment, 1890.

Coffin, Charles Carleton. *Drum-Beat of the Nation*. New York: Harper & Brothers, 1899.

_____. *Stories of Our Soldiers: War Reminiscences, by "Carleton" and by Soldiers of New England*. Boston: The Journal Newspaper Co., 1893.

Cogar, William B. *Dictionary of Admirals of the U.S. Navy, Volume I, 1862–1900*. Annapolis, MD: Naval Institute Press, 1989.

Currier, John J. *Ould Newbury: Historical and Biographical Sketches*. Boston: Damrell and Upham, 1896.

Davis, William C., ed. *The Confederate General*. 6 vols. Harrisburg, PA: National Historical Society, 1991.

Derby, Perley, and Dr. Frank A. Gardner. "Elisha Story of Boston and some of his Descendants." *The Essex Institute Historical Collections* 50 (October 1914): 297–312.

Devereux, Arthur F. "Some Account of Pickett's Charge at Gettysburg." *Magazine of American History* 18 (July 1887): 13–19.

Dix, Morgan. *Memoirs of John Adams Dix*. 2 vols. New York: Harper & Brothers, 1883.

Ellery, Harrison, and Charles Pickering Bowditch. T*he Pickering Genealogy*. 3 vols. Cambridge, MA: University Press, 1897.

Emerson, William A. *Leominster, Massachusetts, Historical and Picturesque*. Gardner, MA: Lithotype Publishing Co., 1888.

Federal Publishing Co. *The Union Army*. 8 vols. Madison, WI: Federal Publishing Co., 1908.

Harrington, Fred Harvey. *Fighting Politician: Major General N.P. Banks*. Philadelphia: University of Pennsylvania Press, 1948.

Harris, William C. *Lincoln and the Border States: Preserving the Union*. Lawrence: University Press of Kansas, 2011.

Headley, P.C. *Massachusetts in the Rebellion*. Boston: Walker, Fuller, and Co., 1866.

Hedrick, Mary A. *Incidents of the Civil War*. Lowell, MA: Vox Populi Press, 1888.

Heidler, David S., and Jeanne T. Heidler. *Encyclopedia of the American Civil War*. New York: W.W. Norton, 2000.

Heitman, Francis B. *Historical Register and Dictionary of the United States Army*. 2 vols. Washington, D.C.: Government Printing Office, 1903.

Hincks (Hinks), Edward W. *Extracts from Speech by General Edward W. Hincks, of Cambridge, at Peabody, November 5th, 1883*. Cambridge, MA: William H. Wheeler, 1883.

Hollandsworth, James G., Jr. *Pretense of Glory: The Life of General Nathaniel P. Banks*. Baton Rouge: Louisiana State University Press, 1998.

Hornblow, Arthur. *A History of the Theatre in America From Its Beginnings to the Present Time*. 2 vols. Philadelphia: J.B. Lippincott Co., 1919.

"How Marblehead Fishermen Saved the Constitution." *The Sailors' Magazine and Seamen's Friend* 52 (March 1880): 80–81.

Hunt, Roger D., and Jack R. Brown. *Brevet Brigadier Generals in Blue*. Gaithersburg, MD: Olde Soldier Books, 1997.

Hunter, Mark C. *A Society of Gentlemen: Midshipmen at the U.S. Naval Academy, 1845–1861*. Annapolis, MD: Naval Institute Press, 2010.

Hurd, D. Hamilton. *History of Essex County, Massachusetts*. 2 vols. Philadelphia: J.W. Lewis & Co., 1888.

Ingraham, Charles A. *Elmer E. Ellsworth and the Zouaves of '61*. Chicago: University Press of Chicago, 1925.

Jensson, The Rev. J.C. *American Lutheran Biographies*. Milwaukee: Houtkamp, 1890.

Kelley, Bruce C., and Mark A. Snell. *Bugle Resounding: Music and Musicians of the Civil War Era*. Columbia: University of Missouri Press, 2004.

Lamb, John W. *A Strange Engine of War: The "Winans" Steam Gun and the Civil War in Maryland*. Baltimore: Chesapeake Book Company, 2011.

Lockwood, John, and Charles Lockwood. *The Siege of Washington: The Untold Story of the Twelve Days that Shook the Nation*. New York: Oxford University Press, 2011.

Malone, Dumas, ed. *Dictionary of American Biography*. 22 vols. New York: Charles Scribner's Sons, 1935.

Martin, Michael J. *A History of the 4th Wisconsin Infantry and Cavalry in the Civil War*. New York: Savas Beatie, 2006.

Martin, Tyrone G. *A Most Fortunate Ship: A Narrative History of Old Ironsides*. Annapolis, MD: Naval Institute Press, 1997.

McAfee, Michael J. *Zouaves: The First and the Bravest*. Gettysburg, PA: Thomas Publications, 1991.

McGraw, Robert F. "Minutemen of '61: The Pre–Civil War Massachusetts Militia." *Civil War History* 15 (June 1969): 101–115.

McWhiney, Grady, and Perry D. Jamieson. *Attack and Die: Civil War Military Tactics and the Southern Heritage.* Tuscaloosa: University of Alabama Press, 1982.

Military Order of the Loyal Legion of the United States. *Register of the Commandery of the State of Massachusetts.* Cambridge, MA: The University Press, 1912.

Moore, Frank. *The Rebellion Record.* 11 vols. New York: G.P. Putnam and D. Van Nostrand, 1861–68.

Murray, Stuart. *A Time of War: A Northern Chronicle of the Civil War.* Lee, MA: Berkshire House Publishers, 2001.

Nason, George W. *History and Complete Roster of the Massachusetts Regiments, Minute Men of '61.* Boston: Smith & McCance, 1910.

Osgood, Charles S., and H.M. Batchelder. *Historical Sketch of Salem, 1626–1879.* Salem: Essex Institute, 1897.

Parton, James. *History of the Administration of the Department of the Gulf in the Year 1862.* Boston: Fields, Osgood, & Co., 1871.

Pearson, Henry Greenleaf. *The Life of John A. Andrew.* 2 vols. Boston: Houghton, Mifflin & Co., 1904.

Pegram, John C. "Recollections of the United States Naval Academy." *Personal Narratives of Events in the War of the Rebellion, being papers read before the Rhode Island Soldiers and Sailors Historical Society,* 4th series, No. 11. Providence, RI: By the Society, 1891.

Radcliffe, George L.P. *Governor Thomas H. Hicks of Maryland and the Civil War.* Baltimore: The Johns Hopkins Press, 1901.

Randall, Ruth Painter. *Colonel Elmer Ellsworth: A Biography of Lincoln's friend and first hero of the Civil War.* Boston: Little, Brown and Co., 1960.

Roehrenbeck, William J. *The Regiment That Saved the Capital.* New York: Thomas Yoseloff, 1961.

Scharf, J. Thomas. *History of Baltimore City and County.* Philadelphia: Louis H. Everts, 1881.

Schouler, William. *A History of Massachusetts in the Civil War.* 2 vols. Boston: E.P. Dutton & Co., 1868.

Schurz, Carl. *The Reminiscences of Carl Schurz.* 3 vols., 1907–08. New York: The McClure Company, 1908.

"Secession at the Naval School," *United States Service Magazine* 1 (April 1864): 388–394.

Semmes, John E. *John H.B. Latrobe and His Times, 1803–1891.* Baltimore: The Norman, Remington Co., 1917.

Silverstone, Paul H. *Warships of the Civil War Navies.* Annapolis, MD: Naval Institute Press, 1989.

Soley, James Russell. *The Sailor Boys of '61.* Boston: Estes and Lauriat, 1888.

Steiner, Bernard C. *History of Education in Maryland.* Washington, D.C.: U.S. Government Printing Office, 1894.

Swinton, William. *History of the Seventh Regiment, National Guard, State of New York, During the War of the Rebellion.* New York: Charles T. Dillingham, 1886.

Toomey, Daniel Carroll. *A History of Relay, Maryland, and the Thomas Viaduct.* Baltimore: Toomey Press, 1995.

United States Government. 37th Congress, 1st Session. *Journal of the House of Representatives of the United States: Being the First Session of the Thirty-seventh Congress; Begun and held at the City of Washington, July 4, 1861.* Washington, D.C.: Government Printing Office, 1861.

_____. _____, 2nd Session. House of Representatives, Executive Document 53, *Patent Office Report for the Year 1861-Mechanical.*

_____. _____, _____. Report of the Secretary of the Navy, Senate Executive Document No. 1, *Message of the President of the United States to the Two Houses of Congress.* 3 vols. Washington, D.C.: Government Printing Office, 1861.

_____. _____, _____. Senate Executive Document No. 37, *Letter of the Secretary of War, in answer to a resolution of the Senate of the 30th day of January, in relation to the vessels purchased or chartered for the use of the War Department since the 1st day of April last.*

United States Government. 38th Congress, 2d Session. *Addresses on the Death of Hon. T.H. Hicks.* Washington, D.C.: Government Printing Office, 1865.

The U.S. Nautical Magazine, and Naval Journal. New York: Oliver W. Griffiths, 1856.

United States Naval War Records Office. *Official Records of the Union and Confederate Navies in the War of the Rebellion.* 31 vols. Washington, D.C.: U.S. Government Printing Office, 1894–1927.

U.S. Navy Department. Naval History Division, *Dictionary of American Naval Fighting Ships.* 8 vols. Washington, D.C.: U.S. Government Printing Office, 1970.

U.S. War Department. *The War of the Rebellion: A Compilation of the Official Records*

of the Union and Confederate Armies. 128 vols. Washington, D.C.: Government Printing Office, 1880–1901.
Waitt, Ernest Linden. *History of the Nineteenth Regiment Massachusetts Volunteer Infantry 1861–1865*. Salem: The Salem Press Co., 1906.
Walton Advertising and Printing Company. *The One Hundred Years of the Salem Savings Bank*. Salem, MA: Salem Savings Bank, 1918.
Ward, Susan Hayes. *George H. Hepworth: Preacher, Journalist, Friend of the People*. New York: E.P. Dutton and Company, 1903.
Warren, Richard, and Roger Sturcke. "11th New York Volunteer Infantry (Ellsworth's First New York Fire Zouaves, 1861–1862). *Military Collector and Historian* 39 (Winter 1987), 174–77.
Whipple, George M. *History of the Salem Light Infantry from 1805 to 1890*. Salem, MA: Essex Institute, 1890.
Whitcomb, Caroline E. *History of the Second Massachusetts Battery (Nims' Battery) of Light Artillery, 1861–1865*. Concord, N.H.: The Rumford Press, 1912.
White, James T. & Co. *The National Cyclopedia of American Biography*. 63 vols. New York: James T. White & Co., 1906.
Wilson, William Bender. *History of the Pennsylvania Railroad Company*. 2 vols. Philadelphia: Henry T. Coats & Co., 1895.
Winthrop, Theodore. *Life in the Open Air, and Other Papers*. Boston: Ticknor and Fields, 1863.
Woods, John W. *Woods' Baltimore City Directory*. Baltimore: John W. Woods, 1860.
The Year-Book of the Unitarian Congregational Churches for 1899. Boston: American Unitarian Association, 1899.

Newspapers

Bangor (ME) *Daily Whig and Courier*
Berkshire Eagle (Pittsfield, MA)
Boston Daily Advertiser
Boston Daily Globe
Boston Herald
Boston Journal
Chicago Daily Tribune
Cincinnati Enquirer
Daily Evening Item (Lynn, MA)
Daily National Intelligencer (Washington, D.C.)
Frank Leslie's Illustrated Newspaper
Harper's Weekly
The Liberator
Milwaukee Daily Sentinel
National Tribune (Washington, D.C.)
New York Daily Tribune
New York Herald
New York Illustrated News
New York Times
New York Tribune
The Press (Philadelphia)
St. Louis Globe-Democrat
Salem (MA) *Gazette*
Salem (MA) *Observer*
Salem (MA) *Register*
Scientific American
The Sun (Baltimore)

Census, Military and Manuscript Sources

National Archives and Records Administration, *Eighth Census of the United States*, 1860, Microcopy 653.
National Archives and Records Administration, *Letters Received by the Office of the Adjutant General (Main Series), 1861–1870*, Microcopy 619.
National Archives and Records Administration, *Tenth Census of the United States, 1880*, T9C.
National Archives and Records Administration, *Unfiled Papers and Slips Belonging in Confederate Compiled Service Records*, Microcopy 347.
National Archives and Records Administration, *U.S. Army Generals' Reports of Civil War Service, 1864–1887*, Microcopy 1098.
John P. Reynolds Reminiscences, 1861–1862, Manuscript S-7, Massachusetts Historical Society, Boston.

Internet

United States Patent and Trademark Office website (http://www.uspto.gov/index.jsp), accessed 27 March 2010.

Index

Numbers in **_bold italics_** indicate pages with photographs.

Adelaide 186, 280
Alexandria, Virginia 88, 115–116, 140, 141, 246, 255
Anderson, Maj. Robert 5, 269, 274
Andrew, John A. 9–12, 14–15, 18, 20, 21, 25, 55, 157, 232, 233, 239, 262, 264, 269, 277, 279
Annapolis, Maryland 19–23, 27, 28, 59, 95, 276; U.S. Naval Academy 22–34, **_66_**
Annapolis and Elkridge Railroad 28, 29, 31, 33, 34, 35
Antietam, battle of 45, 48, 268, 274
Appleton, James 268
Ariel 67, 69, 270–271
Ashton, William B. 53
Atwood, Mr. 256–257
Austin, Eleazer 235
Austin, George F. 75, 88, 91, 171
Austin, Mrs. 79

Babbidge, Charles 117, 277
Ball's Bluff, battle of 274
Baltic 67, 271
Baltimore: Barnum's Hotel 223, 283; Battle Monument **_222_**, 223–225; citizens complain about behavior of soldiers 196; citizens visit Union camps 188–189, 194, 211, 214, 277; Druid Hill Park 219; Eighth Massachusetts gives exhibition drill 220–221; Federal Hill 40, 106, 183; hostility of citizens toward Union troops 178, 256, 276–277, 281; Rullman's Bellevue Gardens 175, 227, 280; Washington Monument 176
Baltimore and Ohio Railroad 31, 36, 267
"Baltimore Joe" 140
Banks, Nathaniel 9, 41, 42, 206–208, 212, 245, 281–282
Batchelder, Charles J. 94, 99

Batchelder, George W. 91, 118, 134, 141, 159, 165, 190, 216, 223, 243
Bates, Charles H. 173
Beauregard, P.G.T. 265
Beverly, Massachusetts 13, 254
Big Bethel, battle of 144, 257, 278
Blake, George S. 23–25, 31, 264, 265
Boardman, Frederick A. 282
Boston 21, 27, 28, 64, 65
Boston: Faneuil Hall 12, 13, 14; Massachusetts State House 14–15, **_54_**, 55
Boston Tigers 232, 283
Bragg, Braxton 236
Breed, Bowman B. 149, 158, 257, 280
Brewster, Ethan A.P. 73, 77, 91, 114, 125, 140, 141, 143, 165, 186, 199, 215, 253, 257; intervenes in case of domestic abuse 143
Brown, Elbridge 99
Brown, George W. 18–19
Brown, John 15
Bruce, Daniel 97
Bruce, Robert 200, 281
Bryan, George L. 185–186, 280–281
Bull Run, battle of (1861) 217–218, 280
Bunker Hill Day, celebration of 150–151
Burlington, New Jersey 230
Butler, Andrew 23
Butler, Benjamin **_7_**, **_8_**, 9, 12, 14–15, 17, 18–19, 20–23, 25–31, 36, 40, 56, 59, 60, 63, 70, 95, 106, 144, 157, 241–242, 244, 257, 258, 261–267, 269, 270, 272, 274–277, 279, 281, 283
Butler, John G. 96, 275

Cadwalader, George 40–41
Cambridge 84–85, 87, 245–246, 273
Cameron, Simon 20, 24, 261, 274
Camp Essex 36, 188

289

Centreville, Virginia 218
Chandler and Company 10, 52, 268
Clark, Michael M. 275
Cobb, Leonard D. 175, 250
Coe, Lt. 130, 141, 142, 168–169
U.S.S. *Constitution* **24**–25, 26 27, 30, 31, 35, 45, 62–77, 79, 162–163, 243, 264, 265, 266, 270
U.S.S. *Cumberland* 84–85, 245, 273
Curtin, Andrew 19–20
Curtis, Samuel 35
Cutler, Nathan 85

Dalrymple, Simon O. 71
Davis, Jefferson 28, 114, 266
Dearborn, Charles 80, 141
Devereux, Charles U. 191
Devereux, Charlotte S. 49
Devereux, George H. 49, 55, 69, 155, 158, 168, 169, 235–236
Devereux, Mrs. 140, 158, 255
Dix, John A. 42, 267
Dobbin, George W. 276
Donaldson, Thomas 142, 276, 279
Douglas, Stephen A. 131, 278
Douglass (Douglas), Albert C. 77, 104, 106, 276
Driver, William R. 190
Du Pont, Samuel F. 19

Elkridge Landing, Maryland 36, 249, 252, 276, 278
Ellicott's Mills, Maryland 123, 253, 254, 258, 267, 277
Ellsworth, Elmer 11, **73**, 77, 89, 91, 115–117, 218, 239, 255, 262, 272, 274, 282
Elwell, Andrew 107, 141, 147, 149, 151, 169, 193, 249
Emery, Lt. 248
Emmerton, Charles S. 91, 118, 209, 249
Evans, Alvah A. 91, 223, 247

Fair Oaks, battle of 274
Felton, Samuel 19–20, 264
Floyd, John B. 98, 275
Fort Carroll 186, 281
Fort McHenry 41, 177, 180, 186, **205**, 206–210, 280–281
Fort Sumter: bombardment of 5, 158, 274; effect of surrender on Massachusetts 5–6
Fort Washington 87–88, 246, 273
Fortress Monroe, Virginia 21, 72, 84, 157, 186, 242, 243, 245, 257, 273, 279
Fowler, William T. 127, 278
Franklin Falls, Maryland 193, 212
Frederick, Maryland 258
Fry, Charles 131, 251–252

Galloway, M. 19, 264
Gettysburg, battle of 45, 280
Gillis, James A. 171

Gilmore's Band 37, 188, 232, 235, 267
Glendale, battle of 274
Gloucester, Massachusetts 13
Goodwin, John A. 261
Gray, George C. 91, 165, 192, 223, 247, 251
Gray, William H. 282
Griswold, A.W. 17

"Hacker" 170, 234
Haggerty, Peter 23, 265
Hale, Henry A. 141
Hall, Dr. 101, 109, 113, 136, 167–168
Hall, Harry S. 78, 83, 166
Hamlin, Hannibal 245
Hardy, Augustus 117
Harpers Ferry, (West) Virginia 15, 36, 99, 120, 253, 257
Harriet Lane 67, 71, 271
Haven, Mr. 247
Havre de Grace, Maryland 23, 60, 264
Henry, Alexander 19
Hepworth, George H. 139, 256, 278–279
Herrick, Moses S. 275
Hicks, Thomas H. 18–20, 25, 27, 28, 31, 208, 263, 280–282, 283
Hill, William A. 10, 91, 96, 120, 126, 130, 134, 135, 144, 148, 151, 223, 247
Hinks (Hincks), Edward W. **6**, 12, 17, 43–45, 91, 106, 107, 139, 144, 149, 151, 156–158, 169, 171, 180, 184–185, 188, 193–194, 196, 207–208, 210, 214–215, 220, 232–234, 238, 242, 249, 254, 258–259, 266, 268, 269, 274, 279, 282
Hinks, Mrs. 131, 139, 158, 255
Hudson, Capt. 186
Hugh Jenkins 183, 280
Huntington, Private 85

Independence Day, celebration of 187–189, 281
Ingells, Ephraim A. 158, 280
Ives, Stephen B. 191

James A. Stevens 76, 272
Jersey City, New Jersey 17, 43, 230–231
Johnson, Daniel H. 134, 141, 255, 278
Jones, Edward F. 120, 123–125, 127, 131, 139, 145, 250, 252, 254, 256, 275, 276, 283
Jones, Roger 275
Josephine 271

Kane, George P. 18–19, 41
Keene, Laura 77, 272
Kenly, John R. 42, 283

Lake, David G. 250
Lander, Frederick W. 266
Latrobe, John H.B. 142, 276, 279
Lee, Frank 173
Leeds, George 238, 284
Lefferts, Marshall 19–21, 27, 28, 29, 59, 231, 266

Index

Lewis, Albert H. 119
Lewis, William D. 212, 282
Lincoln, Abraham 6, 28, 35
Lovejoy, Owen 44
Lovejoy, Perley R. 220, 282
Lowd, Albert J. 141, 279
Lowd, Mark 255
Lowe, Lieut. 143
Luscomb, Charles 104
Luscomb, Pvt. 71
Lyle, Peter 282
Lynn, Massachusetts 13, 53, 54, 55, 91, 171–173, 186, 229, 247

Manchester Brass Band 87–188, 234–236, 283
Mansfield, Charles H. 59
Marblehead, Massachusetts 13
Martin, Knott 117, 123–125, 127, 131, 132–133, 135, 144, 164, 167, 169, 252–254, 257–261
Maryland 19–23, 25, 26, 28, 30, 60–65, 162, 264, 265, 270
Maryland units: Fifth Maryland Infantry 219
Massachusetts units: Cook's Massachusetts Battery (Cook's Company, Massachusetts Light Artillery) 36, 37, 100, 103, 106, 116, 119, 151, 212, 250, 275; Eighth Massachusetts Infantry 15, 263; Fifth Massachusetts Infantry 88, 140, 218, 271, 273; First Massachusetts Infantry 151; Manning's Battery, Massachusetts Light Artillery 235–236, 283; New England Guards 232; Nineteenth Massachusetts Infantry 47, 48, 49, 268; Second Massachusetts Battery 280; Sixth Massachusetts Infantry 36, 40, 59, 100, 104, 106, 116, 131, 145–147, 149–152, 167, 175, 178, 179–180, 183, 212, 229, 248–250, 252, 253, 256, 269, 275, 276, 279, 283; Twentieth Massachusetts Infantry 225
Massachusetts Volunteer Militia 9
Matthews, Edmund O. 23, 25
Merryman, John 40
Miller, Morris S. 266
Millersville Bridge 34
Monroe, Timothy 17, 35, 106, 277
Monticello 71, 271
Moody, Convers 200, 250–251, 257
Morris, W.W. 281
Morse, Augustus 151, 279
Mount Clare, Maryland 174, 182, 211–212, 219, 225, 267
Mount Vernon, Virginia 87, 246, 273

New York, New York 16–17, 57, 74–83; Astor House 57, 77–82, 137, 138, 231, 244, 245, 272, 273; Barnum's Museum 79, 114, 272; Park Barracks 231, 283
New York units: Eighth New York State Militia 100, 106, 117, 248; Eleventh New York Infantry (Ellsworth's Zouaves) 77, 89, 91, 115, 218, 255, 272, 274, 282; First Regiment United States Chasseurs (65th New York Infantry) 231; Fourth New York Infantry 227; Ninth New York State Militia 119; Seventh New York Infantry 19–21, **27**, 28, 29, 30, 31, 33, **34**, 35, 36, 43, 59, 60, 64, 65, 79, 119, 127, 157, 231, 241–242, 244, 266–267, 269, 275, 277, 283; Seventy-first New York State Militia 88, 246; Third New York Infantry 227; Thirteenth New York State Militia 175, 188–189, 193, 196–197, 200–201, 210, 212, 214, 217, 219–220, 227, 228; Twentieth New York State Militia 81–82, 212, 272; Twenty-second New York Infantry 82; Twenty-third New York Infantry 180
Newburyport, Massachusetts 13, 33
Niagara 74, 82, 271
Nichols, Benjamin 85
Nichols, James W. 190

Odell, Charles 141, 142, 255
Oliver M. Pettit 76, 272

Palmer, William L. 114
Parsons, Joseph M. 10
Patterson, Robert 19
Payne, Eleazar 222, 282
Peabody, S. Endicott 235
Pennsylvania units: Eighteenth Pennsylvania Infantry 212; First Pennsylvania Infantry 253; Nineteenth Pennsylvania Infantry 212; Twentieth Pennsylvania Infantry 212
Perkins, Daniel 191
Perkins, Dr. 191
Perryville, Maryland 19–23, 60–61
Petersburg, Virginia, siege of 274, 280
Philadelphia, Pennsylvania 17, 19, 58–60
Phillips, Willard 118–119
Phippen, George B. 173
photography 78, 79, 81, 146–147, 272, 279
Pillow, Gideon 236
Pittsfield, Massachusetts 13, 270
Pond, Charles 85
Poor, Eben S. 117
Poore, Ben Perley 107, 130, 132, 144, 148, 149, 152, 194, 249, 259, 277
Pratt, George W. 212, 282
"Pratt Street Riot" (Baltimore) 18, 183
Putnam, George D. 52, 65, 84, 91, 109, 123–124, 126, 142, 155, 210, 247

Quint, Mr. 256–257

Relay House, Maryland 36–40, 51, 100–174, 181–182, 186, 247, 267
Revere, Paul 13, 47
Reynolds, John Perkins, Sr. 47
Reynolds, Mary 125–126, 277
Reynolds, Sarah Rebecca 47
Richardson, Henry H. 234

Roanoke 163, 243, 247, 272
Rodgers, George W. 26, 62, 63, 69, 71, 264, 265, 266, 270
Ross, Private 230
R.R. Cuyler 30, 70, 73, 74

Safford, Joseph 94
St. Michael, Maryland 184–185
Salem, Massachusetts 8, 54–55, 234–239
Salem Light Infantry: pre–Civil War history 10–12
Schouler, William 233, 238, 261, 283
Schurz, Carl 265
Scott, Winfield 29, 37, 41, 247, 259, 265, 266, 274, 282
Seward, William 276
Shaw, Cyrus P. 156
Shepard, J.B. 53
Shepard, S.D. 53
Short, Joseph: and patent knapsack 101, 276
Silsbee, Mary 158
Silver, Peter 161, 280
Simpson, Daniel 148, 279
Smith, Abel 212, 282
Smith, Fred 206, 227
Smith, Samuel H. 69
soldier life: baseball 218; boxing 72; camp inspection 251–252; drill 134, 140–141, 166, 171, 215, 277, 278; expedition to Calverton 216–217; expedition to Hollingworth 120–123, 252–254, 257–259; expedition to St. Michael 183–186; flag presentations 157, 200, 220, 229, 241–242, 282; football 200–202; humor 84, 111, 113–114, 165, 171, 172–173, 195, 230; interaction with African Americans 145, 156, 281, 283; mail 37; pay 126, 202–203, 205, 277–278, 284; punishments 159, 204, 278, 281; quarters/shelter 104–106, 130, 136–138, 174–175, 179, 194–195, 249, 256, 271, 276, 278, 283; rations/food 37, 60, 64, 67, 96, 100, 135, 182, 199, 250, 265, 270, 275, 281; religious services 83–84, 109, 150, 167–168, 218, 243–244, 251, 273; sentry duty 197–198; sham battle 128, 278; singing/music 113, 132, 136, 142, 147–149, 152, 165, 190–192, 214, 277
Springfield, Massachusetts 16, 269
Staten, Edward H. 140, 279
Stephens, Paran 270
Stetson, Charles 272

Steuart, George H. 42, 175, 267, 280
Stevens, George O. 69
Stimpson, Archer 80
Stone, Ebenezer W. 9
Sumner, Charles 35
Swasey, William R. 128, 250
Sweetland, Alonzo ("Du-dah") 84, 100, 103, 104, 136

Taney, Roger B. 40
Tilghman, Samuel O. 184–186, 192, 215, 280–281
Titus, Erastus 80, 272
Trimble, Isaac R. 264

uniforms and uniform items *2*, 37, 55, 79, 128–130, 192, 201, 204, 208–210, 213, 219, 226, 250, 254, 282
Upshur, John H. 69, 271
Upton, William B. 126, 191
Usher, Roland G. 158, 202, 279–280

Ward, J. Langdon 127
Ward, William R. 80–82, 272
Washington, D.C.: 35, 88, *93*, *96*; Capitol Building 89–91, 92, *98*, 163, 247, 273–274, 275; White House 96–97
Watson, Benjamin F. 256
Webb, Stephen P. 8, 55, 236–237
Webster, Daniel 35
Webster, Fletcher 225
Welles, Gideon 23–24
Whittredge, Charles E. 77, 111, 251
Wildes, George D. 55, 169, 238, 239, 269
Wiley, William 10
Williams, Charles F. 75, 77, 78, 119, 134
Wilson, Henry 9
Winans, Ross: and steam gun *99*, 101–104, 248–249, 253, 276
Winthrop, Theodore 30, 35, 44, 267, 275, 279
Wisconsin units: Fourth Wisconsin Infantry 219, 221, 222, 223, 225–226, 282
Woodbury, Isaiah 235
Worcester, Massachusetts 16, 56
Wyatt and Parsons Quadrille Band 238

Zouave cheer 58–59, 202, 234, 272
Zouave Drill Club 235

www.ingramcontent.com/pod-product-compliance
Lightning Source LLC
Chambersburg PA
CBHW051211300426
44116CB00006B/515